# Foundations of CentOS Linux

Enterprise Linux On the Cheap

Ryan Baclit, Chivas Sicam,
Peter Membrey, and
John Newbigin

**Foundations of CentOS Linux: Enterprise Linux On the Cheap**

Copyright © 2009 by Ryan Baclit, Chivas Sicam, Peter Membrey, and John Newbigin

The Evolution Mail Client logo is a copyright of Evolution project and was printed with permission.

ISBN-13 (pbk): 978-1-4302-1964-4

ISBN-13 (electronic): 978-1-4302-1965-1

Printed and bound in the United States of America 9 8 7 6 5 4 3 2 1

Trademarked names may appear in this book. Rather than use a trademark symbol with every occurrence of a trademarked name, we use the names only in an editorial fashion and to the benefit of the trademark owner, with no intention of infringement of the trademark.

President and Publisher: Paul Manning

Lead Editor: Frank Pohlmann

Technical Reviewers: Peter Membrey and Ann Tan-Pohlmann

Editorial Board: Clay Andres, Steve Anglin, Mark Beckner, Ewan Buckingham, Tony Campbell, Gary Cornell, Jonathan Gennick, Michelle Lowman, Matthew Moodie, Jeffrey Pepper, Frank Pohlmann, Ben Renow-Clarke, Dominic Shakeshaft, Matt Wade, Tom Welsh

Coordinating Editor: Debra Kelly

Copy Editors: James A. Compton, Heather Lang, Patrick Meader, and Sharon Terdeman

Compositor: Bob Cooper

Indexer: BIM Indexing and e-Services

Artist: April Milne

Cover Designer: Anna Ishchenko

Distributed to the book trade worldwide by Springer-Verlag New York, Inc., 233 Spring Street, 6th Floor, New York, NY 10013. Phone 1-800-SPRINGER, fax 201-348-4505, e-mail orders-ny@springer-sbm.com, or visit http://www.springeronline.com.

For information on translations, please e-mail info@apress.com, or visit http://www.apress.com.

Apress and friends of ED books may be purchased in bulk for academic, corporate, or promotional use. eBook versions and licenses are also available for most titles. For more information, reference our Special Bulk Sales–eBook Licensing web page at http://www.apress.com/info/bulksales.

The information in this book is distributed on an "as is" basis, without warranty. Although every precaution has been taken in the preparation of this work, neither the author(s) nor Apress shall have any liability to any person or entity with respect to any loss or damage caused or alleged to be caused directly or indirectly by the information contained in this work.

The source code for this book is available to readers at http://www.apress.com.

*I dedicate this book to all current and future users of Linux.*

*—Ryan Baclit*


*To Anna. May all your dreams come true.*

*—Chivas Sicam*


*For my granddad, Bill "Pappy" Membrey. Without his unwavering support and guidance (not to mention patience), I would not be where I am today.*

*—Peter Membrey*


*To my fiancée, Jenna.*

*—John Newbigin*

# Contents at a Glance

# Contents

# About the Authors

**Ryan Baclit** started to use Linux during his college days at De La Salle University. His natural interest in computer technology prompted him to study the operating system and its tools. Knowing that he needed to learn more about open source technology to advance in Linux and the proper use of open source tools, he enrolled in Bluepoint Institute of Higher Technology's Total Linux course in 2005. After graduating, he eventually became an instructor T that institute. As an instructor, he usually teaches open source programming tools like Bash shell scripting and software analysis and design with UML. When not playing with Linux, he studies manga illustration, reads manga, and collects anime toys.

**Chivas Sicam** works as an entrepreneur and IT consultant. Chivas takes pride in being part of the DOST-ASTI (Department of Science and Technology Advanced Science and Technology Institute) Bayanihan Linux project. His team has advocated the use of open source software for the computing needs of government agencies, schools, and small and medium-size enterprises in the Philippines. He also scored 100% in his RHCE exam in March 2005. He enjoys technology, road trips, and keeping up-to-date on news of the Utah Jazz.

**Peter Membrey** lives in Hong Kong and is actively promoting open source in all its various forms and guises, especially in education. He has had the honor of working for Red Hat and received his first RHCE at the tender age of 17. He is now a Chartered IT Professional and one of the world's first professionally registered ICT Technicians. Currently studying for a master's degree in IT, he hopes to study locally and earn a PhD in the not-too-distant future. He lives with his wife, Sarah, and is desperately trying (and sadly failing) to come to grips with Cantonese.

**John Newbigin** has been passionate about Linux for more than 10 years. In that time he has channeled much of his enthusiasm into writing a number of tools and utilities. Ironically it is his Windows programs such as RawWrite for Windows and Explore2fs that have generated the most interest, though they all help to bring Linux to a larger audience.

John's involvement with CentOS dates back to the early days when it was still part of the CAOS Foundation. From late 2003 until mid-2009 when the product was retired, John was the CentOS-2 lead developer. He still helps out on the other releases where possible.

In between working on CentOS and his other programs, John still finds time for his day job as a Linux systems administrator, where he continues to find new and exciting ways to use Linux networking, file systems, and security.

# About the Technical Reviewer

 **Ann Tan-Pohlmann** has experience in many fields, including slinging regular expressions, watching Linux servers, writing telecom billing systems, being an obsessive-compulsive spreadsheet user, and arguing about machine learning. She is learning Italian, has forgotten most of her Mandarin, trains cats using Cat-Kwan-Do, and sings Videoke to survive the Manila night. She currently does GUI development for a telecom testing company in her day job.

# Acknowledgments

Thanks to all of the following:

Dad, Mom, Joel (who gave me my very first Linux CDs), Eric, and Adrian. They were always there to help me push forward when challenges got tough.

Bluepoint Institute of Higher Technology. They gave me the proper training to have concrete Linux skills for the enterprise and to interact with their wonderful BLUE community.

Chivas and Frank. You two introduced me to the world of writing books with Apress.

The CentOS community. They created the alternative Linux distribution to RHEL for the use of all.

The rest of the open source community. They have shown a commitment to providing great open source software.

God. If it were not for Him, I would not have everything I have now.

—Ryan Baclit


I would like to thank the people of Apress for their support in this endeavor.

—Chivas Sicam


The one person I would really like to acknowledge is my wife, Sarah.

Despite being pregnant through the majority of the work on this book, and despite somehow managing to seemingly suffer all the potential side effects of pregnancy (which the doctor joyfully insisted was "completely normal"), she always had a smile for me. I can honestly say that after pulling an all-nighter (alas, entirely my own fault), there could be no better sight. So, please allow me to thank her for her unlimited patience and tolerance. She is my best friend, and I love her dearly. Without her love and support, I would never have been able to finish the book.

—Peter Membrey

# Introduction

Community Enterprise Operating System, or CentOS, is an enterprise Linux distribution. It was developed by the CentOS Project community using the source code of the commercial Linux distribution from Redhat, the Redhat Enterprise Linux (RHEL). They created CentOS to have a free alternative to RHEL and to have a Linux distribution that's as stable as its commercial counterpart and can keep up with the requirements of the enterprise. Using CentOS is a good choice to learn Linux not only for its RHEL roots but also for its compatibility, quality, and support.

CentOS is binary compatible with the RHEL because it was built using the source code of RHEL. Also, the developers made sure to adhere to the redistribution rules of RHEL when they built CentOS so it would be a truly free alternative to the original.

CentOS is continuously being developed by its core developers and its community. They make security and software updates and quality assurance measures to maintain the stability of the distribution. The packages they build for CentOS are placed on their distributed mirror network to allow users to download and install software on their system manually if needed. Because of the core developers and its community, CentOS is able to have a constant release upgrade schedule to allow users to use new software and to support new hardware. They are also increasing in numbers, and that means there's always a better CentOS after each release.

CentOS has an interactive community, and you can ask them for assistance (go to http://centos.org) if you need it. You can send email to community members to share ideas or ask for solutions on the problems that you may have encountered while using CentOS. For business users that plan to use CentOS on their organization, they can avail of commercial support for CentOS through companies that specialize in it.

## The Book

*Foundations of CentOS Linux: Enterprise Linux on the Cheap* was written for beginning to intermediate level administrators who want to learn Linux using CentOS. This book was designed to be a hands-on type of book to enable you to grasp Linux concepts fast. Starting with Chapter 1, you will be given background and instructions on how to install CentOS in your computers properly. Then you will install CentOS on your computers. This pattern continues throughout the book to optimize your Linux learning experience.

The CentOS systems that you will install in Chapter 1 will also be used with the other topics of the book such as shell scripting, securing your system, and setting up servers for network services. While reading the book and learning CentOS, you are also learning how to use the RHEL distribution at the same time. The scripts and server software that you will learn can also be used on a running RHEL system. This forms a strong foundation not only for both CentOS and RHEL but also for the core Linux concepts.

Here is a brief summary of what each chapter covers on the book:

Chapter 1 will give you a walkthrough on how to install CentOS into your computers. You will be given advice on how to prepare for your first Linux installations such as where to get an install CentOS DVD and having a checklist for an enterprise server setup and enterprise workstation setup. After this chapter, you now have at least two working CentOS machines that are good enough for you to experiment with Linux.

Chapter 2 will introduce you to the command-line interface of Linux using the Bourne-again shell or BASH. With BASH, you will be able to find out who is currently logged in, see the concepts behind the Linux filesystem and why the directories are arranged like that, and how to manage directories such as making symbolic links (or shortcuts) or removing directories. If you ever get stumped on any of the shell commands, you will be given an overview on how to get help about it using the man pages.

Chapter 3 will show you how to customize your installed CentOS systems depending on your requirements. You will be given an overview of the Linux boot process, the importance of a bootloader, the runlevels your systems can use, and configuring the system services needed to be started at boot. In addition, you will see how you can configure other system settings such as the keyboard, the current language, the system networking, the graphical adjustment, and the printer.

Chapter 4 will dig deeper into the realm of storage. You will learn how to manage storage devices such as preparing and adding hard drives and what filesystems you can use for them on your system. You will be shown how to set them up for redundancy using RAID or have an extensible partitioning capability with the Logical Volume Manager.

Chapter 5 will show you how to manage users on your systems. You will learn how to add, remove, and modify users, and change passwords on both the graphical desktop and on the command-line interface. Armed with the concepts of Linux users, you will know how to put restrictions on the amount of storage space users can access through the use of disk quotas.

Chapter 6 will introduce you to the X Windows, the base system that is used by graphical Linux applications such as the GNOME Desktop. You will also learn how to use the GNOME Desktop controls like menus and buttons. Later, you will see how you can use your desktop to connect to another X Windows server for remote graphical administration.

Chapter 7 will show you how to manage packages in your system. You will learn how to install, update, and remove packages, and use repositories to further streamline package management in your system.

Chapter 8 will give you a background on basic Linux security to secure your system. You will know how to configure the system logger and view log files to monitor your system in case of a break-in. You will also see how to schedule tasks for automation. Lastly, you will learn how to use Linux-PAM to have a central way of authenticating users with PAM-enabled applications.

Chapter 9 will show you advanced methods of securing your system. You will learn how to use digital certificates for encryption, install and configure intrusion detection tools to detect unwanted attacker break-ins, and monitor system consistency through packages and additional tools. You will be introduced to how to apply a strict security mechanism in your system through SELinux policies.

Chapter 10 will show you how to secure your system on the network. You will learn how to create firewall rules to prevent unwanted traffic and attackers from entering your system through the network. You will also see how to use tcp_wrappers that can provide security for services that can interface with it. To have a secure way to save your system log files, you will learn how to configure a central log server in this chapter.

Chapter 11 will show you how to install and configure different network services on your servers. Some of these network services include the secure shell (SSH) for encrypted connections and the Network Time Protocol server to have synchronized time data on your network. You will see that CentOS is enough to provide the required network services on your network.

Chapter 12 will introduce you to some of the open source databases that you can use with CentOS. These include MySQL and PostgreSQL. You will learn how to install and configure each database system and see how to run database queries on them. You will also see the similarities and differences among database systems, which will aid you in choosing the one that is right for you based on your requirements.

Chapter 13 will show you how to use web services with the Apache Web Server. You will be able to install and configure Apache to serve web pages and scripts such as PHP. If you plan to manage multiple domains using Apache, you will learn that using the virtual hosts.

Chapter 14 will introduce you to the available file services that you can use on your system. These services are FTP to distribute files, NFS to share files with fellow Linux/Unix computers, and Samba to share files on your Windows network. You will also be given a walkthrough on how to share a printer on your Samba server to allow Windows computers to have a central print server.

Chapter 15 will show you how to provide email services on your network. You will see how to install and configure mail servers to send email and IMAP/POP3 servers to retrieve emails.

Chapter 16 will introduce you to the directory services. You will know how to provide central authentication on Linux- or Unix-only computers and to hybrid systems. This will make user credentials available to computers that can use your directory services.

Chapter 17 will introduce you to the Linux kernel, the core of your CentOS system. You will learn about the different types of kernels you can use, manage additional kernel capabilities through modules, and make yourself a new kernel. Having kernel building techniques on hand will be advantageous because you get to customize your system as you wish.

Chapter 18 will teach you about virtualization, the technology that companies and organizations use to save on cost and energy. You will learn about the various virtualization technologies that you can use later. You will experience virtualization using Xen by creating new separate instances of CentOS systems within your current CentOS system.

Chapter 19 will teach you about the basics of Linux troubleshooting to prepare you for situations when your system cannot boot as expected. You will learn how to use the rescue environment to enter your system to know why it cannot load, and fix it. You will know how to find the correct partitions and directories of your unbootable system to begin your repairs.

After you finish this book, you will have a better grasp of the basics of Linux in general and CentOS in particular that will be essential when you learn other advanced Linux administration techniques in your career. You can get an even more advanced Linux book, and you will find that it is much easier to understand because of what you have learned in this book. If you are an aspiring Redhat Certified Engineer, reading this book will give you an edge when using review materials aimed for the RHCE exam. You will better understand the mock exam questions and mock setups that the RHCE reviewer teaches you because you will be able to associate what you have learned in this book to your practice sessions with the reviewer.

If you are already an experienced Linux administrator and want to learn CentOS using this book, you will still find some useful advice that can add to your experience. This book will serve as a reference book that you can use from time to time for common commands and base server setups.

Welcome to the world of Linux with CentOS!

Ryan Baclit

# CHAPTER 1

∎∎∎

# Installation

In this chapter, you will learn how to install CentOS. To make good use of this book's information about how to set up and use enterprise services, we recommend that you have at least three computers connected to a LAN (local area network), with one connected to the Internet. Two computers will be used as enterprise servers, while the other computer will be used as an enterprise workstation.

However, if you do not have these resources at the moment, you can use free virtualization software such as Virtual PC (http://www.microsoft.com/windows/downloads/virtualpc/default.mspx) or VMware Server (http://www.vmware.com/products/server/) to simulate running several computers in one computer. We recommend VMware Server because it's easy to adjust the network connections to match the requirements above, and we've never encountered problems using the graphical user interface. The only limitation is that you won't be able to see the performance and reliability of CentOS if it is running on virtual machines instead of running standalone.

So you've decided to learn CentOS, the cheapest enterprise Linux operating system available. When we say cheap, we mean cheap! You can actually download CentOS for free from this link: http://isoredirect.centos.org/centos/5/isos/i386/. We recommend, though, that you obtain the DVD ISO so that everything you need is in one DVD.

However, whether you download the CD or DVD ISOs, if you have a slow Internet connection, it could take months to download the images. You can try alternative sources such as asking a favor from a friend to download them for you, or you can borrow the CDs or DVD from friends if they already have the images. You can also join the local Linux community to ask for assistance. Check out http://www.linux.org/groups/ to find a group suitable to your location.

Lastly, if all else fails, and if you have a few bucks to spare, you can opt to purchase the discs online and have them shipped to your doorstep. One of the web sites you can visit to purchase the CDs or DVDs online is OSDisc, http://www.osdisc.com/cgi-bin/view.cgi/products/linux/centos.

If you're able to get the image files, though, you need to burn them onto a CD/DVD yourself. You will need blank CDs or a DVD and a CD/DVD burner and software. The instructions for burning a CD/DVD of CentOS are available at http://www.centos.org/docs/5/html/CD_burning_howto.html. This link provides instructions on burning your CentOS images once you have downloaded them in both Windows and Linux.

## Preinstallation Steps

At this point, you will be installing CentOS as a server on one computer and as a workstation on a second computer. The server should have at least two network interfaces: one for connection on the Internet and the other on the LAN. Before you start, you need to obtain the information about connecting to the Internet from your Internet Service Provider (ISP). With this information in hand, connecting to the Internet while installing the server will be a breeze. The other computer will only need to be connected to the LAN. In the chapters ahead, you will learn how to share the Internet connection from the server via gateway or proxy. Also, the computers that you will be using need to be compatible with CentOS.

More often than not they are compatible, but sometimes there are peripherals such as hard disk and network cards that are not supported by the operating system. Based on experience, these are usually new devices. You can check https://hardware.redhat.com/ to see if your hardware supports CentOS. If not, you will need to replace the parts or the whole system, or wait for drivers to become available.

Table 1-1 details how we will set up the servers, and Table 1-2 lists the settings for the enterprise workstation.

*Table 1-1. Enterprise Server Setup*

| Property | Value |
| --- | --- |
| Boot loader password | aBd12_!Gc |
| IP Address(eth0) | 192.168.3.1 |
| Netmask(eth0) | 255.255.255.0 |
| IP Address(eth1) | <settings based on your ISP provider> |
| Netmask(eth1) | <settings based on your ISP provider> |
| Hostname | srv1-manila.example.com |
| Gateway | <settings based on your ISP provider> |
| Primary DNS | <settings based on your ISP provider> |
| Secondary DNS | <settings based on your ISP provider> |
| Root Password | @2Yt5#bCC |
| Fullname | Jaime Sebastian Sicam |
| Password | TR,34,AUy! |

*Table 1-2. Enterprise Workstation Setup*

| Property | Value |
| --- | --- |
| Boot loader password | Ghx_1B7$3 |
| IP Address | 192.168.3.20 |
| Netmask | 255.255.255.0 |

*Table 1-2. Enterprise Workstation Setup (continued)*

| | |
|---|---|
| Hostname | wrkstn1-manila.example.com |
| Gateway | 192.168.3.1 |
| Primary DNS | 192.168.3.1 |
| Secondary DNS | 192.168.3.2 |
| Root Password | 1(Am,nP)! |
| Username | ryan |
| Fullname | Ryan Constantine Baclit |
| Password | 4Pr*m@,Ll7 |

# Installation

Now, let's move forward and start the installation process. Turn on your computer, put the CD/DVD in the CD-ROM/DVD-ROM drive, and wait until you see the installation screen. If the installation screen fails to show up, you may need to change the BIOS setting to boot into CD. Once it is up, follow these steps to set up CentOS.

1. You should be able to see the installation screen as shown in Figure 1-1. You have the option to run the installation in graphical mode simply by pressing Enter. If you do not select any option, in 60 seconds, the installer will proceed in graphical mode. In this mode, you can use the keyboard and mouse to navigate the menus. However, if you want the installation to run faster, or you have problems running installation in graphical mode, you can opt to install it in text mode by typing linux text at the prompt and pressing Enter.

2. Once you've made this choice, you will only be able to use the keyboard in navigating the installation menus. For other parameters you can use for installation you can navigate the help menus by pressing the function keys F1 to F5. F1 displays the main menu, where you are right here. F2 provides other boot options that are helpful if you are not able to install CentOS through text or graphical mode:

   - Run the installer with no hardware probing. This is useful when the installer fails to boot when it fails to identify a particular hardware in your system such as firewire.
   - Test the CD for defects to see if your installation fails due to a CD error.
   - Run rescue mode, where you use the installation CD as a rescue environment on a system that has CentOS installed but fails to boot.
   - Install a driver disk, usually for hardware devices such as the NIC or hard disk for CentOS to be able to operate these devices.
   - Install Linux through the network via LAN or via the Internet. With the Internet option, however, you ideally need broadband to complete the installation in less than a few hours.
   - Use an installer update CD so that the software installed on your computer is updated.

- Test your RAM for defects. When you test the memory, you usually leave the test running for days to make sure that RAM is not the cause of any installation problems.
- Set the screen resolution of the graphical installation should you have problems.
- If memory cannot be detected, you have the option to specify the size of your memory manually.

3. Also, these options can be combined, as you can see by pressing F4. F5 shows you that entering linux rescue as an option allows you to enter the rescue environment.

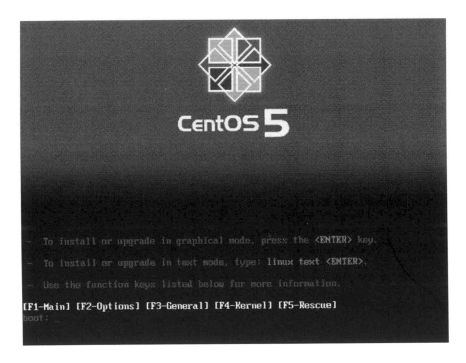

***Figure 1-1.*** *You have the option to install CentOS in graphical or text mode, or specify other options to troubleshoot the installation process or rescue an existing CentOS installation.*

4. The next screen, shown in Figure 1-2, allows you to test the CD for defects. We recommend that you do so now, so that you can rule out the CD as an issue should the installation fail. You can navigate the entries by using the Tab key or arrow keys and pressing Enter to select a choice.

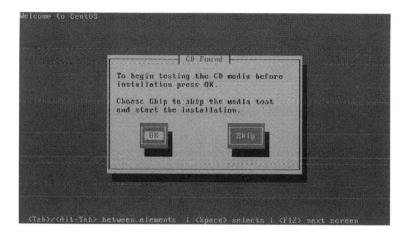

*Figure 1-2. You have the option to test the CD media for defects.*

**5.** Once the media has been tested or if you chose to skip the test, you will see the graphical installation screen shown in Figure 1-3. You can click the Release Notes button to obtain information about the version of CentOS that you are installing. Click Next to continue.

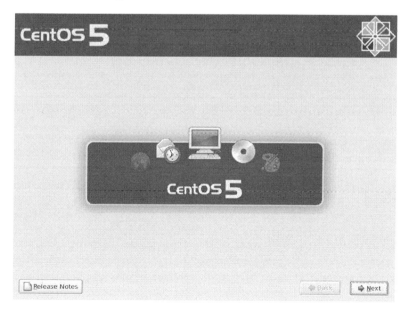

*Figure 1-3. You can check the release notes to learn more about the version of CentOS you are about to install.*

5

**6.** The next step is to choose the language used in the installation process, as shown in Figure 1-4. The default is English, but if you select a different language here, that language will be reflected as soon as you click Next.

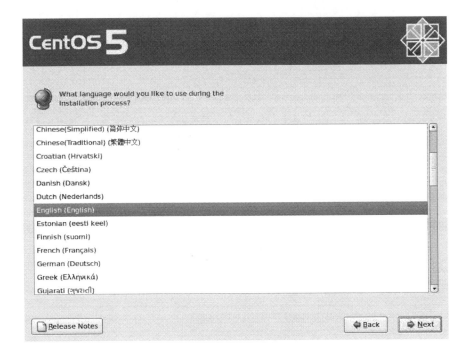

*Figure 1-4. You can choose the language used during the installation process.*

7. Next you can select the keyboard layout appropriate for your keyboard as shown in Figure 1-5. Select the appropriate keyboard and then click Next.

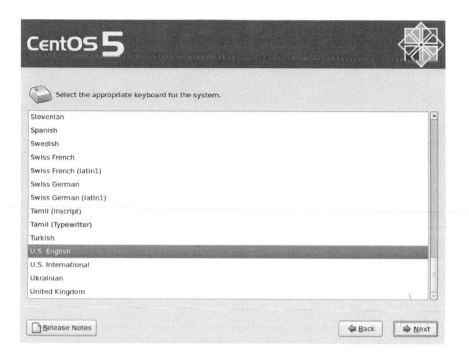

*Figure 1-5. You have the option to choose the appropriate keyboard layout for your keyboard.*

**8.** If your hard disk is unformatted (has never been used until now), or the partition table of the hard disk is corrupt, the dialog shown in Figure 1-6 will appear. Click Yes to initialize the hard disk to create a new partition table on the hard disk, effectively preparing the hard disk for partitioning.

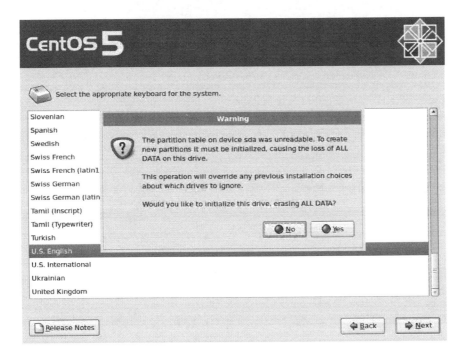

*Figure 1-6.* *The message appearing when the partition table on the hard disk needs to be re-created to prepare the hard disk for partitioning.*

---

■ **Caution:** Please ensure that the hard disk does not contain any valuable information, because you will not be able to recover your data if you click Yes here.

---

9. The next step is creating partitions on the hard disk, as shown in Figure 1-7. The purpose of partitioning is to allocate meaningful portions of the disk space to the CentOS based on how it will be used. The first option allows you to select the partitioning type:

- *Remove All Partitions on Selected Drives and Create Default Layout:* This option allows you to consume all disk space on the selected hard disks for CentOS; the disks will be automatically be partitioned for you. Any existing operating system installed on the hard disk will be erased in favor of CentOS.
- *Remove Linux Partitions on Selected Drives and Create Default Layout:* This option allows you to consume only partitions used in existing Linux installations for CentOS on the selected drives, which will automatically be partitioned for CentOS. This option is typically used for *dual-booting;* that is, choosing which operating system to use at boot time. Normally, this option is used for workstations where users can choose to boot into Windows or Linux.
- *Use Free Space on Selected Drives and Create Default Layout:* If your hard disk has a free, unused partition on the selected drive, it will be consumed by CentOS and will be partitioned automatically. Normally, when Windows is installed on the hard disk, it uses one partition that consumes all the disk space. You will need a third-party tool such as Partition Magic to resize the Windows partition and create an unused partition that can be used for CentOS.

■ **Note:** Unfortunately, at the time of writing, the CentOS installer cannot resize the Windows partition. However, there are LiveCD (http://www.livecdlist.com/) Linux distributions such as Ubuntu that can resize Windows partitions on the fly, so that you don't need to purchase commercial third- party tools such as Acronis Partition Manager or Partition Magic to partition your hard drive.

- *Create Custom Layout:* This is the most advanced of the four options; it allows you to create, edit, and delete partitions as you please. Once you're a seasoned CentOS user, you will likely opt to use this setting since you can tune the partitions based on how the server or workstation will be used.

10. Assuming that there are no existing operating systems on the hard disk, or that any existing operating systems can be deleted, choose Remove Linux Partitions on Selected Drives and Create Default Layout.

11. The second option allows you to select which hard drive will be used for CentOS. If you have several hard disks, they will be listed here unless the disks are configured as a hardware RAID.

■ **Note:** RAID (Redundant Array of Independent/Inexpensive Disks) is a hard disk setup that allows you to tune the performance and reliability of your data storage. See http://en.wikipedia.org/wiki/Redundant_array_of_independent_disks for more information.

**12.** With the third option, Advanced Storage Configuration, you can use a SAN (Storage Area Network) in CentOS through the iSCSI protocol but this isn't in common use at present and is outside the scope of this book.

**13.** Finally, you have the option Review and Modify Partitioning Layout. Check this option so that you can see on the next screen how the partitions will be allocated on your hard disk(s) and be given the opportunity to revise the partition layout if necessary.

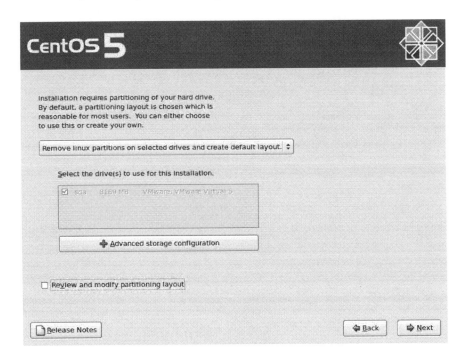

*Figure 1-7. This menu allows you to create partitions on your hard disk with a default layout or to manually do it yourself.*

**14.** Click Next to continue. At this point, you are warned that all existing Linux partitions will be deleted in favor of this installation. Select Yes, since this is the first time you will be installing Linux on your system.

**15.** If you chose the Review and Modify Partitioning Layout option, you will see the partitioning scheme shown in Figure 1-8. In this screen you can review how the partitions are designed and edit them as well. As you've noticed, the hard disk is physically divided into two partitions, one for boot and the other for LVM (Logical Volume Manager). The boot partition contains the files needed to boot CentOS; these are the boot menu configuration and kernel files. LVM allows you to easily adjust or create a virtual/logical partition combined from physical partitions from several hard disks. It is the easiest way of allocating more disk space to a partition while it is still being used. At the moment, there are two logical partitions created under LVM, swap and root (/). The swap partition is used for swapping in and out data to and from the RAM. Normally, the swap size is twice the size of the RAM for optimum performance. The root or (/) partition contains the Linux filesystem. This is where the operating system, applications, and data will be stored. You'll find more information about the Linux filesystem in Chapter 2. Click Next to continue.

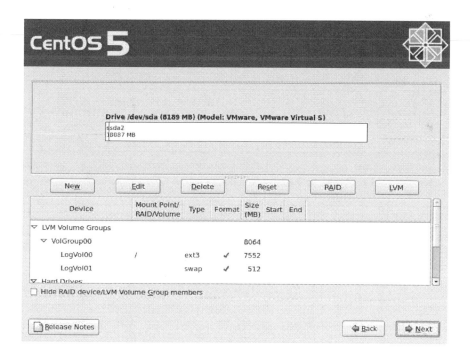

*Figure 1-8. The partitioning scheme.*

**16.** The screen shown in Figure 1-9 allows you to configure the boot loading options.

- The first two options allow you to install a boot loader or not. You need a boot loader to boot Linux, so just keep the current settings. You only use the second option if there's another Linux distribution installed in the system and you would rather configure that boot loader to boot this CentOS installation.
- The next option allows you to add operating systems to boot from this boot loader. Normally, if you are dual-booting with Windows, this entry is already available in the list. However, if you are dual-booting with another Linux distribution, you would need to add that entry here.
- The next option allows you to provide a boot loader password. Select this entry and supply the password in Table 1-1 or Table 1-2, depending on whether you're installing CentOS for the server or workstation. The boot loader password is necessary because without a password, anyone can modify the boot settings and in the worst case, it can be manipulated in such a way that anyone could have system-level access on your computer without having to key in any password.
- The last option, Configure Advanced Boot Loader Options, allows you to set the partition on which the boot loader record will be installed, the drive order and additional options and kernel parameters. Typically, these options can be left unchanged.

**17.** Click Next to continue.

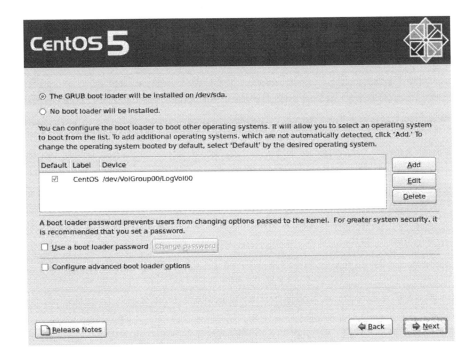

*Figure 1-9. Boot loader settings are configured in this screen.*

**18.** In the screen shown in Figure 1-10, you will set up the network devices, hostname, and miscellaneous settings.

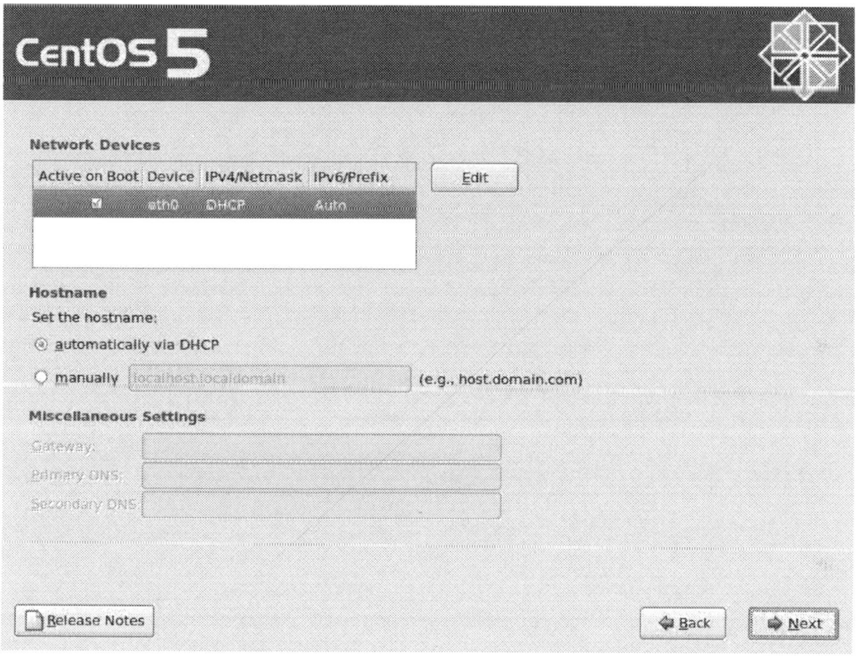

*Figure 1-10. Network settings are configured in this screen.*

**19.** Select a network device and click Edit. Supply the information listed in Table 1-1 or Table 1-2 as shown in Figure 1-11. Under IPv4, select Manual Configuration and supply the IP address and Netmask. IPv6 or the next generation IP addressing is not applicable in our setup, so remove the check from Enable IPv6 Support.

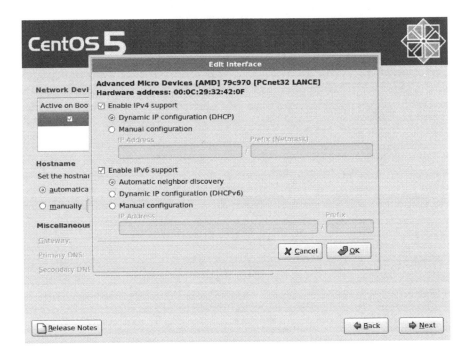

*Figure 1-11. You can set the IP address and netmask of your network device manually or receive the settings through Dynamic IP configuration (DHCP).*

**20.** Take note that on the server, you will be setting up two network devices, one for Internet access and one for the LAN. On the workstation, you will only need to edit one network device.

**21.** For the hostname, set the name of host manually, as shown in Tables 1-1 and 1-2. The hostname is basically the computer name.

22. The miscellaneous settings are used to configure the gateway and DNS settings. The gateway is used for routing. For the server, accessing other networks such as the Internet will go through the gateway server of your ISP provider. For the workstation, it will use the server as the gateway to connect to other networks such as the Internet. This is the best way to control the Internet traffic going in and out of the workstation. It filters what the server can access and forces the workstation to go through that server to access other networks. The DNS or Domain Naming System translates hostnames into IP addresses and vice versa. On the server, use the DNS provided by your ISP until the chapter on DNS, where we set up our own DNS service. For the workstation we use the server for DNS, which will work once the DNS service is configured on the server.

23. Click Next to continue.

24. In the screen shown in Figure 1-12, you can configure the time zone of your system. Choose the area of your time zone by clicking the city nearest your computer location on the map or by selecting an entry from the list. If you need the time to be updated for daylight savings time accordingly, keep System Clock Uses UTC checked. Click Next to continue.

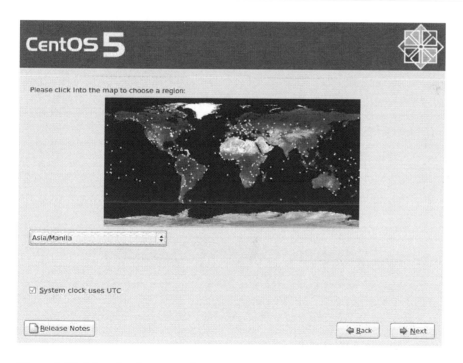

*Figure 1-12. Select the time zone of your system.*

**25.** In the screen shown in Figure 1-13 you will set the password of root, the administrator of this system. With root access, you have full control of the system, so you need to provide it with a password that is difficult to guess but easy to memorize so that you don't need to write it down. It should use more than seven characters, with uppercase and lowercase letters, digits, and special characters. You can use mnemonics such as converting your special phrase "I'm a Jazz Fan, I rock!", into "1'm@JF,1r!" For now, just provide the password listed in Table 1-1 or Table 1-2 and click Next when you're done.

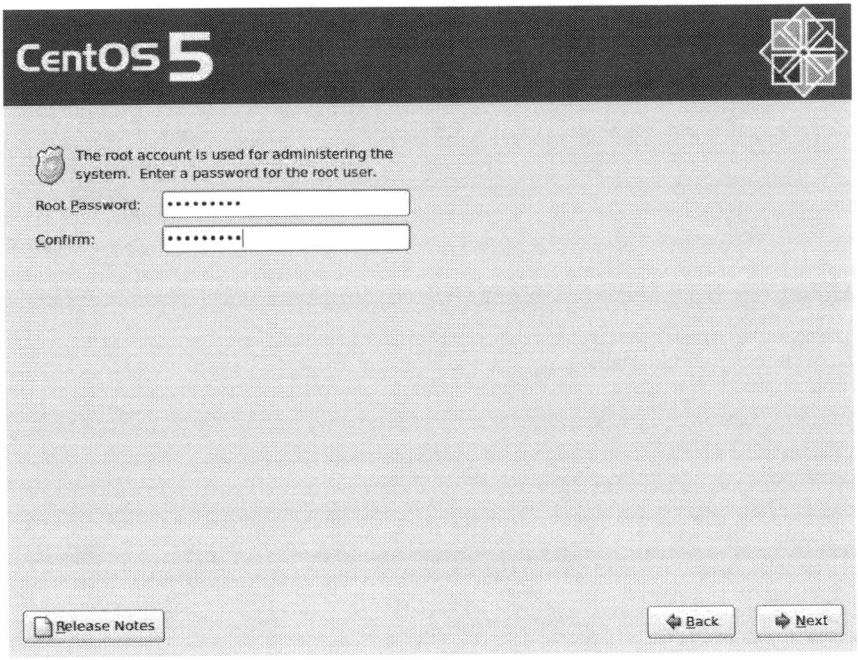

*Figure 1-13. Set the administrator password for your system.*

26. In the next screen, you have the option to select what software packages will be installed in your system, as shown in Figure 1-14. By default, CentOS is set to install the Gnome desktop environment. For now, just leave the option as is for both the server and the workstation. In later chapters you will learn how to install and remove software yourself.

27. You can also add third-party online repositories, such as CentOS Extras. These repositories are useful when the software you need is not in the base CentOS repository but is available elsewhere.

28. At the bottom, you have the option to customize the software packages in detail. For now, just ignore that and accept the option Customize Later.

29. Click Next to continue.

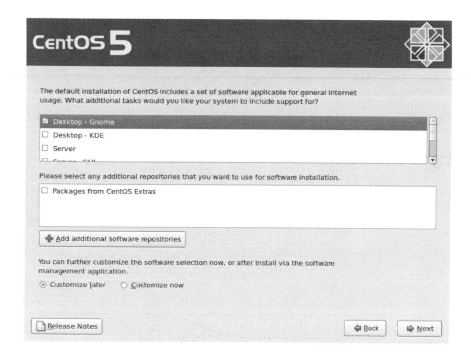

*Figure 1-14. You can choose the software to be installed in your system.*

**30.** The next screen, shown in Figure 1-15, prompts you to click Next to proceed with the installation. Installation logs will be stored in the /root/install.log file. These logs are useful for seeing if any errors occurred during the installation. A *kickstart* file based on the installation options you have chosen will be stored in /root/anaconda-ks.cfg. This type of file is useful if you want to apply the installation options you've chosen here to other servers. It provides a faster way to install the same setup on other servers than setting the same installation options on each server manually. Click Next to continue.

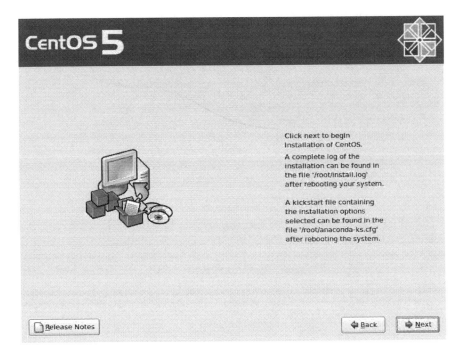

*Figure 1-15.* Clicking Next will start the installation process.

**31.** During the installation process, the partitions are being created permanently and software is being installed on the hard disk. As shown in Figure 1-16, advertisements for CentOS are displayed in the middle of the screen, while the status of the installation is shown through the progress bar at the bottom.

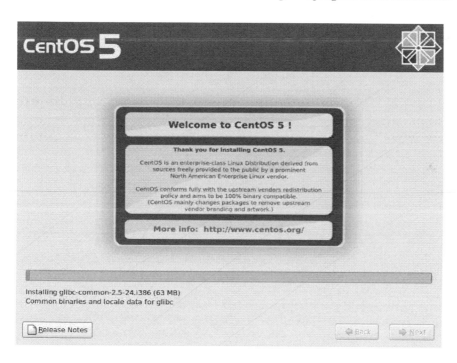

*Figure 1-16. CentOS is being installed on the system.*

**32.** Once the software is completely installed, the confirmation screen will appear, as shown in Figure 1-17. At this point, it's time to reboot the system. Click Reboot.

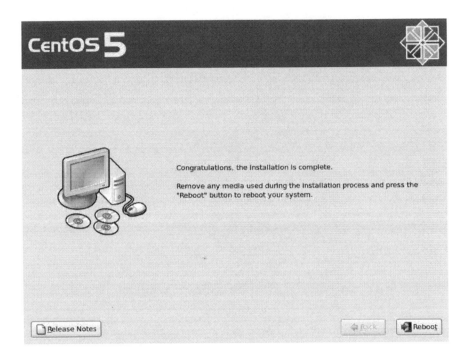

*Figure 1-17. Installation is now complete.*

33. After the system reboots, the newly installed CentOS will boot up. As shown in Figure 1-18, there are a few post-installation steps before you are able to log in to the system.

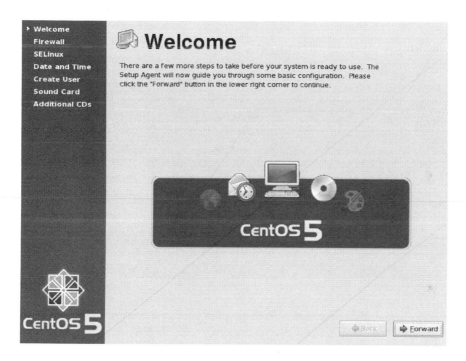

*Figure 1-18. The welcome screen of the post-installation steps.*

34. Click Forward to start the post-installation steps.

**35.** The screen to configure the firewall will appear, as shown in Figure 1-19. The first option, Firewall, allows you to enable or disable the firewall. The second option, Trusted Services, allows you to select which services on your system can be accessed through the network. By default, SSH (Secure Shell) is the only one set. SSH is useful for allowing computers over the network to access the system in a remote secure shell. The final option, Other Ports, allows you to specify services on your system that can be accessed through the network but are not defined under Trusted Services. For example, if your server is configured to run as a chat server such as Jabber, you would need to specify that port 5222 should be open so that chat clients can access the Jabber service your server is offering.

**36.** There's no need to change anything in the firewall settings, since SSH is enough for now. Click Forward to continue.

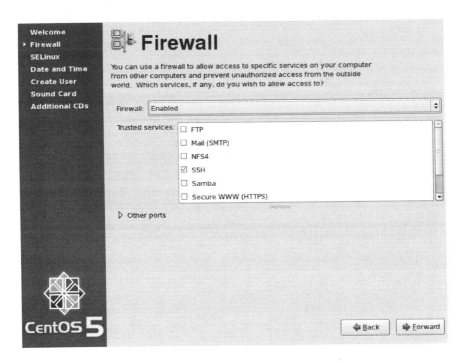

*Figure 1-19. Incoming connections on services can be permitted in the Firewall settings.*

**37.** The next setting to be configured, as shown in Figure 1-20, is SELinux (Security Enhanced Linux), which was developed by the NSA to provide security policies that harden the system considerably even from the administrators themselves. You can leave the default option unchanged and continue by clicking Forward.

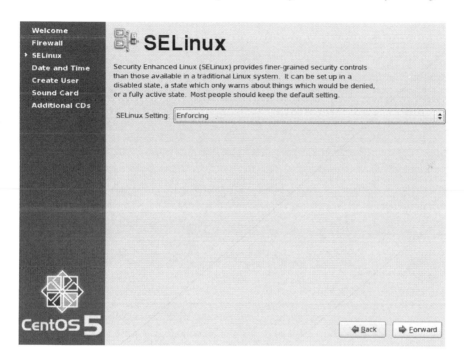

*Figure 1-20. SELinux settings can be configured here.*

**38.** The next setting to configure is Date and Time, as shown in Figure 1-21. You can opt to change the date and time manually by editing this information on the Date & Time tab. However, we recommend that you configure the system to use NTP under the Network Time Protocol tab so that the system will periodically poll time servers to keep your time up to date based on the selected time zone set during installation. This effectively prevents the effects of clock skews.

---

■ **Note:** For more information on clock skews, see http://en.wikipedia.org/wiki/ Clock_skew.

---

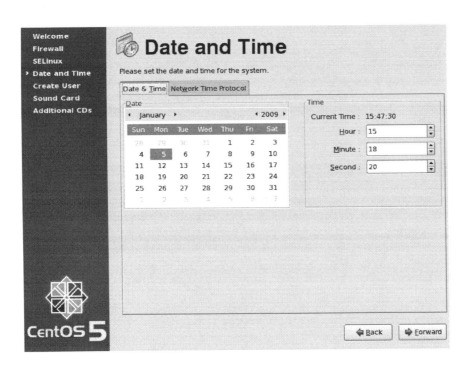

*Figure 1-21. You can configure the date and time manually, or use Network Time Protocol to update the system time periodically from time servers.*

**39.** The next step is to create a regular (nonadministrative) user, as shown in Figure 1-22. A regular user is able to use the system but cannot change its overall configuration, such as adding, updating, or deleting software installed by the administrator or creating other users. You can also verify account details by configuring CentOS to check from a network authentication service such as NIS or LDAP. You will learn how to authenticate accounts from a network authentication service in the later chapters. For now, provide the details of the regular user as stated in Tables 1-1 and 1-2. Click the Forward button to continue.

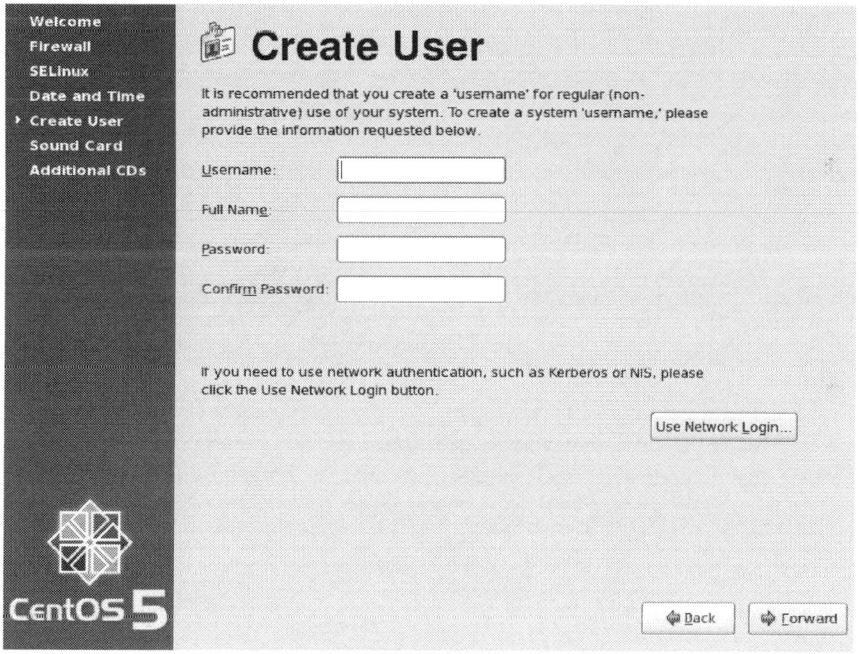

*Figure 1-22. You can create a regular user from this screen.*

**40.** In the next screen, shown in Figure 1-23, you can test your sound card if CentOS was able to detect one. If a sound card was detected, a Play button will appear. Click the Play button and listen to confirm that you can hear the sound. This is useful if you are installing CentOS on a workstation where you may listen to audio. Click Forward to continue.

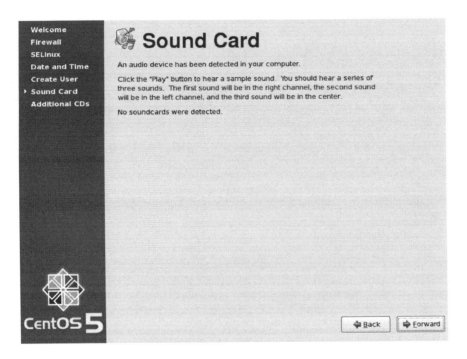

*Figure 1-23. You can test the sound card in this screen.*

**41.** The next screen, shown in Figure 1-24, is for adding third-party software through CDs. As far as we know, there are no third-party software CDs you can install in CentOS at this time, so just click Finish.

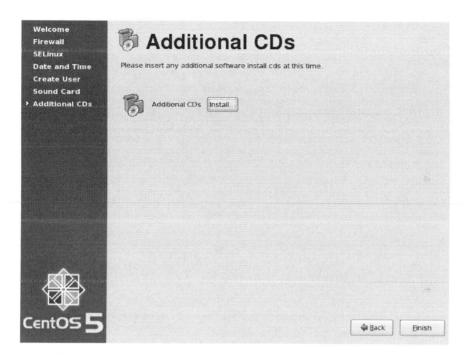

*Figure 1-24. You can add third- party software by installing additional CDs.*

**42.** At this point, you may now log in to the system via the login prompt as shown in Figure 1-25. You can log in as root or the regular user account that you created during installation.

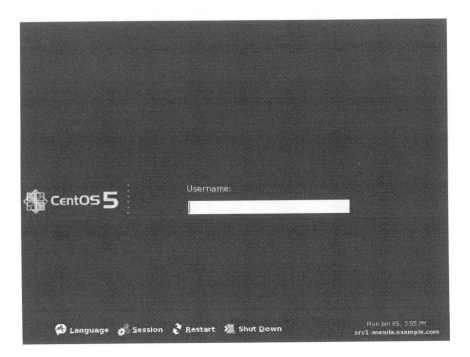

*Figure 1-25. Login prompt.*

**43.** Let's try logging in as root. Type **root** in the Username box and press Enter. In the screen that appears, you'll see a Password box; type the password you created for root and press Enter. If you were able to provide the right credentials, you be able to see the desktop as shown in Figure 1-26.

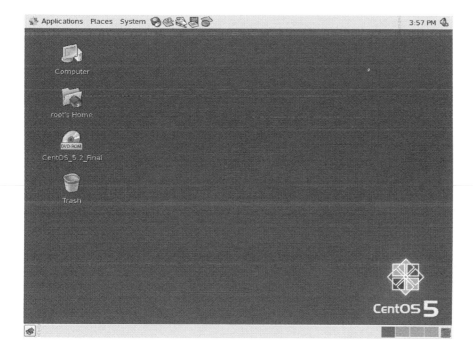

*Figure 1-26. The Linux desktop is shown after authentication.*

Finally, CentOS has been installed as a server and is up and running. To install it as a workstation on a separate computer, repeat the steps but use the settings in Table 1-2 as a guide for setting up the workstation.

# Troubleshooting

Should you have trouble installing CentOS in your system, you may want to try Googling the error messages to see how other users were able to overcome the problem. You can also ask for help from Linux forums and mailing lists. Finally, you can try working on the problem yourself by checking out the troubleshooting section of the online installation guide for assistance:

```
http://www.centos.org/docs/5/html/Installation_Guide-en-US/ch-trouble-x86.html
```

## Summary

Congratulations! You are now able to install CentOS on two different systems. Repetition helps you be more comfortable in setting up a CentOS installation on your own. Proceed to the next chapter to learn more about the command-line interface, Bash, which is used by most Linux system administrators to manage Linux servers rather than its GUI counterpart.

# CHAPTER 2

■ ■ ■

# Bash

System administration can be done using either text-based utilities (such as Bash, the Bourne-again shell) or graphical tools. There are more text-based utilities than graphical tools, however, and there are cases where it is more convenient to use one or the other. There are also cases where you must rely solely on text-based solutions, such as running the rescue environment. As a system administrator, you will be using a combination of both, deciding case by case which is best to get the job done.

In this chapter, you will learn the basics of running commands and text-based utilities as well as creating and running scripts. You will also learn how to get information should you get stuck. Graphical tools are discussed throughout the book alongside the systems they manage.

## Working with the Command-Line Interface

There are three conventional ways of running the command-line interface. You can use virtual consoles, a graphical terminal, or remotely log in through a secure shell.

The virtual consoles are text-based consoles similar to the VT100 terminals that were used to run Unix in the days when personal computers were not yet available. These consoles are used to run programs on the system, input data, and display output. CentOS provides six consoles by default, which are accessible by pressing Alt+F1 to F6, where each function key represents an individual console. However, if you're in graphical mode, you would need to hold Ctrl+Alt and select a terminal from F1 to F6. You can also navigate from one console to the other by holding Ctrl and pressing the left or right arrow key. In order to use the console, you must supply your username and password. To go back to graphical mode, press Alt+F7.

---

**Note:** For more information about VT100 terminals, see http://en.wikipedia.org/ wiki/VT100.

---

In graphical mode, simply log in to the graphical desktop and then run the terminal application by selecting Applications ➤ Accessories ➤ Terminal. This application is called the Gnome Terminal.

You can also log in remotely through the remote login service called SSH (secure shell). You can use this service from an SSH client such as PuTTY in Windows or from a Linux, Unix or Mac console. This service is accessible on the network if the firewall allows access to it.

▓ **Tip** You can allow incoming SSH requests by adding SSH to the trusted services using the Security Level Configuration tool, which you can find in System ➤ Administration ➤ Security Level and Firewall or by entering the command `system-config-securitylevel`. See Chapter 10 for more information about network security. SSH is allowed by default.

From the console, run the command ssh `<username>@<IP Address>` where *username* is the username of your account and *IP address* is the IP address of the Linux host. You will be prompted to provide the password of your account.

▓ **Note:** You can get a copy of PuTTY from `www.chiark.greenend.org.uk/~sgtatham/ putty/download.html`.

At this point, you are actually running a *shell*. The shell is an environment where you can interact with the system in text mode. It provides you with a prompt to key in your commands. Once you invoke a command it will do your bidding.

The prompt itself provides useful information, as shown in Figure 2-1. The information enclosed inside the square brackets comprises the current working user, the hostname of the system, and the present working directory. The current working user and hostname are separated by the at symbol (@), while the hostname and present working directory are separated by a space. In this case, the username, hostname, and current directory are juan, srv1-manila, and ~, respectively. The tilde (~) refers to the home directory of the user. The symbol after the closing square bracket can be either a dollar sign ($), denoting a regular user, or a hash symbol (#), denoting that the user is the system administrator.

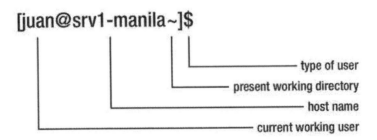

*Figure 2-1. Dissection of the command prompt*

## Identifying the Working User

Let's start by running your first command, whoami, which prints the username of the user running the shell. If you logged in as juan, for example, then the user running the terminal is also juan. You can verify this by executing the command as shown in Listing 2-1. Take note that as a regular user, you will not be able to make system-wide changes. You need to log in as root to do that. Also, the commands are case-sensitive, so issuing the command Whoami will lead to an error.

***Listing 2-1.*** *Running Your First Command*

```
[juan@srv1-manila ~]$ whoami
juan
```

The next command to be learned is how to switch to a different user; specifically, switching to the root user. This is more prudent than logging in as the system administrator directly. If you log in as root at the start, all programs you run from the desktop will run with system administrator privileges, which could lead to accidents. It is safer to run programs as root only when you need root's privileges. So the next command is called su, or switch user, which is used to change the current working user to another user. The command to type on the terminal is su -, which says that you would like to log in as root within this shell. If you key in the root password and then press Enter, the prompt will now end with a #, which denotes that the shell is now running as the root user. Again, you can verify the user running the shell by issuing whoami as shown in Listing 2-2.

---

▓ **Tip** If you would like to switch to a user other than root, all you need to do is pass the username as an argument. For example, to switch to David's account, just invoke su - david.

---

***Listing 2-2.*** *Switching to the Root User*

```
[juan@srv1-manila ~]$ su - root
Password:
[root@srv1-manila ~]# whoami
root
```

As root, you can now do system administration tasks such as managing users, running services, and performing maintenance. To log out from root, type the command exit and then press Enter. This will revert the shell to the previous user.

Before we go further with other commands, you need to understand how data is stored in your system. Here's a quick look at the Linux filesystem.

## The Linux Filesystem

Computer files are basically data that is stored on media such as hard disks, CDs, floppy disks, and memory sticks.

These files can contain programs, databases, images, music, movies, text documents, and so on. To organize files, we group them in directories or folders. For further organization, directories can also be placed inside other directories. (In the Unix world, folders are strictly called directories, but in this book, we will use these terms interchangeably.)

---

▓ **Note:** Any item inside the filesystem is a file. A directory is a special type of file that can contain other files and directories.

---

All directories are placed under one main directory, called the root directory, which is represented by the slash symbol (/).Table 2-1 lists the significant subdirectories.

*Table 2-1. Subdirectories in the Root (/) Directory*

| Directory | Contents |
| --- | --- |
| root | The home directory of root , the system administrator |
| home | Home directories of regular users |
| bin | Shells and command-line utilities, some of which are required to run the system |
| sbin | Command-line system administration utilities, several of which are required to run the system |
| lib | Reusable system libraries needed by programs |
| usr | Programs, configuration settings, libraries, and help files that can be shared with multiple systems |
| usr/bin | Many utilities and applications |
| usr/sbin | Many system administration utilities |
| usr/lib | Many reusable system libraries that are used and dependent on by programs |
| var | Variable data such as logs, database, web files, spool directories for mail, and so on |
| boot | The kernel, initial RAM disk, and boot loader, which are responsible for booting up the system |
| etc | System-wide configuration files |
| lost+found | Files recovered by the file system checker after improper shutdowns such as a system crash or power failure |
| media | Directories used for automatically mounting removable drives such as CD-ROM, DVD, and USB storage devices |
| misc | Directories typically used for mounting NFS directories |
| srv | Data served by your system through services such as web, ftp, or cvs |
| mnt | Folders used for temporarily mounting remote directories (NFS, Samba) and removable drives (CD-ROM, DVD, and USB devices) |

*Table 2-1.* *Subdirectories in the Root (/) Directory (continued)*

| | |
|---|---|
| opt | third-party software applications |
| proc | A virtual filesystem that contains special files used for changing or displaying kernel settings |
| dev | Files that represent the hardware devices in your system and virtual devices supplied by the kernel |
| selinux | A virtual filesystem containing special files used for changing or displaying SELinux settings |
| sys | A virtual filesystem that contains special files used for changing or displaying devices that are hot-pluggable |
| tmp | Temporary files and folders that are deleted periodically by the system |

For now, understanding each subdirectory under the root directory is a tall order. It takes time, but you will understand all of them as you learn how to execute system administration tasks.

## Directory Management

A good way to start learning about the subdirectories under the root directory is to begin with directory management. Table 2-2 lists the directory management utilities at your disposal.

*Table 2-2.* *Directory Management Utilities*

| Utiltity | Description | Usage |
|---|---|---|
| pwd | Displays the present working directory. | pwd |
| cd | Changes the working directory. | cd <directory> |
| mkdir | Creates a new directory. | mkdir <directory> |
| mv | Renames or moves files or directories. | mv <source> <target> |
| ls | Lists the contents of a directory. | ls <directory> |
| rm | Deletes files. | rm <file> [<file2> [<file..>]] |
| rmdir | Deletes an empty directory. | rmdir <directory> |

A shell has a *present working directory*. Many commands process the contents of the present working directory unless explicitly told otherwise. When you run a terminal, the working directory will initially be the home directory of the user. For example, because regular users have their home directories stored in the /home directory, the current working directory for username juan would be /home/juan. To verify the present working directory, use the command pwd, which prints out the present working directory as shown in Listing 2-3.

*Listing 2-3. Displaying the Present Working Directory*

```
[juan@srv1-manila ~]$ pwd
/home/juan
[juan@srv1-manila ~]$ su -
Password:
[root@srv1-manila ~]# pwd
/root
```

## Listing the Contents of a Directory

The ls command is used for displaying the contents of a directory. When executed, it displays the contents of the present working directory, as shown in Listing 2-4. In this example, /home/juan contains an item called Desktop.

*Listing 2-4. Displaying a Directory Listing*

```
[juan@srv1-manila ~]$ ls
Desktop
```

The ls command can be used to display the contents of a different directory by providing it a command-line argument. For ls, the argument is the directory you want to list. The format for using ls with arguments is
 ls <arg1> <arg2> <arg3> ... <argn>
For example, to list the contents of the root directory, just issue the command ls / as shown in Listing 2-5. You could also list several directories by adding more arguments. All you need to do is to separate the arguments with a space.

*Listing 2-5. Directory listing of /*

```
[juan@srv1-manila ~]$ ls /
bin   dev  home  lost+found  misc  net  proc  sbin     srv  tmp  var
boot  etc  lib   media              mnt  opt   root  selinux  sys  usr
```

Try listing the contents of bin and tmp by issuing the commands ls /bin and ls /tmp, respectively.

▓ **Note:** Notice that to display the `bin` and `tmp` directories using `ls`, we added / before the directory names. This is because `bin` and `tmp` are under the / or root directory. However, issuing the commands `ls bin` and `ls tmp` would result in errors, because CentOS would look for these folders under the present working directory (unless the present working directory is the root directory). The problem is that paths can be either *relative* or *absolute*, as discussed later in this chapter.

To see the difference between an ordinary file and a directory in a directory listing, you can pass the option --1, which displays more information about every file listed in the directory. It provides the file type, file permissions, number of links or directories, user ownership, group ownership, size, and the date last modified of each file, as shown in Figure 2-2.

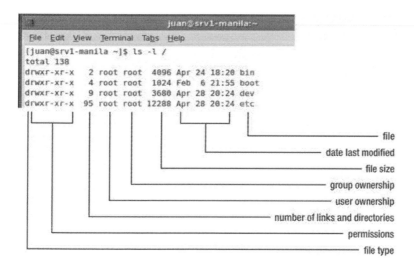

*Figure 2-2. Dissection of the command ls -l*

One file type, the dash (-), represents an ordinary file while the letter d represents a directory. The complete list of file types is enumerated in Table 2-3.

**Table 2-3.** *Linux File Types*

| Symbol | File Type | Description |
| --- | --- | --- |
| – | Ordinary file | Files such as text, image, database, binary, and so on |
| d | Directory | A special file that can contain other files |
| l | Symbolic link | A shortcut or reference to another file |
| b | Block device | Devices that can send and receive buffered or random data such as CD, DVD, and hard disks |
| c | Character device | Devices that can send and receive data in a sequence of characters, such as modems and virtual terminals |
| s | Sockets | Files used for communication within processes in the local system without using network protocols |
| p | Named pipe | Pipes represented in the filesystem |

▓ **Note:** See the "Piping" section later in this chapter to learn how to use a pipe. To learn more about named pipes, see http://www.linuxjournal.com/article/2156.

A symbolic link (or *symlink*) is a shortcut or reference to another file. An example of a symlink is the configuration file for the bootloader, /etc/grub.conf. That file is just a shortcut to the real file, /boot/grub/grub.conf, as shown in Listing 2-6. Here you can see the name of the symlink (/etc/grub.conf) and after the right arrow (->) the location of the real file that the symlink is pointing to.

**Listing 2-6.** *Listing a Symbolic Link*

```
[juan@srv1-manila ~]$ ls -l /etc/grub.conf
lrwxrwxrwx 1 root root 22 Feb  6 14:14 /etc/grub.conf -> ../boot/grub/grub.conf
```

The link is apt because system-wide configuration files should be stored under the /etc directory. You can create your own symlink by issuing the command

```
ln -s <original file> <shortcut file>
```

Deleting the symlink will only delete the symlink and not the original file itself. However, if you delete the original file, the symlink will still exist and any reference made to the symlink will cause an error.

Another type of link is called a *hard link*. Every file has an *inode*, which contains metadata about the file such as its file type, permissions, user ownership, and group ownership. The difference between a symlink and a hard link is that a hard link has the same inode as the original file. This means that even if you delete the original file, for as long as the hard link exists, the file will not be deleted. The only restriction on a hard link is that you cannot create a link across partitions. However, if you need to create that kind of short cut, you can use a symlink. To create a hard link, use the command

```
ln <original file> <shortcut file>
```

The number of links or directories in a directory listing specifies the number of hard links of a file or the number of directories within a directory. Notice in Figure 2-2 that most ordinary files have a value of one unless a file has hard links. Directories, on the other hand, will have a minimum of two. This is because every directory has two special directories, named (.) and (..). The single dot (.) specifies the directory itself. For example, issuing the commands ls /etc and ls /etc/ command. will have the same result, because the single dot represents the etc directory itself. The double dot (..) represents one directory above the specified directory. For example, issuing the command ls /etc/.. lists the contents of the root(/) directory since the directory above /etc is root(/).

Permissions specify what the owner, member of the group, and others can do with the file. User ownership specifies which user owns the file, and group ownership specifies which group owns the file. This will be discussed further in Chapter 3.

The size represents the amount of disk space in bytes that a file occupies. For a more human-readable format, you can use the disk usage command, du -h <directory>/*, to see the file size in kilobytes, megabytes, gigabytes, and terabytes.

The date last modified specifies when the file was last updated. If you run a listing of the /var directory, you will notice that the files there are updated very frequently, especially the files under the log directory, /var/log.

## Traversing Directories

To change the present working directory, use the cd command. This command takes a directory as argument: cd <arg>. Again, we can verify the new working directory by using pwd and ls, as shown in Listing 2-7.

*Listing 2-7. Changing the Present Working Directory*

```
[juan@srv1-manila ~]$ cd /
[juan@srv1-manila /]$ pwd
/
[juan@srv1-manila /]$ ls
bin   dev  home  lost+found  misc  net  proc  sbin    srv  tmp  var
boot  etc  lib   media       mnt   opt  root  selinux  sys  usr
```

Notice that the result of pwd is /, and running ls with no arguments displays the contents of /. This means that the present working directory has been changed to /. Also notice at the command prompt that the symbol ~ has been replaced with the symbol /. When you see the tilde (~), it means that present working directory is the home directory of the user. You will see this symbol again when you cd back to your home directory.

## Absolute and Relative Paths

When passing a file as an argument to a command, you can use either *absolute* or *relative* paths to point to the location of a file. An absolute path specifies the path of the file starting from the root (/) directory.

For example, to change the working directory to /usr/share/doc/zip-2.31 to view the documentation files of the zip utility , you would need to type the command
cd /usr/share/doc/zip-2.31

To change the working directory to view the documentation files of xterm using an absolute path, you would need to start from the root (/) directory and therefore issue the command
 cd /usr/share/doc/xterm-215.

You can make it simpler by using relative paths, since the path starts at the current working directory. Instead of specifying the absolute path, you can issue the command

cd ../xterm-215

which will yield the same result. Besides starting from the current working directory, you can use the tilde to specify that the path starts from your home directory. For example, issuing the command

cd ~/Desktop

means that you want change the working directory to Desktop subdirectory under your home directory.

## Creating Directories

As you already know, directories are used to organize related files. To create your own directory, you use the command mkdir. The format of this command is

mkdir <arg1> <arg2> <arg3> ... <argn>

The directories to be created are based on the arguments passed on to the command. For example, run the command mkdir script in your home directory. This creates a script directory under the present working directory, which on Juan's system is /home/juan. You can use ls to verify that the directory was created, as shown in Listing 2-8.

**Listing 2-8.** *Creating a New Directory*

```
[juan@srv1-manila ~]$ mkdir script
[juan@srv1-manila ~]$ ls
Desktop  script
```

## Renaming and Moving Files

To rename directories and files, use the mv command, which accepts two arguments, *source* and *destination*, as shown below:
mv <source> <destination>

This command renames the *source* to the *destination* name. For example, to rename the directory script that we created into scripts, we issue the command mv script scripts, as shown in Listing 2-9.

**Listing 2-9.** *Renaming a Directory*

```
[juan@srv1-manila ~]$ mv script scripts
[juan@srv1-manila ~]$ ls
Desktop  scripts
```

The same holds true for renaming files. If you pass filenames as arguments, the source file will be renamed to the destination name. Indeed, there is no command called rename in the Linux world. To test this, let's create an empty file, by using the touch command. To create an empty file called test, issue the command touch test, as shown in Listing 2-10.

---

▓ **Note:** Using touch on an existing file updates the file's timestamp to the current time.

---

*Listing 2-10. Creating an Empty File*

```
[juan@srv1-manila ~]$ touch test
[juan@srv1-manila ~]$ ls
Desktop  scripts  test
```

To rename the file to test1, issue the command mv test test1, as shown in Listing 2-11.

*Listing 2-11. Renaming a File*

```
[juan@srv1-manila ~]$ mv test test1
[juan@srv1-manila ~]$ ls
Desktop  scripts  test1
```

You can also use mv to move files or folders to another directory. The destination must be an existing directory, or mv will just rename the source. For example, to move test1 into the script folder, issue the command mv test1 scripts, as shown in Listing 2-12.

*Listing 2-12. Moving a File*

```
[juan@srv1-manila ~]$ mv test1 scripts
[juan@srv1-manila ~]$ ls
Desktop  scripts
[juan@srv1-manila ~]$ ls scripts
test1
```

## Deleting Directories and Files

To free up disk space, you must delete files or directories you no longer need. To delete a directory we use the command rmdir, which accepts a directory as an argument. The command will delete a directory only if it is empty. Try deleting the scripts folder by issuing the command rmdir scripts, as shown in Listing 2-13.

*Listing 2-13. Deleting a Directory That Has Contents*

```
[juan@srv1-manila ~]$ rmdir scripts
rmdir: scripts: Directory not empty
```

The scripts folder contains the file test1, so we need to remove that before we can delete the scripts folder. The command for deleting a file is rm, which accepts a filename to delete as an argument. To delete the test1 file, run the command rm scripts/test1, as shown in Listing 2-14.

*Listing 2-14. Deleting a File*

```
[juan@srv1-manila ~]$ rm scripts/test1
[juan@srv1-manila ~]$ ls scripts
[juan@srv1-manila ~]$
```

As you can see, test1 has now been deleted from the scripts folder. You can now delete the scripts directory, as shown in Listing 2-15.

*Listing 2-15. Deleting an Empty Directory*

```
[juan@srv1-manila ~]$ rmdir scripts
[juan@srv1-manila ~]$ ls
Desktop
```

You can also delete files with similar names using wildcards. For example, to delete files that end with .tmp, you can issue the command rm *.tmp, where * could be zero or more characters.

---

▨ **Caution:** If you need to delete a directory regardless of what files it contains, you can use the rm -rf <*directory*> command. The -r option means recursive deletion, while -f means that it will delete the files without asking for your consent. Be careful when using these options, because you might accidentally delete files you don't want to delete.

---

## Creating and Viewing Text Files

It's essential for you to learn how to create, edit, and view text files. Most configuration files are in plain text, so if all the tools, whether text-based or GUI-based, fail, you can easily fix those configurations yourself using a text editor.

The command to create a text file is vi, which accepts a filename as an argument. To start, we'll create a file called sample.txt. On the terminal, type vi sample.txt and press Enter.

The vi interface starts in its normal mode, where you can scroll, delete, copy, and paste text based on the key or sequence of keys you type. Table 2-4, lists the common actions you can do in normal mode.

*Table 2-4. Common Actions in Vi Normal Mode*

| Key/Command | Description |
| --- | --- |
| Up arrow, k | Move the cursor up. |
| Down arrow, j | Move the cursor down. |
| Left arrow, h | Move the cursor left. |
| Right arrow, l | Move the cursor right. |
| :q | Exit the program. |
| :q! | Exit the program regardless of any changes on the file. |
| :w | Save the file. |
| :wq | Save the file and exits the program. |
| x | Delete a character at the cursor. |
| dw | Delete a word under the cursor. |
| dd | Delete the line under the cursor. |
| /<text> | Search for the specified text. |
| n | Cycle through all the search matches. |
| u | Undo the previous command. |
| yy | Copy a line. |
| yw | Copy a word. |
| p | Paste the copied text. |
| i | Switch to insert mode. |

In order to insert text in vi, you need to switch to insert mode by pressing i. If you see – INSERT – at the lower-left corner of the vi interface, it means you are in insert mode. Type the following text: Hello World!

To save this text as a file, you need to toggle back to the normal mode by pressing Esc. Once you're in normal mode, type, :w and press Enter to save the file. To exit the vi interface, type :q and then press Enter.

The easiest way to familiarize yourself with vi is by learning through the tutorial that comes with it. To run the tutorial, invoke the command vimtutor and do at least Lessons 1 and 2.

---

■ **Note:** If you have trouble using vi, you can also use an editor that's easier to use, called nano. Like vi, it also accepts a filename to edit as an argument. To save your work in nano, type Ctrl+O. To quit, type Ctrl+Q.

---

## Viewing the Contents of a File

How do you view the file you created? Of course, you can use the vi editor to view and edit the file by typing vi sample.txt. However, if you would simply like to view the contents of the file, you can use the cat command. Type cat sample.txt to view the file, as shown in Listing 2-16.

*Listing 2-16. Viewing the Contents of a File*

```
[juan@srv1-manila ~]# cat sample.txt
Hello world!
```

Try viewing the bootloader configuration file by running the command cat /etc/grub.conf.

To read a long file, you can scroll the contents up and down by using Ctrl+PgUp and Ctrl+PgDn, but the console only remembers a relatively small amount, so for really long files this won't help. If you need to scroll through the whole text you can use the more or less command instead of cat. The more command allows you to scroll the content page-wise from top to bottom. You can use the spacebar or the Enter key to scroll down. The less command provides a Vi-like interface that allows you to scroll up and down by using PgUp or u to scroll up and PgDn or d to scroll down. You can also search for a keyword or test using the / key. Try issuing the commands

more /var/log/messages

and

less /var/log/messages

to see the difference.

To view a portion of the top and bottom of a file, you can use the commands head and tail, respectively. The head command will display the first ten lines of a file, while tail will display the last ten lines. However, if you need more or less than ten lines, you can pass the parameter –n<*number of lines*> to both commands to specify the number of lines to be displayed. One very useful parameter for the tail command is –f, which displays the last lines of the file and any new lines appended to the file. This is quite useful for troubleshooting services by monitoring their log files. For example, to monitor the system logs, issue the command

tail -f /var/log/messages

and see what new logs will be stored in this file while troubleshooting.

Finally, if the server is configured to print to a printer, you can print the contents of the file using the lp command. Just provide the filename as argument; for example, lp /etc/grub.conf prints the boot configuration to the printer.

# Text Processing

There are situations where browsing through data is just too tedious, and being able to view the specific data that you want, or to format the data in the manner that you want, will allow you to process it faster. There are several commands you can use to make this happen. This section looks at summarizing, searching, filtering, and formatting text.

Table 2-5 lists the commonly used text processing utilities.

***Table 2-5.*** *Text Processing Commands*

| Command | Usage | Description |
| --- | --- | --- |
| wc | wc <file> | Prints the number of lines, words, and characters in a file. |
| grep | grep <pattern> <file> | Prints lines in a file that matches the pattern. |
| tr | tr <set1> <set2> <file> | Replaces characters in *file* that match *set1* to *set2*. |
| cut | cut <option> | Cuts sections per line in a file. |
| sort | Sort | Sorts lines of text in a file |

The wc (word count) command provides a summary of a text file by displaying the number of lines, words, and characters in it. If you only want to display the number of lines, words, or characters, you can pass the options –l, –w, –c, respectively. For example, to display the number of lines in the password file, /etc/passwd, which translates to the number of users in the system, you can issue the command wc –l /etc/passwd.

The grep command is generally used to search for a pattern in a text file and print it on the screen. For example, if you are looking for the word "error" in the system log, /var/log/messages, the command to be issued would be
grep error /var/log/messages

However, if the search pattern is more than one word, you should enclose the pattern in quotes. For example, if you are looking for "John Smith" in a file called directory.txt, then you should issue the command

    grep "John Smith" directory.txt

By default, grep is case sensitive when matching patterns, but you can make it case insensitive by passing the –i option. Another useful option is –v, which prints everything on the file that does not match the pattern. To search for a pattern in a directory recursively, use the –r option. For example, if you are looking for the pattern "passwd" in any file under the /etc directory, you would issue the command

grep –r "passwd" /etc

Table 2-6 lists the patterns you can use to widen or narrow your search results.

*Table 2-6. Common grep Patterns*

| Pattern | Description |
| --- | --- |
| '[aeiou]' | Matches a single character a, e, i, o or u. |
| '[a-z]' | Matches a single character from a to z. |
| '[a-z][A-Z]' | Matches a single character from a to z and A to Z. |
| '[0-9]' | Matches a single character from 0 to 9. |
| '^<*pattern*>' | Matches a line that starts with a particular pattern. |
| '<*pattern*>$' | Matches a line that ends with a particular pattern. |
| '^[a-z][0-9]$' | Matches a line that only contains a letter followed by a number. |
| '.' | Matches any single character. |
| '<*pattern*>+' | Matches one instance or more of the previous pattern. |
| '<*pattern*>*' | Matches zero instance or more of the previous pattern. |
| '<*pattern*>?' | Matches zero or one instance of the previous pattern. |
| '(abc)+' | Matches a line that contains one or more patterns of 'abc'. |

You can sort the contents of a file in alphabetical order using the sort command. For example, to sort the contents of the password file, you can run the command sort /etc/passwd.

# Standard I/O Devices

Every program in Linux and Unix operating systems apply the concept of I/O streams for passing data into and out of the program. The standard streams are called *standard input, standard output,* and *standard error.*

The standard input by default gets its input from the keyboard. Remember the cat command we used to display contents of a file? By default, it takes input from the keyboard. As a test, at the cat command type anything and press Enter. As soon as you do, everything you typed will be displayed on the screen. Press Ctrl+C to exit cat.

By default, the standard output and error streams send their data to the monitor. This is evident with all the commands that you have executed; the output is displayed on the screen whether it is a successful result or a syntax error.

# Redirection

You can redirect the standard streams to your liking by using the redirection operators >, >>, and <. The greater-than sign (>) denotes that instead of going to monitor, the output will be written to the item on the right side of it. For example, suppose you want to store the output of a listing of the root (/) directory in a file called root.txt. You would issue the command ls / > root.txt. If you try this, you will see that the output is not displayed on the screen, but is instead written to root.txt.

---

■ **Note:** To redirect standard error, you need to append the file descriptor 2 to the operator. For example, try running cat /etc/shadow 2> errors.txt as a regular user. Any errors that arise from this command will be stored in error.txt. The file descriptors for standard input and output are 0 and 1, respectively.

---

The only concern with > is that it overwrites the output file. If you want the new output to be appended to the file, you should use >> instead. Try running ls / >> root.txt and view the contents root.txt to see the difference.

The < operator, on the other hand, redirects standard input. Instead of coming from the keyboard, the input comes from whatever source you specify on the right side of the less-than sign and is passed to the item on the left side. For example, the command cat < root.txt displays the input that comes from root.txt. As another example, the command

```
mysql sampledb < sample.txt
```

imports the contents of a database text file to a MySQL database. You will learn more about MySQL in Chapter 12.

# Piping

Another form of redirection is *piping,* represented with a vertical bar (|) on the command line, which allows you to pass the output of one command as input to another command. Basically, the output of the command on the left side of the pipe symbol becomes the input of the command on the right. For example, to view the contents of dmesg in less, you can issue the command dmesg | less.

Combining piping with text processing is very practical and convenient for formatting data if it is to be processed by several commands. For example, the tr command substitutes one set of characters for another set, and if you want to display the system log but with any occurrence of "error" displayed as "ERROR" so that you can see the errors easily, you would issue the command

```
cat /var/log/messages | tr 'error' 'ERROR'
```

As another example, to print all lines from /etc/passwd that contain root, we would run this command:

```
cat /etc/passwd|grep "root"
```

with the results shown in Listing 2-17.

*Listing 2-17. Using grep and pipe*

```
[juan@srv1-manila ~]$ cat /etc/passwd|grep "root"
```

```
root:x:0:0:root:/root:/bin/bash
operator:x:11:0:operator:/root:/sbin/nologin
```

Finally, another useful command is cut, which you can use to display portions of a line of output. Two practical options are –d and –f. You can format lines of output into columns by using the –d option, where you specify what character denotes the delimiter or separator for a column. The –f option can be used to specify which columns to display. For example, with the password file, you can treat the colons as delimiters, where the first and sixth columns can represent the username and home directory respectively. If you would like to display only these columns, you can issue the command

```
cat /etc/passwd|cut -d ":" -f1,6
```

as shown in Listing 2-18.

***Listing 2-18.*** *Using cut to display portions in a line of text*

```
[juan@srv1-manila ~]$ cat /etc/passwd|cut -d ":" -f1,6
root:/root
bin:/bin
daemon:/sbin
adm:/var/adm
lp:/var/spool/lpd
sync:/sbin
shutdown:/sbin
halt:/sbin
<snipped>
```

If you want the output sorted, you can issue the command

```
cat /etc/passwd|cut -d ":" -f1,6 | sort
```

If you want to store the output in the file users.txt, you can issue the command

```
cat /etc/passwd|cut -d ":" -f1,6 | sort > users.txt
```

# Getting Help

Need help? The shell actually helps you type the appropriate command through *auto-completion*. To use it, press the Tab key. Try typing who and pressing Tab twice. You will be provided three options, who, whoami and whois. If you type a and then press Tab, the shell will complete the command whoami for you. The shell can also auto-complete directory paths as well. Try typing ls /m and pressing Tab twice. You will be provided with three options, media, misc and mnt. If you type e and then press Tab, the shell will auto-complete the command by typing the path media for you.

However, there are many commands, and you need to know how to use them. You can use Google to get your answers, and that is the best place to find most of the solutions to your queries. However, online manuals and documentation are also available in your system. To view the online manual of a particular command, use the command man, which accepts a command name as an argument. For example, to view the online manual of command ls, we run the command man ls. Figure 2-3 shows the results.

*Figure 2-3. The man interface*

You can press the Up arrow or type U to scroll up and the Down arrow or D to scroll down through online manual. Press Q to exit the man interface. To learn more about man, you can also issue the command man  man for details.

Another command used to get online documentation is info, which displays the info files that come with the commands. Try running info  ls, to see this information as shown in Figure 2-4. Use the same techniques as in the man interface for navigating the menu and quitting info.

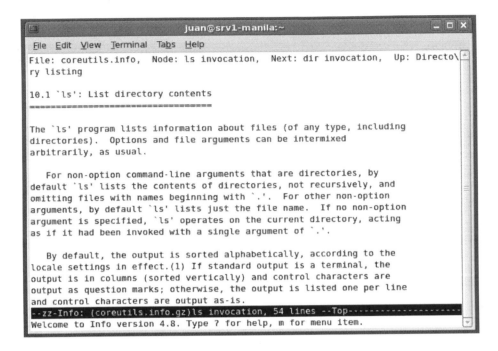

*Figure 2-4. The info command*

You can also get more information by passing the --help parameter right after the command. Try issuing the command ls --help, as shown in Listing 2-19.

*Listing 2-19. Output from the --help Parameter*

```
[juan@srv1-manila bash-3.2]$ ls --help
Usage: ls [OPTION]... [FILE]...
List information about the FILEs (the current directory by default).
Sort entries alphabetically if none of -cftuvSUX nor --sort.

Mandatory arguments to long options are mandatory for short options too.
  -a, --all                  do not ignore entries starting with .
  -A, --almost-all           do not list implied . and ..
      --author               with -l, print the author of each file
  -b, --escape               print octal escapes for nongraphic characters
      --block-size=SIZE      use SIZE-byte blocks
  -B, --ignore-backups       do not list implied entries ending with ~
```

■ **Note:** Not all commands have a man page or –info file or accept the --help parameter.

Another useful command is whatis <*command*>, which provides a brief description of what a command does. The apropos <*keyword*> command, by contrast, displays a brief description of commands that match the keyword. Try running whatis passwd and apropos passwd to see the difference. Listing 2-20 shows the output of apropos passwd.

*Listing 2-20. Using apropos*

```
[juan@srv1-manila ~]$ apropos passwd
chpasswd              (8)  - update passwords in batch mode
fgetpwent_r [getpwent_r] (3)  - get passwd file entry reentrantly
getpwent_r            (3)    get passwd file entry reentrantly
gpasswd               (1)  - administer the /etc/group file
htpasswd              (1)  - Manage user files for basic authentication
lpasswd               (1)  - Change group or user password
lppasswd              (1)  - add, change, or delete digest passwords
pam_localuser         (8)  - require users to be listed in /etc/passwd
pam_passwdqc          (8)  - Password quality-control PAM module
```

Finally, you can browse information about the packages installed on the directory /usr/share/doc. You may find change logs, sample configuration files, readme files, todo files, release info, and other information that you may need.

# Environment Variables

Variables are placeholders for data. You can declare your own variable and place data in it. For example, suppose you would like to declare a variable called A, which contains the value test. To do this, all you need to do is to run the command A=test. The equal sign (=) is used to assign the value on its right side to its left side. In other words, A takes the value of test.

To get the value in the variable A, you can obtain the value in it by prefixing it with the dollar sign ($). For example, there's a command called echo, which is used to display text. Try running the command echo "Hello, world!" and you will see the output "Hello World" on the screen. To display the value in the variable A, you can issue the command

```
echo "The value of A is $A".
```

In addition to assigning the values to a variable explicitly, you can actually store a value coming from a keyboard input. To do this for variable A, run the command read A. Everything you type until you press Enter will be stored in A. Again, you can display the contents of A by running the command

```
echo "The value of A is $A"
```

There are variables that affect the shell, called environment variables. To see what these variables are, just run the command env, which displays the environment variables as well as their corresponding values. Some of these variables, which affect all users, are configured under /etc/bashrc. If you would like to customize these variables for your account only, you can override them from the .bashrc file in your home directory.

One useful environment variable is PATH, which is used to look for binaries and scripts to run. For example, the value of the PATH variable for juan is /usr/kerberos/bin:/usr/local/bin:/bin:/usr/bin:/home/juan/bin. The commands that you have been running are stored in /bin and /usr/bin. If the PATH variable was not set, to issue a command, you would need to specify the full path which is cumbersome. For example, to issue the mkdir command, you would need to run /bin/mkdir if the PATH variable had not been set.

If you are going to customize the value of an environment variable, be sure to use the export command to ensure that the variable is accessible to all future programs and shells you launch. If you don't use export, the change will only be visible to the current shell which is generally not what you want. For example, to change the HISTSIZE variable to 10 in your account only, you would add the following lines in .bashrc:

```
HISTSIZE=10
export HISTSIZE
```

By updating HISTSIZE to 10, you limit the command history to the last ten commands you have executed, instead of the default of 1,000. You can view the list of commands you have executed using the history command or cycle through each command using the Up- and Down-arrow keys.

---

■ **Note:** For more information on environment variables, see http://tldp.org/LDP/ Bash-Beginners-Guide/html/sect_03_02.html.

---

# Creating and Running Your Own Script

A script is basically a list of commands to be run in sequence Until now, you have been running commands one line at a time. Some system administration tasks under are sequences of commands, which you may find yourself running all the time. You can automate these tasks by bundling the commands into a list by writing a script.

For example, use a text editor to create a file called hello.sh with the following contents:

```
echo "What is your name?"
read name
echo "Hello, $name!"
```

The first line displays the text "What is your name?". The second reads keyboard input and stores the value in the variable name. The third line displays "Hello" followed by the value stored in the variable name, followed by an exclamation point (!). To execute this script, we issue the command sh hello.sh. The sh command is used to run a Bash interpreter on your script. You should see a result similar to Listing 2-21.

*Listing 2-21. The Output of sh hello.sh*

```
[juan@srv1-manila ~]$ sh hello.sh
What is your name?
Don Juan
Hello, Don Juan!
```

Let's try another example. Supposing you would like to list the successful and failed login attempts of a particular user, you would use the commands last and lastb, respectively. To filter out logs that pertain to a particular user, you need to use grep. Finally, you would like to enter the username through keyboard input. To do this, let's create logs.sh with the following content:

```
echo "Enter a username: "
read username
echo "Successful login attempts: "
```

```
echo "----"
last | grep $username
echo "Failed login attempts: "
echo "----"
lastb | grep $username
```

As you can see from the code, the pattern to be searched by grep is based on what will be read from the keyboard input. To execute the script, issue the command sh logs.sh. You should see a result similar to Listing 2-22.

*Listing 2-22. The Output of sh logs.sh*

```
Enter a username:
juan
Successful login attempts:
----
juan      pts/1        :0.0            Tue Apr 28 20:27    still logged in
juan      :0                           Tue Apr 28 20:25    still logged in
juan      :0                           Tue Apr 28 20:25 - 20:25  (00:00)
Failed login attempts:
----
juan      tty1                         Wed Apr 29 06:16 - 06:16  (00:00)
```

You will get a permission denied error, as you are running the script as a regular user. You need to switch to root because only the administrator can run the last and lastb commands.

Instead of keyboard input, you may want to use arguments as inputs. Arguments are stored in special variables by default. The first argument is stored in $1, the second in $2, the third in $3, and so on. Again, arguments are separated by spaces. For example, to accept parameters into logs.sh you will need to update the file by replacing it with the following contents:

```
echo "Successful login attempts: "
echo "----"
last | grep $1
echo "Failed login attempts: "
echo "----"
lastb | grep $1
```

As you can see, we replaced the pattern in grep to take the value of $1, which is the first argument that will be passed into the script. To execute the command, enter sh logs.sh juan. You should see a result similar to Listing 2-23.

*Listing 2-23. The Output of sh logs.sh with an Argument*

```
Successful login attempts:
----
juan      pts/1        :0.0            Tue Apr 28 20:27    still logged in
juan      :0                           Tue Apr 28 20:25    still logged in
juan      :0                           Tue Apr 28 20:25 - 20:25  (00:00)
Failed login attempts:
----
juan      tty1                         Wed Apr 29 06:16 - 06:16  (00:00)
```

To run the script without using sh, like the commands you are familiar with, you will first need to place the script in any directory listed in the PATH variable. By default the value of PATH for root is

```
/usr/kerberos/sbin:/usr/kerberos/bin:/usr/local/sbin:/usr/local/bin:/sbin:/bin: ↵
/usr/sbin:/usr/bin:/root/bin
```

In our case, let's place it in root's bin directory. Let's create the bin directory under root by issuing the command mkdir /root/bin. Let's place the script inside the bin directory by issuing mv /root/logs.sh /root/bin.

The second step is adding the default interpreter that will be used to run the script. Without it, if the user is using a shell that is not compatible with Bash, then the script would fail to execute. To ensure that the script will run even if the user is using a different type of shell, you will need to update logs.sh with the following content:

```
#!/bin/bash
echo "Successful login attempts: "
echo "----"
last | grep $1
echo "Failed login attempts: "
echo "----"
lastb | grep $1
```

The she-bang (#!) specifies the default interpreter, which is /bin/bash.

The third step is to make the file executable, like all the other text utilities. To do so, we need to change the permissions and set the file as executable. You can do this by issuing the command

```
chmod +x /root/bin/logs.sh
```

Permissions will be discussed further in Chapter 3.
To test if it works, run the command

```
logs.sh <username>
```

and you should be able to run it successfully. If not, review the three steps.

■ **Note:** The available shells including BASH that can be used are listed in the /etc/shells file.

## Summary

In this chapter, you have learned how to use several text-based utilities that are useful in gathering information about your system. In addition, you are now able to use text processing tools to make the data you gather more presentable. You also learned how to do file management by creating, renaming, deleting and traversing files and directories. Finally, you learned how to create your own scripts, which is essential to make your life easier as a system administrator and be able to read and understand existing scripts as well.

In the next chapter, you will learn how to configure host settings to prepare a machine to be used as a server.

■ ■ ■

# CHAPTER 3

# Client/Host Configuration

In this chapter you will see how to configure your CentOS server so that it matches your needs more closely. Specifically, you'll see how to configure the boot loader, services, the keyboard, language, date and time, network and printer settings.

## The Boot Process

The *boot process* is the sequence of events that transpire starting when you turn on the computer and ending once you reach the login screen. It is essential to have a basic understanding of this process so that you can repair problems that occur during the boot process. Some problems that might arise could be caused by failure to detect hardware such as hard drives or network cards. The system might take a long time to start or certain services might not start automatically as they should. More severely (and less commonly), the system might not be able to boot at all.

### The Boot Loader

In CentOS, the default boot loader is GRUB (GRand Unified Boot loader). It is the program that allows you to choose which operating system you'd like to boot. GRUB can also control how CentOS will boot, by passing special parameters or instructions to the kernel. Generally speaking this is not necessary and is usually only done when the machine has trouble booting or if you need to reset the password. Should you need to troubleshoot this part of the boot process, simply press any key when GRUB starts and it will show you the boot menu as illustrated in Figure 3-1.

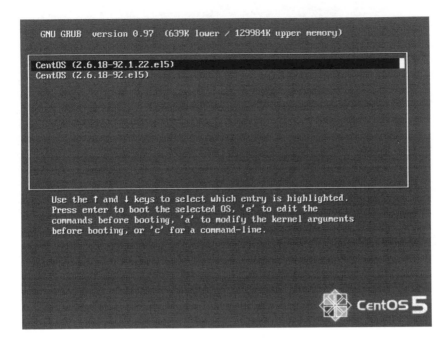

*Figure 3-1.* *This menu appears when you press any key when the GRUB boot loader is running.*

In this menu, you can select a kernel to boot by using the up and down arrow keys to scroll the selection and then press Enter to launch the operating system (although after a fresh install you'll only have one kernel to choose from). The latest kernel is always the default kernel to boot and appears on top. This is because new kernels are appended at the top of list when you perform software updates that include the kernel. It is rare that the latest stable kernel would pose problems in your system requiring you to use the old kernel.

---

■ **Note:** This doesn't happen with modules (device drivers) provided as standard with CentOS, but if you are using a third-party driver (for example with a Storage Area Network) you should double-check that the new kernel is compatible. Otherwise you may find that when you next boot, the device is no longer available. Fortunately, CentOS always keeps the previous kernels, so you can reboot from a previously working kernel. Instructions for building the module should have been supplied by the vendor. Every operating system item under the selection has a batch of GRUB commands used to boot up the system. Press e to edit each command, a to edit just the kernel parameters or c to type commands at the GRUB command prompt. If a GRUB password is set, you need to press p first and enter the password before you can tweak any GRUB entry.

---

For most purposes you'll just need to edit kernel arguments. After you press e, you are presented with the kernel parameters as shown in Figure 3-2.

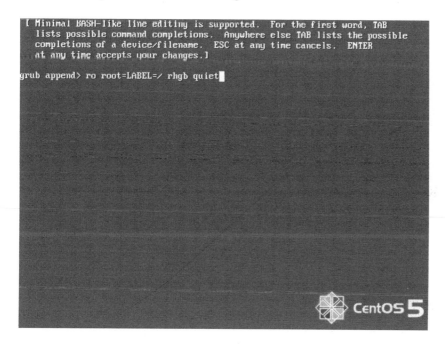

*Figure 3-2. Kernel parameters*

As you can see, four parameters are passed by default to the Linux kernel.

The first is ro, which means the (/) root filesystem will be mounted read-only temporarily so that the file system checker can check the root filesystem without damaging it.

The second is root=LABEL=/, which tells the operating system where the (/) root partition is located. In this case, labels are being used, rather than specific device names, and the kernel will use this information to find the actual root partition on disk. The third and fourth options are for cosmetic purposes; namely, to see less text and more animation. The option rhgb is used to display the graphical boot when booting up. The quiet option limits the text messages seen while booting up. Try to remove the options by pressing Backspace until the only text visible is ro  root=LABEL=/. Press Enter to make changes and to launch the operating system. You will notice that the boot messages are verbose and provide important information for system administrators to examine, as shown in Figure 3-3. If you are troubleshooting boot issues, scan the boot messages for clues.

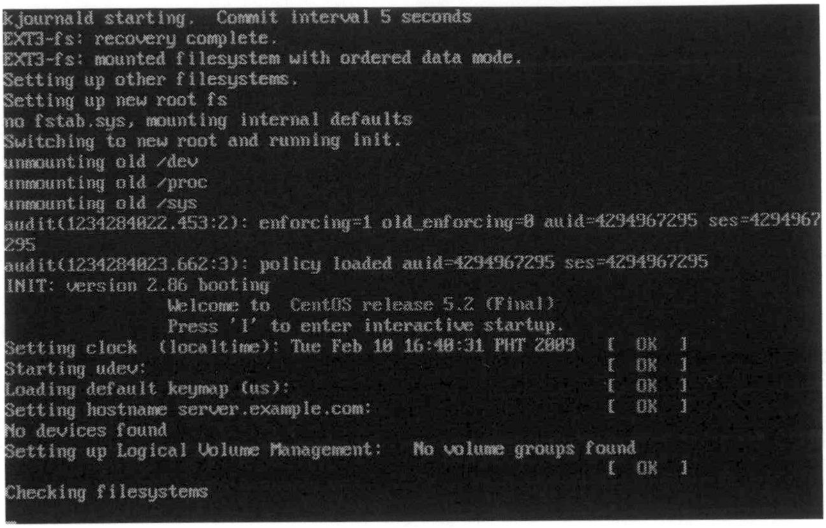

```
kjournald starting.  Commit interval 5 seconds
EXT3-fs: recovery complete.
EXT3-fs: mounted filesystem with ordered data mode.
Setting up other filesystems.
Setting up new root fs
no fstab.sys, mounting internal defaults
Switching to new root and running init.
unmounting old /dev
unmounting old /proc
unmounting old /sys
audit(1234284022.453:2): enforcing=1 old_enforcing=0 auid=4294967295 ses=4294967
295
audit(1234284023.662:3): policy loaded auid=4294967295 ses=4294967295
INIT: version 2.86 booting
                 Welcome to  CentOS release 5.2 (Final)
                 Press 'I' to enter interactive startup.
Setting clock  (localtime): Tue Feb 10 16:40:31 PHT 2009    [  OK  ]
Starting udev:                                             [  OK  ]
Loading default keymap (us):                               [  OK  ]
Setting hostname server.example.com:                       [  OK  ]
No devices found
Setting up Logical Volume Management:   No volume groups found
                                                           [  OK  ]
Checking filesystems
```

*Figure 3-3. Boot messages in text mode*

To add a parameter, just press the spacebar and type the options. Table 3-1 lists the options you may need to add to kernel parameters.

*Table 3-1. Kernel Parameters*

| Parameter | Description |
| --- | --- |
| single | Used to boot to single-user mode, which creates a very basic environment that doesn't start any network services. This mode is used by administrators to repair the system, such as fixing a damaged configuration file or changing the root password. |
| 1 | Has the same effect as passing the parameter single. |
| 3 | Used to run the system in text mode with networking but without X Windows. |
| 5 | Used to run the system in graphical mode. |
| i8042.noloop | Used as a workaround to take control of the mouse pointer in a Virtual PC environment. |
| ide=nodma | Disables DMA on IDE-based drives. |
| mem=*num*M | Used to specify the amount of RAM in MB if the system cannot automatically recognize the amount of memory. |
| nofirewire | Disables the FireWire driver if booting crashes when the FireWire module is booting up. |
| nokudzu | Used to disable hardware detection. |

To make the changes permanent, you need to add these parameters in GRUB's configuration file. The file is located at /boot/grub/grub.conf. Just edit the parameter under the kernel option you need.

For example, if 1 GB of RAM is not recognized by the system, you would need to add mem=1000M under the kernel parameter, as shown in Listing 3-1. You can verify whether your system is able to identify your RAM size by viewing the contents of /proc/meminfo after rebooting the system.

---

▓ **Note:** Although they have a lot in common, it's not unusual for grub.conf files to be slightly different on different machines. Do not worry if yours is not identical to the one shown here.

---

*Listing 3-1. Sample Contents of grub.conf*

```
# grub.conf generated by anaconda
#
# Note that you do not have to rerun grub after making changes to this file
# NOTICE:  You have a /boot partition.  This means that
#          all kernel and initrd paths are relative to /boot/, eg.
#          root (hd0,0)
#          kernel /vmlinuz-version ro root=/dev/hda2
#          initrd /initrd-version.img
#boot=/dev/hda
default=0
timeout=5
splashimage=(hd0,0)/grub/splash.xpm.gz
hiddenmenu
title CentOS (2.6.18-92.1.22.el5)
        root (hd0,0)
        kernel /vmlinuz-2.6.18-92.1.22.el5 ro root=LABEL=/ rhgb quiet mem=1000M
        initrd /initrd-2.6.18-92.1.22.el5.img
title CentOS (2.6.18-92.el5)
        root (hd0,0)
        kernel /vmlinuz-2.6.18-92.el5 ro root=LABEL=/ rhgb quiet mem=1000M
        initrd /initrd-2.6.18-92.el5.img
```

Without the GRUB password (shown in Listing 3-2), anyone could edit the kernel parameters and boot into single-user mode. This would effectively enable them to log in as root without specifying a password. If you did not add a GRUB password during the installation (you were asked if you wanted to set a password on the boot loader setup screen), you can create a password by using the grub-md5-crypt command. It will prompt you for a password twice. The output is your password in encrypted form.

To enable it in GRUB, edit the grub.conf file and append password --md5 followed by a space and the encrypted password between the option hiddenmenu and the first title, as shown in Listing 3-2.

*Listing 3-2. grub.conf with a Password*

```
# grub.conf generated by anaconda
#
# Note that you do not have to rerun grub after making changes to this file
# NOTICE:  You have a /boot partition.  This means that
#          all kernel and initrd paths are relative to /boot/, eg.
#          root (hd0,0)
```

```
#           kernel /vmlinuz-version ro root=/dev/hda2
#           initrd /initrd-version.img
#boot=/dev/hda
default=0
timeout=5
splashimage=(hd0,0)/grub/splash.xpm.gz
hiddenmenu
password --md5 $1$DSfvu$Tv.f9Xr/YFDXvO3CrYAx80
title CentOS (2.6.18-92.1.22.el5)
        root (hd0,0)
        kernel /vmlinuz-2.6.18-92.1.22.el5 ro root=LABEL=/ rhgb quiet mem=1000M
        initrd /initrd-2.6.18-92.1.22.el5.img
title CentOS (2.6.18-92.el5)
        root (hd0,0)
        kernel /vmlinuz-2.6.18-92.el5 ro root=LABEL=/ rhgb quiet mem=1000M
        initrd /initrd-2.6.18-92.el5.img
```

## Kernel, Init, and Runlevels

Once it is loaded by the boot loader, the kernel initializes and configures all hardware and devices. It then mounts the initial RAM disk, which contains the device drivers needed, before the root filesystem can be mounted. The initial RAM disk is responsible for providing modules used to make the root filesystem available if the kernel is not configured to do so itself. Finally, the kernel runs the init (/sbin/init) program to configure the environment (such as setting the hardware clock) and then runs a set of processes.

The init program calls /etc/rc.d/rc.sysinit, which loads modules, initializes software RAID, performs a filesystem check on the root filesystem and then remounts it as read/write, mounts other local file systems (such as /home if you opted to put the home directories on a separate disk), and performs any other initialization that may be required.

The init program calls the /etc/inittab script to determine the default runlevel and the processes to be executed at different runlevels. The default runlevel can be determined by looking for the entry initdefault in /etc/inittab. The format of the entry is id:*runlevel*:initdefault where the runlevel is the default runlevel. You can list the contents of the folder /etc/rc.d/rc*runlevel*.d to determine what scripts will be executed at runlevels that range from 0 to 6. For example, two files you would find in /etc/rc.d/rc3.d are

S10network
K35dovecot

Files that start with S are executed when init enters a runlevel. Files that start with K are executed when init leaves a runlevel. For example, suppose you were to change from runlevel 3 to runlevel 5, by executing telinit 5 (a change that's useful if you want to load the graphical interface). All of the K scripts would be executed before the S scripts in runlevel 5. init will execute the scripts in numerical order i.e. S01 will be executed before S02.

The runlevels for CentOS are defined in Table 3-2. However, although Linux distributions based on Red Hat use this scheme, each Linux distribution may choose to use a different scheme.

*Table 3-2. Run Levels*

| Runlevel | Description |
| --- | --- |
| 0 | System shutdown |
| 1 | Single-user mode, no networking |
| 2 | Multi-user mode, no networking |
| 3 | Multi-user mode, text user interface, with networking |
| 4 | Reserved |
| 5 | Multi-user mode, graphical user interface, with networking |
| 6 | System reboot |

■ **Tip:** You can switch from one runlevel to another by executing `telinit` *runlevel*. For example, if you would like to reboot the system from the console, issue the command `telinit 6`.

If the system is set to boot to graphical interface mode but you would like to run it on text interface mode, edit /etc/inittab and look for:

`id:5:initdefault:`

Replace it with

`id:3:initdefault:`

If the system is set to boot to text user interface mode but you would like to run it in graphical mode, edit /etc/inittab and look for:

`id:3:initdefault:`

and replace it with

`id:5:initdefault:`

■ **Note:** If you have changed the setting to boot to a graphical user interface mode and it fails, it could mean that the graphical packages are not installed. You can install them by typing `yum -y groupinstall "X Window System" "GNOME Desktop Environment"` and pressing Enter.

## Services

The processes that are executed at different run levels are services offered by your system. You can customize what services will be run at different runlevels by using text-based and graphical tools.

The graphical tool is called system-config-services and can be invoked from the command line or from System ➤ Administration ➤ Server ➤ Services to display the window shown in Figure 3-4.

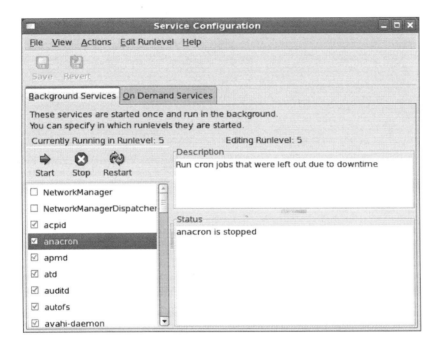

**Figure 3-4.** *The Service Configuration tool is used to start/stop/restart services and manage services to executed in different runlevels.*

You can select a service on the left and choose to start, stop and restart it by pressing the corresponding buttons. To manage which service runs on a particular runlevel, select Edit Runlevel and then choose a runlevel to edit from the menu. The next step is to tick the checkbox corresponding to service you would like to start at that runlevel. To save the changes, click the Save button. Upon reboot, the service will run on the corresponding level.

On the console, you use the chkconfig tool list and specify which services to run at different runlevels. To list the services and corresponding runlevels, type chkconfig --list; Listing 3-3 shows partial results

**Listing 3-3.** *List of services and corresponding runlevels*

```
[root@server ~]# chkconfig --list
NetworkManager  0:off   1:off   2:off   3:off   4:off   5:off   6:off
```

| | | | | | | | | | |
|---|---|---|---|---|---|---|---|---|---|
| NetworkManagerDispatcher | | | 0:off | 1:off | 2:off | 3:off | 4:off | 5:off | 6:off |
| acpid | 0:off | 1:off | 2:off | 3:on | 4:on | 5:on | 6:off | | |
| anacron | 0:off | 1:off | 2:on | 3:on | 4:on | 5:on | 6:off | | |
| apmd | 0:off | 1:off | 2:on | 3:on | 4:on | 5:on | 6:off | | |
| atd | 0:off | 1:off | 2:off | 3:on | 4:on | 5:on | 6:off | | |
| auditd | 0:off | 1:off | 2:on | 3:on | 4:on | 5:on | 6:off | | |
| autofs | 0:off | 1:off | 2:off | 3:on | 4:on | 5:on | 6:off | | |
| avahi-daemon | 0:off | 1:off | 2:off | 3:on | 4:on | 5:on | 6:off | | |
| avahi-dnsconfd | 0:off | 1:off | 2:off | 3:off | 4:off | 5:off | 6:off | | |
| bluetooth | 0:off | 1:off | 2:on | 3:on | 4:on | 5:on | 6:off | | |
| capi | 0:off | 1:off | 2:off | 3:off | 4:off | 5:off | 6:off | | |

As you can see, the first column provides the service name, followed by the runlevels from 0-6, separated by spaces. If the runlevel is followed with :on, the service will run on that level. Runlevels 0 and 6 are used for shutting down and rebooting, respectively, and so services should never be started in these levels. Generally speaking CentOS only runs in runlevels 3 and 5.

To add a service in a particular runlevel, issue the command

```
chkconfig --level runlevels servicename on
```

For example, if you would like the Bluetooth service to run on levels 3 and 5, you issue the command chkconfig --level 35 bluetooth on. To remove a service from a particular runlevel, the command to be issued is chkconfig --level runlevels servicename off. For example, if you don't want the Bluetooth service to run on level 3 and 5, issue the command, chkconfig --level 35 bluetooth off. Again, you can verify these settings by issuing the command chkconfig --list.

To start, stop or restart a service via the command line, you can use the service command. The format is service servicename start|stop|restart. For example, if you would like to restart the Bluetooth service, just issue the command service bluetooth restart. Running service servicename without any options will show a list of options that the command will accept. Many accept more than just start, stop, and restart.

# Keyboard Settings

As you'd expect, there are several ways to change the keyboard layout (, but the most common are to run system-config-keyboard from the command line or select System ➤ Administration ➤ Keyboard to display the window shown in Figure 3-5.

*Figure 3-5. The system-config-keyboard program is used to change the keyboard layout.*

The system-config-keyboard command can also be used in a text-based user interface. The configuration tool will be displayed in text mode. After you select a layout in the list and click OK, the keyboard settings will take effect immediately.

---

■ **Note:** You can find more keyboard configuration settings on the graphical user interface to tweak under Keyboard Preferences, Keyboard Shortcuts, Keyboard Accessibility options under System ➤ Preferences ➤ Keyboard, System ➤ Preferences ➤ Keyboard Shortcuts, and System ➤ Preferences ➤ Accessibility ➤ Keyboard.

---

# Language Settings

To change the overall language settings of the operating system, you can run the command system-config-language or select System ➤ Administration ➤ Language to display the window shown in Figure 3-6.

***Figure 3-6.*** *The language settings*

This tool is also available in text mode. Once you select a language from the list and then click OK, the changes will take effect when you log in again.

# Date and Time Settings

You can use the Time/Date Properties tool to update system date, time, and timezone of your system by running the command dateconfig or selecting System ➤ Administration ➤ Date & Time to display the window shown in Figure 3-7.

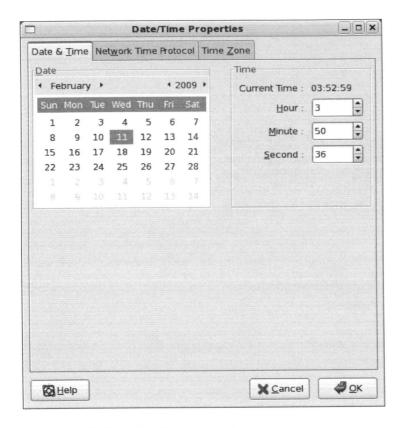

*Figure 3-7. The Date/Time Properties tool*

On the Date & Time tab, the left column allows you to update the date while the right column allows you to update the time. Any changes will be updated to the system date and time as soon as you click the OK button.

On the Network Time Protocol tab, you can allow your system to update its date and time automatically by polling time servers through the Network Time Protocol (NTP), a very useful way of ensuring that clocks on your servers remain accurate and more importantly in sync with each other. When you're running an e-mail server, for example, it's important that the server has the correct time. However, if you're comparing logs between two of your own servers, it's even more important that both machines agree on the time; otherwise, it will make matching up the log files far more difficult.

To use NTP, you need to check the Enable Network Time Protocol option. By default, you are provided with three time servers, 0.centos.pool.ntp.org, 1.centos.pool.ntp.org, and 2.centos.pool.ntp.org, but you can add other time servers available over the network. The Add, Edit, and Delete buttons are at your disposal to update the time server entries. Below them are advanced NTP options, which can be seen by clicking Show Advanced Options. The option Synchronize System Clock Before Starting Service syncs the system time with NTP servers even before the NTP service is started, which is recommended for systems that are always connected to a wired connection such as desktops and servers. The final option, Use Local Time Source, prioritizes the system's hard clock over the time servers. This is useful if your server has an accurate clock such as a GPS radio.

The Time Zone tab allows you to set the timezone of the system. This is also required by NTP as well to determine the date and time set on your system. You may change the timezone by selecting a city from either the world map or the drop down box below. The option System Clock Uses UTC (Universal Time Coordinated) allows for time to be automatically updated for Daylight Savings Time periods.

# Network Settings

In the installation stage, you were only able to configure the network cards of your system, which is the typical network connection for servers. However, if you have other means of connecting to the network, such as using ISDN, modem, xDSL, Token Ring, CIPE and wireless devices you may use the Network Configuration tool by selecting System ➤ Administration ➤ Network to display the window shown in Figure 3-8. The text mode configuration tool counterpart is system-config-network.

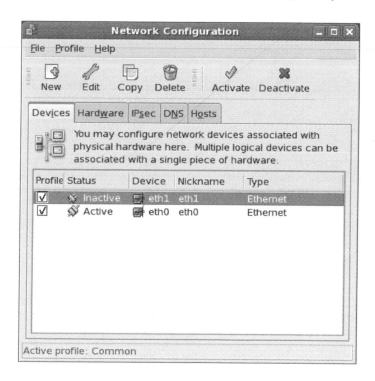

*Figure 3-8. The Network Configuration tool*

To add a new network device, select the Devices tab and then click the New button. You will then follow the wizard as you configure a new network device.

---

■ **Note:** Not all hardware devices are supported by Linux. If you have trouble setting up any network device, you may check http://hardware.redhat.com to see if it is supported. If not, you may still be able to make it work by installing third-party programs such as MadWifi and NDISwrapper.

---

In addition to configuring network devices, you can also configure the DNS settings of the system here. You can supply the DNS settings your ISP has provided for you or use a free DNS service such as OpenDNS (www.opendns.com). The IP addresses provided by OpenDNS are 208.67.222.222 and 208.67.220.220.

# Graphics Settings

The easiest way to configure graphical settings is to use the Display tool by selecting System ➤ Administration ➤ Display; you'll see the window shown in Figure 3-9.

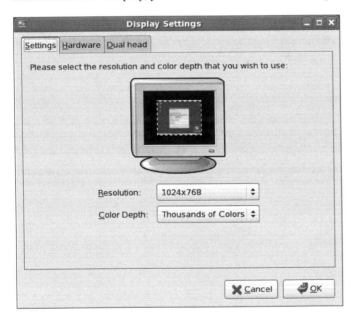

*Figure 3-9. The Display tool*

On the Settings tab, you can select the resolution and color depth of your display. The choices under these two items depend on the type of monitor and graphics card installed in your system.

However, if you find that the resolution is smaller than your monitor and graphics card are capable of displaying, then you just need to select the appropriate monitor and video card under the Hardware tab. You can then go back to the Settings tab to see the updated list for resolutions and then choose the appropriate one.

■ **Caution:** Be sure to select the appropriate hardware, or you might damage your monitor and graphics card! You should read the user manual of your monitor to determine its appropriate resolution.

Finally, you can configure your display to use two monitors in the Dual Head tab. You have the option to use the second monitor as another desktop or an expansion of the first monitor.

To test the new settings, all you need to do is log out from the desktop. The graphical settings will be put in place before you see the login screen.

# Printer Settings

To configure the printer, use the Printer tool by selecting System ➤ Administration ➤ Printing, which displays the window shown in Figure 3-10.

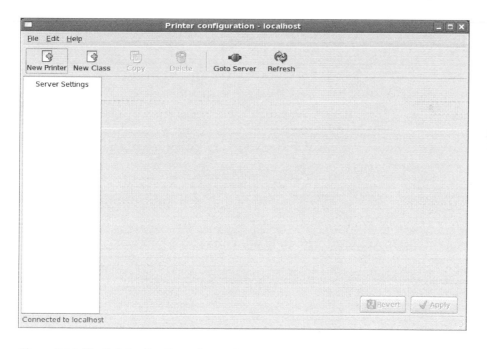

***Figure 3-10.*** *The Printer Configuration tool*

You can install printers connected through the following devices (see Figure 3-11):

*Printer, Serial or USB port:* Used to connect to printers that are attached to your system via the Serial, LPT, or USB port.

*AppSocket/HP JetDirect*: Used to connect to printers that are directly connected to the network using the HP JetDirect interface.

*Internet Printing Protocol:* Used to connect to printers over the network by connecting to Linux systems attached to these printers.

*LPD:* Similar to Internet Printing Protocol but used in older Linux operating systems.

*Windows Printer via Samba:* Used to connect to printers over the network by connecting to Windows systems or Samba-enabled Linux systems that are attached to these printers.

*Other:* Used when none of the previous options meet your needs. It is very rarely used and it is far more likely that you will use one of the other options.

If your printer does not work automatically, there's still hope. Check whether your printer is compatible with Linux by visiting http://www.linuxfoundation.org/en/OpenPrinting and following the instructions for installing the driver for your printer.

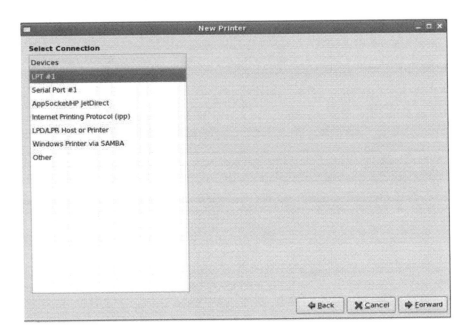

*Figure 3-11. Select which type of printer you want to add.*

# Summary

At this point you should now able to configure basic host settings using text-based and graphical tools. In the next chapter you will delve deeper into configuring your system by managing your disks through LVM and RAID.

# CHAPTER 4

■■■

# Data Storage Management

So far, you've installed CentOS, learned a few key commands, and configured a few basic services. Now, we're going to look at adding additional resilience and reliability to your system. We'll do this by improving how hard drives and partitions are handled. We'll be looking specifically at two technologies: RAID (Redundant Array of Inexpensive Disks) and the LVM (Logical Volume Manager). The first provides redundancy (usually anyway—you'll learn more about this a little later in this chapter when we talk about RAID levels), and the second makes partition management (such as resizing or creating a single partition across two disks) very straightforward.

We'll be putting these technologies to good use in this chapter to create a robust, reliable, and flexible data storage infrastructure. RAID and LVM fix the vast majority of issues administrators have had with data storage over the years, and here, you will learn how to leverage them both to make sure you don't run into the same problems.

## Provisioning a New Hard Drive

For now, let's assume that you want to use your server as a web proxy. Web proxies are a very useful way of speeding up access to the World Wide Web and providing some degree of access control. The idea is simplicity itself. Instead of every individual computer accessing the Internet directly, each should instead pass its request to the proxy server. The proxy server will make the request on behalf of the other computers, and before passing back the web pages, graphics, and other related content, the server stores a copy on its disk. This cached copy is very useful, because if the computers visit popular sites such as Google, rather than downloading the graphics from the Internet, the proxy server can simply return the version it has on disk (assuming the graphic hasn't changed). Obviously, sending an image directly is much faster than trying to download it from the Internet. The only problem is that the web cache can get rather large.

To solve this problem, we need to add another hard disk, which isn't as uncommon as you might think. Servers are often assigned tasks that they weren't originally designed for. Fortunately, a proxy server doesn't take all that much processing power, but it can consume a lot of disk space. Our luck is holding out, because adding a new disk to a server is nice and easy. Although each system is different, the steps are practically the same. Shut down the server; disconnect the power (most motherboards remain energized even if the machine itself is off); install the new hard drive; wire up the new drive; and turn the server back on.

---

■ **Note:** You may need to adjust BIOS settings to enable your new hard disk in your computer.

---

Next, we need to get ourselves a root terminal. Due to the nature of what we're about to do (that is make changes to the system), we need to have full unrestricted access to the hardware and to the filesystem. Once we've got the root terminal, we need to figure out where CentOS has put our disk. Each system is different, so you will probably see something slightly different than I will. However, the principles are the same, so if you follow this guide, you should be OK. First, we're going to use the fdisk -l command to show us what's available on the system (see Listing 4-1).

---

■ **Note:** The fdisk utility can be used to create several partitions in a hard disk. In this case, we just made one.

---

*Listing 4-1. Listing Details of the Hard Disks*

```
[root@server1 ~]# fdisk -l

Disk /dev/hda: 8388 MB, 8388108288 bytes
255 heads, 63 sectors/track, 1019 cylinders
Units = cylinders of 16065 * 512 = 8225280 bytes

   Device Boot      Start         End      Blocks   Id  System
/dev/hda1   *           1          13      104391   83  Linux
/dev/hda2              14        1019     8080695   8e  Linux LVM

Disk /dev/hdb: 10.4 GB, 10485522432 bytes
16 heads, 63 sectors/track, 20317 cylinders
Units = cylinders of 1008 * 512 = 516096 bytes

   Device Boot      Start         End      Blocks   Id  System
[root@server1 ~]#
```

In our example, two disk drives are shown. The first (/dev/hda1) is the original system disk as it holds what appears to be small partition to boot from and an LVM partition for creating logical volumes, as shown in the System column. This is actually the standard partitioning scheme used by CentOS, and you'll probably see it a lot. Looking for this pattern is generally, although not always, a useful way of confirming which disk holds the operating system itself. The second disk doesn't have any partitions yet—not entirely surprising as it's a new disk. If you haven't used a new disk, you should look for partitions that match with your expectations. For example, a disk that has been liberated from a Windows server is likely to show a partition type of NTFS.

The disks themselves are identified by device files. In this example, we have /dev/hda and /dev/hdb. CentOS will automatically detect most disks when the system starts up. If you have a modern machine, you're unlikely to see the prefix hd anymore and will see sd instead. Traditionally, the cheaper IDE (integrated drive electronics) disks would be handled by the IDE driver, while the SCSI (small computer systems interface) driver handled the more-expensive SCSI disks, which had the sd prefix. However, SATA disks are handled by the SCSI driver, so they show up with the sd prefix. As most new systems use SATA, you will see sd a lot more than hd in practice.

Although we can create numerous partitions, doing so seems to be going out of favor. Historically, partitions were very useful, because they sliced up a disk and kept content from one partition affecting another. This was especially handy if any data loss occurred due to filesystem corruption. These days, disks are far more reliable, and with journaling filesystems able to ensure data consistency, lost data is less of an issue. As you'll see in the section on LVM, creating and managing partitions for administration sake is a lot more powerful than creating physical partitions on the disk.

---

■ **Note:** Technically, you can only have four primary partitions in a hard disk. To overcome this limitation, in Linux, you can turn one of those partitions into an extended partition and then add logical partitions. More information can be found at http://en.wikipedia.org/wiki/Hard_disk_partition or check out Chapter 4 of Sander Van Vugt's new book *Beginning Linux Command-line* (Apress, 2009).

---

For our example, though, we're not going to need to do anything fancy, so one partition will do nicely. We're expecting our cache to be very busy, so we want to dedicate the whole disk to storing the cache data. In this case, there really is no benefit in creating more than one partition. To set up the hard disk, we'll use the fdisk command again. This time though, instead of passing it the -l option, we're instead going to pass it the name of the hard disk that we want to work with (see Listing 4-2).

*Listing 4-2. Managing a Particular Hard Disk*

```
[root@server1 ~]# fdisk /dev/hdb
The number of cylinders for this disk is set to 20317.
There is nothing wrong with that, but this is larger than 1024,
and could in certain setups cause problems with:
1) software that runs at boot time (e.g., old versions of LILO)
2) booting and partitioning software from other OSs
   (e.g., DOS FDISK, OS/2 FDISK)

Command (m for help)
```

Follow these steps to create a new partition (see Listing 4-3 as a guide):

1.  Type **n**, and press Enter.

2.  Specify that you will create primary partition by typing **p** and pressing Enter.

3.  At the Partition number prompt, type **1**, and press Enter.

4.  Press Enter to start the partition on the first cylinder of the hard disk.

5.  On the last cylinder prompt, press Enter again so that this partition uses all of the available space on this disk.

6.  Type **p**, and press Enter to have a preview of the partition table. Finally, type **w**, and press Enter to write your changes into the hard disk.

*Listing 4-3. Creating a New Partition*

```
[root@server1 ~]# fdisk /dev/hdb

The number of cylinders for this disk is set to 20317.
There is nothing wrong with that, but this is larger than 1024,
```

and could in certain setups cause problems with:
1) software that runs at boot time (e.g., old versions of LILO)
2) booting and partitioning software from other OSs
   (e.g., DOS FDISK, OS/2 FDISK)

```
Command (m for help): n
Command action
   e   extended
   p   primary partition (1-4)
p
Partition number (1-4): 1
First cylinder (1-20317, default 1):
Using default value 1
Last cylinder or +size or +sizeM or +sizeK (1-20317, default 20317):
Using default value 20317

Command (m for help): p

Disk /dev/hdb: 10.4 GB, 10485522432 bytes
16 heads, 63 sectors/track, 20317 cylinders
Units = cylinders of 1008 * 512 = 516096 bytes

   Device Boot      Start         End      Blocks   Id  System
/dev/hdb1                1       20317    10239736+  83  Linux

Command (m for help): w
The partition table has been altered!

Calling ioctl() to re-read partition table.
Syncing disks.
```

---

■ **Note:** If you see an error that the system needs to be rebooted before it can use the new partition table, just issue the command partprobe twice so that you don't have to reboot.

---

Now, issue fdisk -l again to verify the result as shown in Listing 4-4.

*Listing 4-4. Verifying That the New Partition Has Been Created*

```
[root@server1 ~]# fdisk -l
Disk /dev/hda: 8388 MB, 8388108288 bytes
255 heads, 63 sectors/track, 1019 cylinders
Units = cylinders of 16065 * 512 = 8225280 bytes

   Device Boot      Start         End      Blocks   Id  System
/dev/hda1   *            1          13      104391   83  Linux
/dev/hda2               14        1019     8080695   8e  Linux LVM

Disk /dev/hdb: 10.4 GB, 10485522432 bytes
```

```
16 heads, 63 sectors/track, 20317 cylinders
Units = cylinders of 1008 * 512 = 516096 bytes

   Device Boot      Start        End      Blocks   Id  System
/dev/hdb1              1      20317   10239736+  83  Linux
```

Now that hdb1 is available, it's time to format it. Although the filesystem of choice for CentOS is ext3, you can choose from a wide range of available options. However, most people in the CentOS community will be using ext3, and if you do choose to step off the beaten path, you may find support harder to find if you have trouble.

---

■ **Note:** Filesystems other than ext3 can be used with Linux, including ext2, NTFS, VFAT and ext4, and you may prefer to use one of these based on features such as usability or performance. More information on choosing the best filesystem for your purposes can be found at

http://en.wikipedia.org/wiki/Comparison_of_file_systems.

---

To format the partition for ext3, we use the mkfs.ext3 tool. All we need to do is pass the device partition as parameter to this tool, as shown in Listing 4-5. In this case, it's mkfs.ext3 /dev/hdb1.

***Listing 4-5.*** *Formating /dev/hdb1*

```
[root@server1 ~]# mkfs.ext3 /dev/hdb1
mke2fs 1.39 (29-May-2006)
Filesystem label=
OS type: Linux
Block size=4096 (log=2)
Fragment size=4096 (log=2)
1281696 inodes, 2559934 blocks
127996 blocks (5.00%) reserved for the super user
First data block=0
Maximum filesystem blocks=2621440000
79 block groups
32768 blocks per group, 32768 fragments per group
16224 inodes per group
Superblock backups stored on blocks:
        32768, 98304, 163840, 229376, 294912, 819200, 884736, 1605632

Writing inode tables: done
Creating journal (32768 blocks): done
Writing superblocks and filesystem accounting information: done

This filesystem will be automatically checked every 21 mounts or
180 days, whichever comes first.  Use tune2fs -c or -i to override.
```

Now that we have a partition with a filesystem on it, we need to put it somewhere useful. We need to use the mount command, which will allow us to tell CentOS what filesystem we wish to appear in a given directory. We know that the filesystem is located on /dev/hdb1. The default cache directory used by

Squid (the standard proxy server on CentOS) is /var/cache. To mount the filesystem, we can use the command mount /dev/hdb1 /var/cache/. Let's bring this together. We can verify everything went as planned by using df and mount as shown in Listing 4-6.

*Listing 4-6. Mounting /dev/hdb1 in /var/cache*

```
[root@server1 ~]# mount /dev/hdb1 /var/cache
[root@server1 ~]# df -h
Filesystem            Size  Used Avail Use% Mounted on
/dev/mapper/VolGroup02-LogVol02
                      4.7G  2.4G  2.1G  55% /
/dev/mapper/VolGroup02-LogVol00
                      1.9G   35M  1.8G   2% /home
/dev/hda1              99M   12M   83M  13% /boot
tmpfs                189M     0  189M   0% /dev/shm
/dev/hdb1            9.7G  151M  9.0G   2% /var/cache
 [root@server1 ~]# mount -l
/dev/mapper/VolGroup02-LogVol02 on / type ext3 (rw)
proc on /proc type proc (rw)
sysfs on /sys type sysfs (rw)
devpts on /dev/pts type devpts (rw,gid=5,mode=620)
/dev/mapper/VolGroup02-LogVol00 on /home type ext3 (rw)
/dev/hda1 on /boot type ext3 (rw) [/boot]
tmpfs on /dev/shm type tmpfs (rw)
none on /proc/sys/fs/binfmt_misc type binfmt_misc (rw)
sunrpc on /var/lib/nfs/rpc_pipefs type rpc_pipefs (rw)
/dev/hdb1 on /var/cache type ext3 (rw)
[root@server1 ~]#
```

To unmount the filesystem, we use the umount command. Because CentOS already knows both endpoints, only one endpoint is required to unmount the filesystem. For example, we could use umount /dev/hdb1, as shown in Listing 4-7, or umount /var/cache; either would have the desired effect. Once again, we can use df and mount to verify that this command really worked.

*Listing 4-7. Unmounting hdb1*

```
[root@server1 ~]# umount /dev/hdb1
[root@server1 ~]# df -h
Filesystem            Size  Used Avail Use% Mounted on
/dev/mapper/VolGroup02-LogVol02
                      4.7G  2.4G  2.1G  55% /
/dev/mapper/VolGroup02-LogVol00
                      1.9G   35M  1.8G   2% /home
/dev/hda1              99M   12M   83M  13% /boot
tmpfs                189M     0  189M   0% /dev/shm
[root@server1 ~]# mount -l
/dev/mapper/VolGroup02-LogVol02 on / type ext3 (rw)
proc on /proc type proc (rw)
sysfs on /sys type sysfs (rw)
devpts on /dev/pts type devpts (rw,gid=5,mode=620)
/dev/mapper/VolGroup02-LogVol00 on /home type ext3 (rw)
/dev/hda1 on /boot type ext3 (rw) [/boot]
```

```
tmpfs on /dev/shm type tmpfs (rw)
none on /proc/sys/fs/binfmt_misc type binfmt_misc (rw)
sunrpc on /var/lib/nfs/rpc_pipefs type rpc_pipefs (rw)
[root@server1 ~]#
```

■ **Note:** You won't be able to unmount a filesystem if it's being used. To determine where it's being used, the command `lsof|grep <device name>` is available for troubleshooting. If you see `bash` in that list, chances are good that one of your terminal sessions is actually sitting in that directory. If you find that you are, simply type **cd**, and press Enter. This will take you back to your home directory and release the lock on the directory.

Now that you know our partition works as expected, we need to automate the mounting process. After all, CentOS servers aren't rebooted very often, and forgetting the list of commands you're supposed to run when it boots back up is easy to do. Apart from that, manually mounting partitions is just tedious. Fortunately, we can automated this easily by updating the /etc/fstab file which CentOS uses during booting to determine what filesystems go where:

```
/dev/hdb1       /var/cache      ext3    defaults        1 2
```

The first column specifies the device, and the second column tells CentOS where to mount it. These parameters are identical to the ones we provided manually to the mount command. In this file, columns are separated by spaces, but any whitespace should work; just try to be consistent. The second column tells CentOS which filesystem it should assume is on the disk. Next comes a list of comma-separated values that control how the filesystem is set up. Generally speaking you will use defaults here, which unsurprisingly tells CentOS to use the defaults. The next two columns are more interesting.

The fifth column is mostly there for historical purposes, and it determines whether or not the filesystem needs to be dumped. This information is generally used by the dump command, which is used for taking backups. However, it seems to be rare that anyone uses dump anymore; most prefer to use higher-level tools such as tar or other backup solutions. If this field is not present, it is assumed to be zero, in which case the filesystem will not be backed up by dump.

The final column tells fsck (the tool that verifies and repairs filesystems) the order in which it should check filesystems during a reboot. The root filesystem should always be checked first and should have a value of 1. Other partitions can be given any number, and fsck will check them in that order. Filesystems on the same disk will be checked sequentially one after the other. If you have several disks, however, these will be checked in parallel to take full advantage of the hardware. Otherwise, if this column is set to zero or missing, fsck will presume that that particular filesystem does not need checking.

To check that our new fstab file is working as expected, we can use the mount -a command to tell CentOS to mount all filesystems that it knows about that haven't already been mounted. We can then repeat the checks with df and mount to determine that the new filesystem is available.

# Partitioning a Disk Using RAID

RAID sounds complicated, but the idea behind it is quite simple—and rather cunning. By using at least two disks, we can build a system where the failure of any one of those disks won't result in lost data.

Imagine that you're building a server to store all your company's crucial documents. If you have only one hard disk and that hard disk fails, you would obviously lose everything on that disk, including your extremely important documents. Now, by using RAID (level one, but we'll come back to this in a bit), we can have two hard disks that exactly mirror each other. CentOS will treat them as one disk but everything you store will be written to both hard disks. This means if one of the disks were to fail, the other disk would be an exact copy, and service would be uninterrupted. Of course, you'll want to replace the dead disk as soon as possible, but at least your data is safe. Depending on the type of RAID used, it can also provide a significant performance boost.

That being said, RAID isn't infallible. For example, if the disk controller fails and both hard drives are on the same controller, both disks will become unavailable. If there is a power failure and the disks are plugged into the same power source, they will both go offline. RAID is better than the alternative (i.e., not having RAID), but you must not mistake RAID for a backup solution. You should take proper backups on a regular basis. It may help to think of RAID as a way to protect against short-term hardware faults, whereas backups protect against complete and catastrophic failure.

## Understanding RAID Types and Levels

Generally speaking, there are three types of RAID available: hardware, software, and fake. Hardware RAID is the most expensive and, of course, best solution. In this case, dedicated hardware manages the disks, and the host computer sees only the logical disks the RAID controller creates. This setup makes hardware RAID very easy to use, as the operating system doesn't need to know anything about it. On the other hand, RAID hardware is rather expensive and generally uses proprietary formats, so if your controller fails, you're going to need to get another one just like it to ensure that you can safely get to your data.

Software RAID is the next best thing. In this scenario, CentOS itself manages the RAID array and provides a set of commands (such as mdadm) to set up and manage it. Software RAID isn't as fast as hardware RAID, because the operating system has to send the duplicate data itself, rather than having dedicated hardware do it. However, software RAID can be used with any block device, so it is possible to use RAID to link two USB devices together, for example, or even one USB device, one SATA, and a SAN (storage area network). Because this technology is device agnostic and standard across most Linux distributions, you don't need to worry about vendor lock-in. Some people prefer software RAID over hardware RAID for these reasons, but where performance is key (such as a busy database server), software RAID might not be fast enough.

Fake RAID is describes a technology that provides the basics for RAID but doesn't actually implement it. Instead, fake RAID leaves implementation up to the host operating system. Few people use fake RAID, and it isn't supported under Linux, as software RAID is so much better. Avoid fake RAID like the plague and make sure it's disabled in the BIOS if your motherboard offers it.

There are six different RAID levels. However only the three most common are currently supported under software RAID: RAID0, RAID1, and RAID5.

## RAID 0

In RAID0, disks are logically combined into one big disk, and data is basically distributed evenly on each disk. In this level, hard disk space is maximized to the fullest, but there is no data redundancy: if one disk fails, the data on all disks in the array is lost. Also, reading and writing are fast since reads and writes can be done simultaneously across all the disks.

## RAID 1

RAID1 is also called mirroring, since data on one disk is cloned on another. Data is written to both disks, so generally write operations take longer than on a single disk, but read operations are faster, because CentOS can choose which disk to read from.

If a single disk fails, the system will be able to run from the remaining disk. RAID1 also supports the concept of hot spares—disks that are part of an array but aren't actively being used. These disks don't actually do anything until one of the disks in the mirror fails. When this happens, the failed disk is removed, and the hot spare disk is added to the mirror itself. The data is then copied from the good disk on to the sparc, and the array is brought back up to full strength.

The biggest disadvantage with RAID1 is that for every gigabyte of usable space, another gigabyte is used to provide redundancy. Therefore, if you have one 20-GB disk and one 30-GB disk, the maximum size you can allocate to RAID1 is 20GB.

# RAID 5

RAID5 (also known as "striped with parity") is an attempt to get the best of both worlds. It aims to get as much of the speed of RAID0 as possible while retaining as much of the redundancy of RAID1. What we end up with is a system that can take the loss of a single hard disk (a RAID5 array needs at least three disks) but isn't constrained by RAID1's one-to-one requirement. RAID5 is probably the most common type of RAID found in enterprise environments, as it offers a good compromise between speed and redundancy.

For now, we're going to implement a RAID1 array, although creating a RAID5 array is just as straightforward. To set up RAID properly, you need to have separate disks. Although with software RAID you can create a RAID array on a single disk using two partitions, this obviously wouldn't help you if that hard disk were to fail.

First then, we must undo our changes from the previous section. We need to unmount /var/cache, remove the relevant entry from /etc/fstab, and delete the partition using fdisk.

---

■ **Note:** To delete hdb1, you run fdisk /dev/hdb1. On the menu, to delete a partition, type **d**, and press Enter. Type **1** to delete the first partition, and press Enter. Finally, to make the changes permanent, type **w** to write to the partition table.

---

Shut down the computer, and add another hard disk. We'll be using the two most recently added hard disks as a storage for /var/cache. Turn on your computer; make the BIOS changes necessary to enable your hard disk on your host, and then boot CentOS. Again, run the command fdisk -l to see if the new hard disk is detected (see Listing 4-8). You should see three hard disks labeled hda, hdb, and hdd or sda, sdb, and sdd, depending on how your machine is set up.

---

■ **Note:** The device hdc or sdc is typically reserved for the first DVD or CD drive.

---

*Listing 4-8. Listing Detected Hard Disks*

```
fdisk -l[root@server1 ~]# fdisk -l

Disk /dev/hda: 8388 MB, 8388108288 bytes
255 heads, 63 sectors/track, 1019 cylinders
```

```
Units = cylinders of 16065 * 512 = 8225280 bytes

   Device Boot        Start         End       Blocks   Id  System
/dev/hda1    *            1          13      104391   83  Linux
/dev/hda2                14        1019     8080695   8e  Linux LVM

Disk /dev/hdb: 10.4 GB, 10485522432 bytes
16 heads, 63 sectors/track, 20317 cylinders
Units = cylinders of 1008 * 512 = 516096 bytes

Disk /dev/hdb doesn't contain a valid partition table

Disk /dev/hdd: 10.4 GB, 10485522432 bytes
16 heads, 63 sectors/track, 20317 cylinders
Units = cylinders of 1008 * 512 = 516096 bytes

Disk /dev/hdd doesn't contain a valid partition table
[root@server1 ~]#
```

Let's prepare hdb and hdd for RAID. For hdb and hdd, we'll create one partition like we did in the "Provisioning a New Hard Disk" section.

Once we've done that, we use the mdadm utility to create the RAID array. We'll be creating an array called md0, with RAID 1 from partitions hdb1 and hdd1. To do so, run the command mdadm --create --verbose /dev/md0 –level=1 --raid-devices=2 /dev/hdb1 /dev/hdd1, as shown in Listing 4-9.

**Listing 4-9.** *Creating a RAID1 Array from Partitions hdb1 and hdb2*

```
[root@server1 ~]# mdadm --create --verbose /dev/md0 --level=1 ↵
--raid-devices=2 /dev/hdb1 /dev/hdd1
mdadm: size set to 10239616K
mdadm: array /dev/md0 started.
```

There you have it—a RAID device represented in /dev/md0. To test for any problems, we can use cat /proc/mdstat, as shown in Listing 4-10.

**Listing 4-10.** *Verifying RAID Creation*

```
[root@server1 ~]# cat /proc/mdstat
Personalities : [raid1]
md0 : active raid1 hdd1[1] hdb1[0]
      10239616 blocks [2/2] [UU]
      [======>.............]  resync = 38.5% (3943936/10239616) ↵
finish=1.9min speed=53941K/secunused devices: <none>
```

If there are no problems, we can format md0 using mkfs.ext3, like so:

```
mkfs.ext3 /dev/md0
```

To attach the array to /var/cache, we just add the following line on /etc/fstab:

```
/dev/md0          /var/cache        ext3      defaults        1 2
```

80

To mount the new filesystem, we can use mount -a as we did in the previous section. We can also use the same commands to verify that everything went as planned. Remember that, although we're now using a new device (/dev/md0), it is still treated as a disk, so all the commands that you have practiced before will work equally well here.

Now, you need to create a configuration file for mdadm so that RAID starts perfectly on boot up. You can do so manually, but you can just as easily create the file via the mdadm tool itself by running the following command:

```
mdadm -detail -scan -verbose > /etc/mdadm.conf.
```

This command scans all available disks on the system and looks for RAID markers. It collects all of this information and places it in /etc/mdadm.conf. This information is then used by CentOS during booting to re-create the arrays.

---

▧ **Note:** It's considered best practice by the Linux community that you include a spare disk for RAID 1. This disk will be used to rebuild the RAID array should one hard disk fail. Assuming you have another hard disk, hde, and you created a new partition for RAID1 called, hde1, the command to create the RAID device would be mdadm -create -verbose /dev/md0 -level=1 -raid-devices=2 /dev/hdb1 /dev/hdd1 -spare-devices=1 /dev/hde1.

---

## Checking on RAID

The easiest way to check on software RAID under CentOS is to look inside /proc/mdstat. We did this before when we were verifying the creation of the RAID array. The kernel puts all status information regarding any software RAID in this file. As before, you can use cat /proc/mdstat to examine this file in more depth.

However, this solution relies on the administrator remembering to check the file on a regular basis. Generally speaking, there is no easy way to externally tell if a RAID array is healthy. To get around this, we can tell mdadm to monitor our array for us with the following simple command:

```
mdadm --monitor --mail=your@email.com -delay 1800 /dev/md0
```

This implementation is very straightforward. The monitor option tells mdadm that it should monitor the given array every 1,800 seconds and, if there are any problems, send an e-mail to your@email.com. This way, you will be alerted as soon as any problems are detected, so you can take action.

# Partitioning with LVM

Traditionally on the Intel x86 platform, hard disks have only been able to support four primary partitions. It was possible to increase this number using extended partitions and logical partitions, but though workable, this solution wasn't the most elegant. Unfortunately, you simply couldn't fix the problem, as it would require a fundamental change to the platform, which would break compatibility. For the most part, people just lived with it and with tools available to handle the low level details, it wasn't too much of a problem.

Unfortunately, having a limited number of fixed partitions started to become a real nightmare as disk size and usage increased. For example, traditionally users' files would be stored on a separate partition mounted on /home. Now, if that partition was 20GB and was starting to get full, we would have to find some space. The problem is that this space will come in the form of another partition, and that's just not very useful. There's no way for us to simply increase the size of /home. Instead, we have to mess about splitting home directories across these two partitions. Apart from the obvious nuisance of having to manage two separate disks, we also need to be aware of how we share the space. For example, it might seem perfectly logical if we decided to put all users whose names begin with A to M on the first partition and then N to Z on the second partition. But what if there are more users in one half than the other? Worse, what if there are only a handful of users that use a large amount of disk space, and they all coincidentally end up on the same disk?

These issues are the key problems that LVM was designed to solve. The main features that LVM provides over traditional partitioning schemes are online resizing of partitions and the ability to add and remove disks as well as create partitions on the fly. If this sounds pretty neat, that's because it is! LVM is one of those technologies that, once you start using it, you'll wonder how you managed to get by without it.

■ **Note:** During the install process, CentOS will, by default, set up the disk using LVM. The installer will create a small boot partition (it's not currently possible to boot from an LVM device) and will assign the rest of the space to LVM to create the other partitions that CentOS needs. We will look at this process in more depth later in the chapter.

## Understanding How LVM Works

LVM isn't all that complicated, but you need to get your head around a few new concepts and ideas. We'll look at each of the key parts in turn and show how LVM builds from the raw disk partition all the way up to the logical volumes that are actually used for storing data.

First of all, let's have a quick review of what a hard disk is and how Linux sees it. Regardless of the technology that connects it (such as SCSI or IDE) or whether it has spinning platters or is of solid-state design, a hard drive ultimately presents a chunk of space to the operating system. This space is then usually sliced up into partitions. This slicing used to be done to provide a convenient way to manage "large" amounts of space, as each partition could be effectively treated as a hard disk in its own right. As discussed previously though, this has fallen out of favor and disks are often not partitioned at all these days. You will see what I mean as you read through the rest of this section. So, hard disks provide chunks of space of a predetermined size; that is, a 200-GB hard disk can only store 200GB. The space is made available to the system as a contiguous block and is seen by Linux as a block device.

■ **Note:** "Contiguous" is a fancy term that means "right next to each other." It's often found in technical documentation and usually refers to storage (either on disk or memory) that consists of a single uninterrupted chunk.

Filesystems are created on block devices. It is entirely possible to format a whole hard disk for use with Linux without creating any partitions, although this is seldom done. The problem with filesystems is that they expect a single block of space. In other words, a filesystem cannot cross a partition boundary. This restriction gives rise to the problems we discussed previously about how to upgrade the space available for user home directories. LVM solves this problem by providing a mechanism to collect all the space from a group of physical hard disks and allowing that space to be allocated out to logical volumes at the administrator's discretion.

Figure 4-1 shows a diagram of an example LVM system, and the following sections explore the various aspects of that system in detail.

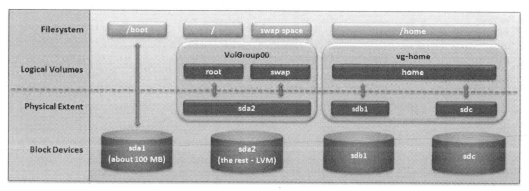

*Figure 4-1. How a system using LVM might look*

## Volume Groups

The most important concept in LVM is probably the volume group. Volume groups (VGs) are where both physical volumes (PVs) and logical volumes (LVs) come together. Volume groups are really just abstractions to make managing disks easier.

Now, given the flexibility we've already talked about, you might be wondering why we need more than volume group. The answer is that we might need to work with more than one type of disk. For example, a CentOS server might have its own local disks, but it might also be connected to a SAN. Generally speaking, when additional disk space is presented to CentOS from the SAN, that disk space will show up in the form of a new partition. Although this makes perfect sense from a SAN point of view, it can be rather unwieldy for the administrator looking after the server. Thanks to LVM, we can create a VG called san and assign all partitions from the SAN to this group. We can create another VG called local for managing the disks local to our server. This way, we can have great flexibility in how we create and manage our disk space, but we also have a clear division between the two types of storage. Of course, there is no reason why we couldn't group data partitions by department, for example, marketing or sales. Although what I've explained here is generally considered best practice, you should create VGs that best express what you're looking to achieve.

## Physical Volumes

PVs are block devices that can be used for storing data and usually take the form of a hard disk partition or a raw disk device.

One of the more powerful features of LVM is that LVM doesn't require a specific, underlying technology as long as it appears to the system as a block device (i.e., it looks and acts like a hard disk). This means that, like software RAID, LVM allows you to combine SCSI, SATA, and USB devices quite happily. Before we can use disks in this way though, we must first tag each as being a PV. We do this with the pvcreate command. In Figure 4-1, the example system has a VG called vg-home that consists of two PGs, sdb1 and sdc. We can mark these disks for use by LVM with the following commands:

```
pvcreate /dev/sdb1
pvcreate /dev/sdc
```

▨ **Note:** Opinion seems to be divided on whether or not you should partition a disk before adding it to LVM; for the most part, it comes down to personal preference.

Now that these PVs have been created, we can create a VG with them using the vgcreate command:

```
vgcreate vg-home /dev/sdb1
```

This will create the VG vg-home or throw an error if it already exists. If you want to add another disk to a VG that already exists (to add more space) you can use the vgextend command:

```
vgextend vg-home /dev/sdc
```

## Logical Volumes

Now that we have a VG (vg-home), we can start using it to create LVs. For this example, let's assume that /dev/sdb1 is 100GB in size and /dev/sdc is 200GB in size. This would mean that vg-home has 300GB of available storage.

The important thing to remember now is that the logical volumes can (and almost always do) have completely different layouts to the disks in the physical layer. This difference is perfectly OK and is one of the most powerful benefits of LVM. Another extremely powerful feature is the ability to resize a partition without having to unmount it first, but we'll come back to that in a second.

First, we're going to create a logical volume. This is actually quite straightforward and involves using the lvcreate command:

```
lvcreate -L 250G vg-home -n home
```

Now, you can begin to see why it's useful to have that vg prefix in there, but let's take the command step by step. The -L 250G tells LVM that you want to allocate 250GB of storage, and vg-home tells LVM where that storage should come from. The -n home portion of the command tells LVM that we want to call the new LV home. Now that we have our LV, let's format it for use:

```
mkfs.ext3 /dev/vg-home/home
```

You will notice the pattern here: /dev/<VG>/<LV>. This pattern makes easy work of keeping track of disk space allocation on a given machine. You use this new device name wherever you would normally have used the real disk partition (such as /dev/sdb1).

▓ **Note:** It's important to remember that, after you've assigned a disk to LVM, you shouldn't attempt to access it directly. Instead, you should refer to it by the device mapper name we discussed.

## Making Sure Your Volumes Work

Now that we have a LV with a filesystem on it, let's get it mounted, so we can see it in action. We're going to mount the new partition on /home:

```
mount /dev/vg-home/home /home
```

Quickly running df -h will show us that there is roughly 250GB free. But what do we do if we want to add another 25GB to the LV? Previously, we'd have needed to jump through hoops, but with LVM, we can do this easily. First, we need to extend the partition, and then, we need to resize the filesystem:

```
lvextend -L +25G /dev/vg-home/home
resize2fs /dev/vg-home/home
```

If you check with df -h now, you should see that you now have roughly 275GB available for use!

▓ **Caution:** You can also shrink filesystems, but doing so can be dangerous and is beyond the scope of this book. However, if you do decide to try it, you must remember to resize the filesystem before you resize the LV. Otherwise, you will corrupt the filesystem, and all of the data on that LV will likely be lost.

## Finding More Information on LVM

This section has provided a whirlwind overview of what LVM can offer, but many more advanced features and other hints and tips are available. The best place for more information on LVM is the documentation at the Linux Documentation Project (http://tldp.org/HOWTO/LVM-HOWTO/), which contains in-depth descriptions of all the LVM features and a complete command reference and a detailed step-by-step guide.

▓ **Note** If you want to mount the disk permanently, simply follow the same instructions we used earlier, only this time, use the device name (/dev/vg-home/home/ in our example) instead of /dev/hdb1.

# Summary

This chapter has given you a broad overview of some of the more advanced features that CentOS makes available for disk management. You've learned about the different types of RAID that are available and how to configure software RAID under CentOS. We've also taken a brief look at LVM and how to set up a volume group and create some logical volumes. This chapter's information is likely to be only the beginning of your storage-related journey but should be more than enough to give you a solid start. In the next chapter, we'll look at user management and how to use both graphical and text-based tools to get the job done.

# CHAPTER 5

■■■

# User Management

During installation of CentOS, you were able to set the passwords for the administrator account known as root and for one regular user. In this chapter, you will learn how to add, edit, and delete users and groups and how to allocate resources to them.

User accounts are essential in an operating system, as they provide real users disk space to store their data and allow access to operating system services, such as desktop systems, e-mail, the Web, and FTP accounts—which services are provided to users is determined by the system administrator.

Sadly, some users abuse the services provided to them, and if these users consume excess resources, there won't be any left for others, which will cause service disruptions. For example, if the server is set up as an e-mail system and users store large attachments in their accounts, in time the disk space in the server will be consumed, and other users won't be able to receive incoming mail. Fortunately, as a system administrator, you have the capability to thwart or limit the disruption through user management and resource allocation.

Every person who needs access to the system should have a unique user account, which ensures security and accountability. The account is secure, because by default, only the user and system administrator have access to the user's data. Users are accountable, because through logs, the system administrator can determine if a user is abusing an account.

In this chapter, we begin by adding a user, which you have already done in the previous chapter, so without further ado, let's get started.

## Managing Users and Groups with the Graphical Interface

In the following sections, we'll walk through the steps necessary to accomplish basic user and group management through the User Manager tool.

### Adding a User

To access the user management tool, simply navigate to System ➤ Administration ➤ User and Groups (see Figure 5-1). On the top of the screen are buttons to add, edit (via the properties button), and delete users; create groups; refresh the account listing; and ask for help. You also have two tabs, Users and Groups, to view the list of users and groups respectively.

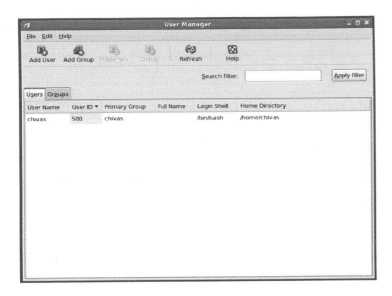

*Figure 5-1. The User Manager tool is used to manage users and groups*

To add a user, click the Add User button. The Create a New User dialog shown in Figure 5-2 will appear.

*Figure 5-2. Fill in the Create New User form with new user details*

In the first half of the form, you will need to supply the username, full name, password, and login shell. The username is the system name you want the user to be identified with. The full name is the user's full name, and this is the only property that is optional. The password is the secret text that proves ownership of the account. The login shell is the default shell used when you run a terminal on your account (using a shell was discussed in Chapter 2).

The second half of the dialog allows you to specify the home directory. By default, the user's username will be used as the name of the home directory created under /home, although this can be changed if you would prefer something different. The "Create home directory" check box will create this directory automatically when the account is created.

Red Hat adopted the policy of assigning users their own private groups with the same names as their usernames, because under Unix-like operating systems, it's very easy to accidentally give people file access that they shouldn't have when there are a lot of shared groups. By isolating users in a dedicated group, the user would have to specifically choose to give another group access and execute commands specifically to make that happen. In other words, it could not be done by accident. Although users can choose to change group ownership of files, only root is able to change user ownership. By default, "Create a private group for the user" will be selected, but if you don't want to use private groups, deselecting this option will add the user to the users group instead. Generally speaking, unless you have a good reason not to use private groups, you should leave this as the default.

The "Specify user ID" option allows you to manually specify the user ID (UID) number if you aren't happy with the default, which will be the next available on the system. If you do specify the UID manually, this number must not already be used by the system. Leaving it unmarked, which is the default, will automatically assign a UID number equal or above 500. This is because, by convention, UIDs 0 to 499 are reserved for system accounts.

Once you are finished, just click the OK button.

If the account creation is successful, you should be able to see the new account in the list of users in the User Manager tool. Aside from that, any files listed under /etc/skel will be copied inside the home directory. Therefore, you can place items on this directory if you would like to add default settings for each newly created user account. For example, if you would like that all home directories have the folder public_html, you may create this directory under /etc/skel.

## Changing User Properties

You can change the properties of the user by double-clicking the user on the User tab list or selecting a user and clicking the Properties button. You will be greeted with the User Properties dialog shown in Figure 5-3, which allows you to change account details and password expiration.

■ **Tip:** To see the list of system users and groups, click Edit ➤ Preferences from the User Manager tool, and uncheck "Hide System users and groups".

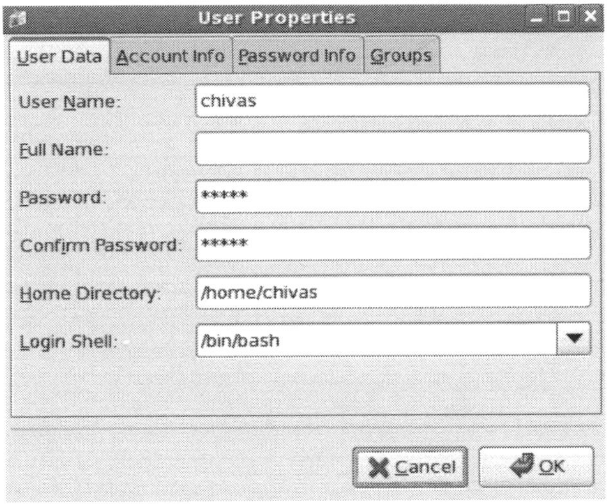

*Figure 5-3. The User Properties dialog allows you to modify the account details of a user*

On the User Data tab, you can update and change any of the details. All are required apart from Full Name, and if you change the password, both password boxes must match. You can update the username, change the home directory, and change the default shell, but generally speaking, doing so isn't advised as it can cause general confusion and misunderstandings. For example, changing the username is technically fine but might confuse users. Changing the home directory will involve moving the user's current directory or setting up a new one, and many scripts depend on the Bash shell and may fail if another is used. For most purposes, the defaults are perfectly fine—only change them if you really need to.

On the Account Info tab, you can specify an expiration date or lock the account. Setting an expiration date is considered best practice, although many people choose not to. Mostly, this choice comes down to personal preference, and depending on what you're using the server for, it could be perfectly acceptable not to set an expiration date. Some companies may have policies that specify that all user accounts must expire after a certain time. For example, an expiration date is a standard security requirement for companies that are PCI (payment card industry) compliant, so that they can process credit card details. You can also immediately disable an account by checking "Local password is locked". Bear in mind, however, that locking the password here only prevents the user from logging in; all the user's services will continue to function, such as accepting e-mail for delivery.

On the Password Info tab, you can set for properties for password expiration, if enabled:

- *Days before change allowed*: Sets the number of required days that need to pass between password changes
- *Days before change required*: Set the number of days the password is valid in the system. Once these days pass, the password will expire.
- *Days warning before change*: Set the number days before password expiration that the user is warned by the system to change the password.
- *Days before account inactive*: Set the number of days before the account will be inaccessible once the password has expired.

On the Groups tab, you can set the primary and secondary groups of the user. You can select only one primary group for a user. The primary group is useful when the user creates files, because the group ownership of these files will be based on the primary group. The user can be part of many secondary groups. We'll be covering groups in detail in the next section.

## Deleting a User

When a user will no longer use the system, you should delete the user to free up the system resources for your services and other users. Deleting a user is as simple as selecting a user from the Users list and clicking the Delete button. You will be prompted to confirm the deletion as shown in Figure 5-4. If the data on the home directory is no longer required, keep the check box checked so that it will be deleted as soon as you click the Yes button. This will free disk space.

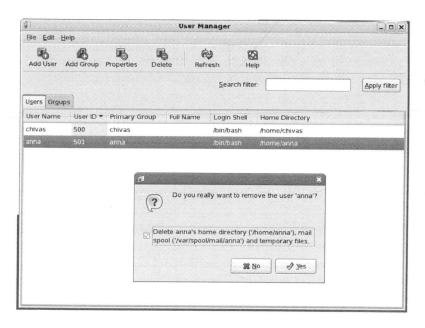

*Figure 5-4.* *Clicking Yes on the confirmation window will delete the user account*

## Adding a Group

A *group* is a collection of users. Groups are useful for applying privileges to a common set of users instead of setting privileges manually per user. Adding a group is also simple; just click the Add Group button from the User Manager dialog, and the Create New Group form shown in Figure 5-5 will appear. All you need to do is supply the group name. If you want to specify a group ID (GID) specifically, you check the "Specify group ID manually" box. Like UIDs, system groups are numbered from 0 to 499, while user groups start at 500. Click the OK button to create the group.

*Figure 5-5. The Create New Group dialog box*

## Changing Group Properties

To edit properties of the group, just click the Group tab in the User Manager window. Double-click the group you want to edit, or select the group in the Groups tab and click the Properties button. Once the Group Properties dialog box appears (see Figure 5-6), you can rename the group in the Group Data tab and add users to the group in the Group Users tab. This group will be added as a secondary group for the selected users. Click the OK button to update the changes.

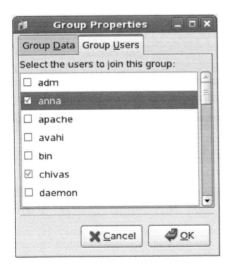

*Figure 5-6. The Group Properties dialog box*

## Deleting a Group

Deleting a group is as simple as selecting a group from the Group tab and clicking the Delete button. You will be prompted for confirmation on deleting the group as shown in Figure 5-7. Clicking Yes will delete the group.

▨ **Note:** You can only remove a group if it is not being used as a primary group by any of the users on the system. If it is, you will receive an error message. You must move those users to other groups before you will be able to delete it.

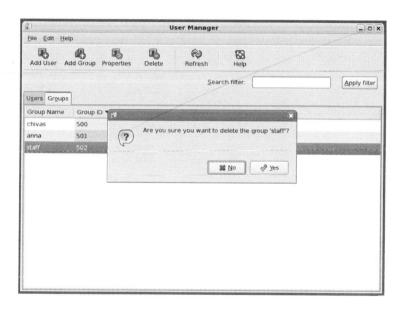

*Figure 5-7. Deleting a group*

# User Management on the Command Line

Now that you know how to use the graphical user interface tools to manage users and groups, you're ready to do the same on the command line.

# Adding a User

To create a user, simply run the command, useradd <username>. This will create a user with the username specified with an automatically selected UID, a private group for the user, and a home directory with the same name as the username under /home.

Follow up useradd by running the command passwd <username> to provide the password of the new user.

You can also pass the parameters for useradd that are listed in Table 5-1.

*Table 5-1. Options for useradd*

| Option | Description |
|---|---|
| -u <UID> | Manually assigns the UID of the user |
| -g <GID> | Manually assigns the GID (primary group) of the user |
| -d <directory> | Manually assigns the home directory of the user |
| -M | Home directory will not be created |
| -m | Home directory will be created, which is the default option for useradd |
| -c <description> | Description about the user, which is usually the full name of the user |
| -s <shell> | The login shell of the user, which is /bin/bash by default |
| -G <grp1>,<grp..>,< grpn> | The secondary groups of the user separated by commas |

# Changing User Properties

The command usermod is used to change the properties of a user. The usage is usermod <options> <username>, and the options are listed in Table 5-2.

*Table 5-2. Options for usermod*

| Option | Description |
|---|---|
| -u <UID> | Manually assigns the UID of the user |
| -g <GID> | Manually assigns the GID of the user |
| -d <directory> | Manually assigns the home directory of the user |

*Table 5-2. Options for usermod (continued)*

| | |
|---|---|
| -e <YYYY-MM-DD> | The date when the account will expire |
| -c <description> | Description of the user, normally the full name of the user |
| -s <shell> | The login shell of the user, which is /bin/bash by default |
| -L | Locks the user account password and effectively disables the account |
| -U | Unlocks the user account password |
| -G <grp1>,<grp..>,<grpn> | The secondary groups of the user separated by commas |
| -a | Used with –G to add users to secondary groups without removing the user's existing secondary groups |

The chage command is used to update expiration date for the user account to stop being accessible. For example, if you would like to set the account expiration date of the user juan to July 23, 2010, you should issue the command, chage –e 2010-07-23 juan.

As for password expiration, you use the chage utility on a user. The usage is chage <options> <username> , and the options are listed in Table 5-3.

*Table 5-3.* **Options for chage**

| Option | Description |
|---|---|
| -m <days> | The number of required days between password changes |
| -M <days> | The number of days the password is valid in the system (Once these days pass, the password will expired.) |
| -W <days> | The number days that the user is warned by the system to change the password |
| -I <days> | The number of days before the account will be inaccessible once the password has expired |
| -E <YYYY-MM-DD> | The date when the account will no longer be accessible |

# Deleting a User

To delete a user, you simply run userdel <username>. This will delete the user account but not the user's directory. If you want the directory deleted also, you need to pass the –r option, as in userdel –r <username>.

## Adding a Group

To add a group, you simply need run groupadd <groupname>. This creates a group with a GID above 500. You can manually assign the GID by using the option -g <gid>. For example, if you want to create a group called students with a GID of 1000, you will issue the command, groupadd -g 1000 students.

## Changing Group Properties

To modify group properties, you simply run groupmod <options> <groupname>, and the options are listed in Table 5-4.

*Table 5-4. Options for groupmod*

| Option | Description |
| --- | --- |
| -g <gid> | Changes the GID of the group |
| -n <name> | Replaces the name of the group name |

## Deleting a Group

To delete a group, simply run groupdel <groupname>. However, you cannot delete a group if it is set the primary group of an existing user.

---

■ **Tip:** You may want to take a look at /etc/login.defs, as it provides the default settings on creating users. For example, the reason why UIDs are automatically equal or above 500 when creating a user is because UID_MIN property is set to 500 in this file. You can also see the man pages for useradd, usermod, groupadd, groupmod, chage, groupdel, and userdel for more information on these commands.

---

### STORING USER, GROUP, AND PASSWORD LISTS

Whether users and groups are created by from graphical tools or command line tools, the information about users, groups, and passwords must be stored. Where? The answer is in the files /etc/passwd, /etc/group, and /etc/shadow. Essentially, you can manually add, edit, and delete items in these files for user management without using any tool except for a text editor.

The /etc/passwd file contains a list of users. Each row shows information about a user, with user properties separated by colons. Take this row item as an example:

```
chivas:x:500:500::/home/chivas:/bin/bash.
```

The first column represents the username of the account.

The second column represents the password of the account. The value x means that the password is not stored here; it's stored in /etc/shadow for security reasons, because /etc/passwd is readable by everyone. If a password is stored in /etc/passwd as in older versions of Linux, a malicious user can run a brute force attack on it to break the password which will then let the malicious user login to the other user.

The third column specifies the primary UID.

The fourth column represents the primary GID.

The fifth column represents the comment section; normally, this contains the full name of the user of the account.

The sixth column is the home directory of the user. In this case, it's /home/chivas.

Finally, the seventh column is the default shell of the user at login. In this case, it's /bin/bash.

The /etc/group file contains a list of groups. Each row shows information about a group, and properties are separated by colons. For example, consider this row:

```
staff:x:502:anna,chivas.
```

The first column represents the group name.

The second column represents the group password. The x means that the password is stored in /etc/gshadow. Group passwords are not used normally, but they are used for nonroot users bestowed the privilege of adding and deleting users in a group.

The third column represents the GID.

Finally, the fourth column represents the users who are part of this group, which are separated by commas.

The /etc/shadow file contains a list of passwords of each user and password expiration details. Each row consists of information about the password of a user. Let's analyze this row:

chivas:$1$XQLzic8C$5CQ9OMD/uBf.1HCouZQAa1:14281:0:99999:7:::

The first column represents the username.

The second column represents the password in an encrypted format (MD5 by default). If this column contains just two explanation points (!!), it means that this user cannot log in.

The third column shows the number of days after January 1, 1970 when the password was last changed. In this case, the password was changed 14,281 days after 1970 began.

The fourth column represents the minimum days that need to pass between password changes. Zero means there's no limitation on changing passwords.

The fifth column represents the number of days that the password is valid. In this case, it would be 99,999 days.

The sixth column represents sets the number days before a password expires that the user is warned by the system to change the password.

The seventh column represents the number of days before the account will be inaccessible after the password is expired.

Finally, the eighth column represents the number of days after January 1, 1970 from which the account is accessible; after these days pass, it will no longer be available.

# Implementing Disk Quotas

You can set up disk quotas on CentOS to prevent users from filling up all of the disk space in the system. You see, a couple of issues arise when there is no more disk space in a system, but ultimately, denial of service for all of the users is the end result. Services cannot run properly if the system cannot store data due to insufficient disk space. For example, when disk space is consumed, users may no longer log in to the system (however, the root user has a special 5 percent reserve on each ext3 filesystem, which can be changed if need be, that ensures that root can gain access and fix things, even if the disk is full). Also, if the system is an e-mail server, no more e-mail can be received by users if the system has no disk space to save incoming messages. With disk quotas, you can control the disk usage for each user and group on a filesystem.

# Enabling User and Group Quotas on a Filesystem

To be able to use user and group quotas, you will need to enable these properties for each filesystem. To enable quotas and persist these settings following reboots, we will add quotas in /etc/fstab.

Typically, quotas are enabled on the filesystem that contain the home directory. On fstab, you will need to append the keywords usrquota and grpquota to the filesystem as shown in Listing 5-1.

*Listing 5-1. Adding User and Group Quota Features on a Filesystem in /etc/fstab*

```
LABEL=/home          /home          ext3          defaults,usrquota,grpquota          1 2
```

In Listing 5-1, usrquota and grpquota were added in the /home partition. These properties will be enabled after you reboot or remount the filesystem. To remount the filesystem manually, issue the command mount -o remount /home. However, you may not be able to remount the filesystem if it's being used.

To verify that these usrquota and grpquota have quota support enabled on the filesystem, check the output of mount -a or cat /proc/mounts, as shown in Listing 5-2. These commands show you the details of filesystems mounted in your operating system. If you see usrquota and grpquota on the filesystem, you can proceed to create quotas.

*Listing 5-2. Remounting the Filesystem with Disk Quotas Enabled*

```
[root@server ~]# mount -o remount /home
[root@server ~]# cat /proc/mounts
rootfs / rootfs rw 0 0
/dev/root / ext3 rw,data=ordered 0 0
/dev /dev tmpfs rw 0 0
/proc /proc proc rw 0 0
/sys /sys sysfs rw 0 0
none /selinux selinuxfs rw 0 0
/proc/bus/usb /proc/bus/usb usbfs rw 0 0
devpts /dev/pts devpts rw 0 0
/dev/hda3 /home ext3 rw,data=ordered,usrquota,grpquota 0 0
/dev/hda1 /boot ext3 rw,data=ordered 0 0
tmpfs /dev/shm tmpfs rw 0 0
none /proc/sys/fs/binfmt_misc binfmt_misc rw 0 0
sunrpc /var/lib/nfs/rpc_pipefs rpc_pipefs rw 0 0
/etc/auto.misc /misc autofs rw,fd=6,pgrp=4366,timeout=300, ↵
minproto=5,maxproto=5,indirect 0 0
-hosts /net autofs rw,fd=12,pgrp=4366,timeout=300,minproto=5,maxproto=5,indirect 0 0
[root@server ~]#
```

# Setting Up the Quota Files

The next step is creating the quota files, which will be used to store quota limits for the users and groups, as well as current disk usage, in the filesystem. You will be using the quotacheck utility to manage quota files and examine disk usage in the filesystem. Particularly, you will be running quotacheck -cugv /home, where /home is the target filesystem, -c performs a new scan on the target filesystem and stores disk usage information in quota files, -u performs the scan for user usage, -g performs the scan for group usage, and -v gives you verbose information on running the command. You should see output similar to Listing 5-3.

*Listing 5-3.* Creating Quota Files

```
[root@server ~]# quotacheck -cugv /home
quotacheck: Scanning /dev/hda3 [/home] done
quotacheck: Checked 11 directories and 12 files
```

The quota files will be stored as aquota.user and aquota.group in the filesystem. Users should be able to read these files so that they can check their quotas themselves by running the quota command. To make these files readable, just issue the commands chmod o+r aquota.user and chmod o+r aquota.group.

# Setting Up Quotas

The next step is setting up quota settings for each user. To edit the quota of a user, we use the edquota utility. Simply issue the command edquota <username> to edit the quota of a particular user. Doing so will enable you to view and edit the quota file of user in vi mode, as shown in Listing 5-4.

*Listing 5-4.* Quota File of a User

```
Disk quotas for user chivas (uid 500):
  Filesystem    blocks    soft    hard  inodes  soft  hard
  /dev/hda3       72         0       0       9       0     0
```

The first column specifies the filesystem where quota is enabled.

The second column specifies the number of blocks, in kilobytes, that have already been used by the user.

The third and fourth columns specify the soft and hard limits for disk usage in kilobytes. Zero values denote no limitation. When the soft limit is exceeded, the system will warn the user, but disk consumption will still be allowed until it reaches the hard limit, or grace period. The grace period can be set in any combination of seconds, minutes, hours, days, weeks, and months.

The fifth column specifies the number of inodes that have already been used. Each file is represented with a unique inode, therefore, this column also represents the number of files the user had in this filesystem.

The sixth and seventh columns represent soft and hard limits of inodes this user can use. Again, zero values denote no limitations. For example, if you want this user to have a soft limit of 10 MB of disk usage, a hard limit of 15 MB of disk usage, a soft limit of 100 inodes, and a hard limit of 120 inodes, you would change the settings as shown in Listing 5-5.

*Listing 5-5.* Sample Quota Management for a User

```
Disk quotas for user chivas (uid 500):
  Filesystem    blocks    soft         hard      inodes    soft    hard
  /dev/hda3       72       10000     15000  9             100     120
```

To save the changes, as in vi, type :wq, and press Enter.

■ **Tip:** If the quota settings will be consistent across users, you may copy the quota settings of one user and apply them to other users by issuing the command `edquota -up <source_user> <user1> <uscr2> <uscr..> <usern>`.

## Setting Grace Periods

To view and edit grace periods for users, just issue the command `edquota -t`. Remember that grace periods are triggered when you have exceeded the soft limits of either disk usage or number of inodes. By default, the grace period for both disk usage and number of inodes is 7 days.

## Managing Quotas for Groups

Setting up quotas for a group is similar for setting up quotas for a user. To set up a quota for a group, you use the `edquota -g <group name>` command to edit the quota for the group. To copy one group's quota settings to other groups, issue the command `edquota -gp <source_group> <group1> <group2> <group..> <groupn>`. To edit grace periods for groups, the command to be issued is `edquota -g -t`.

■ **Tip:** View the help file of `edquota` by running `man edquota` for more information on how to use this tool.

# Enabling Quotas

Finally, to enable quotas on the filesystem, we turn it on by running the command `quotaon <filesystem>` as follows:

```
[root@server ~]# quotaon /home
```

Once, you've enabled quotas, the disk usage and inode limits will be implemented on your users and groups on the filesystem. If you need to turn off quotas, run the command `quotaoff <filesystem>`.

# Reporting on Quotas

To have a summary of quota usage for all of the users, issue the command `repquota -a` as shown in Listing 5-6. To show the quota usage for all of the groups, issue the command `repquota -ag` as shown in Listing 5-7. You can check individual quotas of a user by issuing the command `quota <user>` and check for individual group quotas by issuing the command `quota -g <group>`. Users may check their own quotas by issuing the command `quota` and may check quotas for their groups by issuing the command `quota -g`.

**Listing 5-6.** Summary of Quota Usage for All Users

```
[root@server ~]# repquota -a
*** Report for user quotas on device /dev/hda3
```

101

```
Block grace time: 00:01; Inode grace time: 00:01
                           Block limits            File limits
User              used   soft    hard  grace    used  soft  hard  grace
------------------------------------------------------------------------
root        --  17676      0       0              4     0     0
chivas      --     80   1000    1500             10    15    20
anna        --     56      0       0              7     0     0
```

*Listing 5-7. **Summary of Quota Usage for All Groups***

```
[root@server ~]# repquota -ag
*** Report for group quotas on device /dev/hda3
Block grace time: 7days; Inode grace time: 7days
                           Block limits            File limits
Group             used   soft    hard  grace    used  soft  hard  grace
------------------------------------------------------------------------
root        --  17676      0       0              4     0     0
chivas      --     80      0       0             10   100   150
anna        --     56      0       0              7   100   150
```

# Setting Resource Limits

It's not only excessive disk usage that can cause problems. Services can be disrupted if users bog down the system by running too many things, and eventually, the system could be rendered unusable for others. Luckily, you can also set resource limits on a user session. Resource limits are implemented via PAM (pluggable authentication modules). Though PAM is primarily an authentication mechanism, one of its modules, pam_limits, is responsible for applying resource limits to user sessions. These limits can be viewed and configured in /etc/security/limits.conf.

■ **Note:** For more information on PAM, check http://en.wikipedia.org/wiki/Pluggable_Authentication_Modules.

The syntax of setting a resource limit is:

`<username|@groupname|*> <soft|hard> <resource limit> <value>`

The first property can be a username or group, which means the resource limit will either affect a user or a whole group. If for the limit applies to a user, just supply the username; if it's for a group, prefix the group name with an at sign (@). An asterisk (*) would denote all users are affected by this resource limit.

The second property specifies whether the resource limit is a soft limit or a hard limit. On the soft limit, the user is warned by the system resource limit has been exceeded. The hard limit, on the other hand, is the maximum resource limit, and when a user attempts to exceed this limit, the system logs this behavior and prevents the requested action from taking place. The `<resource limit>` specifies what limitations you can set, such as maximum CPU time, file size, the number of simultaneous logins, and number of processes.

Finally, the `<value>` property specifies the maximum value of the resource limit.

Let's try setting a couple of resource limitations. For example, if you want to limit the maximum logins of the staff group to two, you can do this by adding this limit:

```
@staff          hard            maxlogins       2
```

If you would like to limit the login time for a user, juan, to 1 hour, you may do so by adding a limit to maximum CPU time in minutes like so:

```
juan            hard            cpu             60
```

To limit maximum memory allocated to the staff group to 2 MB, you can set the resource limit memlock in kilobytes as follows:

```
@staff          hard            memlock         2048
```

You can set the maximum size of a file that the staff user can create to 10 MB by modifying the data resource limit in kilobytes like this:

```
@staff          hard            memlock         10240
```

If you would like to limit the number of processes available to juan to 80, you can modifying the resource limit nproc like so:

```
juan            hard            nproc           80
```

# Summary

You are now able to manage users not just by adding, editing, and deleting users and groups but also by limiting the resources these users can access through disk quotas and pam_limits. This will give you much greater control over your CentOS system and will allow you to feel safer deploying a server into production.

In the next chapter, we will be looking at the X Windows system. Unlike Windows where the graphical user interface (or GUI) is built in, with Linux systems, it is an added extra. While you may encounter few Linux servers with X Windows installed, it is, of course, essential for use as a desktop, so it's a vital skill for you to learn.

# CHAPTER 6

■■■

# X Window System

In this chapter, I'll discuss the architecture of the X Window System and how it enables graphical user interfaces for Linux and Unix-like operating systems. I'll also show you how to configure the X Window System to meet your needs, and I'll introduce the GNOME desktop environment and explain how to use the GNOME Display Manager (GDM) to create remote X sessions.

The X Window System, often called X for short, was developed at MIT in 1984 to provide the necessary components for creating graphical user interfaces for Unix and Unix-like operating systems. These components include functions to capture keyboard and mouse input that can be used by applications running on X, and to display windows.

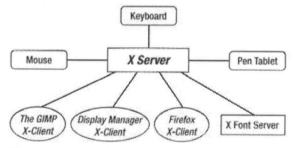

**Figure 6-1.** *The architecture of X Window System*

As Figure 6-1 shows, the X Window System uses a client-server model where the X server provides the user-interface components and the X clients connect to the X server to use those components. Clients can reside on the same computer that hosts the server or on a computer on a completely different network, and may have different architectures and operating systems. This is possible because the X display protocol enables communication between the client and server transparently over the network. The X display protocol can use security measures like SSH tunneling to protect the communication between the client and server on unfriendly networks. As a protocol, it does not dictate how a button and other controls will look like.

Before an X client can connect to X server, it must be able to authenticate itself on that server. If the X client is successful in connecting to the X server, it will start a session with the server and will be able to take advantage of X server's capabilities, such as interpreting keyboard and mouse input. When the X client finishes its session with the X server, it will disconnect and a session cleanup will occur. The program that starts and ends a session is called the X display manager, and it provides the login prompt that lets users authenticate with the system.

The X display manager is not only capable of handling local X client connections, but can also provide remote X clients' connections to its server. You will see later in this chapter how to use the X display manager to create a session from a remote server.

One component required by all X clients is the X font server (xfs), which manages the available fonts X clients can use when connected to the X server. Without the X font server, X clients will not run because they can't properly display any widget that requires text. If you somehow made an X client run without an X font server, you'd see the application window with its icons but no text.

The X Window System is monolithic, meaning that additional functions and libraries must be built into the server prior to its use. If you have a new library for a specific device that you want to use on your X server, you have to get the correct source code, compile it with your library source code, and run the binary with that combination. Newer versions of X may come with support for your device built-in.

# X.Org

The X.Org project represents the current stage of the X Window System. X was originally designed to run on Unix and Unix-like operating systems on x86 hardware. The code base for X.Org is derived from the sources of Xfree86 4.4 RC2.

Development of X.Org is done in collaboration with the freedesktop.org community, which focuses on open-source projects for making modern X desktop environments such as GNOME, XFCE, and KDE interoperable so they can be used on the same architecture, namely X.org, on Unix and Unix-like operating systems.

In contrast with the original X Window System and early versions of X.Org, the newer X.Org now supports modules. This means developers can create libraries and hardware drivers to support new hardware that can be installed without the need to rebuild the whole X Window System from scratch.

CentOS uses X.Org version X11R7.1 and is available whether you select GNOME or KDE during the installation. After installation, the X server binary of X.Org—called Xorg—is executed automatically on runlevel 5. The Xorg binary will consult xorg.conf, its main configuration file (if it exists) and run the commands contained in that file.

---

■ **Note:** Linux runlevels are discussed in Chapter 3.

---

## xorg.conf

The xorg.conf file is located in /etc/X11, and you can use any text editor to open it for modification. This file contains the base configuration commands to run Xorg and to control the available input and output devices for graphical user interfaces.

The xorg.conf file consists of a number of options arranged within several sections. These sections do not have to be in any particular order, and they can contain subsections that can load modules for the enclosing section to use. Like sections, subsections can also contain options that can be used to configure the module that is being loaded.

A section definition has the following syntax:

```
Section "SectionName"
        SectionEntry numericvalues
        SectionEntry stringvalues
EndSection
```

SectionName is the name of the section you are defining in Xorg, and the SectionEntry items are the attributes you want the current section to use. You can include more than one SectionEntry if required. In a section, some attributes may contain one or more values, and these values are separated with whitespaces. The values can be numeric or strings. Numeric values can be integers or floating point and do not require double-quotes. Strings are text values and must be enclosed in double-quotes. To find out which attributes require double quotes, look in the xorg.conf man pages.

You can turn a line into a comment in the configuration file by putting a hash symbol in front of it. Xorg will ignore those lines and you can use them for notes.

Listing 6-1 shows an example xorg.conf file:

*Listing 6-1. A Sample xorg.conf File*

```
Section "ServerLayout"
        Identifier      "Default Layout"
        Screen      0   "Screen0" 0 0
        InputDevice     "Keyboard0" "CoreKeyboard"
EndSection

Section "InputDevice"
        Identifier  "Keyboard0"
        Driver      "kbd"
        Option      "XkbModel" "pc105"
        Option      "XkbLayout" "us"
EndSection
Section "Device"
        Identifier  "Videocard0"
        Driver      "nv"
EndSection
Section "Screen"
        Identifier "Screen0"
        Device      "Videocard0"
        DefaultDepth    24
        SubSection "Display"
                Viewport    0 0
                Depth       24
        EndSubSection
EndSection
```

As you can see, there are four sections defined in this configuration file. Three of these sections are dedicated to the input and output devices found in the system, including the keyboard as specified in the InputDevice section. The system video card is defined in the Device section. Screen display configurations such as the amount of color and which screen resolution size to use are declared in the Screen section. Let's look at the sections a little more closely.

## The Keyboard Section

```
Section "InputDevice"
        Identifier  "Keyboard0"
        Driver      "kbd"
        Option      "XkbModel" "pc105"
```

```
        Option      "XkbLayout" "us"
EndSection
```

The InputDevice section introduces the keyboard section to Xorg, and an Identifier attribute is used to give it a name, which is enclosed in double quotes. The purpose of an Identifier attribute is generally to provide a way of referring to that section from other sections.

The given name for this keyboard is Keyboard0, and this will be used in another section. The Keyboard0 uses the kbd module that is loaded by the Driver attribute to let it communicate with Xorg. The Driver attribute tells Xorg which module to use to communicate with the device corresponding to the section, enabling Xorg to accept values the user types and pass them along to the X clients or applications that require input from the keyboard. The two Option declarations that follow, XkbModel and XkbLayout, can provide additional details on the detected keyboard for Xorg.

Note that an Option declaration takes two arguments; the first indicates the option being set while and the second specifies what it is being set to. XkbModel stands for the model of the keyboard, here pc105, a 105 keys model keyboard. XkbLayout is the layout of the keyboard, the usual United States-style computer keyboard that accompanies most computers. XkbModel and XkbLayout should be set according to the keyboard the computer has.

## The Device Section

```
Section "Device"
        Identifier   "Videocard0"
        Driver       "nv"
EndSection
```

The Device section is created for the detected hardware video card and, like the InputDevice section for the keyboard, has Identifier and Driver attributes. Identifier serves the same purpose here by giving the video card a unique name so Xorg can identify the proper video card (in case you have another video card installed in your computer), and also so you can refer to that Device in other sections. The Driver section for the video card uses the driver attribute to tell Xorg what module to use to run it. You can see that the value for the Driver attribute in the section is called nv and is the module for the open-source driver for Nvidia-based video cards in this case. What you have here will depend on your hardware.

---

■ **Note:** You can change the Driver value later to match the proprietary drivers in this Device section, but be sure you have followed the directions for installing that module within Xorg.

---

## The Screen Section

```
Section "Screen"
        Identifier "Screen0"
        Device      "Videocard0"
        DefaultDepth    24
        SubSection "Display"
```

```
        Viewport   0 0
        Depth      24
    EndSubSection
EndSection
```

In the Screen section you specify items like the resolution or the number of colored pixels that must be used to display images on the monitor. In the Screen section in Listing 6-1, three attributes control the display, Identifier, Device, and DefaultDepth. The Identifier attribute serves the same purpose as in the previous sections; in this case, it has the value Screen0 enclosed in double-quotes. A new attribute called Device is used to tell Xorg which declared video card Xorg must use for this screen to provide the display. You can see that the value "VideoCard0" is used, and refers to the previous Device section. As noted earlier, this is the point of an Identifier attribute—something that can be referred to in other sections. The DefaultDepth attribute found in the Screen section defines the number of colors a pixel can use in bits. The attribute has value 24, the default bit-depth for this screen. This source for the DefaultDepth is found within the SubSection declaration of the Screen section called "Display." The SubSection attribute lets you load modules that can be used within its enclosing Section and has the following syntax:

```
SubSection "ModuleName"
        SubSectionEntry numericvalues
        SubSectionEntry "stringvalues"
EndSubSection
```

ModuleName is the name of the module that must be loaded for this Section and SubSectionEntry are the attributes for this SubSection. The attributes can also take values which can be used to alter the behavior of this SubSection that is going to be used by its enclosing Section.

Within the Display SubSection, the Viewport and Depth attributes are used. Viewport specifies the upper and left coordinates of the initial display. These coordinates act as a marker for Xorg to let it know where to start showing information on the screen when it begins placing pixels in a left-right, up-down sequence for displaying images; Viewport is optional. The Depth attribute is the number of color bits this Display SubSection can use and holds the value 24. So this Display SubSection tells Xorg to use 0 in the upper and left coordinates of the screen as a starting point and to use 24 bits to provide the color depth for the screen display. Because of the DefaultDepth attribute in the Screen section, this Display SubSection is used by default when Xorg runs so you can have several Display subsections with different depths, and the DefaultDepth attribute says which one to use.

You can have more than one SubSection declaration within your Screen section declaration if your video card can support other bit depths and resolutions. For example, let's assume your video card can support the resolution 1024x768 with 16 bits of color depth and 800x600 with 24 bits of color depth. You want the default resolution of 16 bits to be used when starting Xorg and have the other resolution ready if it is needed. You can adjust the Screen section to be similar to the one in Listing 6-2.

*Listing 6-2. A Screen Section for Multiple Bit-Depths and Resolutions*

```
Section "Screen"
        Identifier "Screen0"
        Device     "Videocard0"
        DefaultDepth    16
        SubSection "Display"
                Viewport   0 0
                Depth     24
                Modes "800x600"
        EndSubSection
```

```
        SubSection "Display"
                Viewport    0  0
                Depth       16
                Modes  "1024x768"
        EndSubSection
```

```
EndSection
```

You can see in Listing 6-2 that an additional Display SubSection has been added and with it the Modes attribute. The Modes attribute specifies the resolution to use for the current Display SubSection. The value for Viewport remains the same, but the Depth changes on the second Display subsection. Based on the new requirements, Xorg should use the 1024x768 resolution with 16 bits of color depth when it boots up, and this is specified by the value of DefaultDepth. By default, the second Display SubSection is used by Xorg.

---

▨ **Note:** Doing screen resolution and bit depth changes on the xorg.conf file directly can lead to typos, which can be avoided if you have a desktop environment like GNOME installed on your system. Desktop environments have their own utilities to change sensitive attributes, and using one is recommended over manually changing the file.

---

## The ServerLayout Section

```
Section "ServerLayout"
        Identifier      "Default Layout"
        Screen      0   "Screen0" 0 0
        InputDevice     "Keyboard0" "CoreKeyboard"
EndSection
```

The ServerLayout section defines the overall layout of the input and output devices that Xorg can use in an X session. It ties all the others together. Any section that is not referenced here will not be used by Xorg. ServerLayout includes the Identifier, Screen and InputDevice attributes that are references to Sections that were declared earlier.

The Identifier attribute works as in the other sections, but this time it is used to distinguish this particular layout from other available ServerLayout declarations in the file, if there are any. This might be the case, for example, if you want other configurations for to be used for different X sessions.

The ServerLayout section uses the contents of the declared Screen0 section earlier for its display information. The additional 0's in the Screen option here are optional and useful only if you have multiple display devices. It is safe to leave them alone.

The keyboard for this ServerLayout originates from the InputDevice section for Keyboard0 and is marked as the only keyboard for this system, hence the "CoreKeyboard" keyword. This is why those sections have identifiers–so they can be referred to in this section. The ServerLayout section can be treated as a starting point for the xorg.conf configuration whenever it loads.

## Making a New xorg.conf File

---

▒ **Note:** CentOS still needs the xorg.conf file to run properly because it uses an earlier X.Org server.

---

The newer versions of Xorg have the capability to run without the help of a configuration file. If you need Xorg to use a custom xorg.conf file other than the default to test new display hardware, you will need to make your own. Fortunately, you don't have to do this from scratch because Xorg comes with the option to create one that tries to match what your system can support. You can also use this option for earlier versions of X.Org if you need to create a new xorg.conf file. To create the file, you first must run your system without the X server on the background by using **init 1** as root on a terminal to enter runlevel 1. This is needed by Xorg to be able to probe your system properly. Then run this command:

```
Xorg -configure
```

This will make your screen blink a few times, but it is nothing to worry about; Xorg is trying to detect the attributes of your system's input and output devices. Once this is done, you will be given back the prompt and with it, the generated configuration file called xorg.conf.new in the current directory. This file contains the Section and ServerLayout definitions required by Xorg to run your system in graphical mode. All you need to do is to copy xorg.conf.new into /etc/X11 as xorg.conf, and reload your system. Be sure to backup your old xorg.conf file before overwriting it with the new one, just in case.

---

▒ **Tip:** You can also reload Xorg by pressing the Ctrl+Alt+Backspace keys. Be sure to save all of your open documents because they will be terminated for the reload if your config file does not have DontZap set. The DontZap option prevents you from reloading Xorg using those keys.

---

# The GNOME Desktop

The default installation of CentOS includes a desktop environment to provide a graphical user interface for your Linux computer. It is called the GNU Network Object Model Environment, or GNOME.

If you have installed CentOS using the default options, you will be presented with a login screen. After encoding your credentials, you will see the GNOME desktop, as in Figure 6-2.

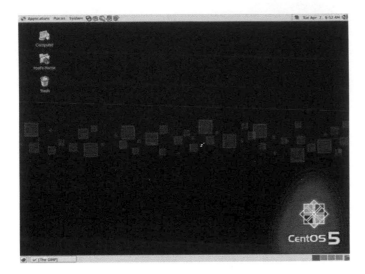

*Figure 6-2. The GNOME desktop for CentOS*

The GNOME desktop was designed to be intuitive, attractive, and easy to use. It can be extended by any developer who knows how to write software based on the libraries underlying the GIMP toolkit (GTK+2.x) and a programming language that can interface with those libraries.

People accustomed to other operating systems are able to grasp the GNOME desktop environment and use it immediately. Clicking on a menu brings up options you can use with that menu. Double-clicking on an icon activates its function. Right-clicking on a control, whether an icon or a launcher that can start an application, brings up a context menu that contains options you can choose. In fact, right-clicking anything is worth a try because there may be a context menu for that control. By clicking and holding the mouse button on an icon, you can drag it, as with other operating systems you have used. Let's take a look at some of the major functions you can use to be productive with GNOME.

## Top Panel

The top panel, shown in Figure 6-3, contains three main menu items, some launchers for quick access, a divider that separates the main menu items from the update applet, the clock applet, and the volume applet for managing sound.

*Figure 6-3. The Top panel*

The main menu items are Applications, Places, and System. Clicking on one of them reveals its corresponding submenu. For example, clicking on Applications displays its contents, and putting the mouse cursor on a menu item with a small triangle shows additional menu items, as shown in Figure 6-4.

**Figure 6-4.** *The Applications main menu*

If you click the Terminal menu item, you'll start GNOME's terminal emulator. With this emulator, you can run Linux commands just as if you were using the real console. I'll present each of the main menu items and discuss what they can do.

## Applications

The *Applications* menu contains software for desktop productivity, organized for a regular desktop user. Choices include applications to create documents with the Office submenu and play multimedia files using the Sound & Video submenu. A separate menu item at the bottom lets you add or remove software from the system. Clicking on that menu item bring up the Package Manager window as shown in Figure 6-5, where you can select an application based on its category and remove it if you want. You can also install new software easily within this window. The Browse tab is shown by default, and you can install or remove a package by its category. Select a category on the left pane, check the package name on the right pane to install it or uncheck the package name to uninstall it. Click the Apply button to put your changes into effect.

113

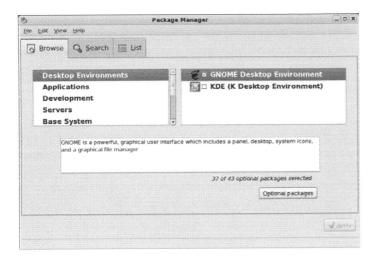

*Figure 6-5. The Package Manager window*

You can search for packages by clicking on the Search tab, which lets you search for all packages, packages that are installed on your system, or available packages that can be installed. This is shown in Figure 6-6.

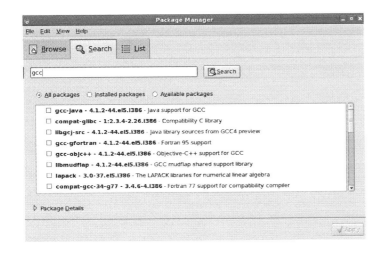

*Figure 6-6. The Search tab of the Package Manager window*

From Figure 6-6, you can give the full name or partial name of the package you want to find in the search box. Clicking the Search button will start the search. You can filter the results by all packages, installed packages, and available packages by clicking the radio buttons. If you check or uncheck a package on the result and click Apply, that package will be installed or uninstalled from your system. You can view the packages in list form by clicking the List tab. This is shown in Figure 6-7.

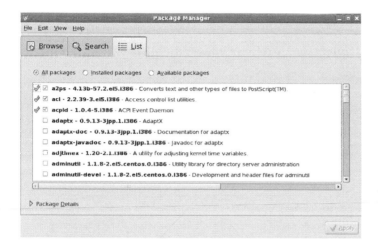

*Figure 6-7. The List tab of the Package Manager window*

In Figure 6-7, the packages are shown as a list in alphabetical order. This is similar to the Search tab except you cannot search for packages. You can filter the results by clicking a radio button. You can add or remove packages by checking or unchecking them and clicking on the Apply button.

The source for packages that can be installed on your system include your CentOS installation media and repositories. If you want to customize the repositories that Package Manager can use, click on the Repositories menu item under the Edit menu.

## Places

The *Places* menu contains items to help you navigate your Linux system, as shown in Figure 6-8. You can see the contents of your home directory using the Nautilus file manager by clicking the Home Folder menu item. You can also see the contents of the file system by selecting the Computer menu item and double-clicking the Filesystem icon. This is shown in Figure 6-9.

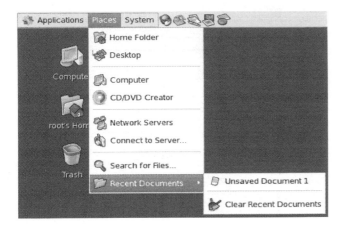

*Figure 6-8. The Places menu for navigation*

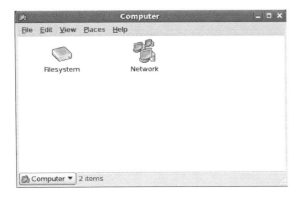

*Figure 6-9. The contents of the Computer menu item*

You can also browse the network and connect to a network server from the Places menu. For example, clicking on the Network Servers menu item brings up the Network window as shown in Figure 6-10.

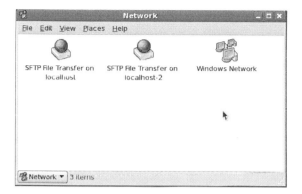

*Figure 6-10. The Network window*

All you need to do to browse the available network is to double-click its icon and the connected computers will show up.

The Places menu also contains a Recent Documents submenu, which holds the files you have opened recently, such as Open Office documents or image files. This serves as a handy shortcut to your frequently used files.

## System

The *System* menu holds the submenus and items for customizing your GNOME desktop and your Linux system, as shown in Figure 6-11. You can change the look and feel of your desktop using the Preferences menu. The Preference submenu contains items that let you customize the keyboard, mouse, and screensavers, for example. The Administration submenu items are those designed for system administration. You can add users and groups using the Users and Groups menu item, and check system performance by clicking on the System Monitor menu item.

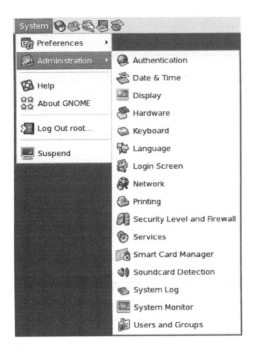

*Figure 6-11. The System menu*

You can put your computer into Suspend mode by selecting the Suspend menu item and turn off the system by selecting Shut Down. You can log out of the system so others can use it by selecting the Log Out item.

## Customizing Menus

You can add menus and menu items for new applications by clicking on System ➤ More Preferences ➤ Menu Layout. This brings up the Menu Layout window that enables you to customize menus on your GNOME desktop, as shown in Figure 6-12.

**Figure 6-12.** *The Menu Layout window*

The Menu Layout window is composed of two panes, menus on the left and menu items on the right. You can add a new menu, a new menu item, or a separator to group related menus or menu items. You can also change the position of a menu item by selecting it on the Items pane and clicking the Move up or Move down button. To add a new Menu, click on the New Menu button and you'll see the Menu Properties window, as in Figure 6-13.

**Figure 6-13.** *The Menu Properties window*

Type the name of your new menu in the Name box. You can put optional descriptive text in the Comment box. The text you provide here will be shown when a user places the mouse over the menu. If you would like to decorate your new menu with an image, you can do that by clicking on the No Icon button and selecting an image. When you're done, your new menu will be created under the selected Menu on the left pane of the Menu Layout window.

Creating a menu item is similar to creating a new menu. On the left pane, you select a menu where the new item should be placed, then click on the New Item button. This opens the Menu Item Properties window, as shown in Figure 6-14.

*Figure 6-14. The Menu Item Properties window*

To create the new menu item, type a name for it in the Name box and, optionally, some descriptive text in the Comment box that will be shown to the user when the mouse is placed over the menu item. You can supply an image for your menu item by clicking on the No Icon button and selecting an image.

Unlike menus, menu items can run commands. You must give the full path of the command that the menu item will start when clicked. You can type the full path of the command in the Command box, or you can select the command on your system by clicking on the Browse button. If you would like to start the command in its own separate terminal window, you can do that by putting a check in the *Run command in terminal* option. This can be useful for studying program output for newly installed software.

## Launchers

On the right side of the main menus are *launchers*, which serve as shortcuts to frequently used programs. You can see five launchers that point to office and email software, such as the Firefox web browser, Evolution email client, Open Office Writer, Open Office Impress, and Open Office Calc. Clicking on a launcher starts the software it represents. You can actually build your own launcher to point to your favorite application by putting the cursor on the middle of the blank space on the top panel and right-clicking on it. This is shown in Figure 6-15.

*Figure 6-15. Where to click to make a launcher on the top panel*

Select the Add to Panel menu item from the context menu that pops up and you will be presented with the Add to Panel window. Click the Create Application Launcher option to open the Create Launcher window shown in Figure 6-16.

***Figure 6-16.*** *The Create Launcher window*

All you need to do to create a launcher now is to provide the name of the software you want the launcher to represent, as well as its system path so GNOME can find it properly. You can use the Browse button to find the path to your software if you prefer, and you can add some comments if you like by putting some text in the Comment box. When you place the mouse pointer over your launcher, the text you used in the Comment box will be shown. This can help other users that will use your launcher. If you have an image file for your software, click the No Icon button and select the image. When you're done, select OK and your new launcher will appear on the top panel.

## Separator, Update, Clock, and Sound Applet

On the right side of the top panel is a separator that is used to divide the most-used main menus and launchers on the left from the two applications, the Clock and the Sound applet, on the far right. The Clock shows the current date and time, which you can modify if necessary. The Sound applet lets you adjust the sound volume for the available detected devices. If there are package updates, the Update applet icon will show itself, and you can click it to view the new packages you can add to your system.

## Bottom Panel

The bottom panel contains the Show Desktop icon, a separator, the Window List applet, the Workspace Switcher, and the Trash applet, shown in Figure 6-17. Clicking the Show Desktop icon hides all open application windows and shows the desktop. The Window List applet next to the Show Desktop icon shows all of the applications currently running. Clicking on the name of a running application in the

Window List applet minimizes its window, and clicking on the name again maximizes it. Clicking another application switches you to that one, of course.

The Workspace Switcher lets you transfer windows from one workspace to another for better organization. Workspaces are virtual desktops that you can use for managing application windows. If you find your current desktop workspace too cluttered, you can move some of the windows to the next workspace by dragging them there or by using the Move to Workspace right (or left) option. You can find this option by clicking on the upper-left button on a window.

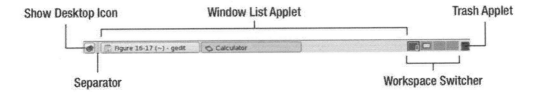

*Figure 6-17. The Bottom Panel with applications*

You can learn more about the GNOME desktop environment by visiting http://www.gnome.org.

# XDMCP Remote Connections

I discussed earlier that the X display manager is responsible for starting and ending an X session to connect the client to the server. If you are using CentOS with the GNOME environment, you use the login screen to start a GNOME session to access your desktop. That screen is GNOME's display manager, the replacement for the original X display manager. Instead of providing just the essentials for starting an X session, the GDM is framed by GNOME desktop components.

The GDM can also use the X Display Manager Control Protocol (XDMCP) to let other X servers start a session within the X server it's running on. With XDMCP, you are actually using the remote server's desktop while working on your own computer. It is like pulling a GNOME session from the remote computer into your computer. When another X server wants to connect to your X server using GDM, the remote X server will send a query packet. If the GDM allows remote connections, it will send a "willing" packet back to the remote X server. After getting the willing message, the remote X server can request that GDM start a session from your X Server, as shown in Figure 6-18.

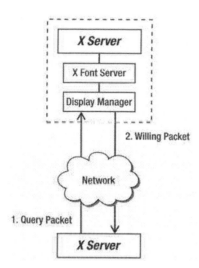

*Figure 6-18. Interaction between the GDM and the Remote X Server*

---

■ **Caution:** Be sure to enable access to the UDP port 177 to have successful XDMCP connections. You can do this by adding a rule on iptables allowing hosts to use port 177 on your system. You can also disable the firewall temporarily by turning it off using `service iptables stop`. Do this only in your practice computers on a secure network.

---

## GDM Configuration

The GDM has a configuration file called custom.conf that is located in /etc/gdm. This is where you enable remote X servers to create sessions with GDM. An example custom.conf file is shown in Listing 6-3.

*Listing 6-3. A Sample custom.conf File for GDM*

```
# For full reference documentation see the gnome help browser under
# GNOME|System category.  You can also find the docs in HTML form on
# http://www.gnome.org/projects/gdm/
#
# NOTE: Lines that begin with "#" are comments.
#
# Have fun!

[daemon]

[security]
```

```
[xdmcp]

[gui]

[greeter]

[chooser]

[debug]

# Note that to disable servers defined in the defaults.conf file (such as
# 0=Standard), you must put a line in this file that says 0=inactive, as
# described in the Configuration section of the GDM documentation.
#
[servers]

# Also note, that if you redefine a [server-foo] section, then GDM will
# use the definition in this file, not the defaults.conf file. It is
# currently not possible to disable a [server-foo] section defined
# in the defaults.conf file.
#
```

The configuration file is divided into sections enclosed in square brackets. The sections include daemon, security, xdmcp, gui, greeter, chooser, debug and servers. These sections contain no options and it is up to you to set whatever options you need to alter the behavior of GDM. The configuration file contains guidelines on what options can be used in the sections in the form of comment lines that start with the hash symbol.

Here is an overview of the sections and some of the things you can do with them in the custom.conf file:

- daemon: Controls the GDM daemon's execution. You can allow automatic or timed logins and change the GNOME greeting program, for example. Automatic logins let users log into GNOME without prompting for a password. Timed logins terminate a user's session at a certain time limit. You can also set the system user and group that GDM will use when running for better security and control.
- security: Defines how users can use GDM and can allow or deny remote TCP connections. You can, for example, use this section to prevent root logins from both local and remote users. You can also configure which PAM module to use with GDM for authentication in this section.
- xdmcp: Allows GDM to use XDMCP to let other X servers start a session on this computer; this is not enabled by default.
- gui: Lets you specify what GTK resource file (gtkrc) file to use on a running session to control the size of the icons or which theme to use.
- greeter: Lets you set the position of the login window, change its logo, or set the welcome message to show to the user.
- chooser: Controls what is displayed when the user runs the XDMCP chooser from the system menu. Choosers list available X servers on the network with XDMCP that users can connect to.
- debug: Makes GDM generate debugging messages in the system log that you can examine if you are experiencing problems with GDM.
- servers: Lets you define the number of standard servers that can run on your system. A standard server is the local X server that runs on this computer. Currently, there is 1 defined in this section as 0=Standard. This means that the first local X server on this computer holds the display number :0.

Adding an option to a section requires the syntax:

`optionname`=*value*

Here, `optionname` is the name of the option that can be used in the section and value is the value to be used on this option. For example, if you don't want the root user to login using GDM, you can change the `AllowRoot` option in the [`security`] section, like this:

`AllowRoot=false`

Every time you change an option in the custom.conf file, you have to restart the X server using `Ctrl+Alt+Backspace` or, if you prefer, reboot the whole system.

There are other options that you can use in your custom.conf file and you can read them in the `defaults.conf` file on the `/usr/share/gdm` directory.

## Reloading Options with gdmflexiserver

If you changed some of the options in the `custom.conf` file, rebooting can be time-consuming. Instead, you can reload selected options from the file, and they will be used by GDM just as if you rebooted the system. To do this, use gdmflexiserver, a tool for reloading options for GDM to use in the current X session.

The gdmflexiserver uses the following syntax:

`gdmflexiserver --command="UPDATE_CONFIG targetsection/targetoption"`

Here, `targetsection` is the section in `custom.conf` that the `targetoption` you just changed belongs to. For example, if you want to let the root user get into the remote X session, you change the `AllowRoot` option within the [`security`] section, like this:

`AllowRoot=true`

Now save the file. Then, instead of rebooting the system to let GDM know about this new rule, run gdmflexiserver at the shell prompt, like this:

`gdmflexiserver --command="UPDATE_CONFIG security/AllowRoot"`

This tells GDM what option has been changed and what section it belongs to. Here, `AllowRoot` belongs to the security section and security/AllowRoot is the proper way to tell gdmflexiserver about that update. If you make a mistake on your `custom.conf` file, such as having a keyword misspelled, gdmflexiserver will not warn you about it. The gdmflexiserver command will ignore that misspelled option and load the valid ones. Make sure to review the contents of your `custom.conf` file in case something is not working as expected.

# Using XDMCP with GDM

To use XDMCP, be sure to have two CentOS Linux boxes with the GNOME desktop ready. The first computer will be named aso and will be the GDM that will allow connections from remote X servers. The second computer will be named pusa and will be the one requesting an X session from the first computer.

To enable XDMCP, you need to add the required options under the [xdmcp] section. Add the following entry under [xdmcp] inside the custom.conf file of aso

`Enable=true`

This tells GDM to enable the XDMCP for remote connections. Find the [security] section and add this line:

```
DisallowTCP=false
```

This lets GDM accept TCP connections from remote computers. Without it, no remote computer will be able to connect to your XDMCP-enabled GDM.

---

■ **Note:** If you are going to connect to `aso` as root, you need to add the lines `AllowRoot=true` and `AllowRemoteRoot=true` inside the [security] section. Connecting with the root account is disabled by default.

---

Once you add those options to their respective sections, save the file and restart the X server and GDM, or update the configuration using the `gdmflexiserver`. You now have GDM with XDMCP enabled on the first computer.

## Requesting an X Session with XDMCP

Next you need to test the first computer to see whether its GDM can accept remote X server requests for a session. You can do this by making the second computer query the first local X server of the first computer directly for an X session. You could also have the second computer nest an X session within its GNOME environment.

## XDMCP with X Query

To query an X server that has its display manager set to accept XDMCP connections, you use the `Xorg` command with the `-query` argument, which makes Xorg query the target X server's display manager for a session. Here is the syntax:

```
Xorg -query targethost targetdisplay
```

Here, `targethost` can be either an IP address or a valid hostname, and `targetdisplay` is the available display you want the new session to be assigned in your Linux box. As an example, if you want to request a session for the pusa computer from the aso server, from pusa press Ctrl+Alt+F1 to get into the first virtual terminal. Log into that prompt to prepare to run the Xorg command. You have to do this instead of using a GNOME terminal shell, or the new session you want to query will cover your current desktop and you'd have to do a lot of switching on the available terminals to get your original desktop back. Next, run the command. For our example, this will be

```
Xorg -query aso :1
```

---

■ **Tip:** You can also use `X -query aso :1` here. The capital `X` is a shortcut for the name of the X server binary, `Xorg`.

---

You can see that the hostname aso was used as the targethost to request an X session. The :1 is the value given for targetdisplay that will be used by the command to hold a created session. The value for targetdisplay can be any number; it always starts with :0 and it is recommended that you omit this value when using XDMCP. That value is always assigned to your local X server if you have one. Better start with :1 and if you want another X session, increment to :2 and so on. Be sure to put the colon in front of the digit when specifying a value for targetdisplay because that's the proper notation that Xorg understands when assigning sessions.

---

■ **Note:** One way to find an available display number is to use the following command:

`ps ax | grep Xorg`

This shows all instances of Xorg running on your computer. Here's an example of the command's output:

`2672    tty    Ss+    49:33 /usr/bin/Xorg :0 -nr -verbose /var/run/gdm/auth-for-gdm-bj7m0e/database -nolisten tcp vt1`

The only part you need to look for is the entry with the highest display number. The output shows :0, which means that the first display :0 is used by your local X server and is the current highest display number. You need to increment that value by 1 for the next free display and that will be :1.

---

Assuming the command runs, you'll see the display manager of the remote session that you can use to log in, as in Figure 6-19.

*Figure 6-19. The Display Manager of the aso computer as seen on the pusa computer*

After logging into the first computer as root within the created session on the second computer, the screen will look similar to Figure 6-20.

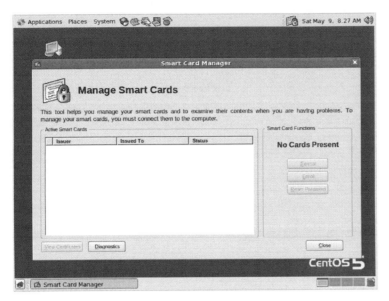

*Figure 6-20. The Desktop of the aso as a Session on pusa*

---

■ **Tip:** You can always get back to your original desktop anytime by pressing Ctrl+Alt+F7. To get back to the remote session, you can press Ctrl+Alt+F8. If you have other sessions open, you can also use the other function keys such as Ctrl+Alt+F9 to activate them.

---

When you finish using the remote session, you can get back to the first virtual terminal by pressing Ctrl+Alt+F1 and then pressing Ctrl+c to get rid of the queried session.

## XDMCP with Xnest

The Xnest is a utility that acts both as an X server and an X client. The Xnest application runs under an X server as a client of that X server. What this client does is provide another X server of its own that other applications can run under. To the Xnest client, the Xnest server is the X server, and vice versa, as you can see in Figure 6-21.

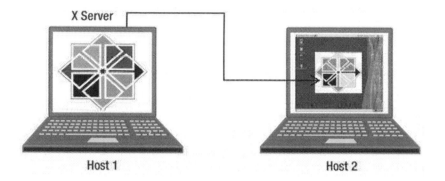

***Figure 6-21.*** *The X server of Host 1 is nested on Host 2's X server using Xnest*

The idea is to create another X server session inside your current X server session. The Xnest command takes the following syntax:

```
Xnest -query targethost targetdisplay
```

Here, targethost is the IP address or hostname of the remote X server you want to be nested in your X session, and targetdisplay is the available display Xnest can use to hold the created nested session in the local server. Much like the Xorg –query shown earlier, the -query argument here makes Xnest query the remote X server; the format of the targetdisplay attribute remains the same.

To run this command, first open a GNOME terminal session on the pusa host. This is where you will run the Xnest utility. Now run the Xnest command on a available target display. To test the Xnest -query along with Xorg -query on targetdisplay :1, use the following:

```
Xnest -query aso :2
```

Here, aso is the targethost and is the first computer, and :2 is the targetdisplay. Notice that I used :2 instead of :1 in this scenario. I did so because the first display, :1, is being used by the Xorg -query command. The value :2 is the next target display and is a good place to put the Xnest session.

---

▦ **Note:** If you accidentally use :1 instead of :2 here, you will see something like this: *Fatal server error: Server is already active for display 1.* No need to panic; Xnest is just telling you that there is another session running on that display. You'll have to use another display number to put the new session in your current X session.

---

After running the command, your desktop will look like Figure 6-22.

*Figure 6-22. An X Session within an X Session*

We're not done yet! One more way to do a remote X session comes next.

# X with SSH

You can use Xorg -query or Xnest -query to create new sessions from different X servers into your computer. However, one problem with both approaches is the way the clients communicate with the servers. The information being passed is not encrypted and is vulnerable to network attacks such as sniffing. If you want a secure remote X session, a better idea is to use Secure Shell (SSH) with X.

---

■ **Note:** SSH will be discussed in more detail in Chapter 11.

---

When you use SSH with X, the current X session that is created will have its communications for both client and server encrypted. All of the benefits of SSH will be applied to the X session for both computers with some minor drawbacks, such as speed. This is unavoidable because, as the information is being passed back and forth to the client and server, it must first be encrypted. Other than that, the session remains the same but is protected.

You can immediately use SSH with X session because the SSH included with CentOS is built with X server support. If you are going to use another version of SSH, make sure it is supported on the X Server that CentOS is using to avoid incompatibility.

Using the aso and pusa computers from the earlier example, here's how to have pusa request an X session from aso using SSH. While in the pusa host, open a GNOME terminal and log into the first computer using the root user. Use the following command:

```
ssh -X root@aso
```

The -X flag in the command tells SSH to forward X session information to your computer with encryption. The root@aso is composed of two parts: the user you want to connect on the first computer (root) and the IP address or host name of the first computer (aso). The @ symbol is a delimiter to tell the user and host information for SSH. Once you give the correct password, you are connected to the first computer and the connection is encrypted with SSH. Now run an X client application from the remote computer to use in your X session. For example, used the GNOME system monitor, gnome-system-monitor to monitor the aso host's activities from pusa.

```
gnome-system-monitor &
```

I placed an ampersand at the end to run the process in the background and to get the shell prompt back so I can run additional commands. After you run gnome-system-monitor, your screen will look like the one in Figure 6-23.

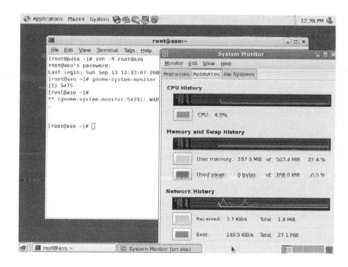

*Figure 6-23. Running gnome-system-monitor from the aso into pusa*

As you can see in Figure 6-23, the system activities of aso are shown in the GNOME System Monitor window. It may look like a local application on pusa, but it is actually running on the other computer, aso.

When you are finished with the remote SSH and X session, close the X application and type exit at the SSH shell prompt. You will be back on your original computer. Closing the shell kills all of the applications running from it.

# Summary

In this chapter, you have learned about the X Window System, its architecture and its open source implementation, Xorg. You also learned how to use the GNOME desktop environment and the Gnome

Display Manager to create sessions from another X server. You saw that it is also possible to provide security in remote X sessions by using the Secure Shell.

In the next chapter, you will see how packages are handled in CentOS and Redhat-based Linux systems.

■ ■ ■

# CHAPTER 7

# Package Management

Linux and Unix-like systems once distributed software only in its source-code form. Users had to get that source code one way or another and build it on their system using the required development tools, such as compilers and interpreters. Only after the software was finished being built could the user run it. This was fine for users who are adept at building software but could be a pain for those who do not understand the build process.

As an answer to this problem, the open source community started to make their own software distribution solutions. Numerous software distribution solutions and package management software tools have been developed and used for Linux and Unix-like systems. This helped administrators at all levels to add, modify, and remove software easily without touching development tools.

In this chapter, you will learn how to install, remove, and update software using RPM and YUM, the two package management tools available in CentOS. You will also learn how to use package repositories to retrieve and remove packages in addition to manually installing and removing each of them.

## RPM

The Redhat Package Manager (RPM) is an open source package management system created by Redhat. RPM is the default package-management tool used by Linux distributions that were derived from the Redhat Linux distribution, which includes CentOS. With RPM, software developers can distribute their software in its binary form. All the developers have to do is pack their software binaries into the RPM format and distribute it. The users will then only need to grab the RPM package and run the RPM tools to install it on their system.

RPM packages can contain not only binaries, but also source code files. This will help other developers who can understand the source code of the distributed package extend the software to make it better. In the next section, you will see how to distinguish RPM packages and to determine which version to download when getting the software you want.

The RPM package management system keeps track of the installed RPM packages in your system by using its own database directory. The database directory is located in /var/lib/rpm and it holds files that the RPM package manager needs in order to reference existing packages and those that have recently been installed or updated. As an RPM user, you do not need to change anything there, because it is used solely by the RPM package management system.

You can spot RPM files almost anywhere, because those files end with rpm. But there more to the filename's extension, as you will see next.

# The RPM Filename Convention

RPM packages use a filename convention to inform users about the nature of the package in addition to its name. In this convention, filenames look like the following:

packagename-version-release-architecture.extension

where *packagename* is the name of the package, *version* is its version number, and *release* holds the current release number of that version. The version of a package is the equivalent of its edition. As with any software, the higher the version number, the more features have been added to it. The release number is an indicator for the changes made to the current version. A higher release number can mean that more fixes were applied to the current version, for example.

The *architecture* is the target hardware architecture this package should be installed to, and *extension* helps differentiate this package from other files.

Here is an example package that can be found inside your CentOS installation media:

bison-2.3-2.1.i386.rpm

This package file has the following values for their filename positions

package name: bison

version: 2.3

release: 2.1

architecture: i386

extension: rpm

This RPM file is the package for the Bison parser generator, a tool used to create compilers. By looking at the RPM file itself, you will have a general idea on what the package contains and whether it is suitable for your system or not.

Before you get any RPM files, it is best to know what kind of computer hardware you have. Most people have an Intel compatible CPU on their system, and the package files that must be used should have at least the i386 value on its architecture part. If you do not get the RPM package with the proper architecture, the RPM tools will complain about its compatibility in your system.

Table 7-1 shows the current architecture values that you need to know in order to differentiate packages built for specific architectures.

*Table 7-1. The Available Architectures of an RPM File*

| Architecture | Description |
| --- | --- |
| i386 | Packages that can be used by machines with Intel-compatible hardware. These include Pentium and Athlon CPUs, for example. |
| ppc | Packages that can be used for machines with the Power PC hardware. An example would be the earlier Macintosh models, such as the iMac. |
| x86_64 | Packages that can be used for machines that have the x86-64 architecture such as Athlon64 and Intel Duo Core. These files in these packages are built to take advantage of the additional machine instructions of x86–64. |
| noarch | These packages are built with no specific target architecture. These are usually library files, documentation and programming language development headers. |

Now that you know the package naming scheme, you will be able to get download the type of package that is correct for your system. It is time to start examining the contents of an RPM file.

---

▓ **Note:** If you see the word src instead of any of the values in Table 7-1, that is a source RPM for that package. A source RPM does not contain the actual assembled tools ready for use but instead human-readable source code files for those tools. For example, the package bison-2.3-2.1.**src**.rpm contains source code files required to build the Bison compiler tools that are inside its binary RPM counterpart, bison-2.3-2.1.i386.rpm. If you are going to use the bison source RPM to install the Bison compiler tools in your system, you must do two things. First, you have to install the source RPM in your system then build the binary package. Second, install the resulting Bison binary package using the rpm command. More of source packages will be discussed later.

---

# The rpm Command

The rpm command is the tool you are going to use to manage RPM packages. With rpm, you can query, verify, install, update and remove RPM packages into your system. The command uses the following syntax

**rpm** *-options filename*

where *-options* can contain one or more options that you want rpm to do with the given RPM file that is represented by the *filename*. You can put the options separately or specify them in concatenated format.

When you specify an option to the rpm command, you can use its long version or its short version. The long version requires you to put a double-hyphen in front of the keyword. For example, if you want to install a package into your system and you want to use the long version, you will use the --install keyword. The short version requires you to put a single hyphen in front of the shortcut letter assigned for the option. Using the installation scenario, the short version of the --install option is -i. You will learn the long version and the short version of the rpm command options when applicable later.

Be sure to be the root user or have root privileges before using the rpm command. Most of the time, rpm will install the files contained in packages into directories that are restricted to regular users. The files in packages will be placed in /usr/bin or /usr/sbin, which only the root user can access.

In the next few sections, you will learn how to use the proper flags in order to get the result you want with the rpm command. You will install the actual RPM packages in the following sections, and it is best that you have your install DVD mounted on your system or install CDs ready to be mounted.

## Installing a Package

To install a package with rpm, you will need to use the --install keyword, or its shorthand, the -i option. This option tells rpm to install the package file that you specify with it. For example, to install the zlib development headers, which are contained the zlib-devel-1.2.3-3.i386.rpm into your system with rpm, you will enter this command:

rpm -i zlib-devel-1.2.3-3.i386.rpm

That will start the install process and will show you something similar to Listing 7-1.

*Listing 7-1. Installing an RPM File*

```
warning: zlib-devel-1.2.3-3.i386.rpm: Header V3 DSA signature: NOKEY, key ID e8562897
```

This message means that the package has been installed in your system, and it tells you that rpm cannot verify the package. This happens if you do not have the public key for that package. It also tells you that the package signature included on the package uses the DSA encryption algorithm. The message will disappear once you put zlib-devel's package signature into your system, which you will do later.

---

■ **Note:** CentOS RPM packages are located in the CentOS directory of your install media. You can run the examples by changing to that directory and entering the rpm commands as you follow the discussion.

---

## Signed Packages

Package maintainers can sign their RPM packages before distribution. When a package is signed, a unique ID number is generated and included with the package. This ID is called the *package signature* and is used by the rpm command to verify that the package came from its original owner.

Signing a package requires the use of a tool that follows the OpenPGP standard (RFC2440), which uses a set of keys to encrypt and decrypt data. One such tool is called the Gnu Privacy Guard or GnuPG, and it can be used to create the required keys to sign RPM packages.

Using GnuPG, the maintainer will create a secret key and a public key, which will be stored in a structure called a *keyring*. The secret key contains sensitive information such as the passphrase that is used to encrypt data. This is never distributed by the maintainer. Its primary use is to encrypt data before being sent. With RPM, the secret key can be used to sign packages.

The public key that was created will be distributed by the maintainer using either HTTP or FTP. Any user that wants to get the public key can download it and use it to verify the maintainer's rpm package. The user will add the public key to his or her GnuPG keyring using the rpm command, which will use that key along with the package signature for verification.

In Listing 7-1, you saw the NOKEY keyword when you installed the zlib-devel package. This happened because you do not have the public key for that package. For the next CentOS packages you will install, you will not see that warning because you will put the public keys of all the packages in your install media into your system.

## Importing Keys

If you are going to install a package that is not included with your CentOS media or that is not created by the CentOS community, it is recommended to verify that the package really came from its owner. You can do that by using the package signature of the package that has been created using an OpenPGP tool such as GnuPG. With that, you must get the public key of the package and import it to your system's GnuPG keyring. After you import the public key, you can verify packages before installation or install the package without any NOKEY warnings.

To add a public key into your keyring, you will use RPM's --import command, which has this syntax:

```
rpm --import gpgkeyfile
```

where *gpgkeyfile* is the file that contains the package's GPG key.

Your CentOS install media includes the GPG key file called RPM-GPG-KEY-CentOS-5. That file contains the GPG keys for all the RPM packages of CentOS 5. With this file, you can verify the packages that you can install from the CentOS installation discs and its website. You will use the following command to put the contents of the RPM-GPG-CentOS-5 key file into your system, assuming that you have mounted the CentOS DVD:

```
rpm -import /media/CentOS_5.2_Final/RPM-GPG-CentOS-5
```

If there are no problems during the GPG key file import, you will return to the command prompt. You can now verify packages from the CentOS DVD before installing or proceed with the install without seeing the NOKEY warning message.

## Verifying Packages

In practice, you do not immediately install an RPM package that you just downloaded to your servers without knowing where it came from or if it is really valid. You want to do this verification because the unknown package you are going to install may be malicious software instead of the legitimate one. The rpm command can be used to verify packages with its --checksig command, which checks the package signatures the algorithm used for its digest header. Digest headers can be used to check whether the package you have downloaded is consistent with the source where you got it.

The --checksig command uses the following syntax:

```
rpm --checksig target_package
```

where *target_package* is the package file that you want to verify. It is assumed that before you verify a package, you must have imported its GnuPG public key into your system. As an exercise, verify the Bison package using this command:

```
rpm --checksig /media/CentOS_5.2_Final/CentOS/bison-2.3-2.1.i386.rpm
```

After it runs, it will display

```
/media/CentOS_5.2_Final/CentOS/bison-2.3-2.1.i386.rpm: (sha1) dsa sha1 md5 gpg OK
```

which means that the bison package has no problems and is verified because its signature matches its public key in your system. The output also tells you that the package uses the SHA1 algorithm for its digest header. You can learn more about SHA1 by visiting http://www.faqs.org/rfcs/rfc3174.html.

## Adding More Output

When you install a package using the -i flag and there are no problems, the command will do its job and exit. Otherwise, if you do not have the public key of that package, it will display an information message that rpm cannot verify the package, similar to Listing 7-1. One of the previous two resulting outputs will be shown when using the -i option on its own, and you may want to see some form of indication and additional output when installing packages. You can add more output when using rpm by using the --verbose and --hash flags. You can use their shorthand versions, -v and -h for both options respectively. The -v option makes rpm show more messages while installing and the -h option will print out hash marks as the activity continues. You can use both options to have rpm display more information as the installation progresses and to keep you updated.

As an exercise, you will install the bison-2.3-2.1.i386.rpm package using the new options along with the -i option. You will use this command:

```
rpm -ivh bison-2.3-2.1.i386.rpm
```

The rpm command will install the bison-2.3-2.1.i386.rpm package file and will show you output similar to Listing 7-2.

*Listing 7-2. Installing a Package with the –v and –h Options*

```
Preparing...                ########################################### [100%]

   1:bison                   ########################################### [100%]
```

You can see from Listing 7-2 that rpm shows you what it is doing while it is installing the bison-2.3-2.1.i386.rpm package file. The display progress is shown by the hash marks, which tell you how much of the package has been installed into your system. You can use the –v and –h options with the other rpm options, and you will do that starting with the next section. Also note that the NOKEY warning message did not appear anymore, because you have imported its public key earlier.

If you try to install into your system a package that is already present, rpm will inform you about that. Installing the bison-2.3-2.1.i386.rpm file again, you will see a display similar to Listing 7-3.

*Listing 7-3. Installing a Package That Is Already on the System*

```
Preparing...                ########################################### [100%]

Package bison-2.3-2.1 is already installed.
```

You may have noticed that rpm did not show the full filename of the package after it has informed you about its existence. Once a package file has been installed with rpm, packages are referred to by their name only for easier access.

---

■ **Note:** If you need to reinstall the package because you accidentally removed an important file in your system that it requires, you can add the —replacepkgs command with the -i option.

---

If you get a warning that a file in the package you are installing has been installed by another package, you can override it by adding the --replacefiles option.

## Package Dependencies

Both the Bison and zlib packages can be installed immediately because they do not depend on any libraries or files that are located in other packages. However, some package files depend on other packages to run properly. For example, try installing the gcc-4.1.2-42.el5.i386.rpm package using the following command

```
rpm -ivh gcc-4.1.2-42.el5.i386.rpm
```

You will be greeted by the "failed dependency" message, as shown in Listing 7-4.

*Listing 7-4. Dependency Message for the gcc-4.1.2-42.el5.i386.rpm Package When Installing It*

```
warning: gcc 4.1.2-42.el5.i386.rpm: Header V3 DSA signature: NOKEY, key ID e8562897
error: Failed dependencies:
        glibc-devel >= 2.2.90-12 is needed by gcc-4.1.2-42.el5.i386
        libgomp = 4.1.2-42.el5 is needed by gcc-4.1.2-42.el5.i386
        libgomp.so.1 is needed by gcc-4.1.2-42.el5.i386
```

The rpm command finished with an error and did not install the gcc-4.1.2-42.el5.i386.rpm package. This happened because the rpm command checked its database files and found out that the files in the gcc package will not be able to run as expected, because of the missing files and packages. The missing items for the gcc package include the libgomp.so.1 and the glibc-devel and libgomp packages.

To fix the dependency problem, you will have to install each of the missing packages before the gcc package file. Here are the packages that you need to install manually to put the gcc package into your system:

- kernel-headers-2.6.18-92.el5.i386.rpm

- glibc-headers-2.5-24.i386.rpm

- glibc-devel-2.5-24.i386.rpm

- libgomp-4.1.2-42.el5.i386.rpm

- gcc-4.1.2-42.el5.i386.rpm

You can install the packages one by one, or put them all together in one line, like this:

```
rpm -ivh kernel-headers-2.6.18-92.el5.i386.rpm glibc-headers-2.5-24.i386.rpm …
```

After installing the packages in order, you will now have the gcc compiler tools in your system.

---

■ **Note:** If you want to install a package even if rpm tells you that has dependencies on other packages, you can do so by using the --nodeps option. With this option, rpm will continue installing the package, ignoring its dependencies. Do this only if you are certain that the package you are installing can be used without the files in the packages it depends on.

---

# Upgrading a Package

With RPM, it is now possible to upgrade the packages in your system, once you have the newer version of the target package you want to upgrade. When you do an upgrade, the rpm command will remove the old package from the RPM database directory and its files from the system. The new package will be installed and will be added onto the system's RPM database directory along with its files.

You can upgrade a package by using the --upgrade or –U option. For example, if you have a package for gcc called gcc-4.1.2-43.el5.i386.rpm, you can replace the existing gcc package in your system with this command:

```
rpm -Uvh gcc-4.1.2-43.el5.i386.rpm
```

That will uninstall the files the old gcc package holds in your system and replace them with the files in the new package.

When you upgrade a package, you are actually installing it. You can use the -U option in place of the -i option when installing new packages. Using the -i option when installing a new package in place of an old one will inform you that the package is already installed on your system. With the -U option, installation will proceed normally, only doing the install part of the process.

---

■ **Note:** Be careful not to use the -U option when you are upgrading your kernel. The new kernel might not work and may cripple your system if you do an upgrade, because the old working kernel will be uninstalled in the process. The best approach is to install using the -i option, because that will install the new kernel and leave the old working kernel alone. Another advantage is that the new kernel package will automatically update the GRUB configuration file so that it can use the new kernel the next time you reboot.

---

## Removing a Package

You can remove unwanted packages with RPM by using the --erase or -e option. You only need to specify the name of the package when removing it from your system.

For example, if you are not going to use the zlib-devel package on any programming projects soon, you can remove it with rpm by entering

```
rpm -e zlib-devel
```

You will be given back your prompt if there were no problems during the removal of the package.

If you try to remove the zlib-devel package, everything goes fine because no other package on the system depends on it at the moment. The same is not true if you try to remove the glibc-devel package you installed earlier, as shown in Listing 7-5.

*Listing 7-5. Removal of a Package That Is Being Used by Other Packages*

```
error: Failed dependencies:
        glibc-devel >= 2.2.90-12 is needed by (installed) gcc-4.1.2-42.el5.i386
```

You will have to remove the dependent packages on the glibc-devel package before you can remove it completely from your system.

---

■ **Note:** If you really want to remove a package that you don't need, and you are certain that the other packages that depend on this package can still work after the removal, you can also use the --nodeps option, just like the installation earlier.

---

## Querying a Package

When you have an RPM package and you are unsure whether it is already installed on your system or not, you can query it on the RPM package management system. A query will make rpm search for that package in your system and show you whether it is on your system or not. To query with rpm, you will use the --query or -q option and the target package name. For example, you want to check if the bison package if it exists, you can use this command:

```
rpm -q bison
```

The rpm command will show you bison-2.3-2.1 as the result because we already have it on the system. Trying the command on zlib-devel, like this:

```
rpm -q zlib-devel
```

will make the rpm command display the message "package zlib-devel is not installed". This happened because we intentionally removed that package earlier and it is not in the RPM database directory. If you want to list all of the packages installed in your system, you can combine the --q with the --all or -a command, with no package name, like this:

```
rpm -qa
```

This can be useful if you want to find a package on your system by filtering the output using the grep command. You will pipe the contents of the rpm query and provide grep with a pattern to define what you want to find. Here is the structure of the filter:

```
rpm -qa | grep keyword
```

For example, if you want to look for every package whose name contains the word "office," you can use this command:

```
rpm -qa | grep office
```

That in turn will show you all of the Openoffice.org packages on your system.

## Information and File Contents of a Package

If you want to know more about the packages that are installed on your system, you can use the --info or -i command in addition to the -q command. This will print out the description of the package; the syntax is

```
rpm -qi packagename
```

Take note that the -i command being used with the -q command is not the same as the --install command, which installs packages and also uses the -i shorthand.

To print out the package description of Bison, you will enter this:

```
rpm -qi bison
```

For the packages that you want to know more about but have not installed on your system, you need to use the --provides or -p option. Assuming that you have your CentOS media mounted, you are in the /media/CentOS_5.2_Final/CentOS directory, and you want to find out more about the yum-3.2.8-9.el5.centos.1.noarch.rpm package, you will use this:

```
rpm -qip yum-3.2.8-9.el5.centos.1.noarch.rpm
```

RPM will display the contents shown in Figure 7-1.

```
[root@localhost CentOS]# rpm -qip yum-3.2.8-9.el5.centos.1.noarch.rpm
Name        : yum                       Relocations: (not relocatable)
Version     : 3.2.8                          Vendor: CentOS
Release     : 9.el5.centos.1             Build Date: Tue 10 Jun 2008 06:13:47
 AM PHT
Install Date: (not installed)           Build Host: builder16.centos.org
Group       : System Environment/Base   Source RPM: yum-3.2.8-9.el5.centos.1
.src.rpm
Size        : 2331786                       License: GPLv2+
Signature   : DSA/SHA1, Sun 15 Jun 2008 07:23:03 AM PHT, Key ID a8a447dce8562897
URL         : http://linux.duke.edu/yum/
Summary     : RPM installer/updater
Description :
Yum is a utility that can check for and automatically download and
install updated RPM packages. Dependencies are obtained and downloaded
automatically prompting the user as necessary.
[root@localhost CentOS]#
```

*Figure 7-1. Description of the yum package*

To see the contents of a package file before installing it, you can use the --list or -l command. For the YUM package's file contents, you will do this

```
rpm -qlp yum-3.2.8-9.el5.centos.1.noarch.rpm
```

If you want to know which package a file came from, you can use the –filesbypkg or -f option with the -q option. This will print out the name of the package the specified file came from. For example, to know which package the gcc file in /usr/bin came from, you will use this:

```
rpm -qf /usr/bin/gcc
```

It will print out gcc-4.1.2-42.el5, its source package.

## Source RPMs

The RPM packages that you have been installing, removing, and querying so far contain program binaries and are also called binary packages. These program binaries, once installed, can be used immediately on your system. You already know that a package whose name contains the word src is a source package. This means it contains the source code of its equivalent binary package. For example, the bison-2.3-2.1.i386.rpm binary package has all of its source code inside the bison-2.3-2.1.src.rpm source package. You can work with binary packages in a fashion similar to, but not identical with, source packages.

You will use source packages if you are a developer or if you want to rebuild the software according to your Linux system. If you are a developer who wants to understand how the Bison package works or you want to modify it for certain purposes, you can do that by installing its source package. After installing a source package, you can browse its source code and create a new binary package that contains your customized code to be used on your system. If the program binary from a binary package does not run after you have installed it, and if you have its source package, you can build a new binary package from it. Then install the new binary package in place of the original one. You can also opt to create the binary packages from the source packages for increased security because you know that the result of the build really came from your system.

# The Spec File

When you install a source package, its source code files will be placed in the /usr/src/redhat/SOURCES directory. You can study source code files from there and make changes if necessary. A file with the same name as the package will be placed inside the /usr/src/redhat/SPECS directory. That file is called a spec file and it contains instructions required to build the binary packages from the source files of the source package. The instructions inside the spec file can be interpreted by the rpmbuild command that can be used to build the binary packages. The basic usage of the rpmbuild command will be discussed in the next section.

The contents of a spec file start with the preamble, which contains general information about the spec file in the form of attributes. These include a summary of what the package is all about and what version it is. The syntax of each preamble attribute is

*attribute_name*: *attribute_value*

where *attribute_name* is the name of the attribute of the preamble and *attribute_value* is the value that you want to assign to the attribute. Here is an example attribute:

Summary: A GNU general-purpose parser generator.

The next part of a spec file is the body. Each part of the body is separated by a section, and its name starts with a % symbol. The section contents follow and can contain additional information about the source package or scripts for building the binary package, for example. Here is the build section from the bison.spec file

```
%build
%configure
make
```

When rpmbuild sees the %build section, it will run the section's body, which contains the %configure section. Then the contents of the %configure section will be executed to start building the binaries that will be included in the resulting binary package.

Listing 7-6 shows a sample snippet of the bison's spec file containing the preamble and the %description section.

*Listing 7-6. Some Contents of the bison.spec File*

```
Summary: A GNU general-purpose parser generator.
Name: bison
Version: 2.3
Release: 2.1
License: GPL
Group: Development/Tools
Source: ftp://ftp.gnu.org/pub/gnu/bison/bison-%{version}.tar.bz2
URL: http://www.gnu.org/software/bison/
Prereq: /sbin/install-info
BuildRoot: %{_tmppath}/%{name}-root
BuildRequires: m4 >= 1.4
Requires: m4 >= 1.4

%description
Bison is a general purpose parser generator that converts a grammar
description for an LALR(1) context-free grammar into a C program to
parse that grammar. Bison can be used to develop a wide range of
language parsers, from ones used in simple desk calculators to complex
```

programming languages. Bison is upwardly compatible with Yacc, so any
correctly written Yacc grammar should work with Bison without any
changes. If you know Yacc, you shouldn't have any trouble using
Bison. You do need to be very proficient in C programming to be able
to use Bison. Bison is only needed on systems that are used for
development.

If your system will be used for C development, you should install
Bison.

With the spec file from Bison's source package, you can build the equivalent binary package that you can install on your system using rpmbuild.

You can learn more about spec files and building custom RPM packages by visiting http://www.rpm.org.

## The rpmbuild Command

The rpmbuild command is used to build both binary and source packages that can be used with the rpm command. If used on a source package, rpmbuild will take the package's spec file and use it to build the binary packages. Here is the syntax

rpmbuild givenoption target

where *givenoption* is the option that you want to pass to rpmbuild and the *target* can be a spec file or a source package that you want to use with the option. To build a binary package given a spec file called myspec.spec, you will use the –bb option with rpmbuild like this

rpmbuild –bb myspec.spec

That will initiate the build process from the commands contained in the myspec.spec file.

The rpmbuild command can also be used to create your custom source or binary packages, but we will only cover how you can use this command to build the binary packages using the spec file from its source package. Making a custom spec file to create your own package with rpmbuild requires you to learn spec file commands and sections that are beyond this book.

## Building a Binary Package from a Source Package

Take the following steps to build a binary package from a source package:

1. Install the rpm-build package by using yum install rpm-build as root. The rpm-build package will create the required directories to build RPM packages inside the /usr/src/redhat directory and install the rpmbuild command. Building binary packages using rpm-build also requires the gcc package, which you installed earlier using the rpm command.

2. Create the mockbuild user with useradd mockbuild. Package maintainers often use the mock package to build their packages in a chroot directory using a non-root user such as mockbuild for added security. If the package you are installing was created using mock, the package will require the mockbuild user to be present on your system. If you do not add this user to your system, the rpm command will inform you that it cannot find the mockbuild user and associate the files of the source package to the root user. You can find out more about mock by visiting http://fedoraproject.org/wiki/Projects/Mock.

3. Download the source package of the bison package from a CentOS mirror, such as http://centos.arcticnetwork.ca/5/os/SRPMS/bison-2.3-2.1.src.rpm, into root's home directory and install it using rpm -ivh bison-2.3-2.1.src.rpm. This will install the source files and the spec file called bison.spec in the /usr/src/redhat directory.

4. Change to the /usr/src/redhat/SPECS directory and run the command rpmbuild -bb bison.spec to start building the binary package. You will see a lot of output when the build process is taking place; just wait until it finishes.

■ **Note:** Similar to installing packages, rpmbuild will tell you about any missing packages that the source package requires. You have to install those packages before you can continue with the build.

5. When the build finishes, you will find the created binary package of bison in the /usr/src/redhat/RPMS directory. Inside that directory are subdirectories named after the known Linux system architectures. For example, if you are running CentOS on a PC-compatible hardware using the i386 architecture, your bison binary packages will be in the /usr/src/redhat/RPMS/i386 directory.

Now that you know the basics of the rpm command, you are ready to install individual RPM packages into your system. One disadvantage of using RPM when installing packages is package dependencies. There are packages that require other packages to be installed before you can install the actual package, similar to the gcc package. There is another package management system that you can use to avoid this minor disadvantage by grabbing packages from a central storage location, it's called YUM and is discussed next.

# YUM

The Yellowdog Updater, Modified (YUM) is a package management tool for RPM. It uses a central directory for RPM packages, called *repositories*, that is used by the yum command when managing RPM packages. Repositories can be inside local directories, FTP servers, or even HTTP. These repositories can be added to give more package sources that will aid YUM when installing RPM packages, for example. When you install a package using YUM, it will not only install the package for you but also get the dependent packages that are required by the package you are installing and verify those packages before installing. This eliminates the need to manually find and install packages that are required by the package you are trying to install. In addition, YUM will find the correct public keys to the downloaded package and add them to your keyring. After adding the keys, YUM will verify each package and inform you about its validity to help you decide whether to continue installing it to your system.

YUM is a good tool not only for installing packages but also for package removal. If you remove a package that other packages depend on, YUM will help you take care of it. First, YUM will find all the dependent packages of your target package and prepare the package for removal. Second, if you proceed with the removal of your target package, YUM will remove the dependent packages and then the target package.

There are other things you can do with YUM, as you will see shortly. The yum command takes on the following syntax

**yum** command packagename[ packagename1 packagename2 .. packagenameN] where *command* is the action you want yum to accomplish with the package and *packagename* is the name of the package you are using with yum. You can specify more than one package that you want to install with yum, provided yum is configured to find it on one of its defined repositories, which you will learn about later. When you do specify multiple packages, the package names must be separated by a space.

## Installing Packages with YUM

To install a package using yum, you will use the `install` command. For example, if you want the Subversion source code control system for your development team to use, you will run the following:

```
yum install subversion
```

This will start the installation of the Subversion package, and yum will also look for its dependent packages to be installed as shown in Figure 7-2.

```
---> Package perl-URI.noarch 0:1.35-3 set to be updated
---> Package neon.i386 0:0.25.5-10.el5 set to be updated
--> Finished Dependency Resolution

Dependencies Resolved

=================================================================
 Package          Arch        Version          Repository      Size
=================================================================
Installing:
 subversion       i386        1.4.2-4.el5      base            2.3 M
Updating:
 neon             i386        0.25.5-10.el5    base            101 k
Installing for dependencies:
 perl-URI         noarch      1.35-3           base            116 k

Transaction Summary
=================================================================
Install      2 Package(s)
Update       1 Package(s)
Remove       0 Package(s)

Total download size: 2.5 M
Is this ok [y/N]: []
```

*Figure 7-2. Installing the subversion package using yum*

By answering y on the prompt, you instruct yum to begin installing the subversion package and downloading its dependency packages, such as `perl-URI.noarch`. After the installation, the subversion package will be on your system.

## Removing Packages with YUM

Removing a package with YUM will also remove its dependent packages, if there are any. To remove a package using the yum command, will use its `remove` option. For example, if you do not need the gcc package anymore, you can remove it from your system by entering

```
yum remove gcc
```

You will see a summary screen that will ask if you really want to remove the package, as shown in Figure 7-3.

```
--> Running transaction check
---> Package gcc.i386 0:4.1.2-44.el5 set to be erased
--> Processing Dependency: gcc = 4.1.2-44.el5 for package: gcc-c++
--> Running transaction check
---> Package gcc-c++.i386 0:4.1.2-44.el5 set to be erased
--> Finished Dependency Resolution

Dependencies Resolved

===============================================================================
 Package              Arch         Version          Repository        Size
===============================================================================
Removing:
 gcc                  i386         4.1.2-44.el5     installed         9.6 M
Removing for dependencies:
 gcc-c++              i386         4.1.2-44.el5     installed         6.5 M

Transaction Summary
===============================================================================
Install      0 Package(s)
Update       0 Package(s)
Remove       2 Package(s)

Is this ok [y/N]: ▮
```

**Figure 7-3.** *Removing packages with yum*

Responding **y** here will remove the gcc package from your system. Note that g++ will also be removed, because it depends on the gcc package.

## Updating Packages with YUM

If you know that there are updates for a specific package and you want those to be applied to your system using YUM, you can do that by using the update command. For example, if you want to update the gcc package to a newer version, you will use this command:

```
yum update gcc
```

Similar to both the install and remove commands, the update command will also prompt you about the following packages to be updated along with the target package, as shown in Figure 7-4.

```
---> Package libgomp.i386 0:4.3.2-7.el5 set to be updated
---> Package cpp.i386 0:4.1.2-44.el5 set to be updated
---> Package libgcc.i386 0:4.1.2-44.el5 set to be updated
--> Finished Dependency Resolution

Dependencies Resolved

================================================================================
 Package              Arch       Version            Repository        Size
================================================================================
Updating:
 cpp                  i386       4.1.2-44.el5       base             2.7 M
 gcc                  i386       4.1.2-44.el5       base             5.2 M
 libgcc               i386       4.1.2-44.el5       base              94 k
 libgomp              i386       4.3.2-7.el5        base              67 k

Transaction Summary
================================================================================
Install       0 Package(s)
Update        4 Package(s)
Remove        0 Package(s)

Total download size: 8.1 M
Is this ok [y/N]: []
```

*Figure 7-4. Updating the gcc package with yum*

Answering **y** will make YUM download the updated packages and apply it to your system. If there are no updated packages, YUM will terminate and inform you that the target package you want to update is still current.

## Searching Packages with YUM

You can also use YUM to find the available packages that can be installed from its repository list, by using the search command. For example, if you want to know what packages will be added into your system when you install the bison package, you will enter this:

```
yum search bison
```

The search command in YUM is not restricted to complete words. You can also search packages by using only a part of the package name, if you are not sure exactly what are you looking for. As an example, if you know that there is a parser generator tool that starts with the letters *b* and *i*, and you want to look for it using YUM, you can run this command:

```
yum search bi
```

You will see a list of all the packages YUM can install that start with the letters *bi*.

## Adding Sources for YUM

CentOS repositories and media are not your only sources for YUM packages. You can add more repository sources into your system by creating *repository* files. A repository file is a text file that YUM references when performing package management functions. Repository files are placed in the /etc/yum.repos.d directory. It uses the following syntax

[*repositoryname*]

```
# comment

attribute=value
:
attribute=value
```

Where [*repositoryname*] is the name of the repository that YUM can use to reference additional repositories. You have to enclose the name in square brackets to let YUM know about that repository. You can alter the configuration of the repository file by specifying an *attribute* and its new *value*. Lines are terminated by carriage returns, and you can add notes by using comment markers, the hash symbol.

There are two repository files included in your base install of CentOS, and they are located in the /etc/yum directory. The repository files are CentOS-Base.rcpo and CentOS-Media.repo; they contain source files for the mirror websites and DVD or CD that contains packages. Open the CentOS-Media.repo file using a text editor and you will see the contents shown in Listing 7-7.

*Listing 7-7. One of the Included Repository Files in CentOS*

```
[c5-media]
name=CentOS-$releasever - Media
baseurl=file:///media/CentOS/
        file:///media/cdrom/
        file:///media/cdrecorder/
gpgcheck=1
enabled=0
gpgkey=file:///etc/pki/rpm-gpg/RPM-GPG-KEY-CentOS-5
```

In Listing 7-7, you can see that the name of the repository is [c5-media] and it contains five attributes. The name attribute holds the human-readable name of this repository and is required. You can also use repository variables, such as $releasever, that will be replaced by the actual value when YUM uses this repository. This will inform the user about what the repository contains.

---

▓ **Note:** Repository variables always start with the $ symbol. You can find out more about them in the yum man pages.

---

The baseurl holds the location of the directory or directories that contain packages for this repository and it is also required. It uses the following format

```
protocol://location
```

where *protocol* can be http, ftp or for local filesystems, file. The *location* contains the path for the repository directory. In Listing 7-6, you saw three local filesystem locations, which are used by yum when fetching packages from this repository.

The gpgcheck attribute makes YUM verify packages that are being fetched by the repository. This is similar to verifying individual RPMs earlier, but this time for YUM. Its value is 1, and yum will have to verify packages during the installation.

The enable attribute tells YUM that this repository is active. Packages can be downloaded from this repository without the need to enable external yum command-line options such as --enablerepo to explicitly use this package.

The gpgkey attribute specifies the GPG key file that the repository uses to verify the packages it contains. The value pointed to here will be used by YUM while retrieving packages and before installing them to your system.

As an example, you will create a repository file called compiler.repo that will contain the packages needed to install gcc on CentOS. Using a text editor, create an empty file named compiler.repo inside the /etc/yum.repos.d directory and add the content shown in Listing 7-8.

*Listing 7-8. The compiler.repo Repository File*

```
[compiler]

name=This is our first repository file
baseurl=file:///var/tmp/compilerpackages/
enabled=1
```

Note that you also called the repository [compiler] to match the repository filename for now. The name attribute describes our first repository, and the packages will be placed inside the /var/tmp/compilerpackages directory specified by the baseurl attribute. You activated the repository by using the enabled attribute set to 1. If you want to activate the repository manually, you can do that by using YUM's --enablerepo command with the name of the target repository as its argument. Assuming you want to enable the compiler repository at the terminal, you can use yum --enablerepo=compiler.

Save this file and you will create the repository directory next that will be used by this repository.

# Creating Repositories for YUM

You will now create a repository that contains the packages required to install the gcc package using yum.

1. Install the createrepo package using either rpm or yum. For rpm, use rpm -Uvh createrepo-0.4.11-3.el5.i386.rpm

2. Create the new directory that will become the repository. For our exercise, you will create the compilerpackages directory within /var/tmp by entering mkdir /var/tmp/compilerpackages

3. Copy the packages required to install the gcc package. Go into your CentOS DVD or CDs and copy the following:
   kernel-headers-2.6.18-92.el5.i386.rpm
   glibc-headers-2.5-24.i386.rpm
   glibc-devel-2.5-24.i386.rpm
   libgomp-4.1.2-42.el5.i386.rpm
   gcc-4.1.2-42.el5.i386.rpm

   into the /var/tmp/compilerpackages directory by using the cp command.

4. Run the createrepo binary with the path of the new repository directory as its argument: createrepo /var/tmp/compilerpackages

5. This will make the required metadata files and directories inside the /var/tmp/compilerpackages directory that can be used by YUM when fetching files.

6. You can test the new repository by running yum install gcc. The output will look similar to Figure 7-5.

```
[root@localhost ~]# yum install gcc
compiler                 100% |=========================|  951 B
primary.xml.gz           100% |=========================|  2.3 kB
compiler  : ################################################## 5/5
base                     100% |=========================|  1.1 kB
updates                  100% |=========================|  951 B
addons                   100% |=========================|  951 B
extras                   100% |=========================|  1.1 kB
Setting up Install Process
Parsing package install arguments
Package gcc - 4.1.2-42.el5.i386 is already installed.
Resolving Dependencies
--> Running transaction check
---> Package gcc.i386 0:4.1.2-44.el5 set to be updated
--> Processing Dependency: libgomp >= 4.1.2-44.el5 for package: gcc
--> Processing Dependency: libgcc >= 4.1.2-44.el5 for package: gcc
--> Processing Dependency: cpp = 4.1.2-44.el5 for package: gcc
--> Running transaction check
```

*Figure 7-5. The [compiler] repository being used by YUM*

---

■ **Note:** You need to run `createrepo` on your repository directory any time you add or remove packages. This will update the metadata files inside the repository directory for YUM to use.

---

If you want to know more about YUM, you can visit its web site at `http://yum.baseurl.org`.

# Summary

In this chapter, you have learned how to use the RPM package management system to install, update, verify, and remove packages in your system. You also learned how to use the YUM tool to install packages and create new repositories.

In later chapters, you will be using YUM extensively to install server packages that you can use with CentOS. This will help us install the proper packages at a much faster pace so you can learn about the open source servers.

# CHAPTER 8

■■■

# Basic Linux Security

You've been introduced to some of the major features of CentOS from its installation up to managing user accounts. It is now time to look at how you can manage your system's security by imposing restrictions and browsing important files that CentOS uses to keep you, the administrator, up to speed. This can be done using logs and modules that can enhance the security of your system. Once you get the hang of logs and modules, you can also use CentOS's task automation facility to run commands that you may often use.

## System Logger

The system logger is a tool that logs messages of the Linux kernel. The information contained in the logs can include sources not just specific to the Linux kernel but also for other applications that it uses. These include mail logs and automation logs generated by the cron command, which will be discussed later.

The system logger is run by its daemon called syslogd, and it is started during boot up. Once syslogd runs, it will record information that the kernel or its related applications may output in its primary log file, the messages file. This file is located inside the /var/log directory, along with the other log files that other applications may use.

The messages file is a text file that is continuously updated by syslogd when important events that require logging are given by the kernel. Whenever a new log entry generated, the syslogd daemon will append that entry into the messages file. The entry takes on the following syntax:

```
date time hostname message
```

where date and time holds the date and timestamp when the event happened. The hostname contains the hostname of this machine, and message is the information about the event.

An example log entry is shown in Listing 8-1.

*Listing 8-1. A Log Entry in the Messages File*

```
May 16 11:11:33 localhost avahi-daemon[4355]: Registering ↵
new address record for 192.168.1.11 on eth0.
```

You can see here that the log was made on May 16 at 11:11:33 a.m. You can also see that the time is in timestamp format, which includes seconds for accuracy of the entry. The log entry was generated by this computer, localhost, using the avahi-daemon service with the process number 4355 used to identify that. The last part is the reason why this log entry has been recorded: this log was made to inform the administrator that the avahi-daemon assigned the IP address for this machine to 192.168.1.11 on the first hardware network card, eth0. For developers of the avahi-daemon, the number inside the square brackets (4355) may be of interest because that is the process ID of the service. That can be used as an aid for fixing problems, if there are any.

---

■ **Note:** The source machine that generated the log entry is not only limited to your computer, localhost. It is possible to have the source come from other computers by making your computer a central system log server. This is discussed further in Chapter 10.

---

You can view the full contents by opening it with a text editor. If you are only interested in the latest activities that the kernel had done, you can view the bottom log entries by using the command tail /var/log/messages. That will show you the last ten lines of the messages file that contains the recent activity being made by your system.

If you notice various system information, such as mail server messages and login messages, gets logged in the messages file, those additional information came from syslog's other log files for specific functions. For example, the maillog file holds e-mail log messages generated by your email server, such as sendmail. Another is the secure log file. It holds user login attempt messages made by the login program that is used by Linux to let users log in locally. It also holds SSH (secure shell) login messages when it lets remote users enter the system (see Chapter 11). Both maillog and secure log files follow the log entry format of the messages file and are located inside the /var/log directory.

You can manage the entries that get logged and even change the log entry destination by changing the syslogd's configuration file.

## Using syslog.conf

The syslog.conf file is the main configuration file of the syslogd daemon. This text file is located inside the /etc directory. The file contains rules on what kind of entries gets logged and where it is being recorded. Each rule comes in the form

```
selector          action
```

where selector is the facility and priority of that facility to be recorded and action does what must be done when the condition of the selector gets satisfied. An example rule is shown in Listing 8-2.

*Listing 8-2. A Rule in the syslog.conf File*

```
# Log cron stuff
cron.*                                        var/log/cron
```

In Listing 8-2, the selector is cron.*, and the action is /var/log/cron. This rule will record all automated task information that is generated by the crond daemon, and those will be placed inside the cron file inside the /var/log directory. Lines that start with a hash are comments and are ignored by syslogd.

## Selectors

The selector in a rule consists of two parts, the facility and the priority. The facility and priority is separated by a period and takes on the following format:

```
facility.priority
```

The facility part of a selector is a set of fixed sources of system information that can be recorded by syslogd. These are the daemons: lpr, mail, cron, mark, news, syslog, user, uucp and local. There are seven local facilities, and these are named as local0 up to local7. Table 8-1 shows what each facility can do in a rule.

*Table 8-1. Selector Facilities*

| Facility | Description |
|----------|-------------|
| daemon | This facility will get messages from the system daemon and system daemons that do not have their own facility value. |
| lpr | Printer servers will use this facility to send printer related messages |
| mail | Mail servers use this facility to send mail information such as e-mail timestamps and failure status messages. |
| mark | This sends system messages at a fixed interval and is for internal use only. |
| news | If you have a news server on your system, messages generated by that server will be come from this facility. |
| syslog | This holds messages from syslogd daemon. |
| user | This holds messages that are generated by processes, like server programs, started by a user. |
| uucp | UUCP uses this facility to send messages. |
| local0–local7 | These are reserved for local use in the system and can be assigned certain sources that can be recorded. In the syslog.conf file, local7 is used to record boot up messages. |
| cron | The crond daemon uses this to send messages. |
| authpriv | These are security information messages. |
| kern | Messages generated by the Linux kernel. Useful for Linux kernel development. |

With the sources defined, you can adjust the amount of information that the facility can generate and record on the specified action by specifying any number of the priorities shown in Table 8-2. In Table 8-2, the priorities are arranged in ascending order.

*Table 8-2. Selector Priorities*

| Priority | Description |
|----------|-------------|
| debug | Debugging information generated by programs. |
| info | General information messages. |
| notice | A notification that certain behaviors of a process that should be observed. |
| warning | A warning message for processes that may affect the system. |
| crit | A critical warning for certain events, such as software or hardware problems. |
| alert | A warning message for the system that informs users for malfunctioning programs that may affect the system. If you see this kind, check the system immediately. |
| emerg | An emergency message, such as notification of kernel problems that can lead to system instability. |

For example, if you want to have general information about the behavior of your newly installed mail server running on your system, you can use this selector:

`mail.info`

where `mail` is the facility and `info` is the priority. You can also make a single rule generate additional messages by appending them with a semicolon. For example, if you want the `mail` facility to generate debug messages in addition to the general information priority information, you can use this:

`mail.info;mail.debug`

You can also use a comma to separate the priorities instead of adding another selector pair:

`mail.info,debug`

This selector will generate both general information messages and mail server debug messages that can be recorded on its action. You are not only limited to adding messages in the priority part, because you can also add facilities that can generate messages for a specific priority. You will also use a comma to add the facilities. For example, if you want general information for both `cron` and `mail` facilities, you can use this:

`mail,cron.info`

That will make the selector generate messages from the `mail` and `cron` facilities using the `info` priority.

Instead of specifying both facility and priority one by one using commas and semicolons respectively, you can use wildcards in the form of asterisk. Using wildcards will tell syslogd to use all of the facilities or priorities. From our first example selector for `cron`, we see this:

`cron.*`

The selector will tell syslogd to generate messages from the `cron` facility for all priorities. This is the same as

```
cron.debug,info,notice,warning,crit,alert,emerg
```

If you want to filter out certain priorities while using wildcards, you can do it with the negation operator (!). The negation operator will tell syslogd not to get messages from a specific priority. For example, if you want all kinds of messages except coming from the warning priority, you can use the following selector:

```
mail.*;mail.!warning
```

When you specify a priority for a facility, syslogd will record messages starting from that priority up to the highest priority. If you do not want that behavior, you can create a selector using the single priority operator, the equals sign. That will force syslogd to log messages for that facility or facilities on that priority. For example, if you only need messages from the mail facility with the warning priority, you can use this:

```
mail.=warning
```

Or if you do not want any messages from the warning priority with the mail facility, you can use the negation operator in front of the single priority operator:

```
mail.!=warning
```

You can use the none keyword in place of the priority in the selector to tell syslogd not to use any priority when recording messages.

```
cron.none
```

This will not log messages coming from the cron facility.

## Actions

An action in a syslog rule is the destination where the messages generated by its associated selector are recorded. This destination is called a logfile and it can be in the form of a regular file, a named pipe, a terminal, a remote computer, or a list of users. Expanding further the list of users, you can also have the action to be sent to every user on the system.

Regular files will save the messages on the filename specified for the action. You have to give the full path of the file for syslogd to know where to put the messages generated by the selector. In Listing 8-2, the regular file where the messages generated by the cron facility will be saved on the text file called cron located in /var/log.

If you want to continuously see the contents of the cron file, you can use the command tail –f /var/log/cron. The –f flag of tail will show new entries being added to the target file. You can terminate this command by using ctrl-c.

```
*.info                          /var/log/newserver
```

You can monitor the output of that server later by opening the newserver text file. If you want to continuously see the contents of the newserver file, you can use the command tail –f /var/log/newserver. The –f flag of tail will show new entries being added to the target file. You can terminate this command by using ctrl-c.

Using the terminal method will show the messages that the selector generates in a target terminal. You can use terminals 1 through 4 to view the messages. For example, if you want to see the messages being generated in terminal 2, you can use /dev/tty2 as the action for that selector.

```
*.info                          /dev/tty2
```

You can use the key combination Ctrl+Alt+*target terminal* to switch between terminals. The *target terminal* is the function key with the terminal number you want to switch to. With /dev/tty2 set, you can press Ctrl+Alt+F2 to view the messages. To go back to your Gnome desktop, you can press Ctrl+Alt+F7.

If you do not have Gnome installed, it is advisable that you use /dev/tty5 up to /dev/tty8 to view log messages. This way, the first four terminals will be free for your use.

If you have a central syslog server and you want to send log information on it, you can by specifying the hostname of that server as the action using this format:

```
@servername
```

where servername is the name of the central syslog server. The @ symbol tells your local syslogd daemon that messages for this selector should be passed on that remote server. For example, if you want to send log messages to the host pusa, you can use this:

```
*.info                           @pusa
```

You can also specify certain users on your system that will receive the log messages from the selector by giving their usernames as the action. Multiple users can receive the messages from the selector by separating their usernames with a comma. For example, if you want to send log messages to ging and bake, you can use this:

```
*.info                           ging,bake
```

provided that these users exist on your system. You can also use the wildcard operator (*) in place of the user list to tell syslogd that the messages must be sent to all users.

When trying out these example rules, you will need to restart the syslogd daemon to update itself with your configuration. Be sure to run service syslog restart after any changes you make in the syslog.conf file.

## Detecting Intruders with the System Logger

The log messages produced by the system logger can be used to detect intruders in your system. You can browse the system logger log files, such as the messages file or the secure file in the /var/log directory, to find out whether the attacker moved into your system. It also gives you some idea what was done during his attack.

Because of the detail that the system logger generates, intrusion detection tools were created to help Linux administrators detect attackers that have tried to get in or got into the system. Some of these intrusion detection tools include Tripwire (http://sourceforge.net/projects/tripwire) and Snort (http://www.snort.org). These tools are capable of finding out what an attacker has changed inside your system and reporting the changes to you via e-mail. You have to download and install the tools and configure them before you can use them.

What happens, though, if you are still in the middle of choosing the right intrusion detection tool to use on your system? How do you find the entries that will tell you that an attempted or successful system break-in happened to your Linux server? You can tell by looking for the common behavior of attackers like failed login attempts and failed su attempts using the secure file. The secure log file in /var/log contains syslog entries from login programs, such as login or SSH. To know if there is someone trying to get into your system, look for the FAILED keyword into your secure log file. You can use the grep command that can retrieve specific text using a keyword or pattern from a file. The syntax is

```
grep givenpattern targetfile
```

where givenpattern is your suspected service or server software that the attacker is using to get into your system. That can also be a keyword generated by a service such as login. You can use regular expressions here if you know how. The targetfile is the log file that you want to search using the search pattern you gave in givenpattern.

For failed local logins, you can use the command grep FAILED /var/log/secure retrieve those log entries. A sample output of the command is shown in Listing 8-3.

*Listing 8-3.* *Failed Login Attempts Retrieved from the Secure File*

```
Aug 19 07:19:55 localhost login: FAILED LOGIN 1 FROM ↵
(null) FOR root, Authentication failure
Aug 19 07:19:57 localhost login. FAILED LOGIN 2 FROM ↵
(null) FOR root, Authentication failure
Aug 19 07:20:01 localhost login: FAILED LOGIN 3 FROM ↵
(null) FOR root, Authentication failure
Aug 19 07:20:04 localhost login: FAILED LOGIN SESSION↵
FROM (null) FOR root, Authentication failure
Aug 19 07:20:08 localhost login: FAILED LOGIN 1 FROM↵
(null) FOR root, Authentication failure
Aug 19 07:20:11 localhost login: FAILED LOGIN 2 FROM↵
(null) FOR root, Authentication failure
```

From Listing 8-3, you can find out that someone is repeatedly trying to log in as the local root user. If you see this pattern, consider talking to your users and asking if anyone of them is trying to log in as root. Similar entries will show up if an attacker tries to find a way in to your system remotely using telnet or ssh by looking for a system user with a weak password. Listing 8-4 shows a remote attacker with an IP address of 192.168.1.10 using ssh to randomly find valid users and crack in to the Linux server at 192.168.1.13 using the command grep ssh /var/log/secure. The Linux server has a valid user called ging as a start.

*Listing 8-4.* *An Attacker Attempting to Break into the System by Guessing Usernames*

```
Aug 19 09:02:12 localhost sshd[4771]: Invalid user chivas from 192.168.1.10
Aug 19 09:02:12 localhost sshd[4772]: input_userauth_request: invalid user chivas
Aug 19 09:02:15 localhost sshd[4771]: Failed none for invalid ↵
user chivas from 192.168.1.10 port 48852 ssh2
Aug 19 09:02:15 localhost sshd[4771]: Failed password for invalid ↵
user chivas from 192.168.1.10 port 48852 ssh2
Aug 19 09.02.15 localhost sshd[4771]: Failed password for invalid ↵
user chivas from 192.168.1.10 port 48852 ssh2
Aug 19 09:02:15 localhost sshd[4772]: Connection closed by 192.168.1.10
Aug 19 09:02:18 localhost sshd[4774]: Invalid user frank from 192.168.1.10
Aug 19 09:02:19 localhost sshd[4775]: input_userauth_request: invalid user frank
Aug 19 09:02:20 localhost sshd[4774]: Failed none for invalid ↵
user frank from 192.168.1.10 port 48854 ssh2
Aug 19 09:02:21 localhost sshd[4774]: Failed password for invalid ↵
user frank from 192.168.1.10 port 48854 ssh2
Aug 19 09:02:21 localhost sshd[4774]: Failed password for invalid ↵
user frank from 192.168.1.10 port 48854 ssh2
Aug 19 09:02:21 localhost sshd[4775]: Connection ↵
closed by 192.168.1.10
Aug 19 09:02:26 localhost sshd[4776]: Failed password for ging ↵
from 192.168.1.10 port 48855 ssh2
Aug 19 09:02:26 localhost sshd[4776]: Failed password for ging ↵
```

```
from 192.168.1.10 port 48855 ssh2
Aug 19 09:02:26 localhost sshd[4777]: Connection ↵
 closed by 192.168.1.10
Aug 19 09:02:34 localhost sshd[4778]: Failed password for ging↵
 from 192.168.1.10 port 48856 ssh2
Aug 19 09:02:34 localhost sshd[4778]: Failed password for ging ↵
 from 192.168.1.10 port 48856 ssh2
Aug 19 09:02:34 localhost sshd[4779]: Connection closed by 192.168.1.10
```

The sample chunk retrieved from grep ssh /var/log/secure in Listing 8-4 shows the attacker trying to see if the victim computer has the chivas user and trying to log with it. The attacker fails and tries the user frank. Still the attempt fails, but on the third try, with a lot of patience and luck, the attacker manages to get a valid system user ging. The attacker's cracking program will now concentrate on the ging user and see if it has a weak password. You might be thinking that the attacker's IP address is the same as your local network address. Do not be fooled, because IP addresses can be faked and attackers use that to hide themselves while doing their attacks.

The last scenario is when a local system user is trying to use the su command repeatedly. This may mean that someone got into your system with a user's weak password. You can use the command grep su: /var/log/secure to look for su commands being used on your system. If something comes up, open the secure file using a text editor and try to find a pattern like the one shown in Listing 8-5.

*Listing 8-5. A Local User Trying to Become root Using su Multiple Times*

```
Aug 19 09:16:08 localhost sshd[4817]: pam_unix(sshd:session): ↵
 session opened for user ging by (uid=0)
Aug 19 09:16:12 localhost su: pam_unix(su:auth): authentication ↵
 failure; logname=ging uid=501 euid=0 tty=pts/2 ruser=ging rhost=  user=root
Aug 19 09:17:14 localhost last message repeated 3 times
Aug 19 09:26:27 localhost last message repeated 5 times
Aug 19 09:27:33 localhost last message repeated 2 times
```

In Listing 8-5, you can see that the attacker got in the Linux server with the ging user, most likely because the ging user has a weak password. After getting in, the attacker immediately started to become root by using the su command repeatedly. This is shown after the first authentication failure entry. If you see this pattern, I recommend that you change the compromised user's password immediately if the server cannot be put offline.

The situations in this section may come from some low-level attacker, but an attack is an attack. If you get into these situations, you must apply additional security measures that you will learn in Chapters 9 and 10.

# Automating Tasks with cron

When you have other server software packages that require administration, chances are those hold sensitive data that require protection. Some examples are database servers and file servers. You will need to create backups for those computers at regular intervals to have the data available again in case of a server breakdown.

But creating backups at a certain time manually can be a pain. You may forget to make one, and that can be a problem. To make things easier for you, CentOS has a facility to automate tasks using the crontab command.

# Using crontab

The crontab command lets individual users specify tasks that must be run at certain times or continuous intervals. When a user creates a schedule, the crontab command will create a text file with the same name as the user who made the schedule inside the /var/spool/cron directory. This file is called the crontab file, and it will be checked by the cron daemon for commands that are required to be run on the defined schedule.

When you are creating crontab files, crontab uses an assigned text editor to help users type in crontab commands. In CentOS and with most distributions, the default text editor assigned for crontab is the vi text editor.

# Using cron.allow and cron.deny

The cron.allow and cron.deny files let you specify which users are permitted to use the crontab command. Both files located in the /etc directory. Only the root user can make changes to those files. Also, the presence of either file will affect how access of the crontab command will be given to users.

If you want to restrict certain users from making crontab files, you can do that by adding their username inside the cron.deny text file found in the /etc directory. Make sure that the cron.allow file does not exist for this to work.

If you want to allow only specific users to create crontab files, you can add their usernames in the cron.allow file. Other users that are not included in this file will not be able to make crontab files. The cron.deny file must not be present for this to work also.

If you try to make both cron.deny and cron.allow files and put a username in both files, the cron.allow file will take precedence. For example, if you added ging to both cron.deny and cron.allow, that user will be able to create crontab files.

If both files are not accessible in the /etc directory, only the root user can make crontab files.

# Working with the crontab File

To create your own crontab file, you need to type the following command:

```
crontab -e
```

That will start the assigned editor for crontab where you can type in your tasks for the cron daemon to run.

## The crontab Task

With the crontab file open, you can now add tasks for commands that you want to run for a scheduled time. Before adding anything to the opened file, you have to know the syntax of a task. A task is divided into the schedule part and the command part. It is created by using the format

```
minute hour dayofmonth month dayofweek          your_command
```

where minute is the minute part and hour is the hour part of the time you want to run your command. You can also schedule your command within a specific day or days in a month or a certain month by filling in both dayofmonth and month fields. If you want to schedule the command on a certain day of the week, you can also fill the dayofweek part of the task. After putting the schedule, you will put the command that you need to run on the your_command command part.

The values that you can put in the schedule part are given in Table 8-3.

*Table 8-3. Possible Schedule Part Values*

| Schedule Part | Value |
| --- | --- |
| Minute | 0–59 |
| Hour | 0–23 |
| Day of the month | 1–31 |
| Month | 1–12 |
| Week | 0–6 for Sunday through Saturday, respectively |

The hour value is on a 24-hour format, where 0 is midnight and 23 is 11 p.m.

You are now going to test crontab on your system. You will make crontab create an empty text file called testcrontab inside your home directory 3 minutes after the current time on your machine. Assuming that the current time is 10:47 a.m. and you want to make the file on 10:50 a.m., you can use this command:

```
50 10 * * *          touch /root/testcrontab
```

Because the default text editor is vi, all the things you have learned on using the vi editor can be applied here. Saving the file will update the crontab entry for the current user and the cron daemon will start running the command when the schedule becomes right. After 3 minutes, check your directory (/root for now), and you will see an empty text file called testcrontab appears.

Here is another example. Assume that you are a database administrator, and you have to create a backup of the database directory using the shell script called makebackup.sh located in your home directory every Friday 11:00 PM. You can use the following crontab task for this:

```
0 23 * * 5          sh /root/makebackup.sh
```

In the previous example, the command part of the task uses the sh command to run the makebackup.sh script. You can arguments on the commands you want to automate with crontab just like running it on the shell by hand.

If you noticed, the sample crontab task uses asterisks in place for the other attributes of the schedule part. This is called the wildcard operator, and when you use it, crontab may put any value on it. You do not have to worry about the current value the asterisk contains, because the cron daemon will prioritize the schedule attributes that you have assigned values.

You can make use of the wildcard operator by putting a denominator value to make your task run at a constant interval instead of a fixed schedule. You can create tasks that can run every 5 minutes or 2 hours, for example. For the makebackup.sh script, if you want to run it every 2 hours starting now, you can use this:

```
* */2 * * *          sh /root/makebackup.sh
```

Be sure to observe the behavior of your tasks automated this way to get the proper results.

## Browsing Available Tasks

You can browse the available assigned tasks that you have created with crontab by using the -l argument. The -l argument will list all of the tasks on the crontab file that will be used by the cron daemon. You can try this out by using crontab -l on your terminal.

## Removing Tasks

You can remove tasks in your crontab list by commenting the entry, removing the entry or clearing the whole crontab command.

When you comment a task, you must put a hash mark (#) in front of the entry like this:

```
#* */2 * * *          sh /root/makebackup.sh
```

This will make crontab ignore the task and is useful if you are trying to fix something on it.

If you do not need the task anymore and you do not want to clutter your crontab file with comments, you can remove the unwanted entries by simply deleting them. Be sure to save the changes to update your crontab file.

The last way to get rid of crontab tasks is to remove them all at the same time. You can do this by using the -r argument of crontab that removes the crontab file for the current user. When you create new tasks using the -e argument, crontab will create a new blank crontab file for you to use.

# Pluggable Authentication Modules

Linux applications have ways of authenticating users. These can range from usernames and passwords to using certificates and keys in protecting information. The multiple schemes of authentication can be good and bad at the same time. Good, because the security features applications provide protects the data it administers, like the credentials of a database server. Bad, because different applications must use different security mechanisms to authenticate and permit users before usage. This can lead to maintaining different password files and permission files for the different services as shown in Figure 8-1.

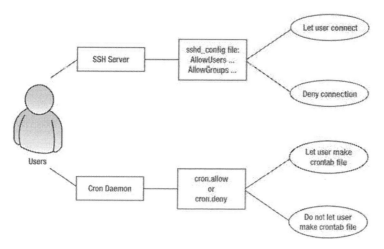

*Figure 8-1.* *A user will require separate accounts for each service for authentication.*

In Figure 8-1, both the SSH server and cron daemon use their own configuration files to authenticate users before allowing usage. For SSH, you can list the users and groups that can connect to the SSH server by using the `AllowUsers` and `AllowGroups` directives in the `sshd_config` file. For the cron daemon, you can list the users not allowed to make `crontab` entries by using the `cron.deny` file as discussed earlier. You have to maintain both `sshd_config` and `cron.deny` files to authenticate users for these services.

A solution to this problem is to create a central authentication method that can be used by the applications. This method must be modular to allow applications to load the modules when needed. The application should be able to use the method to authenticate the user before granting access to the application's services. The authentication method uses PAM (the pluggable authentication modules available in Linux and other Unix-like systems). The PAM implementation being used in CentOS is called Linux-PAM and is available at `http://www.kernel.org/pub/linux/libs/pam/`.

Linux-PAM is a set of system libraries that lets system administrators choose how applications must authenticate users. It includes PAM modules, which an application can use to verify users. Some of these PAM modules let the application retrieve the user's credentials from the `passwd` file after authentication. Others restrict use of an application by a certain time. These PAM modules are used in the rules of the application's PAM configuration file. The primary requirement of an application to be able to use Linux-PAM is to be developed using the Linux-PAM development libraries or Linux-PAM API. Without Linux-PAM support, the application will not be able to use Linux-PAM for authentication. This is shown in Figure 8-2.

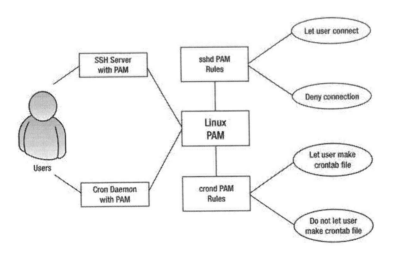

*Figure 8-2. PAM-enabled applications use PAM to authenticate users.*

In Figure 8-2, a PAM-enabled application is used by the user. Before access is granted, both PAM-enabled application and Linux-PAM will do the following to authenticate the user:

1. The PAM-enabled application uses the system's Linux-PAM to authenticate the user.
2. Linux-PAM will use the configuration file of the PAM-enabled application to determine which PAM modules to load.
3. Load a PAM module, and check if it satisfies the given credentials of the user.

4. The current module's verification result is returned to Linux-PAM. Linux-PAM checks the retrieved verification result. If the verification result is successful, go back to step 3 to load the next module, and then repeat step 4 until all modules have been loaded. If all modules evaluated success, the user is authenticated. Proceed to step 5. If a verification result fails, the user is not authenticated; head to step 5.

5. Return the result of the verification to the PAM-enabled application.

6. If the PAM-enabled application sees that the user is authenticated, it will allow usage to its service.

7. If the PAM-enabled application sees that the user is not authenticated, deny the usage of the application's service.

Assume that both the SSH server and cron daemon from Figure 8-1 are PAM-enabled. Instead of maintaining the sshd_config file for the SSH server and the cron.deny file for the cron daemon, the administrator will use the PAM configuration files of each service and will specify the needed modules on their PAM configuration files. Linux-PAM will handle the authentication process. This shows the advantage of PAM over using separate authentication methods for each application. The administrator will only configure the PAM configuration files of the PAM-enabled applications to use the needed modules to authenticate users. You will learn that starting in the next section.

## Understanding PAM Rules and Configuration Files

In Figure 8-2, each PAM-enabled application has its own rules. These rules are used by Linux-PAM to know what modules to load to determine whether to allow or deny a user access to the application. A rule is composed of a name, a type, a control value, and a module. If the module can take arguments, that is also included on the rule. Here is the syntax of a PAM rule:

```
servicename servicetype control modulepath modulearguments
```

where servicename is the name of the PAM-enabled application. The servicetype is the management group that will be used for this rule. The control part of the rule will define the resolution that PAM will use evaluating this rule. The modulepath are the modules that will be used for this rule. The modulearguments is optional and will hold the arguments that the associated modules can use. Here is an example of a rule taken from the cron daemon's PAM configuration file called crond in /etc/pam.d:

```
auth        sufficient    pam_rootok.so
```

In the sample line, the servicetype is the auth management group the control part is sufficient, and the modulepath has pam_rootok.so as the module to be used for this rule. There is no servicename part for this rule, because that is replaced by the configuration file's name. If you like, you can add it like this:

```
crond       auth          sufficient      pam_rootok.so
```

PAM will use this rule without a hitch. Composing rules with a servicename part is necessary if you have to put all of your PAM rules inside a single configuration file. This configuration file is called pam.conf, and it must reside inside the /etc directory.

The other way to make rules for each PAM-enabled application is to create separate text file with the same name as the application and put the rules in it. These files must reside inside the /etc/pam.d directory. This is the method used in CentOS and other modern Linux distributions. Looking back at Figure 8-2, the SSH server has its rules in the sshd file while the cron daemon's rules in the crond file. If the pam.d directory exists, Linux PAM will ignore the rules inside the pam.conf file if there is one on the /etc directory. Some rules inside the crond PAM configuration file are in Listing 8-6.

*Listing 8-6. The Rules in the First Part of the crond PAM Configuration File*

```
auth          sufficient        pam_rootok.so
auth          required          pam_env.so
auth          include            system-auth
```

From Listing 8-6, you can see two rules after our first rule, and it has the same servicetype part. This is fine, and you can add rules on a servicetype if need fine control on a specific management task. This feature is called the rule stack, and you can add rules separated by lines. The Linux-PAM will evaluate the rules like a stack starting from the first line. The result of the evaluation will be used when evaluating the second line. Like in a stack, the first line gets popped off and thrown out, except for its result. From this process, Linux-PAM will know if it is going to grant or deny the service to the user, because it will refer to the final result of the popping process.

The last line on Listing 8-6 uses the include control value that will include all the lines from the file in the modulepath part that matches the management task for this rule. Once the evaluation reaches this rule, the rule will open the system-auth PAM configuration file and get all the lines of that file that have the auth management task on its servicetype part. Assuming that the file has been loaded and all of the auth management tasks have been retrieved, Listing 8-6 will now become Listing 8-7 in memory.

*Listing 8-7. The auth Management Tasks Added on the Rules*

```
auth          sufficient        pam_rootok.so
auth          required          pam_env.so
auth          required          pam_env.so
auth          sufficient        pam_unix.so nullok try_first_pass
auth          requisite         pam_succeed_if.so uid >= 500 quiet
auth          required          pam_deny.so
```

After that, evaluation will continue starting from the third line with the pam_env.so module.

Now that you know what a PAM rule is and how Linux PAM evaluates it, you will learn more of the parts of the rule starting with the *servicename* part.

## servicename

The servicename part of a rule is the name of the application that will use this rule. Every PAM-enabled application that gets initialized will be assigned a name that can be referenced by PAM. When the PAM-enabled application needs to authenticate a user, it will identify itself to your Linux PAM.

During identification, Linux PAM will look for the entries in pam.conf for the servicename part that contains the applications name then apply the rules on the application. If there is no pam.conf, the PAM system will look for the file that has the application's name and apply the rules inside the file.

---

■ **Note:** There is a service name called other, and it acts as a catchall for PAM rules or applications that do not have a PAM configuration file. It denies access to all rules by default. You can check its PAM configuration file on /etc/pam.d named other.

---

## Management Groups

The designers of PAM observed that there is a pattern when an application is authenticating a user and decided to categorize them as management groups. The four management groups that you can use are auth, account, session, and password. The servicetype part will hold the chosen management group that will be used by this rule.

The auth management group will authenticate users by making them provide identification information such as usernames and passwords. It is also used to associate the user to a group for restriction to the service such as giving read-only permission.

The account management group will authenticate users based on account management. This will allow users on the system at a certain time of the day or specify where a user can log into, such as a specific console or terminal.

The session management group controls the session of the user after authentication has been accomplished. The session activities include mounting of directories or changing certain files and recording when the user logged in and logged out.

The password management group is used when the user authentication token is being updated, which can happen if the user is changing a password for example.

## Control

The control part of a rule is its guard condition. The value it holds will determine if the evaluation of the next rule in the rules stack will proceed after the module in the modulepath of the current rule fails on authentication. Some control values are strict that a single failure will not render the application give service to the user. Others are lenient where the result of the rule will not affect the remaining rules to be evaluated.

There are several control values that you can use in making rules. The four most-often used are the required, the requisite, the sufficient, and the optional control values.

The required control value requires the module to succeed before access can be granted for this service. The result of this rule will be returned after all other rules of the same management type have been evaluated. A sample stack is shown in Listing 8-8.

**Listing 8-8.** *Stacked auth Management Tasks with required Control Values*

```
auth          sufficient    pam_rootok.so
auth          required      pam_env.so
auth          required      pam_unix.so nullok try_first_pass
```

In Listing 8-8, evaluation starts with the first line, and the pam_rootok.so results in success. The second line is evaluated, and pam_env.so fails. The fail result is kept, and the third line's result is discarded. Because a rule failed with the required control value, the final result of the authentication with the auth management task is failure. This will be returned to the application.

The requisite control value is similar to the required control value if the module is successful. If the module fails, the evaluation will not continue to the next rule. The return value of the requisite control value will be the result of the first rule with the required or requisite control value to fail. A sample stack for the requisite control value is shown in Listing 8-9.

**Listing 8-9.** *Stacked auth Management Tasks with All Three Types of Control Values*

```
auth          sufficient    pam_rootok.so
auth          requisite     pam_env.so
auth          required      pam_unix.so nullok try_first_pass
```

Assume that the evaluation is on the second line that contains the requisite control value, and the pam_env.so module fails with the PAM_BUF_ERR value. Instead of moving to the next line, the evaluation stops and Linux-PAM will return program control and the PAM_BUF_ERR value to the application.

The sufficient control value will let authentication continue if the module is successful in execution. Back in Listing 8-6, if the pam_rootok.so module runs successfully on the first line, the evaluation will stop and return success to the application. If the rule fails, evaluation will continue and the failed result will not affect the next rule.

Things are different for a rule that has the sufficient control value if a rule before it that has the required control value fails. If that happens, the successful result of the rule will be ignored because of the earlier required rule.

The optional control value is—surprise, surprise—optional and will be used if this is the only rule with this control value in the service's PAM configuration file.

## modulepath

The modulepath part will contain the PAM module that will be used for this rule. Most of the time, only the filename of the module is used on this part like this:

```
auth          sufficient     pam_rootok.so
```

Linux-PAM assumes that the pam_rootok.so module file can be located on the default PAM modules directory, /lib/security or for 64-bit versions of CentOS, /lib64/security. You can specify the full path if your PAM module file is in another directory.

Some of the modules that you can use on a rule can take arguments that can affect how it runs. The argument will be placed on the modulearguments part like this:

```
auth          required      pam_unix.so nullok try_first_pass
```

The pam_unix.so module can take arguments, and on this rule, it uses nullok and try_first_pass as its arguments. Multiple arguments to a rule can be given as long as those are separated with spaces. If an argument requires spaces, you have to enclose it with square brackets like this:

```
auth          required      pam_unix.so nullok try_first_pass ↵
[sample_argument=pam rocks]
```

Take note that the sample_argument given to pam_unix.so is fictional. Consult the module's documentation for the actual argument if there are any.

## Testing PAM

You have seen how Linux-PAM works and the rules it uses during authentication. Let's see if we can use Linux-PAM for crond. We are going to use the pam_time.so module that lets us restrict access to PAM-enabled applications to a schedule that we can set. The module is only usable to the account management group. The schedule and applications can be set on the module's configuration file, called time.conf and located in the /etc/security directory. The file will hold the rules for the applications that you want to restrict. You can set rules for applications like this

```
services;ttys;users;times
```

where services is the name of the service or application that requires a scheduled restriction. The ttys value will be the terminal to which this rule will be applied. The users portion will be the selected users to which this rule be applied. The times slot will contain the allowed day and time when the application can be used by the users of this rule. There are many ways to configure a rule, but you are going to use the line in Listing 8-10.

*Listing 8-10. Rule to Restrict the ging User from Using crond and sshd*

```
crond;*;ging;!Al0000-2400
```

In Listing 8-10, the first line tells pam_time.so that the crond application on all terminals for the ging user will unusable at all times. The expression !Al0000-2400 is read like this: The exclamation point means negate; the Al keyword means "all days of the week," and the value 0000-2400 is the 24 hours of the clock in military format. In short, the ging user is scheduled not to use crond 24 hours a day, 7 days per week. Obviously, this rule is far too restrictive, and this range is used just for testing. Add Listing 8-10 at the bottom of time.conf and then save it.

■ **Note:** Listing 8-10 assumes that the ging user is already present in the system. If not, you can create it by using useradd ging and setting the password by using passwd ging. Run both commands as root.

## Testing pam_time.so with crond

In this example, you are going to create a dummy task with crontab to monitor if the pam_time.so module is really restricting the ging user when using crond.

1. Log in as the ging user on a separate terminal. As an example, use /dev/tty2 by pressing Ctrl+Alt+F2 and logging in as ging from there. You will be given a prompt.

2. Run the command crontab -e, and enter the following task:

```
*/1 * * * *          echo Hello!
```

3. This task will start running after you save the file and will continue to run every minute. It will print out the "Hello!" text using the echo command. Save the file, and you will monitor the progress next.

4. If you have Gnome running, go back to your desktop by pressing Ctrl+Alt+F7. Open a terminal, and run the command tail -f /var/log/cron. That will show you the recent log entries that crond makes to monitor the task of the ging user. A sample output is shown in Listing 8-11.

*Listing 8-11. The Dummy Task Running Smoothly*

```
Aug 22 00:59:53 localhost crontab[6588]: (ging) BEGIN EDIT (ging)
Aug 22 01:00:01 localhost crond[6591]: (ging) CMD (echo gigingang)
Aug 22 01:00:03 localhost crontab[6588]: (ging) REPLACE (ging)
Aug 22 01:00:03 localhost crontab[6588]: (ging) END EDIT (ging)
Aug 22 01:01:01 localhost crond[4243]: (ging) RELOAD (cron/ging)
Aug 22 01:01:02 localhost crond[6601]: (root) CMD (run-parts /etc/cron.hourly)
Aug 22 01:01:02 localhost crond[6602]: (ging) CMD (echo Hello!)
Aug 22 01:02:01 localhost crond[6609]: (ging) CMD (echo Hello!)
```

5. Add a rule to use the pam_time.so module on the account management group. Open the crond PAM configuration file called crond in /etc/pam.d, and add the pam_time.so module on top of the account stack like in Listing 8-12.

*Listing 8-12. pam_time.so Added to the account Stack*

```
account       required    pam_time.so
account       required    pam_access.so
account       include     system-auth
```

6. We used the required control value to make sure that the rule gets enforced when it is successful. Save the file.

7. Monitor the contents of the cron log file that is being shown by the tail command. Wait for a few minutes, and see if some PAM message appears, like the one shown in Listing 8-13.

*Listing 8-13. crond Being Denied for the ging User*

```
Aug 22 01:03:01 localhost crond[6616]: Permission denied
Aug 22 01:03:01 localhost crond[6616]: CRON (ging) ERROR: ↵
failed to open PAM security session: Success
Aug 22 01:03:01 localhost crond[6616]: CRON (ging) ERROR: ↵
cannot set security context
```

You can see in Listing 8-13 that the ging user cannot run the dummy task because of the pam_time.so module's rule in Listing 8-12. With PAM, you did not need to use the cron.deny file to deny the ging user.

After you have finished with the pam_time.so example, you can return things to normal for the ging user by adding a hash symbol to the rule or by removing it.

## Finding Other PAM Modules

There are other PAM modules that you can use in addition to the examples in this chapter. These are documented in the PAM *System's Administrator's Guide* that is included with your system. You can browse the guide in several formats on /usr/share/doc/pam-0.99.6.2. You can also use other PAM modules to add capabilities like authentication with an OpenLDAP server.

# Summary

In this chapter, you have learned how to control the syslogd system logger to control log files in CentOS and redirect log output to other sources, such as the terminal. You also learned how to automate tasks with crontab by using the correct syntax in making a task. Pluggable authentication modules provide you a central way of authenticating applications that are built with PAM support, and you learned about the proper way that PAM does to evaluate modules.

The next chapter will focus on the advanced security configuration that you can use with CentOS and will augment the current basic security skills you have learned in this chapter.

# CHAPTER 9

■■■

# Advanced Security

Maintaining security is an important aspect of administering a CentOS server. One component of maintaining security is to prevent disclosing information to untrusted parties. Another important security measures include detecting a potential break-in attempt. And, if an intrusion is successful, it's important to detect and clean up after a successful intrusion.

In this chapter, we will look at how to prevent disclosing information by encapsulating network traffic inside a secure, encrypted channel. These channels are secured with digital certificates and the secure socket layer. We will also look at using SELinux to prevent unauthorized services from reading files. We will also look at how SELinux can help us prevent an intrusion and ways of detecting an intrusion if one does occur.

## Using Digital Certificates

Perhaps the most common method for securing network protocols it to use Transport Layer Security (TLS). You might be familiar with the name Secure Sockets Layer (SSL), which is basically the old name for TLS. Developers often use the terms interchangeably, and for practical purposes, we can consider them the same thing. Some versions of SSL have security weaknesses, so we will use the term TLS to denote the more secure recent versions.

TLS provides a number of security benefits over plain TCP. It uses cryptographic protocols to prevent data from being intercepted or modified, and it provides the ability to authenticate both the server and the client. The authentication process relies on public key cryptography, using a certificate to protect a distinguished name with a public key. A distinguished name can be anything, but typically it is the full DNS name of your server. Certificates are issues by a Certifying Authority (CA), which publishes a *root certificate*. A root certificate signs every certificate issued by a CA; the root certificate is a special kind of certificate held by the CA that a site can use to sign other certificates. Significantly, a root certificate isn't signed by any certificates, except itself. It acts as the root of a tree of certificates. Developers must configure client applications to trust the root certificate, which means that such applications implicitly trust any certificate signed by a root certificate.

We can use digital certificates to identify users, organizations, and programs. In this chapter, however, we will focus on identifying network services and the HTTPS web service specifically.

CentOS uses a tool called OpenSSL to manage digital certificates. This tool evolved from an earlier tool known as SSLeay (each letter is pronounced separately—the "eay" part derives from the initials of its original author, Eric A. Young). Today, most open source security applications take advantage of the now ubiquitous OpenSSL library. OpenSSL includes many modes of operation, and it creates and manages most of the files you come across when using digital certificates.

# Creating Certificates

We need to do some general housekeeping before we dive in and start creating certificates. It's critical that we map out our certificate strategy, or we can end up with certificate files spread all over our organization. Convention holds that you nominate a single host to act at the repository level for all our certificates that you request and create. From this repository, you can copy certificates to any server that requires them.

A directory structure such as /srv/cert/<year> works well because most commercial certificates must be regenerated every year or every certain number of years. You need to pay careful attention to file permissions to ensure that only authorized users can read these files, particularly any private keys. If you don't manage the certificate files as root, then you need to use a special group for creating certificate managers. Listing 9-1 lists the commands that you can run by root to create such a directory.

*Listing 9-1. Creating a Directory to Store Certificates*

```
mkdir /srv/cert
groupadd certificates
chown root:certificates /srv/cert
chmod 02770 /srv/cert
usermod –a –G certificates chivas
```

Let's assume that you want to provide a TLS-protected web site called https://www.example.com/. When users visit your site you don't want them to have to perform any special tasks to view the web site. To achieve this, you require a certificate issued by a trusted CA. Every web browser comes with a built-in list of certifying authorities that it trusts. Normally, a CA pays for the privilege of being included in the default list trusted CAs in a browser. To cover that cost, the CA typically charges a fee for issuing a certificate.

To obtain a certificate, you must first produce a Certificate Signing Request (CSR). The CSR contains information about your organization and the site you wish to protect. You package this information into a single file that makes it easy to send to a CA. The CSR is protected by a key to prevent any of the information you save from being altered.

Creating a CSR requires several steps. First, you must produce a key. You do this using OpenSSL in genrsa mode; you must specify an output file name for your key. The hostname with .key extension makes it easy to track this file. You must also specify the size of the key in bits: 1024 is adequate for most certificates, but more secure certificates might require a larger key, such as 2048 bits. You should check with your CA to determine what size key it requires. This command specifies your file name and the number of bits in its key:

```
openssl genrsa -out www.example.com.key 1024
```

This command creates the www.example.com.key file in PEM format. This is a text-based format, but it's not human readable. You can view the file using a text editor; see Listing 9-2 for an example of what a PEM file should look like.

*Listing 9-2. Contents of www.example.com.key*

```
-----BEGIN RSA PRIVATE KEY-----
MIICXQIBAAKBgQC1zCjriMcA7ZlBLj2HlJbjlVmr9whxqabYCSLfPMqOpdmSpOJ9
OKVIkAJuaRO+4TCyE+/QqjOt6nxbbOBnem9RC/NNp2tUGXhu+KAw33GwEjOHAe19
UYc2rVqFk6o2GZyEFn/h2pHvqmzv4hSfxZTcBrjJGOA1
-----END RSA PRIVATE KEY-----
```

PEM format is convenient for email, but it's hard to tell whether your file is valid because it is not human readable. You can inspect the key in text format with this command:

```
openssl rsa -noout -text -in www.example.com.key
```

Keys aren't exciting to read, but you should check make sure that you can decode your key successfully; doing this ensures that your file isn't corrupt (see Listing 9-3).

*Listing 9-3. Text Version of an RSA Key*

```
Private-Key: (1024 bit)
modulus:
    00:b5:cc:28:eb:88:c7:00:ed:99:41:2e:3d:87:94:
    96:e3:95:59:ab:f7:08:71:a9:a6:d8:09:22:df:3c:
    c9:1b:40:35
```

■ **Note:** Generating the key requires a source of random data. Most computers don't have an absolutely random source of data, so they must make do with pseudo-random data. To get good pseudo-random data, you must seed the random number generator with entropy. Under CentOS, OpenSSL obtains entropy from the kernel via /dev/urandom. The CentOS initialization scripts ensure that a minimum amount of entropy is saved across a reboot, so you don't typically have to take any extra steps to obtain enough entropy for OpenSSL.

You need to protect your key to prevent unauthorized users from reading it. A user who can obtain your key can impersonate your server. You should set the key files with file-system permissions to restrict access only to the users who perform certificate management. You can also add a passphrase to your key as an additional protection to prevent unauthorized access. A passphrase works like a password; it prevents anyone from accessing the key unless that user knows the secret passphrase. This sounds good, it has a downside: setting a passphrase on your key means you cannot start your secure services without supplying the passphrase manually. If you plan to start the service automatically when your server boots, then you cannot use a passphrase; instead, you must rely on filesystem permissions to keep the key safe.

You can add or remove the passphrase using OpenSSL. This command creates a new file as specified by the -out parameter that contains the key, but is protected by the passphrase:

```
openssl rsa -in www.example.com.key -des3 -out www.example.com.secure.key
```

Now assume you try to read the key now with this command:

```
openssl rsa -noout -text -in www.example.com.secure.key
```

After you use this command, you are prompted for the passphrase. After adding a passphrase, you should delete the unprotected file because you no longer need it.

Use this command to remove the passphrase:

```
openssl rsa -in www.example.com.secure.key -out www.example.com.insecure.key
```

The file specified by -out now contains a copy of the key without any passphrase. You have a key, so you can continue to create a CSR. The next command prompts you for various pieces of information:

```
openssl req -new -key www.example.com.key -out www.example.com.csr
```

Listing 9-4 shows the output from the command. The text in bold indicates user input, while some prompts include default values indicated with square brackets. You can accept the default values by pressing enter.

*Listing 9-4. Creating a CSR*

```
You are about to be asked to enter information that will be incorporated
into your certificate request.
What you are about to enter is what is called a Distinguished Name or a DN.
There are quite a few fields but you can leave some blank
For some fields there will be a default value,
If you enter '.', the field will be left blank.
-----
Country Name (2 letter code) [GB]:
State or Province Name (full name) [Berkshire]:
Locality Name (eg, city) [Newbury]:
Organization Name (eg, company) [My Company Ltd]:Example Company
Organizational Unit Name (eg, section) []:Information Technology Department
Common Name (eg, your name or your server's hostname) []:www.example.com
Email Address []:

Please enter the following 'extra' attributes
to be sent with your certificate request
A challenge password []:
An optional company name []:
```

As you might expect, this code saves the CSR to the file specified by the –out parameter. This file is also PEM-encoded, which (again) means it would be good for email, but it isn't human readable. Before you proceed, you should check that the contents of the CSR are correct again. Mistakes can be very costly at this stage if you're using a commercial CA. The next command shows the CSR in a human-readable format:

```
openssl req -noout -text -in www.example.com.csr
```

Listing 9-5 shows what your CSR might look like. You should also ensure that the information contained in the Subject field is correct. You use this information to identify your organization and the name of the service you want to secure. If there are any errors, you can re-create the CSR and supply the correct values. You will also note that the modulus is the same as for the key you created earlier.

*Listing 9-5. A Text Version of a CSR*

```
Certificate Request:
    Data:
        Version: 0 (0x0)
        Subject: C=GB, ST=Berkshire, L=Newbury, O=Example Company,
            OU=Information Technology Department, CN=www.example.com
        Subject Public Key Info:
            Public Key Algorithm: rsaEncryption
            RSA Public Key: (1024 bit)
                Modulus (1024 bit):
                    00:b5:cc:28:eb:88:c7:00:ed:99:41:2e:3d:87:94:
                    96:e3:95:59:ab:f7:08:71:a9:a6:d8:09:22:df:3c:
                    d1:67:d5:d8:81:3a:d0:65:a5
```

```
        Exponent: 65537 (0x10001)
Attributes:
    a0:00
```

Sometimes it can get confusing which key was used for which certificate. You can identify the key by the modulus field, but it can be tricky to compare this field manually. You can use the diff command to compare this field by supplying the OpenSSL output for the key and for the CSR:

```
diff -qs <(openssl -rsa -noout -modulus -in www.example.com.key) \
    <(openssl req -noout -modulus -in www.example.com.csr)
```

This command reports whether your files are identical, which indicates the keys match. Otherwise, they differ, which means that the key in question is not the correct key for the CSR.

At this point, you need to send your CSR to a certifying authority to sign. Once the CA validates your identity, it creates a certificate and sends it back to you. Every CA is different in cost, required documentation, and time to deliver your certificate back to you. You should take this into account before purchasing a certificate. Some CAs allow you to get a trial certificate at no cost. In the preceding example, you store the CSR as text that you can copy easily into an email or web form. You use web forms to submit the CSR with most CAs; you—note that you don't need to send the key to the CA.

When you receive your newly signed certificate, you can inspect it with this command:

```
openssl x509 -noout -text -in www.example.com.crt
```

Every certificate and CA will include different fields, but it's important to check the Issuer and Validity dates. You can see some sample output Listing 9-6. Again you can see the modulus field, which matches the key.

*Listing 9-6. Text Version of an X.509 Certificate*

```
Certificate:
    Data:
        Issuer: C=GB, ST=Berkshire, L=Newbury, O=Example Company,
            OU=Information Technology Department, CN=Example Root
CA/emailAddress=ca@example.com
        Validity
            Not Before: Apr 22 23:35:47 2009 GMT
            Not After : Apr 20 23:35:47 2019 GMT
        Subject: C=GB, ST=Berkshire, L=Newbury, O=Example Company,
            OU=Information Technology Department, CN=www.example.com
        Subject Public Key Info:
            Public Key Algorithm: rsaEncryption
            RSA Public Key: (1024 bit)
                Modulus (1024 bit):
                    00:b5:cc:28:eb:88:c7:00:ed:99:41:2e:3d:87:94:
                    96:e3:95:59:ab:f7:08:71:a9:a6:d8:09:22:df:3c:
                    d1:67:d5:d8:81:3a:d0:65:a5
```

■ **Note:** This certificate in Listing 9-6 has been self-signed by a CA called Example Root CA. You will learn how this works in the next section.

# Deploying Certificates

You now have a certificate, and you want to use it to secure your network services. The first step is to copy the key and the certificate files to the server that runs the service. Even if this is the same server you used to create the CSR, you need to copy the files into a new directory because the files will have different permissions. Once you have the files in place, you can configure the service to use them.

CentOS comes with a /etc/pki/tls/private directory that you can use for most services. For extra security, you should tighten the permissions on this directory. As root user, you can accomplish that tightening with this command:

chmod 0700 /etc/pki/tls/private

CentOS also ships with several other directories in /etc/pki/tls that we will touch on later.

You might find it cumbersome to copy the certificate and key file separately, but you can combine them both into a single file known as PEM format. You can use a text editor to create the PEM file, but it's just as easy to create it from the command line, as shown in Listing 9-7.

*Listing 9-7. Creating a PEM Certificate*

```
cp www.example.com.key www.example.com.pem
echo "" >> www.example.com.pem
cat www.example.com.crt >> www.example.com.pem
echo "" >> www.example.com.pem
```

---

■ **Note:** The echo "" command adds a blank line to the file. Keeping a blank line between components in the PEM file is required for some services to parse the multiple components correctly.

---

Now you can copy the PEM file into the /etc/pki/tls/private directory. Configuring Apache is now a matter of editing /etc/httpd/conf.d/ssl.conf and setting SSLCertificateFile to point to your new PEM file. You can comment out the SSLCertificateKeyFile because you're not using a separate key.

---

■ **Note:** You must install mod_ssl before Apache can serve pages using HTTPS. If you don't have mod_ssl installed, you can use the yum install mod_ssl command to install it. You might also have to configure your firewall to allow connections on port 443.

---

You configure most SSL-aware services in a similar way.

## Configuration Files

You entered the value for each field manually at the appropriate prompt in the first certificate you created. If you find that you have to create many certificates, then you can create a configuration file that contains these values already incorporated as the defaults. This ensures that every certificate contains consistent values for your company identification, and it can help you avoid costly mistakes.

The OpenSSL configuration file consists of several sections that different subcommands of OpenSSL can take advantage of. The sample here focuses on the [req] section, which you use when making CSRs.

Start by making a local copy of the default OpenSSL configuration file with this command:

```
cp /etc/pki/tls/openssl.cnf /srv/cert/example.cnf
```

Next, edit example.cnf and find the line containing [req distinguised_name], which indicates the start of the section. Immediately after this, you can see a number of lines with the name, <field>_default. You can edit the values for each of these fields as required. While editing the file, you can also comment out this unnecessary line:

```
email_address = Email Address
```

You can also comment out this line in the [req] section:

```
attributes = req_attributes
```

Once you finish your edits, you can save your updated configuration file. Of course, you can come back and make additional edits later. Listing 9-8 shows the relevant parts of the configuration file that you use for http://example.com, displaying the suggested changes in bold.

*Listing 9-8. Configuring example.cnf*

```
[ req ]
distinguished_name                = req_distinguished_name
#attributes                       = req_attributes
[ req_distinguished_name ]
countryName                       = Country Name (2 letter code)
countryName_default               = AU
stateOrProvinceName               = State or Province Name (full name)
stateOrProvinceName_default           = Victoria
localityName                      = Locality Name (eg, city)
localityName_default              = Melbourne
0.organizationName                = Organization Name (eg, company)
0.organizationName_default            = Example Company
organizationalUnitName            = Organizational Unit Name (eg, section)
organizationalUnitName_default        = Information Technology Department
#emailAddress                         = Email Address
```

You have customized your configuration file as required; now you can generate your CSR with this command:

```
openssl req -config example.cnf -new -key www.example.com.key \
    -out www.example.com.csr
```

You can see that the default values are the correct values for your site, and you can accept them by pressing the "enter" key. The only value you need to input is the Common Name, which is the name of the server you want to secure. Once you create the CSR, you can proceed to get it signed, as already demonstrated.

# Intermediate Certificates

So far we have touched only on two types of certificates: the root certificate and the server certificate. These certificates have a trust relationship that resembles a tree. One root certificate can sign many server certificates. It's possible to expand this tree-like structure, and many commercial CAs do exactly that. They use their root certificate to sign an intermediate certificate, which is used to sign the server certificates.

There are many reasons for using this intermediate certificate. The root certificate key is normally kept well-protected in a locked vault, and no one is allowed to access it. CAs store this intermediate certificate key in a more accessible location, using this certificate to sign server certificates. It also allows different intermediate certificates to be generated for different geographical locations, so the work of signing server certificates can be distributed.

If your CA tells you it's using an intermediate certificate, then you need to include the intermediate certificate in your service configuration, so clients have enough information to validate your server's certificate. Your CA provides the intermediate certificate to you or tells you where you can download the file.

Your CA typically stores this file in PEM encoding, much like your key and server certificate. You need to deploy this file in the same way as you deploy your server certificate. If you use a PEM file to store your key and your server certificate together, then you can also include the intermediate certificate to keep all the relevant files together. Note that some services—Apache in particular—require that you configure the intermediate certificate explicitly, and separately, from server certificate. The Apache configuration for an intermediate certificate looks like this:

```
SSLCertificateChainFile /etc/pki/tls/certs/intermediate.crt
```

# Certificate File Formats

The certificates you've learned about so far are known as X.509, which is a standard format for digital certificates. Despite being a standard format, there are many different ways to encode these certificates. PEM encoding is the most common encoding or file format under CentOS, but other platforms commonly employ other file formats and encoding techniques (see Table 9-1).

*Table 9-1. File Types for Digital Certificates*

| Extension | Description |
| --- | --- |
| .key | PEM encoded RSA or DSA private key |
| .csr | PEM encoded Certificate Signing Request |
| .crt | PEM encoded X.509 Certificate |
| .pem | PEM encoded file often used to hold a key and certificate in a single file |
| .der | DER encoded certificate |
| .p7b .p7c | PKCS#7 encoded certificate |
| .pfx .p12 | PKCS#12 encoded key and certificate |

OpenSSL can convert between these formats, but each format has a slightly different syntax. Rather than details pages of options, you can consult this list for the basic commands to convert between different formats (see Table 9-2).

**Table 9-2.** *Converting Between Common Formats*

| Conversion | Command |
| --- | --- |
| PEM Certificate to DER Certificate | `openssl x509 -outform der -in www.example.com.crt -out www.example.com.der` |
| DER Certificate to PEM Certificate | `openssl x509 -inform der -in www.example.com.der -out www.example.com.crt` |
| PEM RSA Key to DER RSA Key | `openssl rsa -in www.example.com.key -outform DER -out www.example.com.der.key` |
| DER RSA Key to PEM RSA Key | `openssl rsa -inform der -in www.example.com.key -out www.example.com.pem.key` |
| PEM Certificate to PKCS#7 Certificate | `openssl crl2pkcs7 -nocrl -certfile www.example.com.crt -out www.example.com.p7b` |
| PCKS#7 Certificate to PEM Certificate | `openssl pkcs7 -print_certs -in www.example.com.p7b -out www.example.com.crt` |
| PEM Certificate and Key to PKCS#12 Certificate and Key | `openssl pkcs12 -export -out www.example.com.pfx -inkey www.example.com.key -in www.example.com.crt` |
| PKCS#12 Certificate and Key to PEM Certificate and Key | `openssl pkcs12 -in www.example.com.pfx -out www.example.com.pem -nodes` |

## Signing Your Own Certificates

It can be expensive to use a commercial CA. This cost is often unwarranted for in-house services and can quickly become exorbitant if you wish to offer many services. One solution in this scenario is to use self-signed certificates. You can begin the process of self-signing a certificate by creating the CSR and signing it with the command:

```
openssl x509 -req -days 365 -in www.example.com.csr -signkey \
    www.example.com.key -out www.example.com.crt
```

This certificate will be valid for one year, as specified by the –days parameter. If you don't want to create new certificates every year, you might want to use a longer period, such as 1095 days, which is about three years.

This is a stand-alone certificate that has no certifying authority that can be trusted. Anyone can create a self-signed certificate, which means someone else can create a certificate with your server name in it. This means there is no protection against a user being tricked into visiting a rogue server and potentially disclosing sensitive information. However, a self-signed certificate still provides transport security, so the data being exchanged cannot be intercepted or altered by anyone.

Another solution for zero-cost certificates is to create your own CA. By creating your own self-signed CA, you can issue as many certificates as you need at no cost. Unlike a commercial CA, you can also configure the certificate to be valid for as long as you want, so the burden of recreating certificates annually is reduced. You can also configure clients to trust your CA root certificate, which allows them to validate that the server they are talking to is authorized by you.

You must implement a few steps to maintain your own CA, but it doesn't have to be a daunting or complex task. You can acquire a toolkit for doing this called ssl.ca version 0.1 from the OpenSSL web site at this URL: http://www.openssl.org/contrib/ssl.ca-0.1.tar.gz.

This package contains scripts that do the hard work for you. After extracting the files, you need to edit new-root-ca.sh and change the value for days on line 49. The default value is 10 years, but unless you want to have to reissue certificates in the future, you should make it longer—perhaps 10000 days. You can also edit sign-server-cert.sh and change the value for days on line 48. This is the length of time that your server certificates will remain valid. You can choose a more modest value for this, such as 1095 days or three years. Once you edit these scripts, run new-root-ca.sh to create your CA.

---

■ **Warning:** Don't forget the passphrase for your root certificate because there is no way to recover from a lost passphrase. You should record the passphrase in accordance with your company's security and escrow policy.

---

Once you create your certificate, you can copy ca.crt to /etc/pki/tls/certs, where it will be available to validate any certificates that have been signed by this certificate. You will also need to import this certificate into every client that contacts the server. For most web browsers, opening this file is enough to prompt the browser to import the certificate. Often you will need to select the level of trust you want to assign to the certificate—the default options are usually sufficient. In some browsers, you might be prompted to select which services to use the certificate for. In these cases, select the Identify Web Sites option (or similar). You can also host the file on your HTTP web site and allow users who wish to use HTTPS to import the certificate before connecting. A client's configuration should be complete once a browser imports the certificate. Most clients can also bypass this step and connect even though the server certificate isn't trusted. We want to set up a trusted service in this example, so I don't recommend you bypass this step.

You can now generate certificates as required, starting with the CSR that you create in the usual way. Save your CSR to the ssl.ca directory using the common name as the base of the file name, such as www.example.com.csr. Now sign the certificate with this command:

```
./sign-server-cert.sh www.example.com
```

Doing so brings up a prompt that asks you for the passphrase for the root certificate and then asks you to confirm the details for the new certificate. If everything is correct, you can sign the new certificate and save it in the ssl.ca directory.

You now have a certificate in the www.example.com.crt file. You can verify whether the new certificate has been created correctly with this command:

```
openssl verify -CAfile ca.crt www.example.com.pem
```

Specifying the root certificate with the CA file parameter enables you to confirm that the new certificate will be trusted by anyone who trusts your CA. You can now use the certificate to create your PEM file, as shown previously.

## Go Wild

So far all the certificates have had a single common name value: the DNS name of the server to be entered into the web browser to access the page. Technical restrictions in the HTTPS protocol require that you have one IP address per common name if you want to host multiple HTTPS sites on the same server. It's not common practice, nor is it supported by many commercial CAs, but it is possible to add multiple common names to a single certificate. You could use this ability with your own CA to offer multiple services within your organization, but without having to utilize multiple IP addresses. A certificate that matches more than one name is often referred to as a wildcard certificate.

There have been many attempts to standardize the use of multiple names and wildcards, but there remains no universal solution at this time. Different browsers use two main naming formats to implement this wildcard behavior. One format requires listing each name that you want to use in full. The other format uses regular expressions to embed many names in a single entry. If you want your certificate to work will all browsers, you must implement both approaches in your certificate. To supply multiple values to OpenSSL, you must save them to the configuration file you use to generate the CSR. The order of names is also important to some browsers, so you might want to experiment with different configurations. Listing 9-9 shows the relevant parts of an example OpenSSL configuration file that generates a CSR for `www.example.com` and `webmail.example.com`. Note that entries 0 and 1 are fully qualified domain names, while entry 2 is a regular expression.

***Listing 9-9.*** *Configuring Multiple Common Names*

```
0.commonName = Common Name (First FQDN of your server)
0.commonName_default = www.example.com
1.commonName = Common Name (Next FQDN of your server)
1.commonName_default = webmail.example.com
2.commonName = Set of common names (Netscape-supported expansion)
2.commonName_default = (www|webmail).example.com
```

You might also like to experiment with an X.509 extension called the `subjectAltName` extension. As with the common name, support for this extension varies from browser to browser.

# Intrusion Detection

Intrusion detection focuses on monitoring the network and the filesystem to detect unwanted or unexpected access. Many different schemes exist for performing this monitoring and what to do when anomalies are detected. In this section, I'll walk you through how to use a pair of tools that let you monitor the filesystem for unexpected changes, the RPM database, and AIDE.

I'll also walk you through using netfilter to detect and log unauthorized network-connection attempts.

The most common sign of an intrusion to your system is the presence of what is called a root kit. A root kit is a collection of tools that can range in function from gaining root access to the system, to covering up the tracks left from the root exploit, to hiding the root kit, to ensuring that the root kit remains active and opening back doors into the system. The method of gaining root access can vary, and most root kits try all known exploits and often some unknown ones, too. Often, a security vulnerability allows user-level access to the server before the root kit manages to find a root exploit. To limit the ability of a root kit to gain user-level and root access, it is essential that you install all security updates as they become available.

The methods used by root kits to cover up their tracks are often quite ingenious. At a minimum, most root kits alter log files to remove any trace of their activities and install trojan executables that will hide their files, processes, and network connections.

Named after the wooden horse used by the Greeks to gain access to Troy, a trojan executable is a program that appears to do a certain job when it runs, really does something else. The kind of trojan you might see in a root kit is a version of ls, which shows all files as the normal ls would, except for the files deposited by the root kit. In this way, the kit remains invisible to anyone looking for it using ls. Similarly, it might have a version of rm that cannot delete the root kit files, netstat for network connections, and so on.

The root kit often installs a back door into the system that allows the cracker access at a later stage. It might also join what is called a botnet and await further instructions. A botnet is a command network crackers can use to talk to many systems at once. IRC is often used to command a botnet. Crackers often use botnets comprised of many systems to launch distributed denial of service (DDOS) attacks.

The root kit might also patch the original exploit used for the intrusion, thereby preventing any other crackers from gaining access to the system.

## Monitoring the filesystem with RPM

The main filesystem monitoring tool available in CentOS is the RPM database. This database is maintained by the package management tool, RPM. Every file installed from an RPM package is tracked in this database. You can compare the information in the database to the actual files on the filesystem to generate a report of the differences. Some of the differences found indicate valid changes made by the system administrator, but any unexplained differences might be evidence of an intrusion.

The main benefit of using RPM is that every CentOS system comes with an RPM database that is automatically kept up-to-date as you install and uninstall software—you don't need to do anything to maintain the database.

The RPM command includes a mode of operation that lets you verify your installed packages, which you invoke this with the -V parameter. You can verify a single package with this command:

```
rpm -V <package name>
```

You can verify a single file with this command:

```
rpm -V -f <file name>
```

You can also verify all installed packages with the rpm -Va command. You should expect some changes when you run a verify command, and the report provides some information to help determine if the change requires further investigation. Listing 9-10 shows some examples of the output you might receive on a typical CentOS server.

*Listing 9-10. Sample rpm -Va output*

```
S.5....T c /etc/yum.conf
....L... c /etc/pam.d/system-auth
missing    /usr/share/mimelnk/application/pdf.desktop
S.5....T   /usr/share/icons/hicolor/icon-theme.cache
```

The first two lines are marked with a c, which indicates that they are configuration files. You can expect configuration files to change, so you can ignore these safely. This column can also contain other codes to indicate documentation and license files. Table 9-3 shows the possible file codes and what they mean.

*Table 9-3. Verify File Type Codes*

| Code | Type of file represented |
| --- | --- |
| c | Configuration file |
| d | Documentation file |
| g | Ghost file with no contents |
| l | License file |
| r | Read me file |

The next line of output is marked with the word missing, which indicates that the file is missing from the filesystem. Missing files can indicate an intrusion, an accidental deletion by the administrator, or a poorly packaged application. The output doesn't explain why the file is missing, but in this case a packaging conflict with a third-party PDF viewer is suspected. Typically, you can restore a missing file by reinstalling the appropriate package, as I will demonstrate later in this chapter. It might also be a sign of intrusion if system or security files are missing without an explanation. I'll also cover what this might look like and how you might recover from it later in this chapter. The last file listed is a cache file, which you can also expect to change from time to time.

The verify command displays a summary of changed attributes when it detects a change in a file. A number of letters and symbols indicate the different attributes that the RPM database tracks. The first and last files listed in Listing 9-10 show the codes S, 5, and T. These codes indicate changes in the file size, the MD5 checksum, and the timestamp. These three codes are typical of a normal file change, but they can still be cause for concern. As with the other examples, I will cover how some of these changes might have more security significance than others. For example, U, G, and M signify changes to the user, group, and file permissions, all of which are significant changes. On the flipside, changes to timestamps don't typically indicate a problem. You can find the complete list of codes in Table 9-4.

*Table 9-4. Verify Attribute Codes*

| Code | Type of change represented |
| --- | --- |
| S | Size of the file has changed |
| M | File mode or permissions have changed |
| 5 | MD5 checksum has changed |
| D | Device node has changed |
| L | Symbolic link has changed |
| U | User ownership has changed |
| G | Group ownership has changed |

*Table 9-4. Verify Attribute Codes*

| | |
|---|---|
| T | Timestamp has changed |
| . | No change detected |
| ? | Attribute cannot be checked or is no longer relevant |

The rpm verify command can show signs of a root kit installation. Listing 9-11 shows some more output from the rpm -Va command. This output is more alarming than the Listing 9-10 because it shows some potential security-related changes. In this case, ls appears to have been modified. It's possible that it has been replaced with a trojan version, which could indicate a root kit. Because ls is a binary executable, it's unlikely that an administrator has modified the file, as you might expect with a changed configuration file.

*Listing 9-11. Sample rpm -Va output*

```
S.5....T   /bin/ls
missing    /usr/bin/top
.....U.. c /etc/hosts.allow
```

Another concern in Listing 9-11 is that the top file is missing. It might be the case that you can still run top, even though the correct version is missing. Root kits are often built to work on many different operating systems. The root kit might support this by placing the top file in a different directory that is still in your search path, such as /usr/bin.

The third entry is also suspicious. Yes, it's a configuration file, but it's related to security, and a permission change here might show that the file has been replaced or altered in such a way that it can be modified by the cracker. Crackers can enable a lot of nasty tricks by changing files and their permissions, particularly configuration files and files marked as suid root. Files stored in /etc, and especially files stored in /etc/security and /etc/pam, are prime targets for root kits, and you should inspect any changes in these directories carefully.

The ls file has been altered, so the output of that program should not be trusted. If this were a real security breach, then a complete response would involve taking the system off line and performing a forensic analysis. You would have to install a new system to make sure no traces of the root kit remain.

You don't have a real root kit to experiment with; instead, you can practice replacing a file by altering it manually. For example, let's look at how you could accidentally overwrite a file:

```
# cd /bin
# ls > sort
```

You realize you have made a typo. You meant to use the pipe | but instead redirected the output of your command and overwrote the sort executable.

First, find out which package the file belongs to using the query file (-qf) option for the RPM tool:

```
# rpm -qf sort
coreutils-5.97-14.el5
```

Now that you know the name of the package, you can remove it from the RPM database with the –e option. When using --justdb, --nodeps, and --noscripts, the RPM tool leaves the files on the disk, which is important, particularly when the package provides essential commands or libraries:

```
# rpm -e --justdb --nodeps --noscripts coreutils
```

Finally, reinstall the package using the yum tool. This replaces the files on disk and restores the package information in the RPM database:

```
# yum install coreutils
```

Finally, verify that the sort program now works correctly:

```
# ls | sort
```

If you need to correct only the permissions of a file or directory, you can use an rpm subcommand called  setperms. This command resets the permissions on all the files in that package. It also has a subcommand called --setugids that corrects the user and group ownerships. As with -V, you can specify a single package, a single file, or all packages. Be aware that --setugids sets all the permissions without checking the current values first. This can have the side effect of clearing the suid bit on certain files. You can avoid problems by running --setperms after you run --setugids. You can combine both of these into a single command: this provides the safest method of correcting the settings. You can run this command to correct the permissions on hosts.allow:

```
rpm --setugids --setperms -f /etc/hosts.allow
```

Alternately, you can use this command to correct an entire package:

```
rpm --setugids --setperms coreutils
```

---

▨ **Tip:** If you intend to upgrade to a new version of CentOS, it's handy to look at a report of the configuration files which have changed files before you commence with the upgrade. You can use the rpm –Va report to learn what you need to configure in the new installation.

---

## Monitoring the Filesystem with AIDE

Yes, the RPM tool proves useful for checking the filesystem for intrusion. However, it's limited in two ways. First, a root kit could also install a trojan version of the RPM tool or alter the RPM database to hide its tracks. Second, the RPM tool doesn't record information about files that it didn't install.

You can solve these problems by taking advantage of a more specialized tool called *AIDE*. This tool is similar to an older tool called *tripwire*. Tripwire is no longer included with CentOS, but it remains available from the EPEL repository. Aide maintains a database of file checksums and permissions; you can protect this database with cryptography or store it on read-only media to prevent tampering.

You install AIDE with this command:

```
yum install aide
```

Aide comes preconfigured for CentOS, so you can begin by initializing the database. You should create the database before you connect to the network for the first time; this helps you ensure that your server has not been compromised. Note that this approach requires installing both the CentOS and the AIDE package from DVD.

The `aide --init` command generates the initial database. This command must perform a complete scan of your system, which will take some time—up to 30 minutes or even longer, depending on size of your installation and the speed of your disks. To use the default configuration for AIDE, you must have SELinux enabled in either permissive or enforcing mode. If you don't have SELinux enabled, see the next section on how to enable it. Once the generation process is complete, you should see the following message:

```
AIDE, version 0.13.1

### AIDE database at /var/lib/aide/aide.db.new.gz initialized.
```

If the initialization succeeds, you must rename the database with this command, which makes your database ready to perform checks:

```
mv /var/lib/aide/aide.db.new.gz /var/lib/aide/aide.db.gz
```

If you have a CD or DVD burner, you can write the newly initialized database to a read-only media, which prevents it from being altered. This is an important security measure for protecting against a root kit that tries to alter the AIDE database to cover its tracks. You should also copy the configuration file and executable to ensure that they cannot be replaced with trojan versions. You can burn these files with the following command:

```
growisofs -Z /dev/cdwriter -R -J /var/lib/aide/aide.db.gz \
    /etc/aide.conf /usr/sbin/aide
```

■ **Note:** There is still a chance that shared libraries or the kernel itself could be modified by a root kit in such a way that AIDE cannot detect the changes. Detecting and protecting against this kind of intrusion is much harder and isn't supported in CentOS.

Once you create your CD, you can use it to compare your system against the database. Begin by making sure your CD is mounted as the root user. If the CD has been auto-mounted, then it might not be mounted as root, and AIDE will complain. You can then check your system with this command:

```
/media/CDROM/aide -c /media/CDROM/aide.conf –A database=file:/media/CDROM/aide.db.gz
```

When you run a check with AIDE, it will re-scan your disk, but this time it will compare against the saved database. When it finds any differences, it prints out a description of the changes. Listing 9-12 shows some typical AIDE output.

*Listing 9-12. Sample AIDE Output*

```
-------------------------------------------------
Added files:
-------------------------------------------------
added: /var/log/audit/audit.log.1
-------------------------------------------------
Changed files:
-------------------------------------------------
changed: /var/log/lastlog
changed: /bin/ls
-------------------------------------------------
Detailed information about changes:
-------------------------------------------------
File: /var/log/lastlog
  Mtime   : 2009-04-17 16:44:20    , 2009-04-17 18:23:11
  Ctime   : 2009-04-17 16:44:20    , 2009-04-17 18:23:11
  MD5     : yjLNYduGTv1HKoKdZIXTZg== , zmhIZSJM8qTrvZitUfOAiw==

File: /bin/ls
  Mtime   : 2009-01-21 17:28:31    , 2009-04-17 18:11:09
  Ctime   : 2009-04-17 15:45:56    , 2009-04-17 18:11:09
```

The first item of interest is the file audit.log.1 that has been added. The files ends in .1 , so you know this is the result of a log rotation, which you can ignore. The next item is also a log file: /var/log/lastlog. There are special rules for dealing with log files, which continue to grow by their nature. This log file is special because it can change, but it doesn't increase in size. You can tell that the contents of the file have changed because the MD5 checksum has changed. Aide has a rule for dealing with /var/log/lastlog by default, but you can alter it to tell AIDE to check only the permissions of this file. The original rule is /var/log/lastlog LSPP; the new rule is /var/log/lastlog PERMS. You can use a text editor to find that line in the configuration file /etc/aide.conf and make the change.

LSPP and PERMS are predefined macros that tell AIDE which attributes of a file to check. LSPP checks all file permissions and changes, whereas PERMS checks only the various file permissions, but permits the data in the file to change. You can find a complete list of the possible attributes to check in the aide.conf man page. The configuration file contains a summary, as well as a description of the various macros. You can ignore the lastlog file completely by adding this rule:

```
!/var/log/lastlog
```

After changing the configuration file, you must update the database with the aide -u command, as I'll discuss momentarily. The order of the rules in the AIDE configuration file isn't too important because AIDE will do its best to process them correctly. However, as a general rule it's recommended that you put more specific rules at the start of the file and more general rules at the end.

The final change I'll cover is interesting because you don't expect the ls binary to change. The reason this file shows up is because it was reinstalled earlier, after it was altered. If the altered file is still present, the size and checksum would also be changed. If you see unexpected changes on your system, that could be evidence of a root kit. To prevent false positives, you must update the AIDE database after making any system changes such as installing updates. You can update the AIDE database with the aide -u command. This update procedure also performs a check at the same time to prevent any changes between the check and the update from going unnoticed. Remember: After you update the database, you should burn the updated copy to CD.

For this form of intrusion detection to be effective, you must perform these checks regularly. You can create a daily cron job by creating a file called /etc/cron.daily/aide (see Listing 9-13).

*Listing 9-13. A Sample AIDE cronjob*

```
#!/bin/bash
CDROM=/media/CDROM
if [ -x $CDROM/aide ] ; then
    $CDROM/aide -c $CDROM/aide.conf -A database=file:$CDROM/aide.db.gz
else
    /usr/sbin/aide
fi
```
  Finally, make the file executable so it can be run by the cron daemon with chmod a+x /etc/cron.daily/aide. You can also run the script manually to start a check.

---

■ **Tip:** cron is a daemon that runs commands or jobs at scheduled times. Scripts stored in the /etc/cron.daily directory run every day at 4:02 AM. You configure the exact time using the file, /etc/contab. The output of these commands is emailed to root.

---

It's also possible to use cryptography to protect the AIDE database from unauthorized changes. The basic principle is that you can generate a public key using GNU Privacy Guard (GPG). After you create the database, you can create a signature of the database using the private component of your key. Before using the database to perform a check, you can compare the signature and verify that the file hasn't been altered. Unfortunately, this cryptographic checking isn't well integrated with AIDE, and it requires some extra scripting. You can find some sample scripts in /usr/share/doc/aide-0.13.1/contrib, or you can obtain some updated scripts called aide_create.sh, aide_check.sh and aide_update.sh from the web site for this book.

---

■ **Tip:** GPG is a free implementation of the OpenPGP standard. It provides public key cryptography, including encryption, signing, and key management. You can find out more information about GPG at the http://www.gnupg.org/ web site.

---

## Monitoring the Network with Netfilter

There are as many ways of monitoring a network as there are network topologies and protocols. Combining all the techniques inevitably turns into a full-time job.
  The most mature open source network intrusion detection program is called *snort*. Snort is extremely powerful, but also quite complex. It doesn't come with CentOS, and I mention it here for the sake of completeness. If you're interested, you can learn more about snort at http://www.snort.org/. For a single host, you're better off adopting a simpler approach to monitoring.
  One such simple approach is to use *netfilter*. Netfilter is component of the Linux kernel that can filter and modify network packets. A netfilter approach works alongside your firewall and allows you to log information about both successful and denied connections. You can also target specific networks, ports or applications for logging.

You configure netfilter with a tool called *iptables*. Iptables can add rules that identify specific packets based on a source port and address, a destination port and address, and many other properties. When netfilter identifies a packet matching the rule, it performs an action such as accepting or rejecting the packet. The action is called a target. Iptables is a modular program, which means you must load specific modules to access some functionality. These modules often map to a kernel module that implements the packet matching.

If you have not yet implemented a firewall, you might want to skip ahead to the next chapter, which covers netfilter in detail and guides you through the process of setting up the netfilter firewall. This is not strictly required because the default firewall configuration is sufficient.

Netfilter has a target called LOG that causes information about the packet to be logged to the standard syslog service. You can take advantage of this target, as well as all the regular netfilter packet matching criteria, such as the address, protocol, port details, and even special packet flags such as the TCP SYN flag.

In contrast to most netfilter targets, the LOG target doesn't terminate the processing of a packet. This means that you can log a packet and then proceed to either ACCEPT or REJECT it.

■ **Tip:** The TCP protocol uses the TCP SYN flag to create a new connection. The client initiates the process by sending a packet with the SYN flag set. The server then replies with both SYN and ACK flags set, at which time the client then sends an ACK flag and the connection is established. This is often referred to as the three-way handshake.

Listing 9-14 shows a command for activating logging for incoming TCP SYN packets on port 22: the iptables -I RH-Firewall-1-INPUT command adds the rule to the incoming packet processing.

*Listing 9-14. Example Command to Log SSH Connections*

```
iptables -I RH-Firewall-1-INPUT -m tcp -p tcp --dport 22 --syn -j LOG
```

-m tcp -p tcp selects the TCP protocol, --dport 22 selects the destination port number, and --syn matches the SYN flag. If all these conditions are matched, the command activates the LOG target. The SSH protocol uses port 22, so this rule identifies new SSH connections. You can connect to the server using SSH after you run the preceding command. If you look in the /var/log/messages log file, you should see a message similar to this one:

```
kernel: IN=lo OUT= MAC=00:00:00:00:00:00:00:00:00:00:00:00:08:00 SRC=192.168.3.1
 DST=192.168.3.1 LEN=60 TOS=0x00 PREC=0x00 TTL=64 ID=21337 DF PROTO=TCP SPT=59674
 DPT=22 WINDOW=32792 RES=0x00 SYN URGP=0
```

The log entry shows the details of the packet that was matched. IN= indicates which interface the packet came in on. In this case, the packet arrived in the lo loopback interface. OUT= shows the output interface, but this interface is available only for forwarded packets, so it's blank in this example. MAC= shows three bits of information. The first six octets show the hardware MAC address of the sender; the next six, the MAC address of the destination; and the final two octets contain the EtherType, or protocol used by the packet.

The value 08:00 is the EtherType for IP version 4. The two MAC addresses are shown as all zeros because the loopback interface doesn't use them. On an Ethernet interface, the MAC addresses would contain real values. SRC= and DST= show the source and destination IP Address, which are the same in this example, but might well be different when you encounter them. LEN= shows the length of the packet.

The next few fields provide some technical details about the IP protocol that you can safely ignore. The next significant entry is PROTO=, which indicates the protocol; as expected, the protocol is TCP. SPT= and DPT= show the source and destination ports—again, the destination is port 22, also as expected. The remaining fields show the technical details of the TCP protocol. The only interesting field here is SYN, which indicates the SYN flag was set.

One thing missing from the log entry is any information that indicates whether this packet was accepted. To fix that, you can use another iptables parameter called --log-prefix to enhance the message. Listing 9-15 illustrates how you can log the packet with a prefix, then perform the accept in the next rule. The rule is also slightly modified from the preceding example to use the state matching module to match a TCP connection rather than using the SYN flag directly. This improves readability of the log rule because it matches the preferred syntax for the accept rule; it also means that the rules are suitable to save to your firewall configuration.

*Listing 9-15. Example Rules for Accepting SSH Traffic*

```
-A RH-Firewall-1-INPUT -m state --state NEW -m tcp -p tcp \
    --dport 22 -j LOG --log-prefix "ACCEPT SSH "
-A RH-Firewall-1-INPUT -m state --state NEW -m tcp -p tcp \
    --dport 22 -j ACCEPT
```

You can also log rejected packets with a catch-all rule. The last rule in the default firewall has these parameters:

```
-j REJECT --reject-with icmp-host-prohibited
```

This stops any processing from being executed against any packet that hasn't been accepted yet. The --reject-with command informs the sender of the packet via ICMP that the firewall rejected the packet. You can log these packets by adding a LOG rule immediately before the catch-all reject rule (see Listing 9-16).

*Listing 9-16. Example Rules to Log Denied Traffic*

```
-A RH-Firewall-1-INPUT -j LOG --log-prefix "REJECT "
-A RH-Firewall-1-INPUT -j REJECT --reject-with icmp-host-prohibited
```

You can use the state matching module to refine your logging of TCP packets. For example, you can log only TCP connection attempts, rather than all TCP packets. After you do this, all non-TCP packets are logged using the not operator (!) and -p, which matches the protocol. Finally, you reject any packet that hasn't been accepted already with a host prohibited packet (see Listing 9-17).

*Listing 9-17. Example Rules to Log Denied TCP Connections*

```
-A RH-Firewall-1-INPUT -m state --state NEW -m tcp -p tcp -j LOG --log-prefix "REJECT "
-A RH-Firewall-1-INPUT -p ! tcp -j LOG --log-prefix "REJECT "
-A RH-Firewall-1-INPUT -j REJECT --reject-with icmp-host-prohibited
```

The next step is to put this all together. You can see a complete firewall configuration suitable for /etc/sysconfig/iptables in Listing 9-18. The sections in bold are the example rules that you've learned about in this chapter. The other lines are the default entries that you'll learn about in the next chapter. If you've already made changes to your firewall, then the contents of your /etc/sysconfig/iptables might be different than those shown in Listing 9-18. If that's the case for you, you might have to enter only the logging rules.

*Listing 9-18. Complete /etc/sysconfig/iptables*

```
# This file is maintained manually
# Do not run system-contig-securitylevel
*filter
:INPUT ACCEPT [0:0]
:FORWARD ACCEPT [0:0]
:OUTPUT ACCEPT [0:0]
:RH-Firewall-1-INPUT - [0:0]
-A INPUT -j RH-Firewall-1-INPUT
-A FORWARD -j RH-Firewall-1-INPUT
-A RH-Firewall-1-INPUT -i lo -j ACCEPT
-A RH-Firewall-1-INPUT -p icmp --icmp-type any -j ACCEPT
-A RH-Firewall-1-INPUT -p 50 -j ACCEPT
-A RH-Firewall-1-INPUT -p 51 -j ACCEPT
-A RH-Firewall-1-INPUT -p udp --dport 5353 -d 224.0.0.251 -j ACCEPT
-A RH-Firewall-1-INPUT -p udp -m udp --dport 631 -j ACCEPT
-A RH-Firewall-1-INPUT -p tcp -m tcp --dport 631 -j ACCEPT
-A RH-Firewall-1-INPUT -m state --state ESTABLISHED,RELATED -j ACCEPT
# Enter your rules below this line
-A RH-Firewall-1-INPUT -m state --state NEW -m tcp -p tcp --dport 22 -j LOG↵
 --log-prefix "ACCEPT SSH "
-A RH-Firewall-1-INPUT -m state --state NEW -m tcp -p tcp --dport 22 -j ACCEPT
-A RH-Firewall-1-INPUT -m state --state NEW -m tcp -p tcp -j LOG --log-prefix "REJECT "
-A RH-Firewall-1-INPUT -p ! tcp -j LOG --log-prefix "REJECT "
# Do not change below this line
-A RH-Firewall-1-INPUT -j REJECT --reject-with icmp-host-prohibited
COMMIT
```

# Security Enhanced Linux

You're familiar with the standard security model used by CentOS at this point. Each file on the filesystem is assigned a user and group owner. A set of permissions is assigned for the user, the group, and for all other users. When you use the ls -l command, you see the permissions listed with a series of letters or dashes similar this: rw-rw-r--.

This method of access control is referred to as Discretionary Access Control (DAC). This approach means that the owner of a file or the root user can, at his discretion, change the permissions and alter the security assigned to the file.

Security Enhanced Linux, or SELinux, is another form of access control called Mandatory Access Control (MAC). MAC differs from traditional DAC because the security is controlled by an administrative policy that the user cannot change. Consequently, the correct permissions are enforced for all users. Be careful not to confuse this MAC with other uses of the term; this is not related to any networking protocols or cryptography.

# Why Use SELinux

The main problem with the traditional DAC model is that many services must be run as the root user, either because they require access to a low numbered TCP port, they need to switch to a user log-in session, or they require access to another restricted resource. Under the traditional DAC model, a compromised or misconfigured service can allow a cracker full access to the system with the ability to bypass all security measures. This is referred to as *privilege escalation.*

SELinux reduces the problems associated with DAC by adding another layer of security checks. If a compromised service is running as root, and it attempts to access a file that the service doesn't need for normal operation, the access is denied. This prevents the compromised service from gaining any further access.

You might be thinking that this sounds a lot like access control lists (ACLs). ACLs can give you fine-grained security, but they are still a form of DAC. Users can alter their own ACLs, and the root user—or any process running as the root user—can alter and bypass any ACL.

CentOS comes preconfigured with SELinux, which has three modes of operation: Disabled, Permissive, and Enforcing. You might recall from Chapter 1 that you are prompted to select your preferred SELinux mode after you install CentOS.

When set to Disabled mode, SELinux is fully disabled, and CentOS provides only traditional DAC security.

The other two modes, Permissive and Enforcing, enable SELinux. When you run SELinux in Permissive mode, any security policy failure generates a warning, but it doesn't prevent access. Only in Enforcing mode does a security policy violation result in an access-denied error.

Note that enabling SELinux doesn't disable the traditional DAC permissions. If the DAC denies access, then the error is returned immediately. If the DAC permits access, then the MAC is consulted.

To follow this section, you should ensure that you have SELinux enabled and running in either Permissive or Enforced mode. You can check your SELinux status with the getenforce command (see Listing 9-19).

*Listing 9-19.* *Checking the SELinux Mode*

```
# getenforce
Permissive
```

# Enabling and Disabling SELinux

You must complete a pair of steps to enable SELinux correctly. Your first step is to edit the /etc/sysconfig/selinux file and ensure it contains either SELINUX=permissive or SELINUX=enforcing. The second step is to request that the filesystem be relabeled with the SELinux context information.

Under CentOS, SELinux context information for files and directories is stored on the ext3 filesystem as an extended attribute. Extended attribute is often abbreviated to EA or xattr. Extended attributes allow you to associate arbitrary metadata with a file or directory. The content of the extended attribute isn't normally of concern to the kernel, but special attention must be paid to this in the case of SELinux. When you disable SELinux, the kernel cannot maintain the context information, so you must correct the context information when you re-enable SELinux.

---

■ **Tip:** A file that lacks context information is allocated the default value, file_t type. This can prevent the file from being accessed by some services.

---

If SELinux is currently enabled, but has been disabled previously, then there is a chance that some files don't have the correct context information. If this is the case, SELinux won't work correctly until the correct context information has been restored.

Restoring the context information is referred to as *relabeling*; you can do this with the `fixfiles relabel` command. The `fixfiles` command has some side effects that can cause problems if the system is already running, so it's recommended that you reboot after running this command. If you have just rebooted to enable SELinux, then you need to reboot a second time. You can prevent the multiple reboots by configuring `fixfiles` to run automatically at boot time. To activate the boot-time labeling, you must create a file called `/.autorelabel` and then reboot. You can create this file with the `touch /.autorelabel` command.

---

■ **Tip:** Some versions of CentOS 5 might print an error like this: `/etc/selinux/targeted` `/contexts/files/file_contexts.homedirs: line 18 has invalid context user_u:` `object_r:user_mozilla_home_t:s0`. If you see this error, then you should run the `genhomedircon` command and then restart the relabel process.

---

You can continue to experiment with SELinux once you have your filesystem labeled correctly with context information and SELinux enabled.

If SELinux is enabled, you can switch from Permissive mode to Enforcing mode—and back again—at any time using the `setenforce Enforcing` or `setenforce Permissive` command. Note that enabling or disabling SELinux completely requires a reboot.

---

■ **Warning:** When running in Permissive mode, files can be allocated with invalid context information. Before switching back to Enforcing mode, you might need to relabel the filesystem to correct the context information, or some services might not be able to access the files.

---

## SELinux Policy

SELinux is driven by a set of rules called a *policy*. CentOS comes with one main policy: *targeted*. You can find other policies on the Internet, but these aren't suitable for a general purpose server. This section focuses exclusively on the targeted policy, which applies restrictions only to services, not to interactive user logins.

Files and directories are called *objects* under SELinux. Other types of objects include network interfaces, sockets, devices, and so on. The main focus of this section will be on how to leverage files and directories. Every object is assigned a context in the same way that all files are assigned permissions.

SELinux is also concerned with processes, or *subjects*. Each subject runs within a specific context known as the *domain*. You should not confuse this domain with DNS or NIS/YP domains.

By default, any new process inherits the domain from its parent process. Once SELinux has allocated a process to a domain, it cannot be changed. The policy can specify rules that cause some new process to use a different domain than its parent. This is called a *domain transition*, and it can occur only when the kernel creates a new process. Later in this chapter, I'll teach you how to turn some of these rules on and off, so you can control which processes run under the control of SELinux.

You might wonder where the first domain comes from if processes inherit the domain from their parents. After the kernel finishes booting, it starts the init process. This process is assigned automatically to the init_t domain. As init starts to run processes, some of them will transition to a new domain. This is how you ensure that every process is assigned a domain to run in.

Processes exist only in memory, so the domain information for the process must also reside in memory. The kernel stores this domain information as a property of a process, much as it stores other properties, such as the process ID and environment variables.

Files get their context information in a different way. When the file is created, the appropriate context for the file is selected and saved to the EA. This context stays with the file, even if the file moves. Files get their context mainly by inheriting it from the directory in which they were created.

A second way files get assigned a context is from a set of rules that form part of the SELinux policy. These rules specify which files will be assigned which contexts, and they override the default the context handed down by the parent directory. A rule can match files with specific names or by using regular expressions. These policy rules also serve as the information source when you relabel the filesystem.

The third method is to change the context of a file manually with the chcon command. This change is recorded permanently in a file's extended attribute. However, you lose this information if the filesystem is ever relabled. You can also apply the default context to a file or directory at any time using the restorecon command.

Although the file context information is stored on disk, it must be loaded into memory before it can be used. When a file is accessed, the metadata is loaded into memory. This metadata includes the file size, timestamps, and permissions for that file. The context string is also loaded into memory, so it's ready to use in the security checks.

## Drilling Down on Context

You can use SELinux to implement several different security models:
- Role-based access control (RBAC)
- Type enforcement (TE)
- Multi-level security (MLS)

The targeted policy follows the type enforcement model, but the ability of SELinux to support other models means that the format of a given context can seem overly complex.

SELinux represents the context using a string made up of three or four colon-separated components. These components represent a user, role, type, and, optionally, a level. Again, these properties are unique to SELinux, so you shouldn't confuse them with user log-ins, file types, and so on. You can see some example context strings in Listing 9-20.

*Listing 9-20. Example Context Strings*

```
system_u:system_r:kernel_t
user_u:system_r:unconfined_t
user_u:system_r:inetd_t:SystemLow-SystemHigh
root:system_r:unconfined_t:SystemLow-SystemHigh
```

Now let's dissect each part of the string. The SELinux user field doesn't represent an actual user, but a class of user. The users available in the targeted policy are root, user_u and system_u. The targeted policy uses the suffix _u as a reminder that this is a user. Similarly, the name of a role ends in _r, and the name of a type ends in _t. Yes, user classes exist, but they don't play an important role in the targeted policy.

The policy can use roles when implementing an RBAC-based security model. Roles act similarly to the concept of a group, where you assign users a set of roles, and then assign roles to a set of domains. The targeted policy defines some roles, but it doesn't make extensive use of them.

The targeted policy uses the type field extensively, as suggested by the name of the model, Type Enforcement. When applied to a process, the type is called the domain. When applied to an object such as a file, it's simply referred to as the type. Your main job as it pertains to SELinux is to ensure that files are allocated the correct type. Note that this type field does *not* indicate the contents of the file; rather, it indicates the purpose of the file.

The level is used for the MLS model. In this model, objects can be allocated an arbitrary security level or range. The values for these levels would be defined by the system administrator, depending on the type of data being stored. In a military application, the range might be from Top Secret to Unclassified.

Note that you can subdivide the levels further, so that people working on one Top Secret project are not permitted to see other Top Secret projects. Again, a system administrator would assign these categories. The internal representation of the level is a string made from an s followed by a number (such as s0). You can convert this numeric representation to a user-friendly string such as TopSecret. This is similar to how you can write a user ID as a number or convert it to a log-in name. Any level that you might see on CentOS is converted to the SystemHigh or SystemLow strings. You might see levels listed in some contexts, but the targeted policy doesn't use the level, and you can ignore it.

To manage the context of your files, many of the standard CentOS tools have been updated with new functionality. For example, ls, id, and ps have been enhanced with a new command-line parameter, -Z. This command-line parameter alters the output to include the SELinux context information. Also, cp has been updated to maintain context information on copied files. A new chcon command allows you to set the context of a file. Listing 9-21 shows a number of commands which will show context information. You should run these and familiarize yourself with reading their output.

*Listing 9-21. Tools for Viewing Context Information*

```
id -Z
ps -Z
ps axZ
ls -Z /etc
ls -Z /bin
ls -Z /var/www
```

Listing 9-22 shows some sample output from the ls -Z /etc command. Specifying -Z shows you the context, as well as the traditional DAC permissions. Note how many of the configuration files are allocated a specific type to represent the service that uses that file. Also, note the different values for the SELinux user. Remember that the only information the targeted policy uses is the SELinux type.

*Listing 9-22. Output of ls -Z /etc*

```
-rw-r--r--  root root  system_u:object_r:adjtime_t        adjtime
-rw-------  root root  system_u:object_r:etc_t            aide.conf
-rw-r--r--  root root  system_u:object_r:alsa_etc_rw_t    asound.state
drwxr-x---  root root  system_u:object_r:auditd_etc_t     audit
-r--------  root root  system_u:object_r:shadow_t         gshadow
-rw-r--r--  root root  user_u:object_r:prelink_cache_t    prelink.cache
-rw-r--r--  root root  root:object_r:etc_t                yum.conf
```

It is important that you become comfortable identifying the domain of processes and the type of files. Start the web server with the `service httpd start` command and then run `ps xZ`. Now, can you identify what domain the HTTPD service is running? What about `init`? Listing 9-23 shows some commands you can use to experiment with the context of files. Practice until you're comfortable identifying and changing the context.

*Listing 9-23. Exploring the Context of a Directory*

```
cd ~
ls -laZ # what is the default context?
mkdir public_html
ls -ldZ public_html # has public_html inherited its context?
restorecon public_html
ls -ldZ public_html # what is the correct context for this directory?
mkdir webfiles
ls -ldZ webfiles # inherits user_home_t
restorecon webfiles
ls -ldZ webfiles # context has not be altered
chcon --reference public_html webfiles
ls -ldZ webfiles # context has been set to match public_html
restorecon webfiles
ls -ldZ webfiles # context has not been altered
restorecon -F webfiles
ls -ldZ webfiles # context has been set back to the inherited user_home_t
```

---

▓ **Note:** There is a service called `restorecond` that is always running. This service can assign the correct context to specific new files and directories automatically. This includes user-specific files such as `~/public_html`. Confusingly, this is only done if the user is show as logged in via UTMP. If you rely on this action, you should always check the context of new files or directories to make sure it has been set correctly.

---

The targeted policy in CentOS usually does the right thing, and you shouldn't need to intervene. The main problem area occurs when users start supplying files to be used by a service. The main case for this is the web server. The Apache web server—named HTTPD under CentOS—has the most complex policy associated with it. For example, you can apply several types that allow you to serve static content, running CGI scripts, saving files, and so on. There are also some restrictions that pertain to connecting to databases that can be turned on and off.

Other services, such as Samba and FTP, can also cause problems. When users upload files over the network, the targeted policy might apply the wrong context; in these cases, access is denied when the files are accessed from another service such as the web server. It is here where you might need to use chcon to correct the context on the files.

# Booleans

You can set flags to enable or disable many parts of the targeted policy. For example, you use flags to set permission for CGI scripts to connect to a database. These flags are referred to as booleans because they must be set to either on or off. You can get a complete list of the booleans available with the getsebool -a command. There are currently over 200 booleans, which control around 130 possible services. The main boolean for each service is named <service>_disable_trans. The default value for the _disable_trans Booleans is off, which instructs SELinux to protect that service. You can disable this protection by setting the value to on. You can also make the setting persist over a reboot; this is important for services you might want to start at boot time. The command to alter a boolean setting is setsebool. Listing 9-24 illustrates how to query and set boolean values. The boolean shows control whether or not samba is permitted to share out users' home directories. Samba will be covered in depth in Chapter 14.

---

■ **Warning:** Disabling transition for a service can cause a problem if files are created with the wrong context. If that happens, the service might not be able to access such files the next time a transition occurs for the service.

---

*Listing 9-24 Altering Booleans*

```
# getsebool samba_enable_home_dirs
samba_enable_home_dirs --> off
# setsebool -P samba_enable_home_dirs on
# getsebool samba_enable_home_dirs
samba_enable_home_dirs --> on
```

---

■ **Tip:** New versions of CentOS let you set individual services to Permissive mode. This technique reduces the problems caused by services running in the wrong domain.

---

Some services have additional booleans that you can use to fine-tune the permissions for that domain. For example, HTTPD includes approximately 20 booleans. There are also some general system settings that control individual commands such as ping and dmesg. The system-config-selinux tool provides the easiest way to manage these flags. This tool comes in the policycoreutils-gui package, which isn't installed by default. You can install the package with this command:

```
yum install policycoreutils-gui
```

After you install the package, you start its GUI by selecting System ➤ Administration ➤ SELinux Management. Figure 9-1 shows the main screen for system-config-selinux.

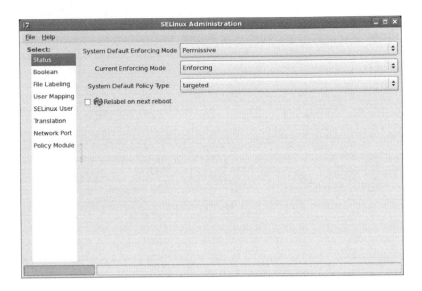

*Figure 9-1.* *The system-config-selinux status screen*

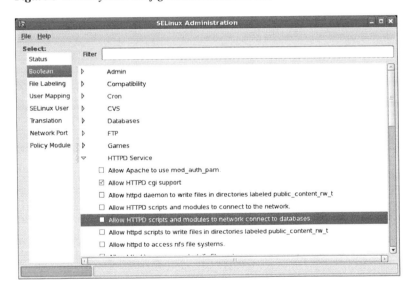

*Figure 9-2.* *The system-config-selinux tool showing booleans*

This GUI combines the functionality of getsebool, setsebool, and semanage into a single interface (see Figure 9-2). It provides an easy-to-read format; be aware that it is also easy to change. Changing a boolean setting can have an immediate impact, so you should be careful not to alter any settings without having a clear understanding what the impact your change will have. You can also change other SELinux settings using this tool, but it's not recommended.

Many of the available context types and booleans are documented in a series of man pages. For example, the httpd_selinux(8) man page contains the details for many context types and booleans that apply to the web server. You can view the man page with the man 8 httpd_selinux command. You can find man pages for the following services:

- ftpd_selinux
- httpd_selinux
- kerberos_selinux
- named_selinux
- nfs_selinux
- nis_selinux
- rsync_selinux
- samba_selinux
- ypbind_selinux

## Access Vectors

A SELinux policy contains a number of rules that called *access vectors*. These rules control the access a subject has to an object. Remember that a subject is a process, and an object is typically a file or directory. For example, consider this rule:

```
permit httpd_t read access to httpd_sys_content_t
```

This rule enables the web server to read and serve files specially marked for access by the web server. If there is no rule that permits access, then the result is to deny access. If the web server tries to serve a file with the user_home_t context, it receives an access denied error because there is no Access Vector that permits it. If the server tries to write to the file with the httpd_sys_content_t context, it also receives an access denied error because there is no access vector. Even setting the permissions on the file so it is world writable would not permit writing to the file because the MAC is still consulted.

When SELinux makes a decision about access, the result is stored in memory in what is called the *Access Vector Cache* (AVC). SELinux also generates a message about the access decision. These messages are logged via the audit daemon and placed in this file: /var/log/audit/audit.log. The format of the AVC messages makes them hard to interpret, but you can use another tool called *setroubleshoot* to process these messages and write them to /var/log/messages in a human-readable format. You can install the setroubleshoot tool with this command: yum install setroubleshoot. This package also comes with a GUI tool that you can use to display the messages. You can do this by accessing the SELinx Troubleshooter option at Applications ➤ System Tools ➤ SELinux Troubleshooter. The SELinux Troubleshooter includes the error message, then explains why the error occurred and the steps required to resolve the problem. Figure 9-3 shows an example where access was denied and setroubleshoot suggests how to resolve the problem.

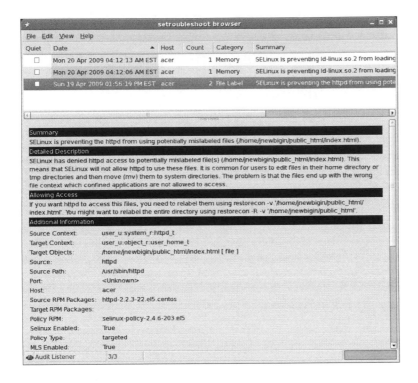

*Figure 9-3. Explanation from SELinux Troubleshooter*

If you encounter a situation where a policy denies access to your service, but no boolean exists to permit access, then you might have to alter your policy to enable access. The policy is essentially a set of rules that you can change. Making changes to the policy is beyond the scope of this book, but you can find many books and online resources that cover this procedure.

## Interactive Users

When a user logs either via SSH or into X11, he is allocated the user_u:system_r:unconfined_t context. This unconfined type puts no extra restrictions on the user and relies on traditional DAC security. The targeted policy has only a few rules that allow the user to change his password and run a handful or other suid commands.

Future versions of CentOS might include a new policy that gives you greater control over what users can do. Already experimental policies exist that allow you to restrict an X11 session for kiosk-style use. Once the future version of the OS refines these interactive policies, CentOS might remove the unconfined policy completely.

# Summary

In this chapter, we looked at three important tasks that provide advanced security for your CentOS server. Specifically, we looked at how to generate and use digital certificates to secure TCP connections with TLS. We also looked at using the RPM and AIDE tools to monitor the disk for unauthorized changes, as well as how to use netfilter to monitor the network for connection attempts. Finally, we looked at the core aspects of running SELinux such as selecting the mode, the importance of context information, and how to maintain it.

In the next chapter, we will take an in-depth look at netfilter and how to build an advanced firewall. We will also look at restricting network services using tcp_wrappers and setting up a central log server.

■ ■ ■

# CHAPTER 10

# Network Security

This chapter covers two common tools for securing your CentOS server against unwanted traffic and users, netfilter and tcp_wrappers. It also looks at how you can use netfilter to configure your server to act as a router and enable sharing of an Internet connection. Finally, you'll see how to set up remote logging to a centralized log server.

## The Firewall

In an ideal world, every service running on your CentOS server would be completely secure from unwanted users on the network, without having to implement anything beyond the built-in access control of the service. Unfortunately, this is not the case with many services you may need to run.

The aim of network security is to ensure that only authorized users can connect to your services and anyone else will be denied access. The major threat to any computer connected to the Internet is crackers, both external and inside your network. Internal security is also important and should not be overlooked.

Crackers are people on the network who are trying to gain unauthorized access to your system. Often these will be on the Internet, but depending on who can use your network, you may also need to protect from internal break-ins as well. The main protection from crackers is to prevent services from being available to users who do not need to use them. If you store sensitive information, you might have to restrict which internal users have access. For example, the payroll departmental file server stores confidential information which should not be accessible to users from, for example, the sales department. To make sure there is no unauthorized access to these files, you can use a firewall. You might also want to restrict remote access to workstations so that only IT department staff members have access.

---

■ **Tip**: Many of the protocols used by CentOS were designed in the early stages of the Internet, when security had not become a serious problem. Rather than redesigning these protocols and causing compatibility problems, it is possible to add security using a firewall.

---

## A Basic Firewall

The first tool we will look at for limiting access to your server is the *firewall*. There are many firewall types, ranging from hardware-based network appliances down to software-based ones that run inside the host. We will be using the Linux software firewall, which is implemented by a piece of software called netfilter. This software runs inside the kernel but some user-space applications are also used to configure it. The main tool used to configure netfilter is called iptables. For this reason, netfilter is often referred to as iptables.

The first firewall we will examine is the default CentOS firewall. CentOS comes with an interactive user-level tool called system-config-securitylevel, which can be run under X11 or from a text-based terminal. This tool gives you the ability to enable and disable the firewall and select which services you wish to allow. It works on what is called a *mostly closed* configuration. What that means is all incoming connections are blocked by default. Any connection you want to allow must be explicitly enabled. In contrast, a *mostly open* configuration would allow all connections except any you have explicitly blocked.

---

▓ **Tip**: A mostly closed firewall will provide greater security than a mostly open one. Converting from mostly open or no firewall at all to a mostly closed firewall can be a daunting task and cause disruptions to live services as you complete the configuration. To prevent this disruption, it is recommended that you implement a mostly closed firewall from the beginning. As you set up and configure each service, it is easy configure the firewall by adding access to that service.

---

Start system-config-firewall either by typing the name into a root shell prompt or using the GUI menu system and choosing System ➤ Administrator ➤ Security Level and Firewall. If you are not logged in as root you will be prompted for the root password. You must be root to alter the firewall. Once you've done that, you'll see the screen shown in Figure 10-1.

*Figure 10-1. Firewall settings in system-config-firewall*

This screen may look familiar to you. You may recall from Chapter1 that as part of the first login procedure you have the ability to configure the firewall with these options. You can of course rerun this tool at any time to make adjustments to you current configuration.

This tool provides a coarse-grained level of control over the basic services that come with CentOS. It also allows you to configure custom services by adding extra TCP and UDP ports. Some services use a number of ports, so selecting a service will permit all the ports associated with that service. Table 10-1 lists all the built-in ports.

*Table 10-1. Default Services Known to system-config-securitylevel*

| Service | Protocol | Port |
| --- | --- | --- |
| FTP | tcp | 21 |
| Mail (SMTP) | tcp | 25 |
| NFS4 | tcp | 2049 |
| SSH | tcp | 22 |
| Samba | udp | 137 |
| | udp | 138 |
| | tcp | 139 |
| | tcp | 445 |
| Secure WWW (HTTPS) | tcp | 443 |
| Telnet | tcp | 23 |
| WWW (HTTP) | tcp | 80 |

The important thing to note about using system-config-securitylevel is that you cannot limit access based on the IP address or network interface (such as eth0) of a connection. This limits the effectiveness of the firewall on a host connected directly to the Internet or another untrusted network. In the next section you will see how you can enhance this firewall to add the required host-based filtering. However, it is still worth using this tool to prepare the basic firewall, which will simplify the next step.

Using system-config-firewall is straightforward. First, make sure that Firewall is set to Enabled and then select each of the services you are running and need to provide access to from the network.

If you are running services that are not listed, you can add your own ports by selecting Add and entering the service name or port number in the Add Port window, as shown in Figure 10-2. You may enter a service name as listed in the /etc/services file. Select the appropriate protocol and click OK. The new service will be listed in the Other Ports section of the dialog. If you have entered a service name, you must check that the port number which has been added is the one you were expecting.

*Figure 10-2. Adding a custom port to system-config-firewall*

Once you have made your selection of trusted services, the configuration is saved to the file
/etc/sysconfig/iptables. Along with your selected services, some default system services and protocols
will be added. It is safe to ignore these extra entries for now. You may wish to examine them in more
detail in the next section. When you select Apply, these rules are loaded into the kernel by running the
command service iptables start.

In most circumstances you will want the firewall to start automatically when the server boots. This is
the default configuration, but you can ensure that it is correctly enabled by issuing the command
chkconfig iptables on. Listing 10-1 shows an iptables configuration file with one rule added. The rule
that will allow connections to the SSH service which runs on port 22 is shown in bold, confirming that it
was selected in the GUI. The lines starting with # are comments, which are ignored when the rules are
activated.

*Listing 10-1. An Example /etc/sysconfig/iptables File*

```
# Firewall configuration written by system-config-securitylevel
# Manual customization of this file is not recommended.
*filter
:INPUT ACCEPT [0:0]
:FORWARD ACCEPT [0:0]
:OUTPUT ACCEPT [0:0]
:RH-Firewall-1-INPUT - [0:0]
-A INPUT -j RH-Firewall-1-INPUT
-A FORWARD -j RH-Firewall-1-INPUT
-A RH-Firewall-1-INPUT -i lo -j ACCEPT
-A RH-Firewall-1-INPUT -p icmp --icmp-type any -j ACCEPT
-A RH-Firewall-1-INPUT -p 50 -j ACCEPT
-A RH-Firewall-1-INPUT -p 51 -j ACCEPT
-A RH-Firewall-1-INPUT -p udp --dport 5353 -d 224.0.0.251 -j ACCEPT
-A RH-Firewall-1-INPUT -p udp -m udp --dport 631 -j ACCEPT
-A RH-Firewall-1-INPUT -p tcp -m tcp --dport 631 -j ACCEPT
-A RH-Firewall-1-INPUT -m state --state ESTABLISHED,RELATED -j ACCEPT
-A RH-Firewall-1-INPUT -m state --state NEW -m tcp -p tcp --dport 22 -j ACCEPT
-A RH-Firewall-1-INPUT -j REJECT --reject-with icmp-host-prohibited
COMMIT
```

■ **Warning:** If you are connected to your server via the SSH protocol, you must make sure that you do not uncheck SSH or you will become disconnected from your server and will not be able to reconnect without physical access to the server.

## An Advanced Firewall

Although `system-config-securitylevel` provides basic firewall control, you may find that you want to configure your firewall with a finer level of control. To achieve this you will need to configure `netfilter` using the `iptables` command. There are three ways to do this under CentOS.

The first method involves entering commands directly at the shell prompt. The rules you enter in this way will take effect immediately and remain in effect until you remove them or reboot the server. This is a good way to check that the syntax of your rule is correct and to test it to make sure that it blocks or allows the correct traffic.

The next method builds on the first method of inputting rules but extends the idea with a method to save the running rules so they will persist over a reboot. This is done by using the `iptables` service. You can also configure the service to save the current rules automatically at shutdown.

The third method involves editing the `iptables` configuration file directly. By maintaining this file you save your rules before they are activated; and when they are activated, all rules are activated at the same time. You can also write comments to explain what your rule is doing, and you can easily copy the configuration from one server to another.

Before you can use any of these methods you need to understand how to build a `netfilter` rule and how to input it using `iptables`. Rules are built up with a number of ways for matching a network packet and with a target or action to take when a matching packet is found. Because we are extending the configuration generated by `system-config-securitylevel`, some of the decisions on how to structure these rules have been made for us.

In order to write effective `netfilter` rules you will need to know a bit about how `netfilter` works. It would be possible to fill an entire book on `netfilter`, so we will just look at a few concepts that are relevant to our firewall. If you want more details on what you can do with `netfilter`, check the `netfilter` web site at `http://www.netfilter.org/`. Readers who want to get their hands dirty with some of the advanced features of `netfilter` may wish to read *Designing and Implementing Linux Firewalls and QoS using netfilter, iproute2, NAT and l7-filter*, by Lucian Gheorghe (Packt Publishing, 2006).

## How netfilter Works

Netfilter works by hooking into the kernel network processing in a few key places known as inspection points. In this section we are focusing on the filtering capabilities of `netfilter`, so we are concerned with packets as they go into and come out of an application and as they are forwarded by the kernel routing module. Although all the processing is done by the kernel, the names for where the processing takes place, INPUT and OUTPUT, have been chosen with the point of view of an application in mind. The name for forwarding packets is FORWARD. There are other places that `netfilter` can hook into. These are called PREROUTING and POSTROUTING and are commonly used for altering the packet addressing. We will touch on these in the section on masquerading.

Each of these inspection points can be used with one or more *tables* called `filter`, `nat`, and `mangle`. Again we are looking at the `filter` table, which happens to be the default table used by the `iptables` program. This table can be used with the INPUT, OUTPUT, and FORWARD inspection points. The `nat` table is used for network address translation, which involves altering the packet addressing. It uses the PREROUTING, POSTROUTING, and OUTPUT inspection points. The `mangle` table allows for arbitrary packet modifications, traffic classification, and shaping. It can use any inspection point. The use of the mangle table is beyond the scope of this book.

Each table contains a number of *chains*. You can think of a chain as a list of rules or instructions to apply to each packet that passes through this point in the network stack. For each inspection point in a table, a default chain is created. You can also add more chains to the table. A chain rule might be to allow or drop a packet or to forward it to another chain for further processing. The rules in the chain are processed in order from first to last. When a rule is found to match the packet, the target associated with that rule is applied and in most circumstances, the processing stops. The name *chain* comes from the ability to jump or chain from one rule to another list of rules.

Already you can see that netfilter can be quite complex, and we have not started to look at the packet-matching options. There are many valid ways in which chains can be constructed. CentOS provides a default configuration, which is a good starting point. The default creates a chain called RH-Firewall-1-INPUT, which is configured to process all packets coming into the network stack and all packets being forwarded by the routing code. This is done by adding to the INPUT and FORWARD chains a rule that unconditionally chains to the RH-Firewall-1-INPUT chain.

A packet that enters the network card on the server may be destined for an application running on the server, or it may need to be forwarded to another server. The concept of input is defined in relation to the application on the server:

- A packet coming from the network to an application will follow the INPUT chain.
- A packet coming from the application will follow the OUTPUT chain.
- A packet, coming in from the network, that will be routed to another host will follow the FORWARD chain.

Although we combine INPUT and FORWARD into one chain, we can still retain fine control by matching based on source and destination address.

It is also possible to restrict outgoing packets, but for most general-purpose servers that is not necessary.

A firewall is implemented by filtering out unwanted packets. Some firewall implementations can only filter based on connection requests and destination ports. This means that a large range of ports has to be left open to allow outgoing connections to function correctly.

Because of the way TCP works, each end of the connection (the client and the server) needs to have a port number. The server port number is normally what is called a *well-known port number*. For example, http uses port 80. The client port number is normally chosen at random by the kernel, often from a high range of port numbers between around 32,000 and 64,000. Once a TCP connection has been established, the client and the server operate in the same way, so if a single packet is inspected in isolation, it is impossible to know if it belongs to an incoming server connection or an outgoing client connection. If packets with a high port number are not permitted, the host will be unable to make outgoing connections. This does not effectively prevent unwanted connections, because a service listening on a high-numbered port will always be permitted.

To solve these problems, netfilter has the capability to perform what is called *stateful packet inspection*. This means it can track the current connections and filter packets based on the direction of the connection. This allows outgoing connections to function correctly without having to set aside ports for them.

Another benefit of a stateful firewall is that it can relate multiple connections to each other. This is useful for some protocols such as Active FTP. In the Active FTP protocol, the client initiates a connection to the well-known port on the server (21). When the client requests a file from the server, the server opens a new connection back to the client. This means that the client is also acting as a server. Unless the client firewall allows this incoming connection, the file transfer will fail. Netfilter has a module that can be loaded to extend its functionality so it can understand the FTP protocol. Once this module is active, it will see when FTP traffic is operating and needs to establish an incoming connection. It can allow this specific connection to succeed without having to open any new ports.

The firewall we will be looking at here only relates to IP version 4. It is possible to build a firewall that supports IP version 6, but this is still a relatively new field. IP version 6 also brings its own complexities, which are outside the scope of this book.

## Viewing the Current Firewall

You can view the list of rules being used by netfilter at any by time by issuing the command iptables -L -n. The -L says to list all the chains and rules in the table, and -n will skip DNS lookups and show IP addresses only. You will see output similar to that shown in Listing 10-2.

■ **Note:** Not all options in iptables can be combined. The command iptables -Ln will list a table called n and is not the same as iptables -L -n, which will list the default table in numeric form. For this reason it is recommended that you always specify each parameter separately.

*Listing 10-2. Viewing the Current Rules*

```
Chain INPUT (policy ACCEPT)
target       prot opt source            destination
RH-Firewall-1-INPUT  all  --  0.0.0.0/0          0.0.0.0/0

Chain FORWARD (policy ACCEPT)
target       prot opt source            destination
RH-Firewall-1-INPUT  all  --  0.0.0.0/0          0.0.0.0/0

Chain OUTPUT (policy ACCEPT)
target       prot opt source            destination

Chain RH-Firewall-1-INPUT (2 references)
target       prot opt source            destination
ACCEPT       all  --  0.0.0.0/0          0.0.0.0/0
ACCEPT       icmp --  0.0.0.0/0          0.0.0.0/0       icmp type 255
ACCEPT       esp  --  0.0.0.0/0          0.0.0.0/0
ACCEPT       ah   --  0.0.0.0/0          0.0.0.0/0
ACCEPT       udp  --  0.0.0.0/0          224.0.0.251     udp dpt:5353
ACCEPT       udp  --  0.0.0.0/0          0.0.0.0/0       udp dpt:631
ACCEPT       tcp  --  0.0.0.0/0          0.0.0.0/0       tcp dpt:631
ACCEPT       all  --  0.0.0.0/0          0.0.0.0/0       state RELATED,ESTABLISHED
ACCEPT       tcp  --  0.0.0.0/0          0.0.0.0/0       state NEW tcp dpt:22
REJECT       all  --  0.0.0.0/0          0.0.0.0/0       reject-with↵
 icmp-host-prohibited
```

---

■ **Tip**: Always use the –n flag to display numeric addresses. Using DNS names in the firewall is unsafe because at boot time when the firewall is loaded, the DNS will not be available, which means your firewall will fail to start. Using –n will remind you to always use IP addresses.

---

The default output from iptables shows six columns of information: the target, protocol, options, source address, destinations address, and protocol-specific options. There is more information, which you can display by using the verbose option, –v. This will add packet counters and interface details. You can also list just one specific chain by specifying a parameter to –L. For example, this command will show only the RH-Firewall-1-INPUT chain and include the counters and interfaces:

```
iptables -L RH-Firewall-1-INPUT -n -v
```

Listing 10-3 shows the result.

*Listing 10-3. Viewing the Current Rules with Counters and Interfaces*

```
Chain RH-Firewall-1-INPUT (2 references)
 pkts bytes target      prot opt in    out    source           destination
    0     0 ACCEPT      all  --  lo    *      0.0.0.0/0        0.0.0.0/0
    0     0 ACCEPT      icmp --  *     *      0.0.0.0/0        0.0.0.0/0↵
            icmp type 255
    0     0 ACCEPT      esp  --  *     *      0.0.0.0/0        0.0.0.0/0
    0     0 ACCEPT      ah   --  *     *      0.0.0.0/0        0.0.0.0/0
    0     0 ACCEPT      udp  --  *     *      0.0.0.0/0        224.0.0.251↵
            udp dpt:5353
    0     0 ACCEPT      udp  --  *     *      0.0.0.0/0        0.0.0.0/0↵
            udp dpt:631
    0     0 ACCEPT      tcp  --  *     *      0.0.0.0/0        0.0.0.0/0↵
            tcp dpt:631
 2352 3001K ACCEPT      all  --  *     *      0.0.0.0/0        0.0.0.0/0↵
            state RELATED,ESTABLISHED
    3   240 ACCEPT      tcp  --  *     *      0.0.0.0/0        0.0.0.0/0↵
            state NEW tcp dpt:22
   35  4106 REJECT      all  --  *     *      0.0.0.0/0        0.0.0.0/0↵
            reject-with icmp-host-prohibited
```

You can see from the boldface row that this rule only applies to a specific interface. In this case, it's the loopback interface, which is called lo. Without the –v flag it looks like all traffic will be ACCEPTED, but in fact only loopback traffic is accepted by this rule.

> ▓ **Tip**: `netfilter` records the number of packets and the total amount of traffic matching each rule. You can view the counters with the command `iptables -L -n -v`. You can also reset or zero the counters after viewing them by using the -7 parameter, like this: `iptables -L -n -v -Z`. You could use this feature to record how much network traffic your server is receiving.

## Building netfilter Rules

Now we are ready to look at how to build our own rules. The most basic options we can specify are the source address and destination address. These are specified with -s and -d, respectively. Each of these parameters can be specified as a single IPv4 address or IPv4 subnet. You should not use DNS names, as the DNS may not be operating when the firewall is started. If necessary you can also *negate* an address, to allow traffic from everywhere except the specified address. Listing 10-4 shows some examples of how to match a source address. If possible you should avoid using the negate syntax because it can be confusing to read. The same result can often be achieved by matching the address but using a different target. Targets are covered later in the chapter.

*Listing 10-4. An Example of Address Matching*

```
-s 192.168.3.20 # packet sent from a single host
-s 192.168.3.0/24 # packet sent from any host on the subnet
-s ! 10.0.0.0/8 # packet has sent from a host not on the subnet
```

For a simple host, specifying the source address is adequate to implement the firewall. A server that is acting as a router has a more complex network setup, and it may be required to specify a destination address as well. This will be covered in more detail later.

> ▓ **Tip**: The ! character has a special meaning to the Bash shell and performs history substitution. Although it is not strictly required when specifying the `iptables` command (because ! is always followed by a space), it is good practice to escape or quote the character. You can escape it with the \ character so it becomes \! or enclose it in single quotes so it is processed as a single '!' character. Forgetting to escape it can cause unexpected history substitution, which will cause you to run potentially dangerous commands.

Sometimes it is sufficient just restricting the traffic to a trusted set of addresses. It is recommended, though, that each service is restricted based on the protocol and port. The two main protocols we will look at are TCP and UDP. The protocol is selected with the -p parameter. Although both protocols operate differently, they have the common characteristic of being uniquely identified with a source address, destination address, source port, and destination port.

Before we can specify details specific to a protocol, we must tell `iptables` so it can prepare to accept the parameters. We do this with the -m parameter, which stands for module. In the case of TCP and UDP, the module name is the same as the protocol name, tcp and udp.

Once we have loaded the module we can specify the source and destination port details using the --sport and --dport parameters, respectively. Each port can be specified as a single port number or a sequential range of port numbers, written as *low number:high number*. You can also negate the port with ! to mean that all ports can be used except for this port. As with host selection, this can be confusing and often it is better to match the port and use a different target. Listing 10-5 shows some example protocol and port matching.

*Listing 10-5. An Example of Protocol and Port Matching*

```
-m state--state NEW -m tcp -p tcp --dport 80 # port 80 is used for http traffic
-m state --state NEW -m tcp -p tcp --dport  5900:5999 # a range of VNC ports
-m udp -p udp --dport 514 # syslog is a udp protocol
-m udp -p udp --sport 123 --dport 123 # ntp uses the same port to send and receive
-m tcp -p tcp ! 22 # all ports except for ssh
```

When you're specifying a TCP rule, the source port is not normally important. Most connections are made with a random high-numbered source port to a well-known destination port.

Many UDP-based protocols set the source port the same as the destination port. Although we could filter based on the source port, it does not provide any advantages, so again we will only filter based on the destination port.

One further option we can use with the TCP protocol is stateful inspection. This requires loading the state module. Once the state module is loaded you can match with --state NEW, which will match only the connection request. Once the connection is established, the packets are matched with another rule, which matches ESTABLISHED and RELATED connections. Listing 10-6 shows how the state module is used. We will use the rules that were automatically added in the default firewall configuration to allow the established and related packets.

*Listing 10-6. Using Stateful Matching*

```
-m state --state NEW -m tcp -p tcp --dport n
-m state --state ESTABLISHED,RELATED
```

The last part of the puzzle before we can build our rules is the target. This tells netfilter what to do when a packet is found to match a rule. The target is specified with the -j parameter. The main targets are ACCEPT, DROP, and REJECT. You can also jump to another chain and begin processing from there.

The ACCEPT target will allow the packet to continue unfiltered which is how you specify the traffic you want to allow.

The DROP target will cause the packet to be thrown away. The sender of the packet is not informed so anyone trying to connect will have to wait until the connection times out before receiving an error.

The REJECT target will throw away the packet but first send an ICMP error message to its sender. This way, the sender knows immediately that the service cannot be used.

Each built-in chain can also have a default target, which is applied to any packet that makes it through to the end of the chain without matching any rules. This default target can be specified with the -P parameter.

---

▓ **Tip**: ICMP is the Internet Control Message Protocol. Its primary use is to inform the client or the server about an error in the network. Common errors are No Route to Host and Connection Refused. This is also the protocol used by the ping command.

---

Using these parameters you will be able to build rules ready to use with iptables. In order to add your rules to the chain you must specify where in the chain to put them. Remember, the rules in a chain are processed in order from first to last. When a match is found, processing stops and the target is applied. There are a few ways to order the rule sequence. The simplest way is with –A, which will append your rule to the end of the chain. This is fine when editing /etc/sysconfig/iptables, but it doesn't work from the command line, because the rule will be added after the final catch-all rule, which rejects all traffic.

You can also use –I for insert. This works at the start of the chain or at any point in the chain. In most cases inserting at the start of the chain with –I is sufficient. You can insert before any rule by specifying a rule number, like this: –I *rule number*. Rules are numbered from 1, so –I 2 will insert the rule into position 2. The rule currently at position 2 will move to position 3, and so on. You can also replace chains at any point in the chain using –R *rule number*. Counting the exact location in a chain can be difficult, so it is often easier to delete the old rule and then insert the new rule at the start of the chain.

Deleting a rule from a chain can also be done in two ways: –D can be used with a rule specification, and the first exact match to that rule will be deleted. Alternatively, you can specify a location in the chain with –D *rule number*, and the rule at that location will be deleted.

---

▓ **Tip**: If you add a rule with the command iptables –I *rule* or iptables –A *rule*, you can remove that rule with the command iptables –D  *rule*.

---

You should now have an idea of the types of rules which can be built. By revisiting the first method for adding rules, using the shell prompt. Listing 10-7 shows some example rules you can try out on the server. After adding each rule, check which workstations can connect to the service. Then remove the rule.

*Listing 10-7. Example rules*

```
# Allow a specific host to connect to all services
iptables -I RH-Firewall-1-INPUT -s 192.168.3.20 -j ACCEPT
# Remove the previous rule
iptables -D RH-Firewall-1-INPUT -s 192.168.3.20 -j ACCEPT
# Allow a specific subnet to connect to all services
iptables -I RH-Firewall-1-INPUT -s 192.168.3.0/255.255.255.0 -j ACCEPT
# Allow anyone to connect to a specific tcp port (http)
#(don't forget to remove the previous rule)
iptables -I RH-Firewall-1-INPUT -m state --state NEW/
 -m tcp -p tcp --dport 80 -j ACCEPT
# Allow a specific host to connect to a specific tcp port (ssh)
iptables -I RH-Firewall-1-INPUT -s 192.168.3.20 -m state --state NEW -m tcp -p↵
```

```
  tcp --dport 22 -j ACCEPT
# Allow a specific subnet to connect to a specific udp port (dns)
iptables -I RH-Firewall-1-INPUT -s 192.168.3.0/24 -m udp -p udp --dport 53 -j ACCEPT
# Prevent a specific host from connecting to a service
iptables -I RH-Firewall-1-INPUT -s 192.168.3.20 -m tcp -p tcp --dport 22 -j DROP
# Prevent a specific host from connecting to a service (contrast with the previous rule)
iptables -I RH-Firewall-1-INPUT -s 192.168.3.20 -m tcp -p tcp --dport 22 -j REJECT
```

Now that you have worked out some rules and tested that they work, you want to ensure that they are applied after a restart. The easiest way to achieve this is to use the command service iptables save. This will save rules that are currently active in the kernel to the file /etc/sysconfig/iptables. It will overwrite the current contents of the file, so this method is only useful if you do not edit the configuration file manually.

The command service iptables invokes the iptables initialization (init) script. This script is automatically run during system startup and shutdown. It is possible to tune some of the actions that this script performs by editing another configuration file, called /etc/sysconfig/iptables-config. Of interest here are the variables IPTABLES_SAVE_ON_STOP and IPTABLES_SAVE_ON_RESTART. If you set IPTABLES_SAVE_ON_STOP=yes, then any time you use the command service iptables stop or shut down or reboot the system, your current iptables rules will be saved. If you set IPTABLES_SAVE_ON_RESTART=yes, then any time you use the command service iptables restart, your current iptables rules will be saved. Using this method for managing the firewall can be handy if you find yourself frequently making manual alterations to the firewall rules. You can still use the command service iptables save when these variables are set to yes.

This method is not foolproof, as it will not save the changes if the server crashes, has a power failure, or for any other reason does not perform a proper shutdown. Also, a result of constantly adding rules to the start of the list is that the rules tend to end up listed in a strange order, which can become difficult to manage. It is also not possible to document with comments what each rule is doing.

The third method we'll describe is to edit the /etc/sysconfig/iptables file directly. In combination with testing at the shell prompt, this provides the ability to maintain a well-documented firewall script, which should always keep the system in a consistent state. To begin, run system-config-securitylevel and apply a blank firewall. Then use your favorite text editor to edit /etc/sysconfig/iptables and change the comments (which are the lines that start with a #) to reflect those highlighted in Listing 10-8. Once you have started to make manual changes to the configuration file you should not run system-config-securitylevel or service iptables save or you may overwrite your changes. You should also make sure that in your /etc/sysconfig/iptables-config file, both IPTABLES_SAVE_ON_STOP and IPTABLES_SAVE_ON_RESTART are set to no.

*Listing 10-8. A Skeleton /etc/sysconfig/iptables File*

```
# This file is maintained manually
# Do not run system-config-securitylevel
*filter
:INPUT ACCEPT [0:0]
:FORWARD ACCEPT [0:0]
:OUTPUT ACCEPT [0:0]
:RH-Firewall-1-INPUT - [0:0]
-A INPUT -j RH-Firewall-1-INPUT
-A FORWARD -j RH-Firewall-1-INPUT
-A RH-Firewall-1-INPUT -i lo -j ACCEPT
-A RH-Firewall-1-INPUT -p icmp --icmp-type any -j ACCEPT
-A RH-Firewall-1-INPUT -p 50 -j ACCEPT
-A RH-Firewall-1-INPUT -p 51 -j ACCEPT
```

```
-A RH-Firewall-1-INPUT -p udp --dport 5353 -d 224.0.0.251 -j ACCEPT
-A RH-Firewall-1-INPUT -p udp -m udp --dport 631 -j ACCEPT
-A RH-Firewall-1-INPUT -p tcp -m tcp --dport 631 -j ACCEPT
-A RH-Firewall-1-INPUT -m state --state ESTABLISHED,RELATED -j ACCEPT
# Enter your rules below this line
# Do not change below this line
-A RH-Firewall-1-INPUT -j REJECT --reject-with icmp-host-prohibited
COMMIT
```

You are now ready to add rules as required to the file. Add your rules between the comments to keep them separate from the default rules. Once you have added your rules you can apply them with the command service iptables start.

Now that the basics of netfilter commands have been covered, the entries in the default firewall configuration should make more sense. Following is a short explanation of each entry and why it is present. Lines that start with *, : and COMMIT are interpreted by the iptables initialization script. The lines that start with -A are rules that are passed by the initialization script to the iptables command.

```
# Select the 'filter' table:
*filter
# Set the default action for the INPUT chain to ACCEPT and set the counters to zero
:INPUT ACCEPT [0:0]
# Set the default action for the FORWARD chain to ACCEPT and set the counters to zero
:FORWARD ACCEPT [0:0]
# Set the default action for the OUTPUT chain to ACCEPT and set the counters to zero
:OUTPUT ACCEPT [0:0]
# Create a new chain called RH-Firewall-1-INPUT and set the counters to zero
:RH-Firewall-1-INPUT - [0:0]
# Make all INPUT packets jump to the RH-Firewall-1-INPUT chain
-A INPUT -j RH-Firewall-1-INPUT
# Make all FORWARD packets jump to the RH-Firewall-1-INPUT chain
-A FORWARD -j RH-Firewall-1-INPUT
# Allow all local loopback traffic
-A RH-Firewall-1-INPUT -i lo -j ACCEPT
# Allow ICMP traffic as required for correct TCP/IP operation
-A RH-Firewall-1-INPUT -p icmp --icmp-type any -j ACCEPT
# Allow ESP traffic, which is a protocol used by IPsec†
-A RH-Firewall-1-INPUT -p 50 -j ACCEPT
# Allow AH traffic, which is a protocol used by IPsec†
-A RH-Firewall-1-INPUT -p 51 -j ACCEPT
# Allow multicast DNS traffic, which can be used with Zeroconf and bonjour†
-A RH-Firewall-1-INPUT -p udp --dport 5353 -d 224.0.0.251 -j ACCEPT
# Allow the Internet Print Protocol (IPP)†
-A RH-Firewall-1-INPUT -p udp -m udp --dport 631 -j ACCEPT
# Allow the Internet Print Protocol (IPP)†
-A RH-Firewall-1-INPUT -p tcp -m tcp --dport 631 -j ACCEPT
# Allow connections that are being managed by stateful inspection
-A RH-Firewall-1-INPUT -m state --state ESTABLISHED,RELATED -j ACCEPT
# Reject any packets which have so far not be matched
-A RH-Firewall-1-INPUT -j REJECT --reject-with icmp-host-prohibited
# Activate the configuration for this table
COMMIT
```

The rules marked with a dagger (†) have so far been left alone because they are included in the default CentOS configuration. If you are not using these protocols, then it is safe to remove them. The rules that are not marked with the dagger are important and should not be altered without understanding the impact of the change.

---

▓ **Tip**: Although exceptions are made for CUPS/IPP in the firewall, the default CUPS configuration is to listen to localhost only. If you do enable network printing, then you should create your own firewall rule that allows only the required workstations to print.

---

## Using CentOS as a Router

A server that has more than one network interface is said to be *multihomed*. An interface is normally a network card such as an Ethernet card. Typically these will be named eth0 and eth1. There are other types of interface, such as the loopback interface, dial-up PPP interfaces, and so on. In this section we will be dealing with two Ethernet interfaces, but netfilter will behave the same for any type of interface.

Although there are many possible configurations for a multihomed host, the simplest is to have each interface on a different IP network, which means that each interface has a unique IP address.

We will look at two ways of handling this configuration under CentOS, first by acting as a router and forwarding traffic between one subnet and another. We will then look at IP masquerading, which allows a private subnet to access the Internet by sharing a single IP address.

It is quite straightforward to turn your CentOS server into a router. All that is necessary is to enable IP forwarding. To do this, edit /etc/sysctl.conf and set net.ipv4.ip_forward = 1. To apply this change, run sysctl -p.

If you have a firewall you must configure which traffic is allowed to be forwarded between interfaces. Because the forwarded packets are processed by the RH-Firewall-1-INPUT chain, you must add a rule to that chain. So far, none of the rules presented have been concerned with which interface the packets are arriving on. A router has multiple interfaces, so this becomes an issue. The iptables command provides parameters to allow you to specify which interface the packet arrived on and will be output on. These are -i and -o, respectively. Each parameter takes the name of the interface such as eth0.

To allow traffic from one network to another, the general rule format is

```
iptables -I RH-Firewall-1-INPUT -i first interface -s first IP subnet \
 -o second interface -d second IP subnet -j ACCEPT
iptables -I RH-Firewall-1-INPUT -i second interface -s second IP subnet \
 -o first interface -d first IP subnet -j ACCEPT
```

Because you need to permit traffic to be forwarded from the first network to the second, and traffic from the second back to the first, you need to have two rules. If you have the subnet 192.168.1.0/24 on eth0 and 192.168.2.0/24 on eth1, you would add these two rules:

```
iptables -I RH-Firewall-1-INPUT -i eth0 -s 192.168.1.0/24 \
 -o eth1 -d 192.168.2.0/24 -j ACCEPT
iptables -I RH-Firewall-1-INPUT -i eth1 -s 192.168.2.0/24 \
 -o eth0 -d 192.168.1.0/24 -j ACCEPT
```

Now that your server is acting as a router, you must also refine your host access rules to include a destination address. This will ensure that rules which permit incoming connections to your server do not inadvertently permit a connection to be made to a host on the other network. Listing 10-9 shows a rule that permits SSH connections from one subnet to the server IP address.

**Listing 10-9.** *Restricting the Destination Address*

```
-A RH-Firewall-1-INPUT -s 192.168.3.0/24  d 192.168.3.1 \
 -m state --state NEW -m tcp -p tcp --dport 22 -j ACCEPT
```

Unless you have been allocated a whole subnet from your ISP, routing alone is not sufficient to get the workstations on the Internet. You must also use a technique called *IP masquerading*.

# Using netfilter for IP Masquerading

So far we have only looked at `netfilter` for filtering packets both from a single network interface and multiple interfaces. If your server has more than one interface, then there are many other things that `netfilter` can do. One very useful feature is IP masquerading. This is often referred to as Network Address Translation (NAT). However, masquerading is subtly different from NAT because we are hiding an entire subnet behind a single IP address. Masquerading is different from filtering and forwarding packets because it requires actually altering the packets for both the IP addressing and the protocol port numbers. The main purpose of IP masquerading is to allow many hosts to access the Internet using a single IP address. Windows users might be familiar with Internet Connection Sharing, which is similar to what can be done with masquerading.

To use masquerading you need to use the `MASQUERADE` target, which can only be used in the `POSTROUTING` chain in the nat table. The table is specified with the -t parameter to the `iptables` command. Along with the `MASQUERADE` target you must specify the output interface. It is the address on the output interface that will be used for the masquerading.

Once masquerading is enabled, you must also add a rule that will permit traffic from the internal network to be forwarded. You must have IP forwarding enabled, as shown earlier. Finally, your routing table must have an entry so that Internet traffic is routed via the masquerading network interface. You will normally have set this up already when you performed your network configuration. Listing 10-10 shows the `iptables` commands that will enable masquerading.

**Listing 10-10.** *Setting Up Masquerading*

```
# Assuming eth1 is the Internet, masquerade internal traffic to the Internet
iptables -t nat -A POSTROUTING -o eth1 -j MASQUERADE
# Assuming our internal subnet on eth0 is 192.168.3.0/24 and
# the scrver is 192.168.3.1, allow the Internet traffic to be forwarded
iptables -I RH-Firewall-1-INPUT -i eth0 -s 192.168.3.0/24 \
 -d \! 192.168.3.1 -j ACCEPT
```

You can use `service iptables save` to save all of these rules so they apply at startup or you can add them to /etc/sysconfig/iptables as previously show.

In order to access the Internet, workstations must have the address of your server (136.186.3.1) as their default router. When connections from the workstations are made over the Internet, the source address will be that of the server rather than that of the workstations.

## Handling Complex Protocols with netfilter

So far, most of the connections we have looked at have been single TCP connections or single UDP packets. There are a number of protocols which for various reasons are more complex than this and require special treatment in netfilter. Some common protocols which require this are FTP, TFTP, and h323. Luckily there is a simple way to activate support for these protocols. The configuration file /etc/sysconfig/iptables-config has an entry called IPTABLES_MODULES. All you need to do is add the name of the required module to this line and restart the firewall. You can get a list of the available modules with this command:

```
ls /lib/modules/$(uname -r)/kernel/net/ipv4/netfilter/ip_conntrack_*.ko \
    /lib/modules/$(uname -r)/kernel/net/ipv4/netfilter/ip_nat_*.ko
```

The conntrack modules are used to help the stateful inspection detect related packets. The nat modules allow the related packets to be rewritten for NAT and masquerading. If you had a workstation with a firewall that blocked all incoming traffic, you would be unable to use a TFTP client unless you load the module ip_conntrack_tftp.

---

■ **Tip**: TFTP is the Trivial File Transfer Protocol. It is a UDP-based protocol which is often used for netbooting and configuring network equipment. It does not provide much security, so it is not suitable as a general-purpose file-sharing protocol.

---

# tcp_wrappers

The tcp_wrappers utility can perform some functions that are similar to netfilter. They will give you some new options in securing your services. Some of the differences between netfilter and tcp_wrappers are summarized here:

- tcp_wrappers can make decisions based on DNS names and usernames, but netfilter cannot.
- tcp_wrappers can pass information about who is connecting to the service, but netfilter cannot.
- tcp_wrappers can display a message banner when it rejects a connection, but netfilter cannot.
- Not all services support tcp_wrappers as they do with netfilter.
- Unlike netfilter, tcp_wrappers must accept a TCP connection before it can be rejected.

CentOS implements tcp_wrappers as a library, which many network services are linked to. Each service uses a unique name, which is referred to as its *daemon name*. Most of the time this is the same name as the executable that runs the service, but that is not always the case. Common daemon names are shown in Table 10-2.

*Table 10-2. Common tcp_wrappers Daemon Names*

| Service | Daemon Name |
|---------|-------------|
| ssh | sshd |
| ftp | vsftpd |
| sendmail | sendmail |
| nfs | mountd |
| telnet | in.telnetd |
| Authd | in.authd |
| Pop | Not supported. Use netfilter instead. |
| samba | Not supported. Configure smb.conf with hosts allow instead. |
| Httpd | Not supported. Configure httpd.conf with allow from instead. |

▓ **Tip**: Sendmail handles tcp_wrappers slightly differently from most services. If a connection is denied you can still talk to the server, but it will not accept any mail.

When the daemon accepts a connection from a client, the tcp_wrappers library reads the configuration files /etc/hosts.allow and /etc/hosts.deny to decide if the connection should be permitted. If the connection is permitted, the service will continue as normal. If the connection is not permitted, the connection is closed and the client is disconnected.

In addition to allowing and disallowing the connection, tcp_wrappers can also take actions of its own, such as logging the details of the connection, sending a message banner, altering the environment variables, and executing arbitrary programs. These provide a powerful way to change the behavior of a service without having to alter the service itself.

Although an application could have tcp_wrappers linked in statically, under CentOS a shared library called libwrap.so.0 is used. The presence of this library indicates that a service is capable of using tcp_wrappers. You can check this using the ldd command, as shown in Listings 10-11 and 10-12.

*Listing 10-11. Checking for tcp_wrappers Support*

```
# ldd /usr/sbin/sshd | grep libwrap
        libwrap.so.0 => /usr/lib/libwrap.so.0 (0x00e53000)
```

*Listing 10-12. A Service That Does Not Support tcp_wrappers*

```
# ldd /usr/sbin/httpd | grep libwrap
no output
```

You can also obtain a list of packages that require `tcp_wrappers` by querying the RPM database (discussed in Chapter 7), as shown in Listing 10-13.

*Listing 10-13. Querying tcp_wrappers Using rpm*

```
# rpm -q --whatrequires libwrap.so.0
tcp_wrappers-7.6-40.4.el5
sendmail-8.13.8-2.el5
quota-3.13-1.2.3.2.el5
conman-0.1.9.2-8.el5
nfs-utils-1.0.9-35z.el5_2
xinetd-2.3.14-10.el5
openssh-server-4.3p2-26.el5_2.1
```

One thing to remember is that when you use `xinet.d` to accept connections, `tcp_wrappers` is automatically available to all services. By default, the daemon name used will be the name of the executable that implements the service. You can override the default by using the `libwrap` service configuration attribute, as shown in Listing 10-14.

*Listing 10-14. Example xinet.d Service, /etc/xinetd.d/telnet*

```
# default: on
# description: The telnet server serves telnet sessions; it uses \
#       unencrypted username/password pairs for authentication.
service telnet
{
        disable = no
        flags           = REUSE
        socket_type     = stream
        wait            = no
        user            = root
        server          = /usr/sbin/in.telnetd
        log_on_failure  += USERID
        libwrap         = telnet
}
```

---

▨ **Note:** The use of telnet is strongly discouraged. It is used in this demonstration as a simple service for learning about network security. On a live network you should use SSH, which is a secure replacement for the telnet service.

---

When you configure tcp_wrappers you must maintain two configuration files. To reduce the complexity of this, it is suggested that you use either a mostly closed or a mostly open configuration rather than mixing some allow rules and some deny rules. In this way you only need to add your rules to a single file. As in netfilter, a mostly closed configuration will deny all connections except those that you specifically allow. A mostly open configuration will allow all connections except those you explicitly deny. It is recommended that you use a mostly closed configuration to retain fine control over who may connect to your server. Listings 10-15 and 10-16 illustrate how to implement each type.

*Listing 10-15. /etc/hosts.deny for a Mostly Closed Configuration*

```
ALL: ALL
```

*Listing 10-16. - /etc/hosts.allow for a Mostly Open Configuration*

```
ALL: ALL
```

Rules for tcp_wrappers are composed of three parts separated by a colon (:). The first part is a list of daemon names as discussed earlier. The second part is a list of which clients to match. They are often identified by IP address but DNS hostnames and usernames can also be used. Some examples are shown in Table 10-3. The third part is an optional list of shell commands to execute. The rules are processed in order, first from /etc/hosts.allow and then from /etc/hosts.deny. The first rule that matches will be used to decide whether to allow or deny the connection, depending on which file the rule comes from. Each list is made up of one or more entries separated by a space or a comma.

*Table 10-3. Examples of tcp_wrappers Client Identifiers*

| Identfier | Description |
| --- | --- |
| 192.168.3.20 | Match a single IP address |
| 192.168.3. | Match a class C IP subnet |
| 192.168.3.0/255.255.255.0 | Match an IP subnet with explicit netmask |
| 192.168.3.20, 192.168.3.21 | Match multiple IP addresses |
| wrkstn1-manila.example.com | Match based on full DNS name |
| .expample.com | Match based on DNS domain |
| ALL | Match all clients |
| LOCAL | Match hostnames without a domain component (localhost) |
| KNOWN | Match IP addresses that have a valid reverse DNS entry |
| UNKNOWN | Match IP addresses that do not have a reverse DNS entry |
| EXCEPT | Used in combination with the other identifiers to reverse the match |

You can also use tcp_wrappers to check what is known as Reverse DNS. Normal forward DNS is used to convert a hostname into an IP address. Reverse DNS is a technique that allows you to convert an IP address into a hostname, and tcp_wrappers can take the IP address of a connection and convert it back into a hostname. It will then take that hostname and look it up in the DNS. If that returns the same IP address, then the reverse DNS is considered to be valid. Not all hostnames and IP addresses have reverse DNS, which can cause problems if you are relying on it.

With some services it is possible to require a certain client username as well as specifying a client identifier, for example chivas@.example.com will allow user chivas from any host with a DNS host name ending with example.com. To find out which user is connecting, tcp_wrappers performs an ident lookup, which involves making a new connection back to the client machine and asking which user is connecting. This process is not very secure so is not commonly used. It can also introduce a long delay while the lookup is performed.

> ▦ **Note:** If you want to perform username-based restrictions, the client machine must be running the ident service. You can install this service with the command yum install authd.

The identifier EXCEPT should be used in combination with other identifies. For example, to permit connections from anywhere but a specific IP address you could use ALL EXCEPT 192.168.3.20.

You can also use comments throughout the configuration files, which provides a convenient way to explain what the rules are doing. Listing 10-17 illustrates a commented /etc/hosts.allow file.

*Listing 10-17. An Example /etc/hosts.allow File*

```
# Allow all local traffic
ALL: LOCAL : severity notice
# Allow only a certain user to ssh
ssh: chivas@.example.com
# Allow internal workstations to ftp
in.ftp: 192.168.3.
# Allow email from servers which have properly configured DNS entries
sendmail: KNOWN
```

When tcp_wrappers does not work as expected, it can be difficult to track down the problem. After checking that your entry in /etc/hosts.allow is correct, the next place to look is in the log files. Each application logs these messages in different ways, so depending on the application, you need to check /var/log/messages, /var/log/secure, and /var/log/maillog.

# Centralized Logging

Many services under CentOS use a standard logging system called *syslog*. You are probably familiar with the log files located in /var/log. Many of these are controlled by syslog. Each service that uses syslog must nominate a *facility* to indicate the type of service it is. There are not enough facilities for each service to have its own unique value, so many services may use the same value. For example, sendmail and dovecot both use the mail facility because they both process email. There are also a number of generic facilities, named local0 thru local7. Under CentOS, some of these are already allocated but you are free to alter them if required. Table 10-4 shows the available facilities.

*Table 10-4. syslog Facilities*

| Facility | Usage |
| --- | --- |
| authpriv | Used for security and sensitive authorization messages |
| cron | Used by the cron and at services |
| daemon | Used by generic services that do not have a dedicated facility |
| ftp | Used by any FTP service |
| kern | Used by messages generated by the kernel |
| lpr | Used by the printing subsystem |
| mail | Used by mail services |
| news | Used by the USENET news service |
| syslog | Used by the syslog service |
| user | Generic user-generated messages |
| uucp | Used by the UUCP subsystem |
| local0 | Available for local customization |
| local1 | Available for local customization |
| local2 | Available for local customization |
| local3 | Available for local customization |
| local4 | Used by clustering software |
| local5 | Used by SpamAssassin, an open source mail filter |
| local6 | Available for local customization |
| local7 | Used for boot time messages |

Each message sent to syslog is also tagged with a *priority*. The priority indicates the importance of the message from debug information thru emergency messages. The available priorities are show in Table 10-5. The priority of a message is determined by the author of the service. Although each priority has a description, there are no hard and fast rules for selecting a priority, and relying heavily on them should be avoided. Generally all priorities from Information and above are of interest and are logged.

*Table 10-5. syslog Priorities*

| Priority | Description | Example |
|---|---|---|
| Debug | Unimportant unless you are debugging a specific problem | A hexadecimal dump of a packet. |
| Information | General information message | A service has accepted a connection. |
| Notice | Normal significant condition | The kernel has detected an unknown piece of hardware. |
| Warning | Warning condition | An operation has failed but will be retried. |
| Error | Error condition | A service has crashed. |
| Critical | Critical condition | File system corruption has been detected. |
| Alert | Condition requiring immediate action | A RAID disk failure has been detected. |
| Emergency | System unusable | The system is overheating. |

When the message is saved to the log file it is also saved with a timestamp and the name of the host that generated the message. Listing 10-18 shows some sample log entries from /var/log/messages and /var/log/secure. Note that the message does not indicate the priority or the facility that was used when the message was sent.

*Listing 10-18. Sample Log Messages*

```
Mar 20 17:12:26 acer shutdown[4215]: shutting down for system reboot
Mar 20 17:14:30 acer kernel: Using APIC driver default
Mar 20 17:14:30 acer kernel: pnp: 00:09: ioport range 0x400-0x4bf could not be reserved
Mar 20 17:14:30 acer kernel: r8169: eth0: link up
Mar 20 17:14:43 acer dhclient: DHCPREQUEST on eth0 to 192.168.2.1 port 67
Mar 21 20:09:10 acer login: pam_unix(login:session): session opened for user↵
 root by LOGIN(uid=0)
Mar 21 20:51:58 acer sshd[14837]: error: Bind to port 22 on 0.0.0.0 failed:  ↵
 Address already in use.
Mar 21 20:52:09 acer groupadd[14854]: new group: name=ecryptfs, GID=105
```

# Configuring the Server to Receive Logs

It is possible to send syslog messages over the network to a central log processing server. To enable the reception of log messages on the server you must edit the configuration file /etc/sysconfig/syslog and add the -r option to SYSLOGD_OPTIONS, as shown in Listing 10-19.

*Listing 10-19. /etc/sysconfig/syslog Edited to Allow Remote Logging*

```
# Options to syslogd
# -m 0 disables 'MARK' messages.
# -r enables logging from remote machines
# -x disables DNS lookups on messages recieved with -r
# See syslogd(8) for more details
SYSLOGD_OPTIONS="-m 0 -r"
# Options to klogd
# -2 prints all kernel oops messages twice; once for klogd to decode, and
#    once for processing with 'ksymoops'
# x disables all klogd processing of oops messages entirely
# See klogd(8) for more details
KLOGD_OPTIONS="-x"
#
SYSLOG_UMASK=077
# set this to a umask value to use for all log files as in umask(1).
# By default, all permissions are removed for "group" and "other".
```

You must then restart the syslog service with the command service syslog restart. Check the file /var/log/messages for the message syslogd 1.4.1: restart (remote reception). If you do not see that message, check that you have edited the file and restarted the service correctly.

If you have already enabled your firewall, then you must add an entry to allow the syslog messages to be received. If you have used system-config-securitylevel, then you can add the port syslog protocol UDP. If you have customized your firewall rules, then you will need to add a rule similar to this:

```
-A RH-Firewall-1-INPUT -i eth0 -s 192.168.3.0/24 \
 -p udp -m udp --dport 514 -j ACCEPT
```

---

■ **Tip**: syslog uses the UDP protocol, which is connectionless. This type of protocol is more susceptible to spoofing or fake IP address information. If you have multiple interfaces, you should specify the interface on which you expect to receive the traffic.

---

After making the configuration changes, remember to activate your new firewall configuration with the command service iptables start. You should now be ready to configure the clients.

## Configuring the Client to Send Logs

Configuring the client requires a simple edit to the /etc/syslog.conf configuration file. All that is required is to add this line to the file

```
*.info          @servername
```

Once the file has been edited you must restart the syslog daemon with the command service syslog reload.

You can test the remote logging with the logger command: echo "Test" | logger. This will cause the message Test to be written to the local /var/log/messages log file and sent over the network to the log server, where it will also be written to the /var/log/messages log file.

The configuration entry *.info will tell the syslog service to send messages from all facilities with a priority of info or higher to the specified log server. You can, of course, alter this to send whichever log entries you want, but sending all messages in this way is simple and still allows the remote log server to separate the logs if required. If you have multiple log servers you can add multiple entries, one for each server. Listing 10-20 shows how you can send mail logs to one server called maillogs and all other messages to a server called logs.

*Listing 10-20. Example syslog.conf Entries*

```
mail.* @maillogs.example.com
*.info;mail.none @logs.example.com
```

░ **Tip**: You can use the logger command from your own scripts to send messages to the log server. See its man page for more details.

# Summary

In this chapter we have looked at the basic CentOS firewall, which uses netfilter. We also looked at how to build and save custom rules for an advanced firewall. We saw how netfilter can enable your server to act as a router and use masquerading to share in Internet connection.

We then looked at using tcp_wrappers, which can restrict services based on DNS information and username as well as IP details. Finally we looked at centralized logging using syslog.

In the next chapter we will look at setting up commonly used services such as OpenSSH, DHCP, and DNS for your network and at using Squid as a web proxy.

# CHAPTER 11

■■■

# Network Services

Networking is a strong attribute of Linux, which was designed from the start to integrate with networks. It can provide a range of network services such as secure remote access, proxy servers, and remote file sharing. When you are tasked with creating a robust network with CentOS, you will find that it has all the tools you need, thanks to its Linux roots.

In this chapter, you will learn how to set up the network services most commonly needed in a networked environment with CentOS. These include secure remote access service with OpenSSH, automatic network information distribution with DHCP, synchronized time with NTP, host lookups with DNS, and web caching with Squid. With CentOS, you will also come to see how manageable it is to assemble these required network services.

## OpenSSH

One of the common remote administration tools available for connecting to Unix or Linux computers is telnet. This tool allows the administrator to send commands using a remote terminal after specifying a user name and password. However, telnet is vulnerable to sniffing attacks, because it sends information in plain form without any encryption and was designed in 1969 for use on secure networks, where cracking and sniffing weren't a problem. The same is true of rlogin and rcp. Security only became an issue much later.

To fix this problem, the computer community began to create a secure alternative for remote administration. One of the early solutions was designed by Tatu Ylonen and is called Secure Shell (SSH), which provides encryption to a connected session. SSH utilizes public-key cryptography to authenticate users. Today, the prominent open source implementation of the SSH protocol is called OpenSSH and is maintained by the OpenBSD community.

With OpenSSH, you will be able to connect to remote machines securely and transfer files with encryption if those machines also support the SSH protocol. By default, CentOS has the remote administration tool for OpenSSH, the ssh command. This allows you to connect from the machine you are currently on to one running an SSH server.

You are going to use the latest version of the SSH protocol, version 2. This version of ssh is modified to prevent attackers from inserting additional data on a secure connection.

## The OpenSSH Configuration File

You control the way the OpenSSH server operates through its configuration file, sshd_config. This file is located in /etc/ssh, and you can view the contents using a text editor. You can include directives such as specifying the interface the OpenSSH daemon must listen on when it is running or how long each user can remain logged in while connected to the server. To specify a directive in the configuration file, follow this syntax:

```
directive_name value
```

where *directive_name* is the name of the directive and *value* is the argument you want to use with that directive. The names of the directives are case-insensitive, but the arguments you specify are case-sensitive. Putting a hash sign (#) in front of a line will make it a comment to be ignored by OpenSSH.

For example, if you want to let OpenSSH listen to a different port number such as 33425 instead of the default port number 22, you will use the Port directive, like this:

```
Port 33425
```

Then restart the OpenSSH server if it is running by using service sshd restart.

---

■ **Note:** If you change some of the OpenSSH directives that can affect connectivity, such as Port, be sure you also include the proper firewall rules so that the new value of the directive can be used by network clients. In the default firewall rules included in CentOS, only the default port number is allowable for the SSH clients.

---

There are many options available in the default configuration file, and some of those are commented out. You can run the OpenSSH server without doing anything on the configuration file and try to use it for practice.

The OpenSSH server is installed by default and is started when you boot your system. If it did not start, you can do it manually by running service sshd start.

## Connecting to the OpenSSH Server

You now have a running OpenSSH server on your system, and it is time to test whether you can connect to it locally. Once the connection is successful, you will see how you can connect to other OpenSSH servers with the ssh and scp commands next.

To connect to a remote computer using ssh, use the following syntax:

```
ssh user@remote_machine [-p port_number]
```

where *user* is the remote user to use in connecting to the remote host, and *remote_machine* can be a valid host name if you have a DNS server properly setup or its IP address if you know it. If you know that the OpenSSH server you are connecting to listens to a different port number, you have to use the –p flag to specify it. As an exercise, try connecting to your own computer as the root user by using the following command:

```
ssh root@localhost
```

In this command, you are making an SSH connection to your computer, localhost, using the default port. The default port is automatically used if you do not specify a different port number using the –p flag during connection. If you want to connect to a remote computer that is OpenSSH-enabled, you can do that by supplying that machine's host name or IP address in the remote_machine part of the command. For example, if you want to connect as the joel user on an OpenSSH-enabled computer named pusa using the default port, you can use ssh joel@pusa.

You will be prompted to either accept or reject a fingerprint value. You can type "yes" here for now to connect. Once you have successfully logged in, the user name in the shell prompt will change to the remote user you have specified during the connection process. After you have finished the required remote administration work, you can leave the session by typing exit.

## Copying Files Securely with scp

You can transfer files securely with OpenSSH by using its scp utility. The syntax of transferring a file from your machine to the remote follows:

**scp** [-P port_number] [-r] **your_file** user@remotemachine:**target_directory**

where *your_file* is the file you want to transfer, and *user* is the remote user you want to receive the file. You can also copy directories by using the optional -r flag. As in the ssh command, *remotemachine* can be either the actual host name of the remote machine or its IP address; what's new here is that after the colon, you specify the directory where you want your transferred file to reside on the remote machine. Again as in ssh, if you know that the OpenSSH server is listening to a port number other than the default, you need to use the -P flag to tell scp which port to use. Let us assume you want to transfer a file called myfile to a remote computer called pusa that has an OpenSSH server listening at 33425. The file should be placed in the home directory of root. To do that, you use the following command:

```
scp -P 33423 myfile root@pusa:/root
```

You have to make sure that the directory of the remote machine you intend to transfer your file exists before sending it. Otherwise, scp will complain that the remote machine does not have the directory you want to use as a drop-off of your file.

## OpenSSH Keys

The previous ssh command and scp commands you have used enabled you to have a secure remote session and copy files with encryption on your local SSH server. The same will be done if you are going to use both ssh and scp to another remote SSH server. This is possible because of the use of public-key cryptography. With public-key cryptography, a pair of keys is created to encrypt and decrypt data. The first is called the private key and the second is called the public key. During the installation of your CentOS system, your SSH server created two private keys and two public keys, and it placed them in the /etc/ssh directory. A private and public key pair is created for both RSA and DSA algorithms to support connections that will use either algorithm.

The private key is used to encrypt and decrypt data during a connection and must be kept by the SSH server. This key must never be distributed, because whoever has it will be able to encrypt and decrypt data as that server, and security will be compromised. The private keys of the SSH server are ssh_host_dsa_key and ssh_host_rsa_key. The former uses the DSA algorithm while the latter uses RSA.

The public key is used to encrypt data that can only be decrypted by its associated private key. This key is fine to be distributed to allow SSH clients to encrypt data that can be decrypted by the server they are connected to. The ssh_host_dsa_pub.key file is the server's public key using the DSA algorithm and ssh_host_rsa_pub.key is the server's public key using the RSA algorithm.

If you want to change the SSH server's private key and public key, you have to make your own using the steps in **Making your own keys** section in this chapter and place those inside the /etc/ssh directory. Then use the HostKey directive to specify the new file that contains your new private key.

For example, if you created a new RSA private key called susi.key and its associated public key, susi_pub.key in /etc/ssh, you would use the HostKey directive like this:

```
HostKey /etc/ssh/susi.key
```

Do not forget to specify the full path of the key for the HostKey to locate the new private key file. Making a new set of keys on a fixed interval will increase your SSH server's security and is important if the current private key is stolen.

## OpenSSH Fingerprints

Earlier, when you connected to your local SSH server, you were asked if you want to accept or reject the local SSH server host because of an unknown fingerprint. The result is similar to Listing 11-1.

*Listing 11-1. The SSH client asking for your connection opinion*

```
[root@localhost ~]# ssh root@localhost
The authenticity of host 'localhost (127.0.0.1)' can't be established.
RSA key fingerprint is b4:d5:3e:81:02:b2:80:8c:dc:c1:c0:c5:0d:eb:f8:6e.
Are you sure you want to continue connecting (yes/no)?
```

The value b4:d5:3e:81:02:b2:80:8c:dc:c1:c0:c5:0d:eb:f8:6e is your SSH server's fingerprint, which is used by your SSH client to check the authenticity of the server. This happens if you connect to an SSH server for the first time. The fingerprint is derived from the remote server's public key.

Included with the fingerprint are the host's name or IP address, the type of encryption algorithm used by its public key (RSA), and the question for the user if he wants to accept it. If you accept the fingerprint by typing "yes," the public key of the local SSH server is saved in the known_hosts file inside the .ssh directory of your home directory. The next time you connect to your local SSH server and you have its public key, you will not be asked again for fingerprint verification. Your SSH client will be able to derive the fingerprint value of your local SSH server's public key in the known_hosts file and compare it with the one being sent by the server during the connection attempt by the user for a match. The same process will apply if you are going to connect to another SSH server.

## Getting the Fingerprint Value

In the following example, you play the role of the client trying to connect to the SSH server on 192.168.1.104. The server's administrator gave you a copy of his SSH server's public key contained in the ssh_host_rsa_key.pub file and you want to know if the fingerprint value derived from that file matches the one being shown on your prompt. To check whether the fingerprint value matches, you are going to use the ssh-keygen command. The syntax is

ssh-keygen -l -f given_public_key_file

where -l informs ssh-keygen to get the fingerprint value of the given_public_key_file being pointed to by the -f flag. After a successful run, you will see the output formatted like this:

size **fingerprint_value** public_key_file encryption_method

where *size* is the actual size of the public key, *fingerprint_value* is the fingerprint value of the key, *public_key_file* is the file that was used, and *encryption_method* is the method used to encrypt the key.

This is the sample output of my run on ssh-keygen. The important part is the highlighted section:

**2048 b4:d5:3e:81:02:b2:80:8c:dc:c1:c0:c5:0d:eb:f8:6e ssh_host_rsa_key.pub (RSA)**

Use the value you get in the second part of the output to match with the fingerprint shown by your ssh client. If it matches, it is safe to connect; otherwise, don't.

## The known_hosts File

After making a successful connection to an SSH server, the SSH client will store the remote host's public key inside the known_hosts file in the user's .ssh directory. This file will serve as a reference to the public keys it has collected from the SSH servers you have connected to. The SSH client will be able to derive the fingerprint values from this file when connecting to a server for verification.

In case the public key and fingerprint value of a server has changed, the SSH client will issue a warning to the user and prevent the connection. The warning includes the offending line number, and you have to keep a note of it. This is for security purposes, and the first thing to do is to ask the server administrator if the SSH keys actually changed. If they did, you have to ask for the new public key and keep it for validation. Next, with the offending line number recorded from the warning earlier, open up the known_hosts file and find the line, then remove it. Reconnect to the server with the new public key and have the fingerprint validated as before.

## Making Your Own Keys

To create your own private and public keys, you will use the ssh-keygen command:

```
ssh-keygen [-t encryption_type]
```

The –t flag tells what kind of encryption you want to use for the keys. Running ssh-keygen without any arguments will create the private and public keys using and encrypt it using the RSA algorithm. This is the same as running ssh-keygen -t RSA. If you want to use DSA, you will run the command using ssh-keygen -t DSA.

---

■ **Note:** You'll learn more about RSA and DSA in Chapter 9, "Creating Digital Certificates."

---

As an example, you can run ssh-keygen without any arguments to create your first RSA private and public key pair. The keys will be created and ssh-keygen will prompt you for where to save the private key and the public key. Accept the default, inside the .ssh directory of your home directory (/root/.ssh). The private key will be created in that directory and you will be asked for a filename. The default id_rsa is fine for now. Next, you will be asked for a passphrase. A passphrase is the password for the private key and it is recommended that you assign one. This will protect the key from being decoded easily if it is stolen. Finally, the public key that can be distributed is created. This is named as the private key but with the .pub extension added (id_rsa.pub). That is the key you are going to give to those selected users you want to allow to connect to the SSH server.

There are other files that can be used inside the ssh directory and you can find out more about them in the man pages of ssh.

# The DHCP Server

Dynamic Host Configuration Protocol (DHCP) is used to give network information to a machine attempting to connect to a network. Network information includes host names and IP addresses, for example. If you have a working DHCP server running, you do not have to assign the required network information manually to each machine of your network, provided they are all configured to send DHCP requests. You can have your CentOS serve as the DHCP server in your network.

To send network information, DHCP follows a sequence of steps in both providing and accepting network information. As shown in Figure 11-1, the interaction involves five messages: DHCPDISCOVER, DHCPOFFER, DHCPREQUEST, DHCPNAK and DHCPACK.

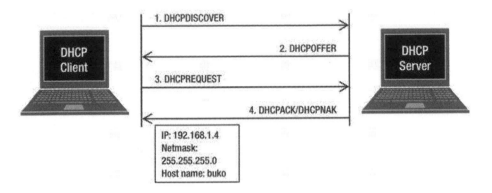

*Figure 11-1. The interaction for network information*

Here is the process outlined in the figure. Assuming a DHCP server is running on the network, a machine that is configured for DHCP joins it physically by getting a network cable connected to its Ethernet card. First, the machine announces that it needs network information to fully join the network. It sends a broadcast query (DHCPDISCOVER) and hopes that a running DHCP server will receive it. Second, the DHCP server receives the broadcast query from the new machine and in turn sends an offer (DHCPOFFER) to the machine. This offer contains the network information needed to connect to the network. Third, the new machine accepts the offer and broadcasts a request (DHCPREQUEST) back to the server. Because the request is broadcast, any other DHCP server will prevent itself from sending new offers to that machine. Finally, the request reaches the DHCP server that made the offer, which accepts it (DHCPACK). The client in turn will configure its Ethernet card to the network information that the DHCP server sent, such as IP addresses and gateway IP. If the server has no free network information in its pool, a DHCPNAK is given back to the client.

The DHCP process can be helpful also when machines on the network need to be replaced. When the new machines are configured to understand DHCP, they can communicate with your running DHCP server and grab network information to join the network immediately.

## Setting Up the DHCP Server

The DHCP server is not included in the default install of CentOS. You will have to install it manually by entering

```
yum install dhcp
```

That will put the configuration files and tools, including the DHCP server binary called dhcpd, in the system.

■ **Caution:** Setting up your own DHCP server on a corporate LAN, for example, is likely to cause a huge outage and plenty of disruption. Be sure to plan your DHCP installation to avoid IP conflicts and deploy it in smaller, manageable networks.

## The DHCP Configuration File

DHCP has a configuration file that you can use to control the dhcpd server process and the way network information will be distributed. This file is called dhcpd.conf and is located in the /etc directory. The file is a free-form text file where you can put statements that will control the server. The statements are divided into two types: parameters and declarations. Parameter statements are commands that tell what you want the dhcpd server process to do, such as specifying the domain name your intended clients should use or whether your server must always be followed by your clients when they enter your network. Declaration statements are used to define the network that your clients will use, provide the IP addresses that can be assigned to clients, or apply a group of parameters to a group of declarations.

Parameter statements can also be seen as simple statements, because they are terminated by a semicolon and are contained in a single line. In contrast, declaration statements can have a body that can contain multiple parameter statements and is enclosed in curly braces. Declaration statements do not end with a semicolon.

Comments are specified by putting a hash sign (#) in front of a line. This will cause dhcpd to ignore that statement. You can use comments for notes when your configuration file caters to multiple networks later.

For our example, we will create a configuration file that describes the following for our network.

1.  The network will represent ten machines in the IP address range of 192.168.1. In the network, three machines will be given special roles: the DHCP server (your computer), the gateway server, and the domain name server.

2.  The gateway server will have the IP address 192.168.1.1, the DHCP server will have the IP address 192.168.1.2, and the domain name server will have the IP address 192.168.1.3.

3.  The remaining IP addresses are prepared for the other machines that will join this network.

Open the dhcpd.conf file in /etc using a text editor and you will find that the file contains only comments. You will add the required parameter and declaration statements to represent the network requirements above. Put the contents of Listing 11-2 in the configuration file.

*Listing 11-2. The Parameter and Declaration Statements for Our Fictional Network*

```
# Global section

ddns-update-style none;
option routers 192.168.1.1;
option domain-name-servers 192.168.1.3;

subnet 192.168.1.0 netmask 255.255.255.0 {
```

```
# Local section

    range 192.168.1.4 192.168.1.10;
}
```

In Listing 11-2, you can see that there are three parameter statements and one declaration statement. Inside the declaration statement is a parameter statement that tells dhcpd what to do on that network.

The ddns-update-style parameter statement defines how dhcpd will handle dynamic DNS updates from the clients. If your domain name server allows clients to update its zone file, then newly added clients will be able to add themselves as resource records in the zone file. If they have successfully added themselves in the domain name server, the server can now resolve those machines when queries are made to them. For now, there is no need for you to do dynamic DNS updates; therefore, that option is set to none. You'll learn more about domain name servers and zone files later in this chapter.

The line

```
option routers 192.168.1.1;
```

tells the system to use 192.168.1.1 as the router or gateway IP address when it is handing network information to the new clients. This is the IP address that the clients will use in the gateway parameter of their operating system.

The line

```
option domain-name-servers 192.168.1.3;
```

assigns 192.168.1.3 as the primary domain name server that the clients will use when resolving host names and IP addresses when using the Internet and services while in the network. It is possible to add more domain name servers, and all you have to do is to separate them with a comma.

The declaration line

```
subnet 192.168.1.0 netmask 255.255.255.0
```

is where you describe the network that the dhcpd process will handle. You will have to specify the network and its subnet properly using the IP address and netmask notation. In this example, you declared that your dhcpd server will administer the 192.168.1.0 network for the 10 machines.

Inside the subnet declaration statement is a parameter statement that identifies the starting and ending IP addresses this declaration statement will use. Because ten machines have been assigned in your network, the first ten IP addresses have been given in the range. The starting and ending IP addresses of the range statement must be separated by a space and should end with a semicolon.

The configuration file is divided into two sections—the global section and the local section. The parameter statements in the global section are applied to the declaration statements. They are used in each local section if it does not override them. Any time a new machine joins the network, whatever values are assigned on the option routers and domain name servers will also be included in the network information given for that machine.

Each time you make changes to the configuration file, always reload the server to have those changes applied, by using service dhcpd restart.

## Assigning Fixed Addresses

DHCP allows you to assign fixed IP addresses and hostnames for certain machines. All you need to use is the host declaration statement, which has the following syntax:

```
host given_hostname {
```

```
        hardware ethernet target_MAC_address;
        fixed-address target_IP_address;
}
```

where *given_hostname* is the hostname you want to assign for the machine, *given_MAC_address* is the MAC address of the target machine, and *target_IP_address* is the IP address that you want to give for that machine. You can get the IP address and MAC address of a Linux computer using the `ifconfig` command. Assuming that you want to assign 192.168.1.4 as buko for the client that has the MAC address of 00:16:3E:6B:BC:16 and 192.168.1.5 as saging for the client with the MAC address 00:16:3E:3F:2D:BF, you will use the host declaration statements shown in Listing 11-3.

*Listing 11-3. The Host Declaration Statements for the Target Machines*

```
host buko {
    hardware ethernet 00:16:3E:6B:BC:16;
    fixed-address 192.168.1.4;
}
host saging {
    hardware ethernet 00:16:3E:3F:2D:BF;
fixed-address 192.168.1.5;
}
```

Any time those machines with the given MAC addresses load, they will be assigned their hostnames and IP addresses. Make sure that the additional host declaration statements that you will make do not contain IP addresses that will conflict with any subnet range in the configuration file, or DHCP will become confused and will not run.

---

■ **Note:** Subnet declaration statements are for dynamically assigned IP addresses, while host declarations are for statically assigned IP addresses.

---

## Organizing with Groups

Later, when your configuration file grows because of additional machines and fixed IP addresses, you need to have a way to organize the statements. Fortunately, there is a declaration statement just for that purpose, called the group declaration. The group declaration has the following syntax

```
group {
    parameter_statements;

    declaration_statements {
        parameter_statements;
    }
}
```

You can enclose parameter statements and declaration statements in a group declaration statement. There can be more than one group statement in the configuration file, and you can nest them if required. For example, suppose a new router with the IP address 192.168.1.20 and two new domain name servers with the IP addresses 192.168.1.18 and 192.168.1.19, respectively, have been added to the network. These two machines will be used by the buko and saging computers only. To create that setup, you will use the group declaration statement shown in Listing 11-4.

*Listing 11-4. The group Declaration Statement for the Hosts with Fixed Addresses*

```
group
{    option routers 192.168.1.20;
     option domain-name-servers 192.168.1.18,192.168.1.19;
     host buko {
         hardware ethernet 00:16:3E:6B:BC:16;
         fixed-address 192.168.1.4;
     }
     host saging {
         hardware ethernet 00:16:3E:3F:2D:BF;
         fixed-address 192.168.1.5;
     }
}
```

Whenever those machines load, they will use the new router and new domain name servers assigned for them only.

To find more statements available to use, consult the man pages for dhcpd.conf.

# The NTP Server

When you are about to begin providing any kind of service using your CentOS installation, it is highly recommended that you put in a facility to synchronize time. You might think that the local timestamps of the individual machines are sufficient, but there will be cases where that would be inadequate. For example, try to check the time set on your machine against your friend's laptop. It is most likely that the both of you may have the same hour but the minutes may well be different. Now ask yourself which time is the most correct one, between the two machines? You can declare yours as official, but the same could be said by your friend.

That's a very simple example, but it can extend to production systems that require accurate time. Some applications include system log servers, database replication, and time tracking systems. When some intruder messes with your system, the first thing to ask is when it actually happened. If you do not have a synchronization scheme available, it would be awkward to report to the authorities that the attack took place at your machine's time. This would make investigation difficult because no one is sure if the system remained intact after the attack.

The answer to this problem is to use Network Time Protocol (NTP) as the mechanism to synchronize timestamps in your machines. Network Time Protocol was designed to synchronize time through the network using a common time scale. The time scale is usually in Coordinated Universal Time (UTC) by default.

NTP is organized according to levels, known as *strata*. Strata on the highest level are the real source of synchronized time data. Public time servers reside on that level and are connected to stratum 0 devices such as atomic clocks, GPS clocks, and other types of radio clocks. Strata one level lower from the highest refer time to them. These are also known as second-level strata. The more strata are concatenated, the lower they become. The lowest stratum is 16, which is assigned to newly run servers. Figure 11-2 shows how the strata are grouped into levels.

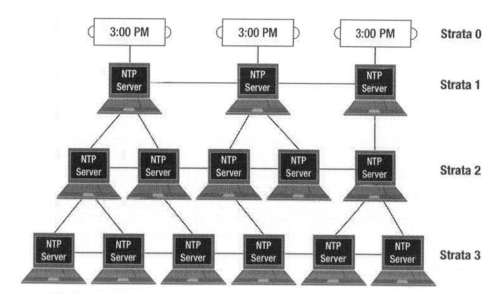

*Figure 11-2. The time servers starting from stratum 0 up to stratum 3. The levels can span up to 16 strata.*

It is not a strict rule that client time servers can refer only to machines a level higher than themselves as servers. There can also be servers residing on the same stratum that can distribute time data. For example, in a three-NTP machine setup, the first server receives its time data from a public time server. The second machine receives its time data from the first. The third machine gets its time data from the second machine. This in effect makes the second machine the server for the third machine.

But where do the client computers enter when we have a working NTP setup? Client machines can always have their own time servers and connect to the highest strata, but that can be overkill. It also can give inconsistent time stamps, it only works when the Internet connection is up, and it can create hard-to-find time discrepancies. Given the earlier example, our client machines can now set their operating systems to use one of the two time servers that are running on the network.

## NTP CONFIGURATION MODES

There are five association modes or configuration modes available for NTP, and each has its own uses:

1. **Client-Server**: One machine is set up to act as an NTP server, and another will be getting time data from that server as an NTP client. The NTP client is usually a local server in your network that provides time data to other machines.

2. **Symmetric active/passive**: NTP servers are configured to be peers to each other for redundancy. If both peers are present, they will send out symmetric active messages to update

237

each other. If one of the peers goes down, time data will still be available because the remaining server will continue to send it.

3.  **Broadcast/Multicast**: This configuration is usually deployed in Wide Area Networks.

4.  **Manycast**: A new feature for NTP version 4 that allows the server to be searched actively by a multicast client.

5.  **Orphan**: NTP can operate in this mode if there are no available time servers to connect to. It will use a local clock driver to simulate a UTC time source.

In this section, you will set up NTP to provide time data in three base configuration modes: client-server, symmetric, and broadcast. Install the NTP server and its tools by entering yum install ntp.

## Client-Server Mode

Using a text editor, open the main configuration file, which is called ntp.conf and located in /etc. Next, find the following entries:

```
server 0.centos.pool.ntp.org
server 1.centos.pool.ntp.org
server 2.centos.pool.ntp.org
```

Your NTP server is already configured as an NTP client when you install it. It gathers time data through the time servers declared by the server command. The server command can accept either the host name or the IP address of the time server it wishes to connect to. You add more time servers, for more availability, by selecting them from http://www.pool.ntp.org. For example, we want to add the time server ph.pool.ntp.org from the Philippines. All we need to do is add another server entry:

```
server 0.centos.pool.ntp.org
server 1.centos.pool.ntp.org
server 2.centos.pool.ntp.org
server ph.pool.ntp.org
```

After adding the new entry, save the file and start the NTP process:

```
service ntpd start
```

or restart if you have the ntpd process running already. If you want to see how things run in real time by watching the log files, you may instead use the following command:

```
ntpd -d
```

This will print out all of the activities NTP does during its operation. You can stop the server by pressing Ctrl+C. When you have finalized things and are ready to put the server into a production environment, you can use the former command.

## Symmetric Active/Passive Mode

We will use another NTP server for this exercise. We will assume that the first NTP server has the IP address 192.168.1.104 and the second has 192.168.1.100. In order to introduce them to each other as peers for a symmetric active/passive setup, we will use the peer command in the configuration file. The peer command takes either the hostname or the IP address of its NTP peer as its argument.

Open the main configuration file of the first machine and add the following line at the bottom:

```
peer 192.168.1.100
```

Save the file. Restart the ntpd process afterward using service ntpd restart. Do the same with the second machine but using 192.168.1.104 as the peer command's argument.

After you've added the peer lines on both machines, they are now running in symmetric active/passive mode. If for some reason the first peer cannot reach any of its public time servers but the second one can, the former will request the latter for time data. The time data will then be distributed to its clients.

## Broadcast Mode

In our next setup, the first machine will play the role of the NTP server that has access to the public time servers, and the second will be the client NTP server. The first machine will broadcast the messages, while the second machine will listen to them. After receiving a message, the client will start to retrieve time data from the server. Therefore, the first machine will play the role of the server and the second machine the client.

1. Put a hash sign (#) in front of the peer command we added earlier. This will make it a comment so the ntpd process will ignore it: # peer 192.168.1.100

2. Add the following lines at the bottom:

   ```
   broadcast 192.168.1.255
   disable auth
   ```

3. The broadcast command will send out messages on the network it has been assigned to. In the example, it will announce to every NTP client that starts with the IP address 192.168.1. The disable auth line will let us run the setup without authentication for practice. By default, broadcasting requires security through the Autokey protocol. Save the configuration file and restart the server.

4. For the client, comment out all the server command entries in the configuration file. We will get the time data from the NTP server broadcasts.

5. Still on the client, comment out the peer command entry to ignore it. Then add the following at the bottom of the file:

   ```
   broadcastclient
   disable auth
   ```

The above lines will make the client listen for broadcast messages being sent by an NTP server without strict authentication for testing. Save the file and restart the ntpd process.

You can monitor the progress on how the client and server interact using ntpq's associations command. You'll have to wait a few minutes before you can see action on this one because both machines need to find each other.

## ntpq

You can monitor your running NTP servers using the the NTP query tool, ntpq. With ntpq, you can retrieve information about your NTP server such as its peers and the operations of the ntpd process. The ntpq tool can be run on the command line or in interactive mode. To run the ntpq tool in the command line, use the following syntax:

```
ntpq [given_command] [target_ntp_host]
```

where [*given_command*] is the command that you want to use with ntpq and [*target_ntp_host*] is the NTP server that you want to use ntpq with. Some of the commands that you can use with ntpq on the command line are –p and –i. The –p command makes ntpq print out the peers of the NTP server and –i forces it to run on interactive mode. Leaving out the [*target_ntp_host*] part will make ntpq run interactively on your local NTP server, as shown in Listing 11-5.

**Listing 11-5.** *The ntpq Prompt in Interactive Mode*

```
ntpq>
```

You can enter commands at this prompt to see how your ntpd process is running. For example, to find the peers of your NTP server, you can use the peers command to list them, as shown in Figure 11-3.

```
ntpq> associations

ind assID status  conf reach auth condition last_event cnt
===========================================================
  1 62519 9014    yes  yes   none   reject   reachable  1
  2 62520 9014    yes  yes   none   reject   reachable  1
  3 62521 9014    yes  yes   none   reject   reachable  1
  4 62522 9014    yes  yes   none   reject   reachable  1
  5 62523 9614    yes  yes   none  sys.peer  reachable  1
  6 62524 8000    yes  yes   none   reject
ntpq> █
```

**Figure 11-3.** *A Sample peers Command Output*

The peers output in Figure 11-3 shows the NTP peers of your server and their current state, like the remote peer's hostname or IP address, in the remote field and the stratum in the st column. You can learn more about the peers command in the ntpq man pages.

You can exit the ntpq interactive mode by typing quit or q.

# DNS

The Domain Name System or DNS is a distributed naming system to identify computers on a network. It was developed by the U.S. military to enable computers to have unique names to communicate with each other properly. Before DNS, a computer's hosts file (called HOSTS, for example) was the only way to identify computers by hostname on a network. This file must be updated regularly by hand to inform the computer when a host is added or removed from the network. Because of the manual updates, naming conflicts that can cause confusion among hosts are common. The hosts file is still present on modern operating systems to provide a way to identify computers if there is no DNS on a network. As an example, Linux uses the hosts file in the /etc directory.

To allow computers to have a unique name on DNS, the computer names are arranged on a hierarchy as an inverted tree. This is shown in Figure 11-4.

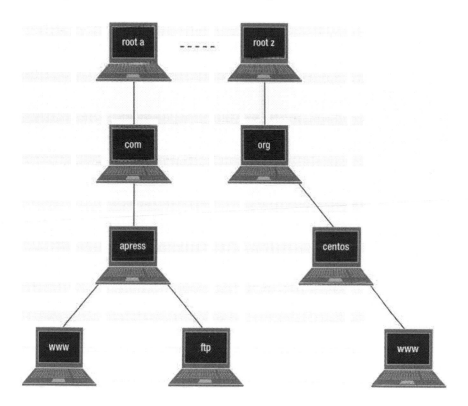

*Figure 11-4. A sample layout of the Domain Name System*

In Figure 11-4, each node is a host with a given name, called the *domain name*. All the domain names in the inverted tree form the *namespace* of the DNS. The domain name identifies not only the host, but the scope or domain it represents. For example, the domain name org identifies hosts that are based on an organization. The com domain name identifies hosts for commercial enterprises. Domain names must be unique horizontally on the tree. There cannot be two com names or two org names, for example, to avoid naming conflicts.

When reading names in the namespace, you start at the target node and then go up to the top. For example, the www node on the centos side becomes www ➤ centos ➤ org ➤ root servers or www.centos.org and root servers. That forms the fully qualified domain name or FQDN for that node.

Domains can have subtrees. For example, the com domain in the diagram has the apress.com domain as its subtree. The org domain also has its own subtree, the centos.org domain. The subtrees within a domain are called subdomains in DNS. These are the hosts related to the domain above them.

At the top level of the tree is a set of servers, called the *root servers,* that are maintained by the Internet Assigned Numbers Authority (IANA). The root servers are authoritative name servers that can give accurate answers for a DNS query. These computers serve as the starting point of a search when finding a host on DNS. They do not have names and are represented as a dot at the end. For example, the `www.centos.org` address shown earlier is actually read as `www.centos.org.`, and the dot is added when the search is about to start.

## Name Servers and Zones

The tree in Figure 11-4 consists of name servers and hosts. Name servers are software that is capable of translating domain names into IP addresses to locate hosts on DNS. They can also perform DNS queries to other name servers to find the accurate answers required in a DNS query. The software can contain host information on a domain that is maintained by an entity such as an organization or a corporation.

Domains and subdomains are usually maintained by an entity. These are called *zones* and contain host information about that entity. Using Figure 11-4, the `apress.com` domain is owned by the Apress publishing company, whose name server has host information for its web server (`www.apress.com`) and ftp server (`ftp.apress.com`). The root servers at the top are on the root zone.

## Name Resolution

Name resolution is used by name servers to find the correct host on the DNS. This is done by recursively querying the authoritative name servers until the accurate answer to the target host is reached. Here is a step-by-step process of how name resolution is used to a DNS query made by a client that wants to load a web page of `www.apress.com`:

1. Get the domain name and divide it at the dots. This will give the client's name server an idea on where to start the query. The FQDN `www.apress.com.` will become `www . apress . com .` after the division.

2. The client's name server will start the query at the root servers for the `com` domain name. In Figure 11-4, those are the name servers at the top, and they are represented by the rightmost dot on the divided FQDN. One of the root servers will give an authoritative answer on the query about the `com` domain name and will refer the client's name server on the `com` domain's name server.

3. The `com` domain's name server is queried next by the client's name server based on the authoritative answer from one of the root servers for the `apress.com` domain name. The `com` domain's name server has authoritative information about the `apress.com` domain and refers the client's name server to the name server of the `apress.com` domain.

4. The `apress.com` domain's name server is queried for the `www.apress.com` domain name by the client's name server. This time, the `apress.com` domain's name server has the host information for `www.apress.com` and returns that computer's IP address to the client's name server. That IP address will be given by the client's name server to the client that requested the query. Having the IP address, both the client and the `www.apress.com` computer will be able to communicate with each other. The web page requested will be sent to the client's web browser using the correct server on the `www.apress.com` computer, the web server.

This process is also used on other servers that require DNS such as those hosting ssh, http, and ftp. If you are going to have an Internet connection in your network, you should install and configure a DNS server. A local DNS server has several advantages; it will help you make faster DNS queries, provide a backup DNS server, and allow you to make your own master server for your zone. In the next section, you will use the tools from the Berkeley Internet Name Domain (BIND) package to set up your own DNS server. BIND is the open source implementation of the DNS and you can install its configuration files and binaries in your system by entering the yum install bind-chroot command as root. We are going to use the BIND package with chroot support to have a secure name server in your system. If an attacker manages to get into your system through BIND, they will only be able to see whatever is inside the assigned chroot directory of the bind-chroot package, /var/named/chroot.

## BIND Utilities

The main tools for running and administering BIND are rndc-confgen, rndc, and named. With these tools, you will be able to create configuration files that your DNS server can use to identify zones and administer the server for maintenance.

### rndc-confgen

The rndc-confgen command is used to generate rndc keys and configuration files for rndc and named. Running it without any arguments will produce output that contains the configuration files for both tools. You must redirect the output into a file and make the required changes to separate them. You'll learn more about this tool when you create your first type of name server.

### rndc

rndc is the command-line administration tool for named. You can control named by issuing commands with rndc, such as getting the status or reloading a zone, for example. The rndc tool uses the rndc.conf file, which is generated by rndc-confgen.

### named

named is the actual name server of the BIND utilities. It is used to create and resolve domains and it uses the configuration file called named.conf, which is also generated by the rndc-confgen tool. You will use named extensively in the DNS section of this chapter.

Additional tools are also included for testing forward and backward name resolution when performing lookups. These include nslookup, dig, and host, for example. Each of these tools will be discussed later when your name server is up and running.

## BIND Configuration Files

Before you can run named and rndc, you need to create their configuration files using the rndc-confgen tool. You will run rndc-confgen without any arguments and save the contents by redirecting them to a file. Do the following to create the configuration files.

**1.** Go to the /var/named/chroot/etc directory and run the following command:

```
rndc-confgen > rndc.conf
```

That will redirect the output into the file called rndc.conf.

Open the rndc.conf file using a text editor such as GEdit and browse the contents. The contents may look like Listing 11-6.

*Listing 11-6. The Configuration Files for rndc and named*

```
# Start of rndc.conf
key "rndckey" {
    algorithm hmac-md5;
    secret "9mt/YqgRTHjiA2H924sfyg==";
};
options {
    default-key "rndckey";
    default-server 127.0.0.1;
    default-port 953;
};
# End of rndc.conf

# Use with the following in named.conf, adjusting the allow list as needed:
# key "rndckey" {
#    algorithm hmac-md5;
#    secret "9mt/YqgRTHjiA2H924sfyg==";
# };
#
# controls {
#    inet 127.0.0.1 port 953
#        allow { 127.0.0.1; } keys { "rndckey"; };
# };
# End of named.conf
```

2. The file contains configuration files for both rndc and named. The configuration file for named is in the commented section below the line

    ```
    # End of rndc.conf
    ```

    and will be ignored by rndc when it is run. You will remove the commented named configuration file and put it into another file called named.conf. Using your text editor, cut the lines starting from

    ```
    # Use with the following in named.conf, adjusting the allow list as needed:
    ```

    until

    ```
    # End of named.conf
    ```

    Put those lines in a new text file called named.conf inside the /var/named/chroot/etc directory and save it. We will focus on this file later.

3. After you've done that, the rndc.conf file should look like Listing 11-7.

*Listing 11-7. The rndc.conf File*

```
# Start of rndc.conf
```

```
key "rndckey" {
    algorithm hmac-md5;
    secret "9mt/YqgRTHjiA2H924sfyg==";
};

options {
    default-key "rndckey";
    default-server 127.0.0.1;
    default-port 953;
};
# End of rndc.conf
```

Save the file.

**4.** The contents of the named.conf file are still commented with the hash symbols and you need to uncomment them so that named can read the commands. After those changes, the named.conf contents should look like Listing 11-8.

*Listing 11-8. The named.conf File*

```
# Use with the following in named.conf, adjusting the allow list as needed:
key "rndckey" {
    algorithm hmac-md5;
    secret "9mt/YqgRTHjiA2H924sfyg==";
};

controls {
    inet 127.0.0.1 port 953
        allow { 127.0.0.1; } keys { "rndckey"; };
};
# End of named.conf
```

Save the file and you are done.

## The Contents of rndc.conf

The contents of the rndc.conf file shown in Listing 11-7 contain two directives, key and options. Both directives are compound and contain options as arguments. In addition, both directives and options are terminated by a semicolon. Directives follow this syntax:

```
directive [directive_name] {
    option_1 option_1_value;
         :
    option_N option_N_value;
};
```

where *directive* is the directive you want to use, and *directive_name* is the name of the directive if it needs one. The value for the *directive_name* is usually enclosed in double quotes. The *options* and their values that are inside the directive are enclosed in curly braces. The options and directives are terminated by semicolons.

The key directive is used by rndc to identify the rndc key to use, so it is equal to the one being used by the target name server. The rndc key's name is "rndckey" and it uses the hmac-md5 algorithm to encrypt its secret key while connecting to the name server. The secret option holds the chosen algorithm's secret key and is encoded in base-64. Both the key name and the secret key value must be enclosed in double quotes.

The options directive tells rndc what additional options it will use while connecting to a name server. The contents of the directive include the server, key, and port that rndc will use while connecting. The default values specified in default-key, default-server, and default-port will be used when rndc is run without specifying explicit values for those arguments. The value for the default-key option must always be enclosed in double quotes.

Lines that are treated as comments have a hash symbol in front of them.

## The Contents of named.conf

The named.conf configuration file in Listing 11-8 is almost the same as the rndc.conf file, except that it is designed for the named domain name server. It also follows the syntax of the rndc.conf file when specifying directives.

---

■ **Note:** The include directive is an exception to this rule because it is a single-line directive.

---

The file also contains two directives, key and control. The key directive behaves the same as the one in rndc.conf and has the same value. This key is used by named to validate clients using rndc to connect to it. If the rndc client has the same key value as the named server, the former can administer the latter.

The controls directive is used by named to determine how to handle rndc clients trying to connect to it. The controls directive allows rndc connections made to the name server locally, and the client should use the "rndckey" value for a successful connection.

This file will contain additional directives later as you learn more about the different types of name servers that you can use.

With the two configuration files, we can now start creating our DNS servers using named.

## Caching DNS

A caching DNS is used to store domain name information that has been accessed recently. This is used to improve DNS query speeds over the network. For example, suppose someone using a freshly started caching DNS tries to visit the URL www.apress.com using a browser. The first run will usually be slow, because the caching DNS will do searches and translations for the target computer of the URL's domain name. Assuming the user visits the site again, he or she will be able to go there much faster because the search and translation information has been cached by the DNS and is immediately given to that user's web browser. Of course the cached information is only available when the caching DNS is running. When it goes out, along with it goes its stored information.

## The hints File

A hints file is required for any caching DNS to do its queries. This file contains the list of root name servers that it can use to start its search, based on the given query. You can get this file by downloading it from http://www.internic.net/zones/named.root or making one yourself using the tool called dig. If you prefer to make your own with dig, be sure to run it periodically to update the contents of the hints file.

Otherwise, the effectiveness of the caching DNS will slowly deteriorate because it is using old root server data in making answers to queries instead of the new root server data available.

The dig and nslookup utilities will prove to be useful in testing out your name servers and will be discussed next.

# dig

The domain information groper (dig) utility lets you interrogate domain name servers. It is flexible and can retrieve answers from the queried servers. The dig utility is often used for troubleshooting because it can show more details about a DNS query. You can also use dig to build a hints file for a caching DNS, as you will see later.

You can run dig by using the following syntax:

dig [-x] *target*

where *target* can either be a domain name or an IP address. Including the –x flag will make dig do a reverse lookup that will get the domain name from a given IP address. Omitting the –x flag will do a forward lookup that will get the IP address of the given domain name. For example, running a reverse lookup on the IP address 127.0.0.1 using dig -x 127.0.0.1 will produce the output shown in Listing 11-9.

*Listing 11-9. The Output of the dig Command*

```
; <<>> DiG 9.3.4-P1 <<>> -x 127.0.0.1
;; global options:  printcmd
;; Got answer:
;; ->>HEADER<<- opcode: QUERY, status: NOERROR, id: 1624
;; flags: qr aa rd ra; QUERY: 1, ANSWER: 1, AUTHORITY: 1, ADDITIONAL: 0

;; QUESTION SECTION:
;1.0.0.127.in-addr.arpa.                   IN      PTR

;; ANSWER SECTION:
1.0.0.127.in-addr.arpa. 86400    IN      PTR     localhost.

;; AUTHORITY SECTION:
0.0.127.in-addr.arpa.   86400    IN      NS      localhost.

;; Query time: 1 msec
;; SERVER: 127.0.0.1#53(127.0.0.1)
;; WHEN: Mon Aug 31 17:42:03 2009
;; MSG SIZE  rcvd: 77
```

This output has three parts. First is some information about the dig tool and the argument for the query. It also contains the global options used when it executed. Second is the answer from the query to the target IP address. The answer contains technical details of the query such as the question that was sent, the received answer, and the authoritative name server of that IP address that gave the answer. The last contains statistics about the query, such as how fast it was run and the size of the message.

## nslookup

The nslookup tool allows you to query DNS servers. It can show you the IP address of the domain name servers from the domain name you specify, or vice versa. The syntax for nslookup is

**nslookup** [*given*]

where *given* can be a fully qualified domain name or an IP address. Assuming you want to know the IP address of the domain www.apress.com, you will use nslookup like this:

nslookup www.apress.com

And the sample output is shown in Listing 11-10.

*Listing 11-10. The nslookup Output for www.apress.com*

```
Server:         127.0.0.1
Address:        127.0.0.1#53


Non-authoritative answer:
Name:   www.apress.com
Address: 66.212.129.45
```

Assuming you want to know the domain name server of the computer in your network with the IP address 192.168.1.7, you will use

nslookup 192.168.1.7

The output will resemble Listing 11-11.

*Listing 11-11. Doing nslookup on a Computer in Your Network*

```
Server:         127.0.0.1
Address:        127.0.0.1#53
7.1.168.192.in-addr.arpa        name = ns1.pvctoyfan.com.
```

## Configuring a Caching DNS

Take the following steps to configure a caching DNS server:

1. Create a hints file called db.cache using dig and place it inside the /var/named/chroot/var/named directory:

   dig @a.root-servers.net . ns > /var/named/chroot/var/named/db.cache

The contents of the db.cache hints file will be needed by named when it initializes itself. This will give a starting point for our caching name server for its searches at the public root servers.

2. Open the named.conf file in /var/named/chroot/etc and add the following entries:

```
options {
        directory "/var/named";
};

zone "." {
        type hint;
        file "db.cache";
};

zone "0.0.127.in-addr.arpa" {
        type master;
        file "db.127.0.0";
};
```

You added an options entry and two zone entries in your configuration file to complete your caching DNS. The options entry has a directory command that tells named where to look for additional files. Because we are using the bind-chroot package, the value given in the directory command is relative to the /var/named/chroot directory. In effect, the /var/named value becomes /var/named/chroot/var/named when named runs. The hints file, db.cache, is inside that directory. More commands can be used here, as you will see later in the other configurations.

The first zone entry tells named that whenever it searches for the public root servers, it must reference the contents of the db.cache file we created earlier. Note that we did not put the directory where it resides before db.cache, because that directory is already known by the server through the options entry.

The second zone entry is a must for any configuration because it tells named that our machine has its own name server to resolve itself and need not do outside queries for it. This is made possible because of the type master command. For example, if we query our default machine name localhost, our name server does not have to go outside our network to find out who owns the localhost name. It will instantly show our machine as the answer.

3. To complete this zone entry, you need to create another file, called db.127.0.0, and it must also be placed inside /var/named/chroot/var/named. Listing 11-12 shows the contents of the file.

*Listing 11-12. The Zone File for Your Local Name Server*

```
$TTL 1D
@                       IN      SOA     localhost.      root.localhost. (
                                1       ; Serial
                                3H      ; Refresh
                                2H      ; Retry
```

249

```
                               1W      ; Expire
                               1D)     ; Minimum TTL
                       NS         localhost.
1                      PTR     localhost.
```

This file contains the details of the second zone entry, which declares your machine as its own name server. The zone file contains the time-to-live variable and the start-of-authority statement for this domain. The attributes include the master DNS server (localhost) for this zone, the email of the admin of this zone (root.localhost.), and additional details about how long the slave servers should wait before connecting to this server for updates. This file also allows reverse name lookups. Reverse name lookups use numeric IP addresses in searching for machines on the Internet, in contrast to regular lookups, which use domain names. You'll learn more in the section on making your own domain.

4. Open the resolv.conf file and add the following at the top of the file:

```
name server 127.0.0.1
```

This line tells CentOS to first talk to our own name server before going anywhere else.

5. We're done! Next, run our name server by issuing

```
service named start
```

6. Try out a query using the nslookup command on www.apress.com:

```
nslookup www.apress.com
```

It will print out an answer like listing 11-13.

*Listing 11-13. Using nslookup on Your New Name Server*

```
Server:         127.0.0.1
Address:        127.0.0.1#53

Non-authoritative answer:
Name:   www.apress.com
Address: 66.211.109.45
```

7. Run the same command again.

The first time you ran the query on www.apress.com, it was a little slow in giving out the answer. But the second time is faster because our name server cached the query, and that is the one given to us. If you look closely at the output, you will see that it gave out a *nonauthoritative* answer. Any query done from a caching-only name server is considered nonauthoritative. So when you first do the query, it is stored in that file, and the second time the DNS server only has to look in the file.

■ **Note:** Only authoritative name servers can give authoritative answers, because their queries are not temporary, unlike caching name servers. You will make an authoritative name server later in this chapter.

For a taste of reverse lookups, try to run dig -x 127.0.0.1. It shows an authoritative answer because of the final zone entry in our current configuration, and there is no other name server that could have a better answer to where localhost is than our own.

## Configuring a Forwarder

It is common today for your ISP to have its own DNS ready for your use. To add a little more speed to your DNS, we will lighten the load on your server by handing whatever we can to the ISP's DNS. Their servers in return will retrieve our name server's queries and give the results back to us. This is advantageous because forcing our local server to do Internet-wide queries every time will be costly in bandwidth and time. Why not just request them from your ISP's DNS server, which is dedicated for that purpose? We will do this in this section.

Assume that you have two name servers owned by your ISP. These have the IP addresses 202.125.123.45 and 202.125.123.46. With these addresses, you can now forward requests to them and retrieve the answer without having your name server do all the hard work.

All we have to do is to add the following in our named.conf inside the options clause:

```
forward first;
forwarders {
    202.125.123.45;
    202.125.123.46;
};
```

Otherwise, it won't work.

The forward first command tells your name server to talk to the name servers declared in the forwarders command and only do the query itself if that fails. Each name server in the forwarders command is asked sequentially if the first is unavailable. Only when all of the forwarders are unavailable will your own name server do the query.

## Configuring a Slave DNS

BIND lets us have redundancy on our name servers through the use of slave name servers. Slave name servers are used to have a backup of the running main name servers in your network. In case the main name server or master DNS server crashes, users can switch to the slave name server to get information from your domain. This is possible because while the slave name server is running, it grabs a copy of the available zones on short intervals. The copy process is also known as the *zone transfer* because the main name server's zone is transferred to the slave name server for backup.

To have a slave name server running in your network that performs a zone transfer on a master name server with an IP address of 192.168.1.1 for the apress.com domain, add the lines shown in Listing 11-14 at the bottom.

*Listing 11-14. The Slave Name Server Configuration For the apress.com Domain*

```
zone "apress.com" {
```

```
type slave;
file "slaves/db.apress.com";
masters {192.168.1.1;};
};
```

In this zone entry, we can see that the type is slave and it references a master name server that has the IP address 192.168.1.1. This will tell the slave DNS on which master DNS to do zone transfers.

---

**Note:** Zone transfer is a type of DNS transaction where zone data from one DNS server is being copied by another DNS server. The actual contents of the zone file of a domain in the primary DNS are copied by the secondary DNS.

---

Whenever the slave DNS server performs a zone transfer, it will save the information in the file called db.apress.com within the /var/named/chroot/var/named/slaves directory. That file will be created on successful zone transfers. However, if you don't see any file related to the master name server and you know it is running, it is likely that the master DNS server does not allow zone transfers. You can check whether the zone transfer has been refused by the master server in the messages file in /var/log. If that happens, you have to ask permission from their DNS administrator to allow you to gather information from them.

If you want to allow your own master name server to permit slave machines to perform zone transfers from it, you can use the allow-transfer command inside the zone entry. The arguments are similar to the masters command. For example, suppose you are administering a name server for Apress named ns1.apress.com, and you have another name server called ns2.apress.com as a backup with the IP address 202.124.124.67. You have configured ns2.apress.com as a slave for ns1.apress.com, and the final thing you need to do is to use the allow-transfer command to let ns2.apress.com perform a zone transfer of ns1.apress.com's zones. To do that, you will use allow-transfer like this:

```
allow-transfer { 202.124.124.67; };
```

## Configuring a Master DNS

If your organization has applied for an official domain name and wants to have its own primary name server that will answer queries instead of a third party, you will need to deploy a master name server. In this section, we will assume that your organization applied for the domain name pvctoyfan.com at a domain registrar and we will set up a machine to host it. Our master name server also has other servers that it needs to resolve, such as FTP and web servers, as well as another name server. These three machines have the IP addresses 192.168.1.7, 192.168.1.8, and 192.168.1.9.

1. Add the entry shown in Listing 11-15 to the named.conf file in /var/named/chroot/etc.

   *Listing 11-15. The zone Statement for the pvctoyfan.com Domain*

   ```
   zone "pvctoyfan.com" {
           type master;
           file "db.pvctoyfan.com";
   ```

```
};
```

We are telling named that it is now going to host the pvctoyfan.com domain as a master name server. The zone details can be found in the db.pvctoyfan.com zone file that will be created next.

2.  Create a file called db.pvctoyfan.com inside /var/named/chroot/var/named with the entries shown in Listing 11-16.

*Listing 11-16. The Zone File for the pvctoyfan.com Domain*

```
$TTL 1D
@               IN      SOA     ns.pvctoyfan.com.       hostmaster.pvctoyfan.com. (
                                1       ; Serial
                                3H      ; Refresh
                                2H      ; Retry
                                1W      ; Expire
                                1D)     ; Minimum TTL
                NS      ns.pvctoyfan.com.

ftp     A       192.168.1.7
www     A       192.168.1.8
ns2     A       192.168.1.9
proxy     A     192.168.1.10
```

Our zone file consists of four major sections identified as resource records. The first is

```
@               IN      SOA     ns.pvctoyfan.com. hostmaster.pvctoyfan.com. (...)
```

This is a start of authority (SOA) resource record. SOA gives information about the zone, its originating machine, and who administers this domain. There can only be one SOA resource record per zone file, and it can be split over several lines.

---

■ **Note:** The @ symbol on the SOA is a shorthand for the domain name that is represented by this zone file. In the example, this will translate into pvctoyfan.com, as that name appears on the zone entry in named.conf

---

The originating computer is our ns.pvctoyfan.com, and the individual who will be assigned to maintain this domain will be hostmaster.pvctoyfan.com. The period after the originating machine tells named to stop resolving when it is encountered. If you accidentally remove the period so that it looks like ns.pvctoyfan.com, the DNS will append pvctoyfan.com as a suffix for ns.pvctoyfan.com. This is visible when you use dig with the missing final period:

```
pvctoyfan.com.          86400   IN      NS      ns.pvctoyfan.com.pvctoyfan.com.
```

instead of

```
pvctoyfan.com.          86400   IN      NS      ns.pvctoyfan.com.
```

in the AUTHORITY SECTION of the answer.

The attributes in the SOA consist of *serial, refresh, retry, expire* and *minimum time to live (TTL)*. *Serial* holds the version format this zone file is following. The value of *serial* is used mostly in slave zone transfers. If the value of *serial* changes and is not the same as the ones held by the slaves, a zone transfer will be done to update the copy of their zones. The *serial* value is also updated on the slaves. The way the *serial* value is updated is internal to the name server. *Refresh* is the amount of time before connecting to a master server for a zone transfer. The *refresh* attribute is useful if the DNS server is configured as a slave. *Retry* is the amount of time required for a slave DNS before doing another zone transfer. This is done if the zone transfer fails from the master DNS server. *Expire* is the duration before a slave refuses to accept connections. In the event the master name server fails, the slave server takes over and considers the time value of *expire* at the time before the zone data it holds becomes invalid. *Minimum TTL* is the minimum time in the event of failed lookups. If these terms scare you, using these values won't do any harm in production environments. If you have noticed, the value for TTL is appended on the $TTL line. This line sets the default expiration for a record without its own TTL value, such as negative or invalid answers from queries. It is fine if we use the same value in the SOA here.

The line

```
NS        ns.pvctoyfan.com.
```

is an *NS resource record* that declares the name server of this domain the zone file is representing. This is our name server's host name. Take note of the period in the end. The same period rule we talked about earlier in SOA also applies here. You can put any number of NS resource records in your zone file.

The lines

```
ftp    A    192.168.1.7
www       A    192.168.1.8
ns2    A    192.168.1.9
proxy      A    192.168.1.10
```

are address resource records or *A resource records* that resolve to the IP addresses of the host names found in this domain. They take the following syntax:

```
hostname         A        IP_Address
```

where *hostname* is the hostname of the machine that will be translated by the IP_Address value on the right side of the **A** keyword.

For example, if we do a dig for ftp.pvctoyfan.com, it will answer with the IP address 192.168.1.7. First, the master DNS server segregates the FQDN and finds the domain name. It will see if it can match the domain name based on its existing zones, and it matches the pvctoyfan.com domain, so the search continues. Second, the master DNS server will search the A records for a match for the given hostname. The hostname ftp matches, and the IP address value on the right side will be returned to the client.

As with NS resource records, you can place any number of A records as needed.

Restart the named server process and try to issue a dig on the web server:

```
dig www.pvctoyfan.com
```

The name server of pvctoyfan.com will answer authoritatively this time, unlike our earlier cache-only DNS server, as shown in Listing 11-17.

*Listing 11-17. The Authoritative Answer to the Query for www.pvctoyfan.com*

```
;; ANSWER SECTION:
www.pvctoyfan.com.      86400    IN     A      192.168.1.8

;; AUTHORITY SECTION:
```

```
pvctoyfan.com.          86400   IN      NS      ns.pvctoyfan.com
```

## Reverse Lookup

After you set up the master DNS server, it can now answer queries from clients by supplying the translated IP address based on the given FQDN. If a client tries to query your master DNS server by giving it an IP address instead of a FQDN, like nslookup 192.168.1.8, your server will not be able to give the correct domain name as an answer. To make your master server answer those kinds of queries, you need to add the right zone entry and create the zone file for your domain to support reverse lookups.

Create a file called db.192.168.1 in the /var/named/chroot/var/named directory with the contents shown in Listing 11-18.

*Listing 11-18. The Zone File for the pvctoyfan.com Domain to Support Reverse Lookups*

```
$TTL 1D
@               IN      SOA     ns.pvctoyfan.com hostmaster.pvctoyfan.com (
                                1       ; Serial
                                3H      ; Refresh
                                2H      ; Retry
                                1W      ; Expire
                                1D)     ; Minimum TTL
                        NS      ns.pvctoyfan.com

7       PTR     ftp.pvctoyfan.com.
8       PTR     www.pvctoyfan.com.
9       PTR     ns2.pvctoyfan.com.
10      PTR     proxy.pvctoyfan.com.
```

The SOA statement remains the same as the one in db.pvctoyfan.com except for the last four statements. Instead of using the A resource record, it uses the PTR record. Similar to A resource records, PTR resource records will translate the last number of the given IP address of a DNS query into its FQDN value on the right side. Save the file, open the named.conf file, and add the following zone entry:

```
zone "1.168.192.in-addr.arpa" {
    type master;
    file "db.192.168.1";
    notify no;
};
```

The value 1.168.192.in-addr.arpa tells named to answer queries that have IP addresses starting with 192.168.1 and find the machine matching the PTR record inside the db.192.168.1 zone file created earlier. Notice that the zone representation for the 192.168.1 network is reversed. This is much like resolving a domain name starting from the root servers, but this time the root server for reverse lookups will be in-addr.arpa. The option notify no tells named not to inform slave name servers if this zone gets updated. You can do otherwise by setting this notify to yes.

Save the named.conf file and restart the master DNS server. Repeat the reverse query for 192.168.1.8 with nslookup, and the DNS server will return the correct FQDN that holds this IP address.

# The Squid Web Caching Server

When you are getting short of network bandwidth, it is time to introduce web caching to your network. Web caching servers, also known as web proxy servers, support the major Internet protocols that are required in a corporate network. The web caching server that you can use in CentOS is the Squid proxy server.

Squid maximizes Internet bandwidth by recycling frequently used web pages through caching. When a user requests a web page, Squid can sometimes serve a copy of content that has been downloaded before rather than downloading it again. To further maximize bandwidth, Squid can also talk to other Squid servers to query web content that is already present, preventing unwanted downloads of the same data. In addition, it also supports access controls that can put restrictions on certain hosts and networks for basic security.

Squid has some limitations in addition to its advantages. Squid can only act as a web cache or accelerator for some protocols, including HTTP, HTTPS by pass-through, and FTP, for example. Some people want support for other protocols, but enabling those on the network requires workarounds. One is teleconferencing software. Though it supports HTTP, it is also dependent on some proprietary protocols that cannot be disclosed. Hence, automatically Squid does not support most of them. It is best to use Squid for what it is good at, web caching.

In this section, we will install Squid and see some of its web caching features.

## Installing Squid

Squid is not installed by default in CentOS. You will install it now by using yum install squid. The binaries and configuration files will be placed in their respective directories.

## The Squid Main Configuration File

Squid configuration files are stored in the /etc/squid directory. There are many files there but the important one is squid.conf, the main configuration file. With it, we can control the behavior of Squid during its execution. The configuration file contains directives that are separated by lines. We can use them to set options such as where to store cached content and the ports that Squid must use. The directives have the following syntax:

```
directivename  givenvalue_1[ givenvalue_2 givenvalue_3 .. givenvalue_N]
```

where *directivename* is the name of the directive that we want to use and *givenvalue* is the value that we want to assign to the directive. Some directives, like cache_dir, can take more than one value. If a directive requires more than one value, those must be separated by spaces. You'll find the other directives you can use with Squid by checking its documentation at http://www.squid-cache.org/Doc/config. Lines starting with a hash symbol are comments and are ignored.

In this section, we will look at the frequently used directives in the configuration file to make our web proxy server run to cache web data.

### The visible_hostname directive

The visible_hostname directive is used to inform system log files and users about the identity of the web cache server when problems appear. The value you assign here will be shown by Squid on the log files and generated information web pages. This directive is required and you must set it before running Squid. Otherwise it will not start.

The syntax of the visible_hostname directive is

visible_hostname *givenhostname*

where *givenhostname* is the hostname to be used by the Squid server. Names assigned to this directive usually start with proxy, such as proxy.apress.com. For our practice, we will name this Squid server proxy.pvctoyfan.com; it is the web proxy server for the pvctoyfan.com domain. Add the following line at the bottom of squid.conf:

visible_hostname proxy.pvctoyfan.com

When Squid needs to inform users about problems or display other information, it will show proxy.pvctoyfan.com as its hostname.

## The cache_dir directive

The cache_dir directive is used to tell Squid the cache directories it can use to store cache information such as downloaded web pages and files. It uses the following syntax:

cache_dir *storagetype targetdirectory storagesize directorycount subdirectorycount*

where *storagetype* is the type of storage this cache can use. You will use the default storage type ufs because it is available after installation. You can use other storage types to optimize your web cache later once you get the hang of Squid. Information about additional storage types can be found at http://www.squid-cache.org/Doc/config/cache_dir.
The *targetdirectory* is the directory in your system that Squid will use to store its cache data. It is recommended that the partition where the directory resides have ample space to accommodate all the cache data Squid will store when it runs.
The *storagesize* value is the size of this cache directory in megabytes. The size you want the cache directory to have depends on the usage of bandwidth. If the web content is increasingly downloaded instead of cached, it is time to add more space for this directory.
The *directorycount* denotes the number of directories the cache directory can hold. The *subdirectorycount* is for the number of subdirectories each of the directory given in *directorycount*. For our example, if the *directorycount* is set to 16, the cache directory specified in *targetdirectory* can have a maximum of 16 directories. Each directory given in *directorycount* can have another 256 subdirectories to store web data if the *subdirectorycount* is set to 256 (1 directory = 256 subdirectories). If a client requests a resource such as an HTML file or image file that is present in one of the cache directories, that resource will be retrieved by Squid and given to the client. Any kind of data that can be stored for caching will be placed in one of the directories pointed to by cache_dir. In the squid.conf file, there is one default cache_dir directive, shown here:

# cache_dir ufs /var/spool/squid 100 16 256

In the default cache_dir directive, the *storagetype* is ufs, the *targetdirectory* is /var/spool/squid, the *storagesize* is 100 megabytes, the *directorycount* is 16, and the *subdirectorycount* is 256. If you want to change any of these parameters, you can uncomment this line, make the changes, and then reload Squid. The default values are sufficient for your practice.
You can use more cache directories for Squid if you have enough hard disk space on your system by adding cache_dir directives. After setting up the hard disk and adding a partition for Squid, put another cache_dir statement for it. Use the command squid -z to initialize the new cache directory and wait for it to finish. Restart Squid using service squid restart and it will now use the new cache directory along with the existing one.

Before you can allow your clients to use your Squid server, you need to enable them by using ACLs and ACL-operators.

## ACLs and ACL-operators

Access Control Lists (ACLs) are directives that can be used to restrict usage to Squid. You can use ACLs to limit which host or hosts have access to the Internet to avoid bandwidth abuse. Squid denies web access to all hosts when it is first installed. You must add some access control lists to allow our network to use the Internet. The syntax of an ACL is

```
acl name type (chosen_type) value
```

where *name* is an identifier for this ACL. You can use any text here but a good practice is to name it depending on its function. An ACL's function depends on the *chosen_type* you give it. One possibility is src, where you control access based on the IP address of the person accessing content. Another is password, where users have to supply a password in order to access content. Most of the time we will use the src type in our ACLs. The *value* is required data that needs to be included depending on the type. It can be an IP address or even a hostname.

The following example ACL allows the localhost computer to access the Internet:

```
acl localhost src 127.0.0.1/32
```
We have chosen the name localhost for this ACL because it serves the localhost machine. The type is src, which represents the source IP address of the localhost computer, 127.0.0.1/32, which in turn is an additional argument for it. This ACL matches the IP address of a specific machine on the network.

ACLs work in conjunction with ACL-operators. An ACL-operator uses the information contained in the declared ACL during its evaluation. ACL-operators are the filtering commands that let Squid control access to the Internet. Here is the syntax for an ACL-operator used for web access:

**http_access** operation target

The http_access ACL-operator performs the required *operation* based on *target*, where the target is an ACL. If the target ACL matches a target IP or host name, the ACL-operator's operation will be applied. Here is an example:

```
http_access allow localhost
```

We are allowing the computer that matches the IP address range contained in the localhost ACL to access the Internet.

There are other ACLs and ACL-operators available for Squid, but these two are enough for now for practice.

## Adding ACLs and ACL-operators

For example, to allow your 192.168.1 network to access the Internet, with the squid.conf file still opened, find the lines

```
http_access allow localhost
http_access deny all
```
and replace them with

```
acl localnetwork src 192.168.1.0/24
http_access allow localhost
```

```
http_access allow localnetwork
http_access deny all
```

Be sure to replace the underlined value with your actual network. Save the file and start Squid using this command:

```
service squid start
```

## How ACL-operators Work

ACL-operators evaluate sequentially starting from the top. This can produce unexpected results if you put things in the wrong order. As an example, if you did something like this to the changes above:

```
acl localnetwork src 192.168.1.0/24
http_access deny all              # Intentionally placed here
http_access allow localhost
http_access allow localnetwork
```

in effect you are denying network access to everybody! Squid will stop at `http_access deny all`. Watch out for these situations.

The next test is to use a computer on your network and have its web browser's connection settings changed to point to the host name (if you have a working DNS) or IP address of the web cache. Put the default port 3128 on the port settings alongside the web cache (proxy_server:3128). Do this on some more computers and have them access the same web site. See if there are any speed improvements. If you want to see Squid run with debugging information, you can run it manually with `squid -d 1`. Also, if you have enabled the firewall in your system, be sure to add a rule to allow traffic to pass for Squid's port number, which is 3128 by default.

---

■ **Tip:** Always use `squid -k parse` to check whether the Squid main configuration file contain errors after you modify it.

---

## Talking to Squid Peers

If you have more than one Squid server, you can have one access cached pages on the other. The content is still only being copied around your local network rather than around the Internet. In addition, this newly acquired content will then be stored in the server's web cache.

You can have your Squid server access a peer web cache server by using the cache_peer directive, which has the following syntax:

**cache_peer** peer_host_name peer_type http_port icp_port

where *peer_host* is the host name or IP address of the other Squid server you want to talk to, and *peer_type* can be parent, sibling, or multicast. The parent and sibling values are usually used for a Squid hierarchy, while multicast is for using multicast to communicate with other Squids instead of ICP. The *http_port* and *icp_port* are the HTTP port number and ICP port number of the peer we are letting our server talk to.

Assume we have three Squid computers, proxy.pvctoyfanparent.com, proxy.pvctoyfansibling1.com, and proxy.pvctoyfansibling2.com. We want to make the last two computers siblings and set proxy.pvctoyfanparent.com as their parent.

Here are the cache_peer directives that proxy.pvctoyfansibling1.com must use when accessing the proxy.pvctoyfanparent.com Squid web cache as a parent and proxy.pvctoyfansibling2.com as sibling:

```
cache_peer proxy.pvctoyfanparent.com parent 3128 3130
cache_peer proxy.pvctoysibling2.com sibling 3128 3130 no-query
```
and for proxy.pvctoyfansibling2.com the entries would be

```
cache_peer proxy.pvctoyfanparent.com parent 3128 3130
cache_peer proxy.pvctoysibling1.com sibling 3128 3130 no-query
```

Putting a no-query on the cache_peer statement for both proxy.pvctoyfansibling1.com and proxy.pvctoyfansibling2.com will prevent those addresses from sending ICP queries to their parent. This will reduce unnecessary network traffic and speed up communication for both machines.

Being a parent peer, proxy.pvctoyfanparent.com can get new data if it does not exist on the cache. That cannot be done for proxy.pvctoyfansibling.com, because it is a sibling peer. As such, it can only borrow data from its other siblings if the requested data is not found in its cache; they can ask the parent to fetch it for them.

## More Squid

There are more ways to configure Squid. One is to have it configured as a transparent proxy server, which can help slow web servers by pretending to be one. Another is to put more complex ACLs and ACL-operators to give you more granularity for your security policy. You can find out more on Squid's home page at http://www.squid-cache.org/Doc/.

# Summary

This chapter has explored some of the network services available in CentOS ready for our use. These include secure transactions with 7OpenSSH, automatic network information distribution with DHCP, synchronizing time accurately with NTP, administering domain names with BIND tools, and finally speeding up web access using the Squid proxy server. All of these will help you provide the required network services as required by the users.

In the next chapter, you will see how to store transactional data through the use of relational database systems. You will see how PostgreSQL and MySQL can help us in giving users a robust data store for their important data.

# CHAPTER 12

■■■

# Open Source Databases

Open source Relational Database Management Systems (RDBMSs) are available in Linux and therefore in CentOS. These systems use the Structured Query Language (SQL), the language of relational databases, to store and manipulate data just like their commercial counterparts. In addition, they include programming libraries that developers can use to interface to them.

In this chapter, you will learn about the two open source RDBMSs that you can use in Linux. The first is MySQL, and the second is PostgreSQL. Both can provide features that you will need for a database, and some of those features, such as database replication, can equal commercial implementations. You will learn how to install and configure both databases, and you'll be able to decide which of them is more suited to your organization.

After you learn the proper way to set up your databases, you will also learn the basics of SQL through CRUD (Create, Read, Update, and Delete), the conceptual model that describes the four major functions of software. This will enable you, the CentOS administrator, to use database objects such as tables and create queries that can give out results from your databases.

## ACID

RDBMSs have the concept of a transaction, such that anything you run on a database, for example a query, is treated as a transaction. You create a statement to send to the system. Next, the system runs your statement, performing, say, a read or write operation. Last, you get the result that you want, retrieving or changing some data on the database. You can safely expect the intended results of your transactions if you are the only user of the database. If others use the same database and are making different transactions at the same time, you might get different results than you expect. Consider the two users doing separate transactions on the same table in a database illustrated in Figure 12-1.

| Transaction_Biboy | Transaction_Jambo |
|---|---|
| read(A); | |
| A = A + 10; | |
| | read(A); |
| | A = A + 20; |
| write(A); | |
| | write(A); == ? |

*Figure 12-1. Two transactions on the same table*

In Figure 12-1, the statements are executed downward and alternate between Biboy's and Jambo's transactions, starting with Biboy. There is a problem with those separate transactions and that is the final value of the variable A, which represents some data on the same table. Let's assume that A starts off with the value of 10. Biboy reads 10 and adds 10 to the next statement, so that A becomes 20. Jambo starts her transaction by reading A, and she also gets 10 because the changes Biboy made have not been saved. Her next statement adds 20 to the current A value, which results in a value of 30. The last write instruction of Biboy saves his A value in the database, and that is 20. In Jambo's final write statement, instead of saving the value 30, she saves the value 20. This happened because the final value of A was overwritten by Biboy, and Jamby's changes got lost. The final value of A should have been 40, but it is rather unclear due to the uncontrolled concurrent activities of both transactions. This situation is called the *lost update problem*. It is one of the problems that RDBMSs face with concurrent transactions.

To counter this and related problems, database designers came up with a set of rules that make a good transaction. The rules are called ACID (Atomicity, Consistency, Isolation, and Durability):

*Atomicity:* Each transaction you make must be completed from start to finish. If it does not finish, the transaction is invalid.

*Consistency:* Each transaction must remain in a consistent state during execution by following the rules imposed on the database, such as foreign keys on tables.

*Isolation:* A transaction must never reveal its updates to other transactions while it is running. This is to prevent incorrect data reads from other concurrently running transactions using the same table, for example.

*Durability:* The transactions must make its changes permanent. In case of system failure, the data must remain intact and usable after recovery.

With ACID, you are guaranteed to make reliable transactions to have better control of your data. You can be confident that your data will remain safe during execution when you run transactions along with others concurrently. Most RDBMSs implement ACID, including PostgreSQL and MySQL. Those RDBMSs have SQL transaction statements such as BEGIN TRANSACTION and COMMIT that you can use to make transactions. Be sure to check their documentation for these statements.

---

■ **Note:** You can learn more about transactions by reading database books. I recommend *Fundamentals of Database Systems* by Elmasri and Navathe (Addison Wesley, fifth edition 2006).

---

# MySQL

MySQL is known as the fastest database system in the open source world. It can process large queries and give out the required results with speed. In addition to its speed, MySQL is also popular with developers and organizations because it is easy to set up and maintain. Web developers often use MySQL with popular programming languages such as PHP and Ruby because it is fast enough to process database queries required by web sites. As a leading database for the web, it also forms the *M* of LAMP—*Linux, Apache, MySQL, and PHP*.

Speed is not the only thing MySQL has in its favor. It also has features for advanced database administrators to use, such as triggers, transactions, and subqueries. The way data is stored and retrieved can also be customized through its available storage engines like InnoDB and MyISAM. MySQL is also available for other operating systems like UNIX and Windows.

---

**MYSQL STORAGE ENGINES**

Storage engines in MySQL define how it stores data in the tables of its databases. Some storage engines are designed for speed, while others are built for using standard SQL language features, such as transactions and foreign keys. The two common storage engines that you can use immediately are MyISAM and InnoDB.

MyISAM is MySQL's implementation of the Indexed Sequential Access Method (ISAM), a fast method for retrieving data that also provides FULLTEXT search capabilities on tables that use this storage engine. MyISAM is supported in all MySQL configurations and is the default storage engine when you do not specify any in creating your tables. Because the focus of MyISAM is speed, it does not support some standard SQL database features. These include transactions and the use of foreign keys for relational integrity. If you need both features, you need to use another storage engine for your tables.

InnoDB was created to provide the missing features of MyISAM and is an improved storage engine. It can recover faster from crashes and has increased data reliability thanks to its ACID compliance. For database users who require relational integrity, InnoDB also supports the creation of foreign keys to enable table joins.

There are other storage engines that you can use, and you can learn more about them at http://dev.mysql.com/doc/refman/5.0/en/storage-engines.html.

---

If you need redundancy in your databases, MySQL has its own replication system that you can use. You can configure replication as a single-master–multiple-slave, or chain setup, where replication of data propagates from the master down to its series of slaves.

Some companies are rather reluctant to use MySQL because it does not include any paid support. In fact, MySQL offers several options for companies that want to have support. One of these is to use MySQL's commercial version, MySQL Enterprise. This provides paid subscription-based support that gives monitors and rules which can help the administrator maintain the MySQL database. You can even avail yourself of the trial offer to see what benefits MySQL Enterprise can give to your organization.

For now, it is best to stick with the open source version of MySQL, the MySQL community server. It is the same as the commercial release but without the support. This is more than enough for you to learn the ropes of using MySQL in your organization within your CentOS system.

# Setting Up MySQL

Add MySQL to your system by issuing two commands. One is for the server:

```
yum install mysql-server
```

This will add the server binaries that you will use to run the MySQL process. It will also add the `mysql` user to your system. The next is for the client:

```
yum install mysql
```

This will install the tools needed to connect to a running MySQL server and do database administration tasks.

After the installation finishes, MySQL tools and configuration files are now installed in your system and ready for use.

## Running the MySQL Server

Run the `mysqld` process by executing `service mysqld start`. It will now start listening for database connections on its default port, 3306.

When you run MySQL for the first time, it will create a data directory in /var/lib called `mysql`. This directory contains the required MySQL system tables needed by the server to provide database functionality to users. Without this data directory, MySQL will not be able to run at all. Be sure to handle this directory with care!

## MySQL Users

MySQL has its own user system. The first role, which is already available after installing MySQL, is the root user. Also known as a *superuser*, this user is capable of creating additional users and manipulating system tables like host permissions, and it can also perform database tasks. It is also capable of granting permissions to non-root MySQL users, for tasks such as creating tables and triggers, using the MySQL system tables. While root is also the name of MySQL's superuser, it is not the same as the root user of your Linux system.

The second role is that of a normal user with no special privileges to use MySQL's system tables. You need to create additional normal users for your intended system users instead of superusers in order to avoid accidental changes to your current configuration. Normal users should be granted privileges on the database and tables that they are going to use, so they can issue SQL statements.

Be warned that the root user does not have a password when it is created. This allows the database administrator to log in to the running MySQL system and do preliminary administration like creating regular users and adding host permissions. It is a good idea to change the password of this user after logging in for the first time in order to maintain security. Running applications with the root user is also a bad idea.

MySQL users are always associated with their originating hosts. This helps MySQL identify valid clients by requiring them to supply not only their user name and password, but also their host name or IP address when connecting. With this authentication scheme, it is not unusual to have a single username associated with different host names in MySQL.

For example, the root user of MySQL can connect to a MySQL server from three hosts: using the `localhost` hostname, using the `localhost.localdomain` hostname, or using the local IP address of the machine, such as `127.0.0.1`. When you attempt to connect to the server using one of the hostnames of the root user, the MySQL server will consult the user system table when authenticating it. If the supplied username, password, and hostname all match, the root user is allowed to connect to the server.

## MySQL Monitor

MySQL includes a terminal client called `mysql` that you can use to administer databases. `mysql` has the following syntax:

```
mysql -u user [database] [-h remote_host] [more options];
```

where *user* is the MySQL username you are going to use to connect to the server, and [*database*] is the target existing database you want to use on your MySQL server after a successful connection. If you omit this, MySQL will assume you just want to enter the server and not use any database. You will have to connect to a database manually once inside the terminal prompt if you do this. If you are going to connect to the server remotely, you will need to use the -h flag and specify the hostname or IP address of the machine you are using. Additional options can be given when connecting by adding them on the [*more options*] part. For example, if the MySQL user you want to use requires a password, you need to specify the  p flag to let you authenticate properly.

To connect to your running MySQL process locally, use the following command:

```
mysql -u root
```

You will be given a mysql monitor where you can do administration tasks, as shown in Figure 12-2.

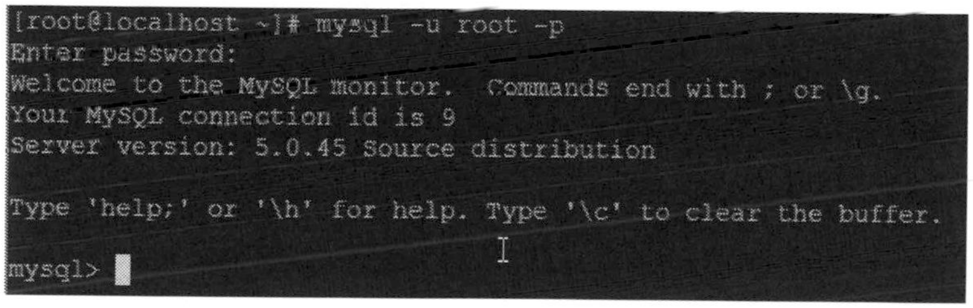

*Figure 12-2. The MySQL monitor*

Now that you have connected to our server using the MySQL root user, it is time to change its password to protect yourself.

---

■ **Note:** Assume that your MySQL server, with the hostname pvcserver.com, has an entry for the root user coming from the host pvctoyfan.com and you want to connect to the server using the machine with the hostname pvctoyfan.com as root. You will have to use this command: mysql -u root -h pvcserver.com.

---

## Securing the MySQL Root User

We will change the password for the root user that is associated with the localhost host name using the SET PASSWORD command. The SET PASSWORD command to change an account password is

```
SET PASSWORD FOR 'target_user'[@'target_host'] = PASSWORD('new_password');
```

In this syntax, *target_user* is the user we want to change the password and *target_host* is the hostname it belongs to. If you do not specify a value for *target_host*, the value defaults to '%' which stands for any host. It is better to add host names or IP addresses to each user so MySQL can help you track them down when needed. The *new_password* is the new password we are going to assign for this user. The PASSWORD() function will encrypt the given password for added security. You need to add a semicolon at the end to tell MySQL to run your command.

1.  Run the following command while inside the MySQL monitor:

    SET PASSWORD FOR 'root'@'localhost' = PASSWORD('root123');

    This command assigns the password root123 for the root user that belongs to the host, localhost. The next time you try to log in with this user without any password, you will not be able to connect to the server.

2.  Try to log in our server using the mysql monitor as the root on localhost without any password:

    mysql -u root

    You will not be able to log in.

3.  To log into the server using the root user's password, add the –p flag at the end:

    mysql -u root -p

    The MySQL monitor will ask you to give a password. Type in root123 and you will be connected.

As an additional exercise, you can also change the password of the root user coming from localhost.localdomain and the IP address 127.0.0.1.

---

▓ **Note:** In the previous exercise, you did not specify an originating host for the root user while connecting. When you do not append the hostname for the machine you are coming from, the mysql command will assume that you want to connect locally to the server. This is treated as mysql -u root@localhost -p, for example.

---

## Creating a Database

Before anybody can use MySQL, databases are needed to store their data. We will create a database called toys by using the CREATE DATABASE command. The syntax of the CREATE DATABASE command is

CREATE DATABASE *new_database*;

where new_database is the name of the database to be created. Note that only users with the CREATE privilege can create databases. Only root has the capability to do this at the moment, though you can let normal users create databases, too, as long as you give them permission using the GRANT command. Privileges, along with the GRANT command, will be discussed later.

To create a database called toys, enter the following:

CREATE DATABASE **toys**;

This will create an empty database called toys that is ready for use. In the next section, you will create a normal user who can use this database, in addition to root.

## Removing a Database

Removing databases is seldom done but if you need to do it, you will need to use the DROP DATABASE command. The syntax is

```
DROP DATABASE target_database;
```

where *target_database* is the database you want to remove. You will see an example in the following exercise.

## Adding a User

After entering the MySQL root user's terminal, you can create a regular user who can use the toys database. In order to do this, you will use the CREATE USER command, which has the following syntax:

```
CREATE USER 'new_user'[@'target_host'] IDENTIFIED BY 'new_user_password';
```

where *new_user* is the username of the user to be created and *new_user_password* is its corresponding password. You can also specify a host or domain name this user belongs to. Add a new user called toymaster in localhost with the password toymaster123, using this command:

```
CREATE USER 'toymaster'@'localhost' IDENTIFIED BY 'toymaster123';
```

After running the command, you can now log into the MySQL monitor using toymaster with its password.

---

■ **Note:** For user-oriented commands such as CREATE USER, DROP USER and GRANT, omitting the [@'targethost'] part is the same as including @'%', which means from any host. This is similar to the SET PASSWORD command earlier. For example, to allow the user toymaster to connect to our server coming from any host, use this command:
```
CREATE USER 'toymaster' IDENTIFIED BY 'toymaster123';
```
It translates to
```
CREATE USER 'toymaster'@'%' IDENTIFIED BY 'toymaster123';
```

---

## Removing a User

There will be times when you have to remove certain users in your MySQL server. An account may go inactive or the user may move to another location. In order to remove a user, you will use DROP USER. Its syntax is

```
DROP USER 'target_user'[@'target_host'];
```

For example, to remove the toymaster user, you would run the following:

```
DROP USER 'toymaster'@'localhost';
```

---

▓ **Caution:** Just like any other activity that involves removal, you have to think twice with this one because once you drop a user, it is gone for good!

---

## Granting Privileges

Now that you have the toymaster user, you need to give it some permission to be able to use the toys database. Without sufficient privileges, the toymaster user cannot do anything useful with the database. To grant permissions, you will use the GRANT command, which has the following syntax:

```
GRANT privileges ON target_db.[target_table] TO 'target_user'[@'target_host'];
```

where privileges are the options you want to permit the user to use on the database. The *target_db* is the database where you want to apply the permitted options (which we'll discuss next), and *target_table* is the table within that database. Both *target_db* and *target_table* can be replaced with an asterisk (*) to denote everything. *target_user* is the username we are giving permissions and *target_host* is the host or domain it belongs to. Be sure to use a superuser account to run this command; otherwise MySQL will not allow you to change privileges.

### GRANTING PRIVILEGES

Here are some of the available privileges that you can use when applying permissions to regular users.

1. ALL: Gives the user every available privilege.

2. SELECT: Allows viewing for the user on a table or database.

3. INSERT: Lets the user add data to the table or database.

4. DELETE: Gives table data removal capability for the user on a table or database.

5. OPTION: Makes the user capable of giving privileges. This essentially transforms it to a superuser on your MySQL server.

You can use these in place of the *privileges* part of the GRANT syntax discussed earlier. There are more privileges to choose from, and you can see them in the MySQL documentation at http://dev.mysql.com/doc/refman/5.0/en/grant.html.

---

You can allow toymaster to do anything to the toys database by running this command:

```
GRANT ALL PRIVILEGES ON toys.* TO 'toymaster'@'localhost';
```

Here you are granting all available privileges, except OPTION, on every table on the toys database to the toymaster user belonging to localhost. With this in effect, the toymaster user can now create tables and run queries while connected to the toys database.

## Removing Privileges

MySQL also lets you remove privileges from a user if necessary. This can be done through the REVOKE command:

```
REVOKE privileges ON target_db.target_table FROM 'target_user'[@'target_host'];
```

This is fairly similar to GRANT. You can easily create an equivalent REVOKE command to a GRANT command because of their similarity. Additional REVOKE options are found in the MySQL documentation at http://dev.mysql.com/doc/refman/5.0/en/revoke.html.

## Getting a List of Available Databases

While inside the mysql terminal as the toymaster user, issue the following command:

```
SHOW DATABASES;
```

As illustrated in Figure 12-3, this will display the available databases in your running MySQL server.

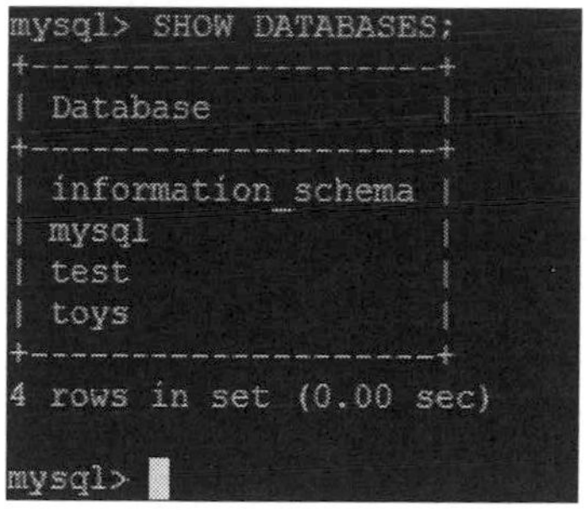

*Figure 12-3. A list of currently available databases*

This is useful when you want to know what databases are already occupying your MySQL data directory to manage server space. In Figure 12-3, we can see the databases available in the data directory. The first is information_schema; this database contains the internal workings of MySQL. You do not have to worry about it because most of the time we will let MySQL manage it. The second is mysql, which contains information about privileges for tables and users. The third is test, a dummy database available for practice. Finally, you can see the toys database you made earlier. Exit from the MySQL prompt after viewing the contents by typing \q and pressing Enter.

## Creating Database Backups

One of the major duties of database administrators is to back up database data regularly. In order to create a backup, you need to use the utility mysqldump, which has the following syntax:

```
mysqldump -u user database [more_options]
```

where *user* is the permitted MySQL user who will create a backup. This is usually the superuser, but normal users with sufficient permissions can also make one. The database argument is the target database that needs to be backed up. Additional options can be used in place of [*more options*], as in the mysql utility.

Unlike the previous commands, mysqldump needs to be run at the shell and not within the MySQL monitor. When the command is run, the backup contents will appear on the screen. The contents must be redirected into a file to save it. To make a backup file called toys.mysql that contains the current contents of our toys database, enter the following command:

```
mysqldump -u toymaster toys -p > toys.mysql
```

After the command runs, there will be a file called toys.mysql that contains the contents of the toys database. This is a regular text file and you can use a text editor to examine its contents.

You can also back up all of the databases at once instead of individually, with this command:

```
mysqldump --all-databases -p > all.databases.mysql
```

---

■ **Caution:** Be sure to make a copy of the backup file before playing with its contents! This is for safety in case you accidentally change its contents. If the contents get modified, chances are that MySQL will not be able to restore the database it contains successfully. Change the contents only if you have enough experience with MySQL.

---

## Restoring Databases Using Backups

At some point in your MySQL administration career, you will be requested to restore database backups from earlier. Incorrect data may have been entered or important database elements such as tables accidentally removed. To restore a backup, take the following steps:

1.  Terminate all current database connections with the target database and inform your users. This is to prevent them from complaining if their database suddenly disappears.

2.  Make a backup of the current running database. This is a safety precaution because we might need its contents later. Be sure not to overwrite the backup that you are going to restore from.

3.  Drop the target problem database.

4.  Create a new database with an identical name to the deleted problem database. This will still be empty and we will add data to it using our backup.

5.  Restore the backup by using the mysql command along with the selected backup file.

## Restoring the toys Database

To illustrate the restoration process, here is a scenario in which the toys database suddenly gets damaged.

1. Log in to the server as the root user and see if the toys database is still intact. If it is there, you will make a backup of it. Exit from the monitor prompt to head back to the terminal.

2. Create a backup of the toys database by running this command:

   ```
   mysqldump -u toymaster toys -p > toys.mysql
   ```

   This will create a toys.mysql backup file in the current directory.

3. Log in to the server again as root. Issue the following command to remove the toys database:

   ```
   DROP DATABASE toys;
   ```

   You can verify that the toys database is deleted by entering

   ```
   SHOW DATABASES;
   ```

4. Create a new toys database by entering

   ```
   CREATE DATABASE toys;
   ```

   It is empty at the moment and you will restore its contents based on the backup file. Exit from the monitor.

5. Restore the database from the toys.mysql backup file with this command:

   ```
   mysql -u root toys < toys.mysql -p
   ```

6. After this step, your toys database is now ready for action as if nothing happened!

# Customizing the MySQL Server Configuration

You can make further changes to the way MySQL behaves through its main configuration file, called my.cnf. The file is inside the /etc directory and its contents are shown in Listing 12-1.

*Listing 12-1. The Contents of the my.cnf File*

```
[mysqld]
datadir=/var/lib/mysql
socket=/var/lib/mysql/mysql.sock
user=mysql
# Default to using old password format for compatibility with mysql 3.x
# clients (those using the mysqlclient10 compatibility package).
old_passwords=1

[mysqld_safe]
log-error=/var/log/mysqld.log
pid-file=/var/run/mysqld/mysqld.pid
```

The configuration file is divided into two sections, [mysqld] and [mysqld_safe]. In the [mysqld] section, you can see that the data directory is located in /var/lib/mysql and the user of the process is the mysql system user. This section can be treated as global because what is defined here is applicable to the succeeding sections.

The [mysqld_safe] section contains options for the mysqld_safe startup script, which adds safety features for the main MySQL server process, mysqld. Some mysqld_safe safety features include the automatic restarting of the mysqld process in case of an error and logging of that error. You can see in listing 12-1 that the errors are placed in mysqld.log using the log-error command while the process ID that it uses is stored using the pid-file command.

As shown in Listing 12-2, you can change the port where the mysqld_safe process listens for database connections to 22522, for example, by adding port=22522 in the mysqld_safe section.

*Listing 12-2. Making the mysqld_safe Process Listen to Port Number 22522*

```
[mysqld_safe]
log-error=/var/log/mysqld.log
pid-file=/var/run/mysqld/mysqld.pid
port=22522
```

Be sure to restart MySQL whenever you make changes in this file, by running service mysqld restart.

There are other configuration options you can use and even recommended configuration files MySQL developers contribute on their web sites. There are configurations for small, medium and large systems that you can use depending on your hardware. All you have to do is download the configuration file you want, replace the one inside /etc, and tweak it according to your needs.

# PostgreSQL

PostgreSQL is a good alternative to MySQL if you need to utilize more advanced database features in your implementation. Known as the most advanced open source database, it supports foreign keys and most SQL92 and SQL99 data types, and it is ACID-compliant. In addition, it can use stored procedures, triggers, and procedural languages that can be used to write stored procedures. PostgreSQL is an object relational database management system, which means that you can have inheritance of attributes from a parent table to another. This is similar to object-oriented programming but at the database level.

Many administrators compare PostgreSQL with MySQL in terms of speed. Out of the box, MySQL is faster because it uses MyISAM as its default storage engine, which supports the features needed by most database users. PostgreSQL can also be on a par with MySQL in terms of speed, but you have to customize its configuration a little bit through its main configuration file and later, in your individual databases. We will examine the contents of the configuration file later to see how we can speed things up a little for PostgreSQL.

## Setting up PostgreSQL

In this section you will install the PostgreSQL server and its client tools. First, run the command

```
yum install postgresql-server
```

to install the server binaries, and then execute

```
yum install postgresql
```

With these packages in place, you can now create databases using PostgreSQL.

## Starting PostgreSQL

Next, start PostgreSQL for the first time and have it create its own data directory, which contains its system tables and configurations. To do this, enter

```
service postgresql start
```

The data directory will be created in /var/lib/pgsql/data. The PostgreSQL server process called postmaster will then listen to database connections on port 5432, its default.

## PostgreSQL Interactive Terminal

PostgreSQL administration can be done using its command-line client called psql, which creates the interactive terminal. With the interactive terminal, you can create database objects such as users and tables as needed. But be warned, you need to be logged in as the real postgres system user before you can use it. The root system user is not available on the default PostgreSQL installation.

The syntax of psql is

```
psql [-U target_user] [-h target_host] target_database
```

where *target_user* is the user we want to connect with. The *target_host* can be a valid host name or IP address of the PostgreSQL server we need to connect. The *target_database* is the name of the database.

### Using the Interactive Terminal

In this exercise you will try the Postgres interactive terminal on the default system database as the postgres user.

Assume that you are logged as the root user. Change into postgres by issuing

```
su - postgres
```

Run the next command to enter the interactive terminal:

```
psql template1
```

This command will connect you locally to the PostgreSQL system database, called template1. After a successful connection your terminal should look like Figure 12-4.

```
Welcome to psql 8.1.11, the PostgreSQL interactive terminal.

Type:  \copyright for distribution terms
       \h for help with SQL commands
       \? for help with psql commands
       \g or terminate with semicolon to execute query
       \q to quit

template1=#
```

*Figure 12-4. **The PostgreSQL interactive terminal connected to the template1 database***

With the interactive terminal, you can now run queries as PostgreSQL's postgres user.

## PostgreSQL Roles

PostgreSQL also has its own superuser and normal users, similar to MySQL. These are called *roles*, and a role can be a database user or even represent a group of database users. You can also apply permissions and options to roles such as tables. PostgreSQL roles are different from Linux system users because they are used solely for administering PostgreSQL databases.

After you install PostgreSQL, it contains a single role called postgres. This is a superuser, and you can use this role to create additional normal roles and databases that other roles can also use.

## Creating a Role

You can create additional roles using the CREATE ROLE command as a superuser. It has the following syntax:

CREATE ROLE new_role_name [more_options];

where *new_role_name* is the name of the new user or role we want to create. You can put additional attributes by filling in the [*more_options*] part that you can apply to the new role. As an exercise, create the toymaster role for PostgreSQL this time by using

CREATE ROLE toymaster LOGIN CREATEDB PASSWORD 'toymaster123';

That will add the toymaster role, which can be used to connect. The command has the additional options LOGIN to let toymaster log into the server and CREATEDB to allow it to make databases. PASSWORD will set a password for the new role that will be used for authentication when logging in remotely. Here, you've set 'toymaster123' as toymaster's password. Next, exit the interactive terminal by typing \q and pressing Enter.

Before you can use toymaster to log in with the interactive terminal, you need to create an equivalent system user for it. Log in as root and create a new user by running useradd toymaster and then switch to that user with su - toymaster. This is required because the installed Postgres server is configured to allow local logins only if the current system username is the same as the database username for added security.

Now we test the toymaster role to see if you can use it. We do this by running

psql template1

As illustrated in Figure 12-5, you are now in the template1 database using toymaster!

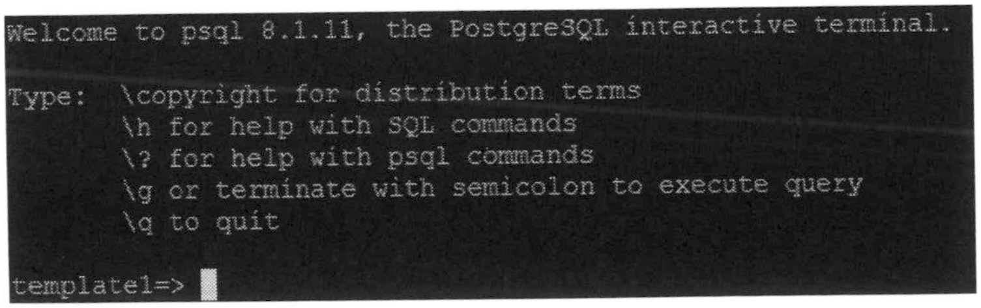

```
Welcome to psql 8.1.11, the PostgreSQL interactive terminal.

Type:  \copyright for distribution terms
       \h for help with SQL commands
       \? for help with psql commands
       \g or terminate with semicolon to execute query
       \q to quit

template1=>
```

*Figure 12-5. The interactive terminal for toymaster*

If you compare Figure 12-4 and Figure 12-5, you can see that the prompt has changed from template1=# to template1=>. This is a way for PostgreSQL to tell you about the nature of the user you logged with in the interactive terminal. As in BASH, if the prompt has a hash (#) sign, the account is a superuser. Otherwise, it is a regular system user.

## Removing a User

You can also remove roles in PostgreSQL through the DROP ROLE command. The syntax for DROP ROLE is

```
DROP ROLE target_role;
```

Just as in MySQL, be sure that the user you are about to remove is actually not used anymore to avoid problems.

## Creating a Database

To create a database in PostgreSQL, we use the CREATE DATABASE command:

```
CREATE DATABASE new_database;
```

where *new_database* is the name of the database we want to create. To create the toys database with the toymaster role, you run

```
CREATE DATABASE toys;
```

The toys database will now be ready to accept tables for later.

## Dropping a Database

To remove a database in PostgreSQL, we use the DROP DATABASE command:

```
DROP DATABASE target_database;
```

where *target_database* is the database to be removed; so if you wanted to remove the toys database, you would use

```
DROP DATABASE toys;
```

But you must not do this at the moment! You will work with the toys database later when we talk about the Create-Read-Update-Delete (CRUD) model later in this chapter.

## PostgreSQL Privileges

Whenever something is created in PostgreSQL such as a table, by default it is owned by its creator. The table created is a PostgreSQL *object*, and there are other object types as well, including triggers, stored procedures, and even roles.

Changes to an object can only be made by its owner or a superuser. If you want to give permissions to other roles to distribute duties like letting them change attributes or add entries to tables, you can do so with privileges.

## Granting Privileges to Objects

The GRANT command lets you assign privileges on an object to a role. It uses the following syntax:

```
GRANT chosen_privilege ON target_object TO target_role;
```

where *chosen_privilege* is the option to be given. The *target_object* can be a table, database or role for example. The *target_role* is the role that will be affected by this GRANT command.

As an example, assume that you have a table called statues, which was created by the toymaster role. Therefore only toymaster can make changes to the statues table. There is another role, called supplier, that needs to view the contents of the table. However, it is not able to do so because the table is owned by toymaster. As toymaster, you can give supplier the ability to see the contents of the table by entering:

```
GRANT SELECT ON statues TO supplier;
```

After you run this command, the supplier role can now see the contents of the statues table. You can see here that SELECT is the *chosen_privilege* you want to give; statue is the *target_object*, and supplier is the *target_role*.

Now assume you have a role called stocklister that acts as a group. The stocklister group can SELECT from and UPDATE the statues table. You can use the GRANT command for the stocklister role:

```
GRANT SELECT, UPDATE on statues TO stocklister;
```

Another role, called contacts, has been created and you want it to have SELECT and UPDATE permissions on the statues table. Instead of manually giving the permission, you can have contacts join the stocklister group by using

```
GRANT stocklister TO contacts;
```

as the postgres user. You have to use the postgres user for now because only that user has enough privileges to allow roles to be added to groups. When the contacts role uses the UPDATE statement on the statues table, it can do it successfully.

Additional privileges that can be used with the GRANT command can be found in http://www.postgresql.org/docs/8.1/interactive/sql-grant.html.

## Revoking Privileges on Objects

When you need to remove privileges on objects for certain roles, you can do so by using the REVOKE command, which has the syntax

```
REVOKE chosen_privilege ON target_object FROM target_role;
```

where *chosen_privilege* is the option to be given, the *target_object* can be a table, database or role, for example, and the *target_role* is the role that will be affected by this REVOKE command.

Continuing from the previous example, assume that the supplier role is to be restricted so that they cannot view the contents of the statues table. To remove the privilege you granted earlier, use the following REVOKE command:

```
REVOKE SELECT ON statues FROM supplier;
```

In this command, the *chosen_privilege* to be removed is SELECT, the *target_object* is the statues table, and the *target_role* that is going to be affected is supplier. The next time supplier tries to peek at the contents of the statues table, he or she will be denied access.

Additional REVOKE options can be found at http://www.postgresql.org/docs/8.1/interactive/sql-revoke.html.

## Changing Role Attributes

If you need to change attributes of a database role, you can use the ALTER ROLE command. This command can change a role's password, make a role represent a group, or permit access to databases. The syntax for ALTER ROLE is

```
ALTER ROLE target_role [WITH] target_option1 [target_option2 … target_optionN];
```

where *target_role* is the role whose attributes you want to change and the *target_options* are the attributes you want the role to use. For example, if you need to change the password for contacts to 'ging', you enter this:

```
ALTER ROLE contacts WITH PASSWORD 'ging';
```

assuming that the stocklister role is not yet capable of representing groups. If you need to give it that capability and let the permissions it has be used by its members, you enter this:

```
ALTER ROLE LOGIN INHERIT stocklister;
```

Any role that joins the stocklister group will be able to log into the PostgreSQL database because it will also take the LOGIN attribute through the INHERIT keyword.

You can learn more about the ALTER ROLE command at http://www.postgresql.org/docs/8.1/interactive/sql-alterrole.html.

## Getting the List of Databases

The list of available databases in PostgreSQL can be seen by using the \l command at the interactive terminal. Figure 12-6 is a screen capture of the current list, assuming you have created a toys database.

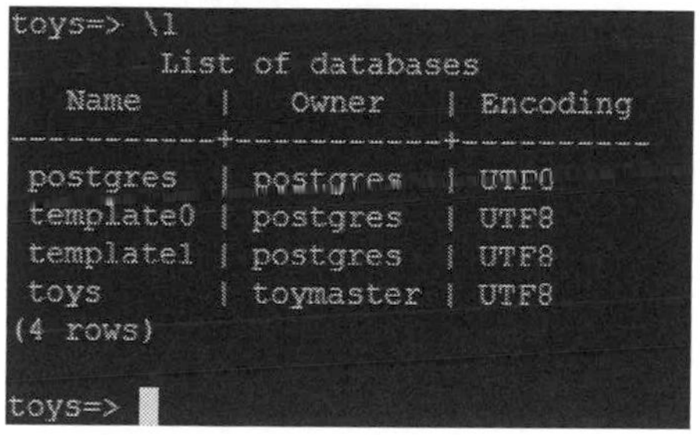

*Figure 12-6. The list of databases in the PostgreSQL server*

After checking the list of available databases, go back to the shell by typing \q at the PostgreSQL interactive shell prompt.

## Creating Database Backups

PostgreSQL comes with a utility called pg_dump to create backups of databases. Its syntax is

pg_dump *database*

where database is the name of the database you want to back up. The contents of the backup will be shown in the terminal and you need to redirect it to a file to save it. To create a backup of the toys database, use

pg_dump toys > toys.pgsql

This will create a text file called toys.pgsql that contains the backup of the toys database. There is also another utility, called pg_dumpall, that can create a backup of all the databases located in /var/lib/pgsql/data. To use it, enter

pg_dumpall > *backup_file*

where *backup_file* is the file that will be used to store the queries required to restore all the databases. Be sure to use a superuser for pg_dumpall; otherwise, only the databases you can see will be saved on the backup.

## Restoring a Database

You can also re-create a database from a backup in PostgreSQL by using the psql command. This command is used for administration not only in interactive mode but from the shell as well. To restore the contents of a backup file to an empty database, you use the following:

psql target_database < backup_file

where *target_database* is the database to be restored and *backup_file* is the file that contains the backup of the database.

Here are the steps to restoring a backup from a file. You will notice that they are similar to the MySQL procedure earlier.

1. Inform all users to log out of the server if they are still connected. This will alert them of the incoming database restoration.

   Create a backup of the damaged database if possible. This can be useful for future investigation or if there was something you needed that was missing from the last backup.

2. Drop the damaged database.

3. Create a new database with the same name as the old one. Be sure to do it with the original owner of the database to have the required privileges.

4. Use the psql command to restore the database from the backup file.

Assuming that we are restoring the toys database as the toymaster user and have done up to step 4, here is the command for step 5:

psql toys < toys.pgsql

We are uploading the contents of the backup file toys.pgsql into the empty database toys. After the command executes, the database will be restored based on the backup file.

# Configuring PostgreSQL

PostgreSQL also has its configuration files in its data directory (/var/lib/pgsql/data) that you can use to alter its behavior. The two most used configuration files are postgresql.conf and pg_hba.conf.

The first, postgresql.conf is the main configuration file of PostgreSQL. Here, you can set the port number it runs on, what options to use on table indexes to speed queries on the server, and even the number of connections you want PostgreSQL to handle. The options are specified with the following format:

```
option = option_value
```

where *option* is the option available in the configuration and *option_value* is its value. You can change the options depending on your needs. If you are going to deploy PostgreSQL in your organization, and some users will connect to this server remotely, it is best to have it listen to remote connections. Change to the postgres system user and open the postgresql.conf file using a text editor. Find the line containing

```
#listen_addresses = 'localhost'
```

and change it to

```
listen_addresses = '*'
```

Save the file and reload the PostgreSQL server as root using service postgresql restart. That will allow users on remote machines to connect to your server.

The main configuration file can be used to tweak PostgreSQL to make it perform better in terms of speed and resource usage. The options are divided into sections such as File Locations, Connection and Authentication, Resource Usage, and Query Tuning, for example. Most of the advanced options are set to a default, which may certainly not meet your organization's demands at first. But if you take some time to change the values of the options, you will see a great performance gain when PostgreSQL is reloaded. As a start, you can play with the Query Tuning section of the configuration file when the load gets tough and check if there are changes in performance. Always remember to reload PostgreSQL whenever you change an option in this file to inform the server process.

There are more properties you can configure with the postgresql.conf file, and you can choose from them in http://www.postgresql.org/docs/8.1/interactive/runtime-config.html.

## pg_hba.conf

The pg_hba.conf file lets you specify hosts or networks that can log into your PostgreSQL server. This file lets you configure which users can connect to which databases from which machines and the method they can use to connect. Each line of the file is divided into five columns: host, database, user, cidr-address, and method.

- The host column defines what kind of host can connect to the server. Most of the time you will specify host here because that will tell PostgreSQL to match incoming connections with TCP/IP. There are other options available if you need stricter matches, such as hostssl, and you can find them at http://www.postgresql.org/docs/8.1/interactive/client-authentication.html#AUTH-PG-HBA-CONF.
- database is the name of the database you want your remote machines to connect to. You can use the default all value but if you know which database your remote users need, it is better to specify it. You can specify more than one database here by separating them with commas.
- user lists the PostgreSQL roles allowed to connect to the specified databases. As with database, you can specify more than one user by separating the names with commas.

- cidr-address specifies the IP address range to match to the machine that connects to this server. For example, if you want to allow hosts in the network 10.0.0.0, you will use 10.0.0.0/24 here. If a machine with the IP address of 10.0.0.25 is allowed, you will use 10.0.0.25/32.
- method lets you specify how PostgreSQL will authenticate hosts that will connect to it. You can let hosts connect without authentication by using trust or refuse them access with reject.

For example, to allow a network 192.168.1.0 with the role toymaster to connect to the toys database, you add this line:

```
host    toys    toymaster    192.168.1.0/24        md5
```

This tells PostgreSQL to let hosts that use TCP/IP using the toymaster user to connect to the toys database. These hosts must belong to the network 192.168.1.0. When authenticating, the server must first check whether the PostgreSQL user toymaster exists. If so, the server will retrieve the MD5-encrypted password from the remote host. When the remote host's password matches to the server's password database, it is allowed to use the toys database.

You can change the behavior of authentication so that you aren't forced to make identical system users for the PostgreSQL users, by changing the ident sameuser entry to something else. For example, you can use md5 so the server still asks the remote host to identify it without having identical system users checked before connecting. As with any configuration file change, you need to reload the server for the modifications to take effect.

Now that you know how to administer both MySQL and PostgreSQL at the system level, it is time to learn about administration at the database level. The next section looks at some fundamental database language that encompasses CRUD.

# CRUD and Databases

CRUD is the acronym for Create, Read, Update, and Delete, the four major functions for software. Software almost always creates, reads, updates, and deletes something, such as lists and data structures. Databases are no exception because they are also software, specializing in storage.

CRUD translates directly to SQL, including both MySQL and PostgreSQL. Whenever an object is created, viewed, updated or destroyed, an associated SQL statement is used for that operation. Table 12-1 shows the association of CRUD to SQL.

*Table 12-1. Mapping CRUD to SQL*

| CRUD Stage | SQL Statement |
| --- | --- |
| CREATE | CREATE |
| READ | SELECT |
| UPDATE | UPDATE |
| DELETE | DELETE |

As systems administrators handling RDBMSs such as MySQL and PostgreSQL, do we actually need to learn all of SQL? Not really, because once you get to know the basics through CRUD, it can largely get you by. For most purposes, only developers who write database-enabled software need to learn more of the language.

In this section, you will learn the basics of the four SQL statements using MySQL and PostgreSQL. You can choose one of the two systems for the exercises for now and repeat them later with the other.

# Creating

Creating anything with SQL involves two statements most of the time: CREATE TABLE and INSERT. With the CREATE TABLE command, we can create tables and auxiliary structures such as keys in the database. When a table is created, we can use INSERT to add entries in it.

The next exercise will create a database for a fictional toy store called PVC Toys that stocks collectible statues and figurines such as popular game and movie characters. You will issue SQL statements to create tables, and later add and remove entries in it.

First, you will create a table in the toys database to add information such as attributes on it. Tables are one of the basic requirements of a database to store information. To make one, you will use the CREATE TABLE command, which has the following syntax:

```
CREATE TABLE table_name
(
attribute_1 attribute_1_type[,
attribute_2 attribute_2_type,
:
attribute_N attribute_N_type]
);
```

The *table_name* argument is the name of the table to create, *attribute_1* is the name of the first attribute in the table, and *attribute_1_type* is the kind of data the attribute is going to hold. Table 12-2 summarizes our plan to make a statues table in our toys database.

*Table 12-2. The Table Structure for the statues Table*

| Attribute Name | Attribute Data Type |
|---|---|
| statuecode | integer |
| statuename | varchar(100) |

The statuecode attribute will take numbers and the chosen data type for it is integer. This will help keep track of how many entries are already in the table, and it gives your figurines a unique identity. The statuename attribute will be take names of toy statues and figurines, and we choose varchar as the data type that can accept up to 100 letters. The varchar data type can actually hold up to 255 characters, but 100 will do for now. The notation in Table 12-2 tells the CREATE TABLE command the size of the statuename attribute in terms of the number of letters it can hold. That should be more than enough for toy names!

To create the statues table, use the command shown in Listing 12-3.

*Listing 12-3. Your first CREATE TABLE Command*

```
CREATE TABLE statues
(
        statuecode integer,
        statuename varchar(100)
);
```

You can see here that *attribute_1* is statuecode and *attribute_1_type* is integer. Similarly, *attribute2* is statuename and its type is varchar. We plugged in the attribute names and their corresponding data types to form the statement to create the statues table. Run this command on the terminal of your running database and the table will be created, as shown in Figure 12-7.

```
toys=> CREATE TABLE statues
toys-> (
toys(> statuecode integer,
toys(> statuename varchar(100)
toys(> );
CREATE TABLE
toys=>
```

*Figure 12-7.* ***Creating a table using CREATE TABLE***

---

■ **Tip:** Queries can be very long, and `CREATE TABLE` is no exception. You can divide the long query in your terminal by separating its parts into lines for readability. If you think what you are typing is long, press Enter to put it into another line. Whitespaces mean nothing, and it is the punctuation that is important. Be sure not to forget the semicolon at the end of your query to complete it!

---

Looking back at Figure 12-7, you might wonder why varchar is used for the statuename attribute when there is an equivalent char data type that can also hold letters. Imagine a pizza box; it represents the data type, and the pizza is the value. If we have half a pizza and we have a char data type, once we put the pizza in the box, we still have to put the whole box in the refrigerator. Space is wasted when there is only a small amount of food within the pizza box. For the varchar data type, the pizza box is cut into the size of the remaining half pizza before being placed into the refrigerator. In short, space is better allocated for character data that has a length we don't know in advance.

## Verifying the Newly Created Tables

After you create the table, you can check for its existence by typing `\d` on the PostgreSQL interactive terminal or issuing `SHOW TABLES;` within the MySQL monitor.

Figure 12-8 shows the MySQL screen after we create the statues table.

```
mysql> SHOW TABLES;
+----------------+
| Tables_in_toys |
+----------------+
| statues        |
+----------------+
1 row in set (0.00 sec)

mysql>
```

*Figure 12-8.* ***The statues table in the MySQL toys database***

## Viewing the Structures of the Tables

We've seen that our tables reside in the toys database. If you want to go further and view the inner details of each table, like the attributes and datatypes it has, you can use

```
\d table_name;
```

in PostgreSQL or

```
DESCRIBE table_name;
```

in MySQL. You can also use DESC as the shorthand for the DESCRIBE command. Figure 12-9 shows the PostgreSQL version of the command in action.

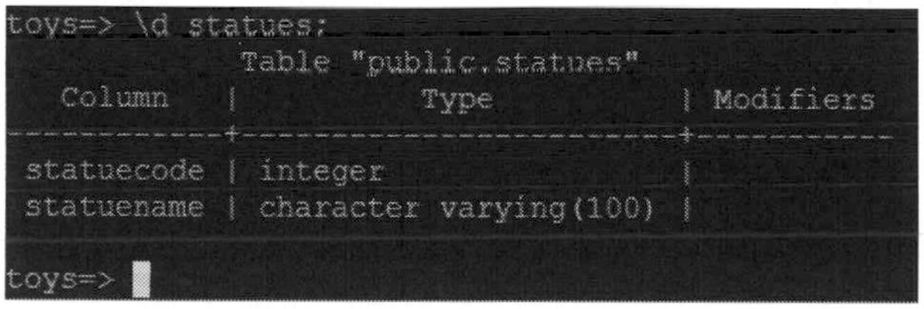

*Figure 12-9.* *The statues table in PostgreSQL*

Now that we know how to check our tables in the databases, we can move on to populating them with the next attribute of CRUD's C, the SQL INSERT statement.

## Adding Entries to the Table

To add entries to a table, we use the INSERT command of SQL. It follows the syntax

```
INSERT INTO table  VALUES (value_1,..value_N);
```

where *table* is the table you want to add an entry to, *value_1* is assigned for the first column of the table, *value_2* for the second column, and so on. The number of values must match the number of columns of the table.

The INSERT statement has another syntax that lets you specify the columns you need to add values to:

```
INSERT INTO table [(target_column_1,..target_column_N)] VALUES (value_1,..value_N);
```

Here, *target_column_1* will take *value_1*, and *target_column_2* will take *value_2*, and so on. The number of column names must match the number of values, and the values are associated with the column names in the statement in order.

As an exercise, type the following queries into the command line of your connected database. These INSERT statements will add two entries to your statues table:

```
INSERT INTO statues VALUES (1, 'Godzilla');
INSERT INTO statues (statuecode, statuename) VALUES (2, 'Cloverfield lizard');
```

Notice that the first INSERT command did not explicitly declare the attribute (or column) association with its value, unlike the second. That is fine as long as the values you assign to have the same type as its column. PostgreSQL will complain if you provide too many arguments, but it will accept too few as long as the types match. MySQL will accept this form only if the values provided match the number of columns. Otherwise, it will reject the statement.

For the first INSERT, we see that the number 1 is assigned to the statuecode column, and Godzilla is paired with the statuename column.

After adding the entries, how do we see if they are really there? We then use the R of CRUD, reading them with the SQL SELECT statement.

## Reading

The proper way to view the contents of a table is to use the SQL SELECT command, which uses the following syntax:

```
SELECT [column_1,..column_N] FROM table [WHERE conditions];
```

We can see that this command has three parts. The SELECT part specifies the columns that we want to look, the FROM part identifies the table the columns belong to, and if we want to restrict the output, we can do so by adding a WHERE part with its conditions. Most real-world database queries specify a WHERE clause; the user finds specific information by defining conditions.

For example, to see all of the contents of the statues table, you would run the following command:

```
SELECT statuecode, statuename FROM statues;
```

You can see in Figure 12-10 that this specified the statuecode and statuename columns for the output, which belongs to the statues table as declared in the FROM part.

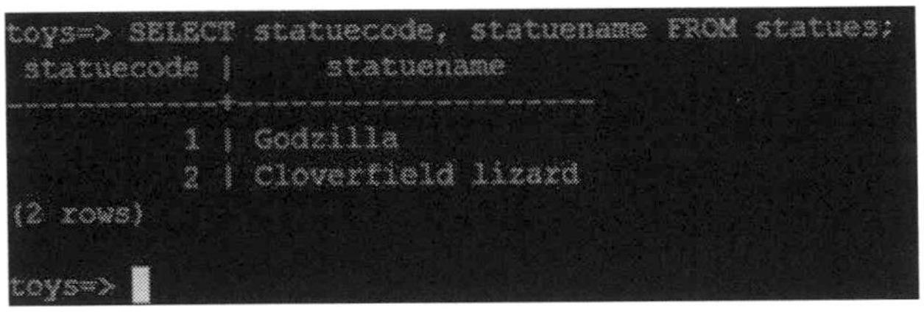

*Figure 12-10. Viewing all of the contents of the statue table*

Here is another query that filters the output to all entries with a statuecode of greater than 1:

```
SELECT * FROM statues WHERE statuecode > 1;
```

Running the query will produce the output shown in Figure 12-11.

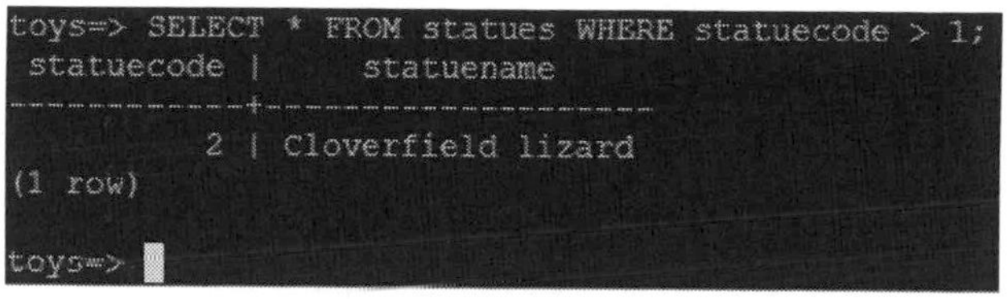

```
toys=> SELECT * FROM statues WHERE statuecode > 1;
 statuecode |       statuename
------------+------------------------
          2 | Cloverfield lizard
(1 row)

toys=>
```

*Figure 12-11. The SELECT statement with a condition*

Why does the SELECT part only contains an asterisk (*)? An asterisk is a shortcut to specify all columns of the table. This can be handy if there are too many columns to type into the SELECT query!

You can now add entries and view them. To modify them, you need to use the U of CRUD, updating.

# Updating

You can change the content of entries using the SQL statement UPDATE, which has the following syntax:

```
UPDATE table SET column_1 = new_value_1[,..column_N = ~CCC
new_value_N]  WHERE conditions;
```

The *table* is the target table that you want to modify. In the SET part, *column_1* is the first target column to update, and *new_value_1* is the value to replace the old value of the table. More than one column can be changed; all you have to do is to separate them with commas. Most of the time, you only change a few entries; this can be done by adding a WHERE part along with its filtering conditions.

---

■ **Warning:** Leaving out the WHERE part on UPDATE can give you a lot of problems, especially if you intend to change only a few rows on your table. It is like saying "I want to update everything on my table using this value," and every row in your table will have the same updated value. You should include a WHERE part in most of your UPDATE statements, unless you really want to do massive updates.

---

In the next set of queries, we will change the column values of statuename from villainous monsters to powerful heroes:

```
UPDATE statues SET statuename = 'Kratos' WHERE statuecode = 1;
UPDATE statues SET statuename = 'King Leonidas' WHERE statuecode = 2;
```

From these statements, you can see that the updates are filtered according to their associated statuecode. When UPDATE sees the condition statuecode = 1, it finds the row entries that have this and then applies the required change as dictated by the SET part. The same is applied to the next query.

Figure 12-12 shows the output of the queries after we run them.

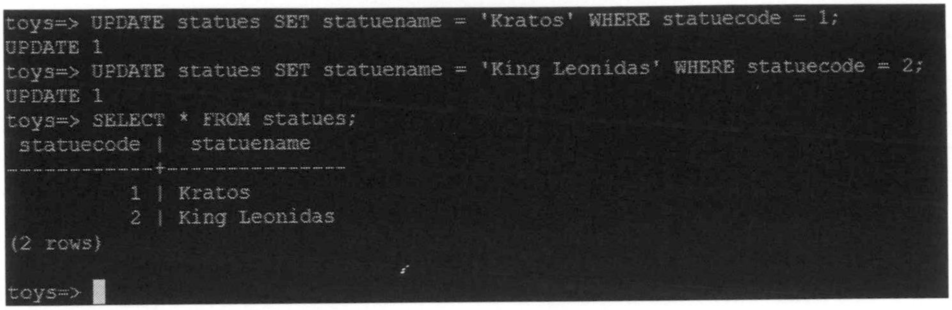

```
toys=> UPDATE statues SET statuename = 'Kratos' WHERE statuecode = 1;
UPDATE 1
toys=> UPDATE statues SET statuename = 'King Leonidas' WHERE statuecode = 2;
UPDATE 1
toys=> SELECT * FROM statues;
 statuecode |   statuename
_____+_____
          1 | Kratos
          2 | King Leonidas
(2 rows)

toys=>
```

*Figure 12-12. Using UPDATE on the statues table*

We now officially have toy statues of famous heroes in our stock! But because of the high demand, our stock slowly reduces, and we need to apply the D of CRUD, dropping or deleting entries.

## Dropping Entries from a Table

Unused entries can be dropped by using the DELETE statement, which has the following syntax:

DELETE FROM *table* WHERE *conditions*;

where *table* is the table that contains the entries we want to remove, and *conditions* pinpoint the entries to remove.

In the next query, we will remove the entry that contains a historical-based statue toy because it has been recently bought. To do that, we run the following:

DELETE FROM statues WHERE statuecode = 2;

The DELETE command will remove the entry that contains 'King Leonidas' because it has the statuecode of 2 as specified in the WHERE part. After the removal, the table looks like Figure 12-13.

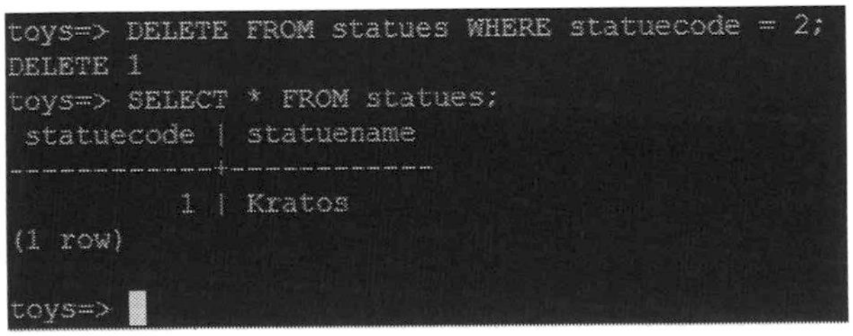

```
toys=> DELETE FROM statues WHERE statuecode = 2;
DELETE 1
toys=> SELECT * FROM statues;
 statuecode | statuename
_____+_____
          1 | Kratos
(1 row)

toys=>
```

*Figure 12-13. After King Leonidas was purchased, we DELETEd his entry from the statues table.*

We need to remind you again about doing DELETEs on databases. Be sure to think thrice before you actually do a DELETE because if you accidentally remove an entry, oh well.

**Caution:** The WHERE part of both UPDATE and DELETE is actually optional. But if you omit it, you are either massively updating all rows in the table or removing a whole table instantly. Be careful!

## Summary

This chapter proves to be a titan in terms of open source databases! We discussed how to properly set up, configure and use both PostgreSQL and MySQL in our system. Users, hosts ,and permissions are a necessity for RDBMS to ensure security. You also learned about basic database administration with CRUD through the main SQL statements.

■ ■ ■

# CHAPTER 13

# Linux Web Services

Web servers are becoming more diverse in the features they offer beyond serving web pages. Scripting languages such as JSP, PHP, and Python are now a major requirement for any web server that must perform server-side processing for web client requests. Secure web connections with SSL are a must for any web site that does transactions and exchanges of sensitive information.

In this chapter, you will learn how to install the Apache web server, one of the first web servers available to provide web content to web browsers. You will also add PHP to Apache to let it interpret PHP scripts, which can generate dynamic web content. With Apache and PHP, you will have a working LAMP setup to build dynamic websites. Finally, you will install OpenSSL on our Apache web server to enable it to have secure HTTP connections.

## The Role of a Web Server

As a network administrator, you need to know what a web server really does. Web servers send resources over the network as required by the client. Resources include web pages, images, and other formats that are understood by both the web server and the web client. This request/response exchange is shown in Figure 13-1.

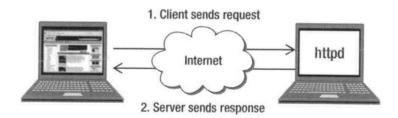

*Figure 13-1. HTTP request/response*

Figure 13-1 depicts the normal process of a user visiting a web site. The user opens a web browser (the client software), types in the web address of the site to visit, and waits for it to load. The web site server receives the request, prepares the web page and its associated images, and then sends it back to the client. The client then loads the web pages of the web site on the user's machine.

These interactions are the basics of the Hypertext Transfer Protocol (HTTP), the protocol of the World Wide Web (WWW). This is the standard for both client and server in making a resource request/response.

---

■ **Note:** You can read more about HTTP and WWW by visiting `http://www.ietf.org/ rfc/rfc2616.txt` and `http://www.w3.org/WWW` respectively.

---

# Apache Web Server

The Apache web server started as the public-domain HTTP server of the National Center for Supercomputing Applications (NSCA). It was created by Rob McCool during the early 90s. Rob left the NSCA during 1994, and that meant no one was left to maintain the web server. A group of webmasters took the initiative to start maintaining the web server's source code through email. They started to make code patches to provide fixes to the web server. Those patches would become the basis of the actual name of the web server: "a patchy" server. Later, a mailing list was set up by Brian Behlendorf and Cliff Skolnick to help the core developers collaborate while further developing the web server.

Apache grew popular not only as an open source tool but also for its capabilities. It can provide HTML and server scripting through CGI and can even integrate other server languages. This made Apache equal to or better than commercial web servers for deployment.

When the user base of the Apache web server continued to grow, the core contributors formed the Apache Software Foundation to give the Apache community a place for interaction and a repository for software. There are now more projects in the foundation's web site (`http://www.apache.org`) along with the Apache web server. Ant is an example, a Java-based build tool that can help Java developers compile batches of source code similar to the make software in Unix and Linux, for example.

In the following sections you will start to set up the Apache web server in your system to see if it provides the HTTP services required by your organization.

# Setting Up Apache

Apache is included in the default install of CentOS. If you had explicitly excluded the server during installation, you can add it to your system with the command `yum install httpd`.

# Testing Apache

Once the Apache server is in the system, you can run it by issuing `service httpd start`. After starting the server, you can open a web browser and type

`http://localhost`

in the address bar. If your server resides on another machine within the network, you can directly access it with your web browser using its IP address:

`http://192.168.1.104`

assuming that the remote machine has `192.168.1.104` as its IP address. This will display the default home page of your web server as shown in Figure 13-2.

Now that you know your Apache server is running, it is time to learn how to customize it according to your needs. The next section shows where you can make changes in Apache.

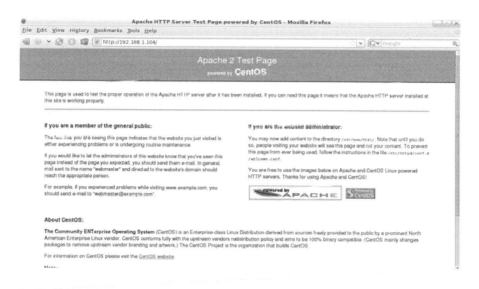

*Figure 13-2. Test page of the Apache web server*

# Apache Server Directories

The Apache server provides you with two directories that you can use after installation. The first is the configuration directory, located in /etc/httpd. The second is the content directory in /var/www.

The configuration directory contains five subdirectories that Apache refers to during its execution. Two of these subdirectories are actual directories, conf and conf.d. The remaining three, logs, modules, and run, are symbolic links to the actual directories.

The conf directory contains the main configuration file, httpd.conf and the magic file, Apache's reference for all known types of files. You will probably never need to look into the magic file unless you are a developer who develops code for Apache. The conf.d directory holds the configuration files for Apache modules.

With httpd.conf, you can change how the Apache server handles HTTP requests and where it finds the web documents in the system. The magic file contains information for Apache's mod_mime_magic module, which is used to classify data properly. Without the file, Apache would have a difficult time distinguishing a Java file from an audio file, for example, and it could put incorrect file headers on the requested file sent to the client. If the server incorrectly sent a requested Java file as an audio file, the client would download the Java file and try to play it using its default media player, which would report an error.

---

■ **Note:** You can learn more about Apache's mod_mime_magic module by going to
http://httpd.apache.org/docs/2.2/mod/mod_mime_magic.html.

---

The logs directory holds the log files produced by the Apache server. These files are the access_log, which contains web server access-related information based on the requests being accepted and responses being sent, and the error_log, used by Apache to record problems it encounters while processing HTTP requests. This is very useful in troubleshooting and doing forensics on a possible cracker attack.

The content directory (/var/www) holds directories that let you store content which can be accessed by clients. They are html, cgi-bin, icons, and error:

html: The default primary web document directory (or formally known as the document root) that lets you store web documents such as HTML files to be accessed by clients. This directory cannot run CGI scripts, but the next one can.

cgi-bin: The default CGI script directory of Apache. It can interpret Perl-CGI scripts by default and have them produce output based on the client's request. Other scripting languages, such as Python, can be used to run files in this directory if required. Be sure to change the permissions of the script you want to be accessed to executable and to thoroughly test it!

**Warning:** CGI scripts are an attacker's favorite entry point to web servers. One problem CGI scripts have is that the script executed by Apache runs with the permissions of the assigned User directive. If that user can access restricted files and directories, the attacker can take advantage of it after entry to damage the system through the web server. Another is that CGI scripts can access system environment variables that can give additional information to the attacker, if the programmer is not careful when using those variables in the script. Before deploying CGI scripts, double-check for these kinds of exploits to avoid this problem. You can read more about securing Apache at http://httpd.apache.org/docs/2.0/misc/security_tips.html.

icons: The default image directory of Apache, it contains images of the Test Page and additional bundled images for your own use. You can also use this directory to store your own set of icons and images for custom web sites. Most sites, however, are deployed as single units, each of which may have its own directory to store images. These days, most Apache administrators see the icons directory only in directory listings.

error: Contains HTTP error messages in multiple languages. If the preferred language of a client is available, it is selected automatically via the MultiViews feature. This applies to all content, not just error messages.

**Note:** More information about the MultiViews feature can be found at http://httpd. apache.org/docs/2.2/content-negotiation.html.

These are the default directories that come with the default installation of Apache. If you need to customize Apache, you will need to change entries in the httpd.conf file. You will see how to do that next.

# The Apache Configuration File

Apache uses the configuration file called httpd.conf, which is located in /etc/httpd/conf. You can open the file and view it using any text editor.

In this file most configuration details are specified using compound *directives*, which can contain attributes in addition to arguments. Here is the syntax of the compound directive:

```
<compounddirectivename argument>
option1 argument
:
optionN argument
</compounddirectivename>
```

where *compounddirectivcname* is the name of the directive and *argument* is the value you want to use with the directive. Inside the compound directive, you can include options that are themselves directives. These options can also take arguments that can change the way the whole compound directive functions. Following all the options, the compound directive is enclosed using the directive's name prepended with a slash, with no arguments. This identifies the end of the compound directive and tells Apache to move on to the next one. Here is an example of a compound directive:

```
<Directory "/var/www/icons">
    Options Indexes MultiViews
    AllowOverride None
    Order allow,deny
    Allow from all
</Directory>
```

This is one of the actual Directory directives that you will find in the Apache main configuration file. You can see here that the argument for the Directory directive is /var/www/icons, and there are four options used. One of the options, Order allow,deny, states that when Apache reaches the /var/www/icons directory, it must evaluate all the allow rules that govern this directory. If there is no match, it will check the deny rules. If there are still no matches on both rules, the request is denied.

The configuration file also contains comments, marked with a hash symbol (#) as in other Linux tools. Comments are ignored by Apache, and you can use them to include notes. This feature will help you later in your Apache administration when you use advanced directives and will also serve as a reminder of your configuration.

## Apache Configuration File Sections

The configuration file is divided into the *global environment* section, the *main server configuration* section, and the *virtual hosts* section. The directives within these sections control the way the Apache web server runs, and you can alter them depending on your needs.

*The Global Environment Section:* This section contains options that can affect the overall operation of the Apache web server. Some of the directives provide the locations of other directories that contain additional configuration files. Also specified here is the *process identification file*, which contains the identifier that is used by the operating system Apache runs on. This identifier will enable the host operating system to terminate Apache if the administrator requires it. You can also control advanced capabilities such as the loading of modules to extend Apache's functionality with, for example, additional scripting languages. Finally, you can manage server pool size, instructing Apache how many processes it can start when serving web clients.

*The Main Server Section:* This provides directives that are specific to Apache's main server process. This process creates and controls the subprocesses that communicate with the server's clients. In this section you can change the main server's name to match the one assigned by your DNS server, so that web clients can find your web server by using its hostname, or you can add more directories for web pages. If additional server-scripting language modules have been loaded, you can specify their file extensions so that Apache can interpret them properly.

*The Virtual Hosts Section:* The options available in this section enable you to maintain multiple domains on your machine. This can be useful if you are in the web hosting business or if your company has subsidiaries that need web presence using your server.

The configuration file's division into these parts is actually not required. The maintainers of Apache adopted this convention to help beginning web administrators understand how the configuration file works. When you gain more experience, you can create your own configuration file to use instead of this one. Because you are learning to use Apache, it is best to use the existing `httpd.conf` file at the moment. Be sure to make a backup, because in later sections you will make a lot of changes to observe how Apache reacts to them.

# Commonly Used Directives

Apache has many directives, and the configuration file includes examples of some of them. In this section, you will learn the common directives that are frequently changed and what each is used for. This will prepare you for the upcoming examples, where you will change the contents of the configuration file to further explore how Apache works.

## Section 1: Global Environment

The directives you'll most often modify in the global environment section are `Listen`, `User`, and `Group`.

### Listen

Syntax:

`Listen newport`

This directive identifies the port number Apache must listen to for incoming HTTP requests. Following the HTTP protocol standard, the port is set to 80 by default. If you need to make Apache listen to a different port, you just change the *newport* value in `Listen`. For example, to have Apache listen to port number 8080, enter this directive:

`Listen 8080`

### User and Group

Syntax:

`User newuser`
`Group newgroup`

These directives provide the system user and system group that Apache will use after it starts. Apache uses this scheme to improve security and avoid advanced attacks that can compromise the system. In our default setup, after the Apache server runs, it will quickly change from the root user into the apache user because of the User apache directive. The same goes for the group; it becomes apache because of the Group apache directive. The apache user and its group are unprivileged, which gives us added security because Apache cannot access files owned by different users.

# Section 2: Main Server Configuration

The directives most often modified in the main server configuration section are ServerAdmin, ServerName, DocumentRoot, and Directory.

## ServerAdmin

Syntax:

ServerAdmin *adminemail*

This enables Apache to tell the user where to send email in case of an internal problem such as an Internal System Error message. The value contained in this directive will appear on the web page that generated the system error.

## ServerName

Syntax:

ServerName actualdomainname[:*portnumber*]

The value you specify in this directive will be used as Apache's hostname when identifying itself. This is used when creating redirection URLs that will be used to find your Apache server. You can also specify the port number that your Apache server uses if it listens to another port, as in this example:

ServerName www.pvctoyfan.com

When URLs redirecting to www.pvctoyfan.com are made by the client, your Apache server will identify itself as the web server of that URL running on the default HTTP port number 80. Your Apache server will be able to accept the client's HTTP requests after the redirection and serve the required web pages.

It is recommended to use a valid domain name for any server being deployed in a production environment. If you don't have a domain name for the server yet, use its IP address as a temporary solution.

## DocumentRoot

Syntax:

DocumentRoot "*targetdirectory*"

This will tell Apache to use the directory you specify here to serve web documents. Although this directive tells Apache where to get requested documents, it does not describe the other attributes, such as how deep into the given directory the client can browse. You control those through the Directory directive.

---

▓ **Note:** Some Apache directives require that their argument be enclosed in quotation marks if it contains spaces or regular expressions. DocumentRoot is one of them. Be sure to pay attention to the argument requirements of a directive you are about to use.

---

If the directory given in the DocumentRoot directive is empty, the default webpage specified in the welcome.conf file is used. This file is located in the /etc/httpd/conf.d directory. Because the DocumentRoot directory (/var/www/html) is empty, Apache used the noindex.html file given in the welcome.conf file when you accessed it for the first time. The noindex.html file is located in the /var/www/error directory and is Apache's test page.

## Directory

Syntax:

```
<Directory targetdirectory>
     option1 arguments
          :
     optionN argumentsN
</Directory>
```

The Directory directive provides additional information about the directories that Apache can use, such as how to display the directory contents and any restrictions on a directory. The options specified in the Directory directive will be applied to the directory it represents. Other directives that use the Directory directive are DocumentRoot, Alias, and ScriptAlias. For example, the DocumentRoot directive that points to /var/www/html uses the following options from its equivalent Directory directive.

```
<Directory "/var/www/html">
     Option Indexes FollowSymLinks
     AllowOverride None
     Order allow,deny
     Allow from all
</Directory>
```

The Directory directive for /var/www/html contains four options that Apache will use when it is going to display its contents for a client. These are the Option, AllowOverride, Order, and Allow attributes.

The Option attribute in the example directive contains both Indexes and FollowSymLinks. When Indexes is used, Apache will be able to display the contents of the /var/www/html directory even if there is no index file present. Apache will be able to do that because it will generate its own generic index file to show the contents of the directory. The FollowSymLinks value will let Apache show the contents of the directory that is given as a symbolic link within the target directory.

AllowOverride lets you specify which directives in the current directory's distributed configuration file, called .htaccess, can override the declared directives for this Directory directive. It is set to None, which does not allow distributed configuration files to change any earlier directives. If you set it to All and there is a distributed configuration file in the directory, any directive that the file contains will be able to overwrite the value of an earlier directive with the same name, thus altering the behavior. You'll learn more about distributed configuration files in the next section.

The Order directive tells Apache what sequence must be followed when evaluating Allow and Deny directives for this Directory directive. In the example, it has allow,deny as its value, which means all the Allow directives must be evaluated first, and then the Deny directives. If there is a match on the Allow directive, the evaluation exits and that is used in resolving restrictions to the client for this directory. If there aren't any matches, the Deny directives are evaluated next. If there are still no matches, the final result is that the client will be denied access to this directory.

Next to the Order directive is the Allow directive, which tells Apache which hosts can access resources on this server. Because this Allow directive is in the Directory directive, it gives out the access rules for the /var/www/html directory that Apache must follow. The value it holds is from all, which lets all users view the contents of this directory.

You can include additional directives within the Directory directive to control how the target directory can be used by web clients.

# Distributed Configuration Files

The distributed configuration files, also known as .htaccess files, contain directives to control specific directories that Apache can use. With .htaccess files, you can customize the directives used by Directory directives that include the AllowOverride directive. The AllowOverride directive lets you use new values of earlier directives within the Directory directive only.

Let's assume that you want the /var/www/html directory's default index file to use index.php, instead of index.html or index.html.var as declared in the main server section of the configuration file. You will have to let Apache apply the contents of the .htaccess file for the /var/www/html directory by setting AllowOverride to all:

```
<Directory "/var/www/html">
    Option Indexes FollowSymLinks
    AllowOverride All
    Order allow,deny
    Allow from all
</Directory>
```

Then create an .htaccess text file in the /var/www/html directory, containing the new DirectoryIndex value that must be used:

```
DirectoryIndex index.php
```

Save both files and restart Apache to have the new DirectoryIndex value applied to the /var/www/html directory

One disadvantage of using .htaccess files is additional overhead for Apache. Each time a directory that uses an .htaccess file is accessed, the file is opened and the directives applied to the directory. It is advisable to limit the use of .htaccess files if possible in your deployment.

Another disadvantage is security. You need to set the proper permissions of .htaccess files to avoid allowing unwanted attackers to take advantage of it. Because .htaccess files can use directives that are applied by Apache, leaving them unprotected can compromise the whole web server.

You can find additional information about distributed configuration files on http://httpd.apache.org/ docs/2.2/howto/htaccess.html.

## DirectoryIndex

Syntax:

```
DirectoryIndex newindexfile1 newindexfile2 .. newindexfileN
```

Use this directive to specify the starting web document to use when a client accesses a web directory without giving a web page. You have probably noticed that whenever you type in a URL such as http://www.apress.com, the starting page is automatically downloaded to your web browser. You did not type anything after the URL. In Apache, what happens is that the URL is translated depending on the value of the DirectoryIndex directive. In the httpd.conf file, we have this:

```
DirectoryIndex index.html index.html.var
```

Thanks to this directive, when the user types in the URL http://www.apress.com, it becomes http://www.apress.com/index.html.

If the index.html file exists within the document directory (/var/www/html/index.html, for example), the site is loaded with it. If the file does not exist, Apache will try to append index.html.var and the URL will become http://www.apress.com/index.html.var. If the file still does not exist, Apache will flag an error.

## Alias

Syntax:

```
Alias referencedirectoryname "actualdirectorylocation"
```

Alias lets you store documents in other directories within the system. This can be useful if you want to organize your web sites by putting them in separate directories other than the one specified in DocumentRoot. You may need to add a Directory directive for the directory you gave an alias to for access permissions to the client.

For example, suppose you want to create an alias for the /var/tmp/toys directory, called toys, that lets users access it by using http://localhost/toys. To do that, you will need to add an Alias directive in httpd.conf:

```
Alias /toys "/var/tmp/toys"
```

Be sure to enclose the actual directory location in double-quotes so that Apache will interpret it properly. Also, check that the /var/tmp/toys directory has read and execute permissions to allow the apache user to access it. You can do that by running chmod 755 /var/tmp/toys in a terminal.

## ScriptAlias

Syntax:

```
ScriptAlias referencedirectoryname "actualdirectoryname"
```

Similar to Alias but applied to scripts instead of HTML documents, the ScriptAlias directive lets you store CGI scripts in directories other than the default /var/www/cgi-bin. You may also need to add a Directory directive to give additional access rights for requesting clients that want to run CGI scripts.

For example, suppose you want to let Apache run CGI scripts inside the /var/tmp/toys/cgi-bin and have it called toys-cgi. You will have to add this line on the configuration file to do that:

```
ScriptAlias /toys-cgi "/var/tmp/toys/cgi-bin"
```

That will let users run the required scripts inside the /var/tmp/toys/cgi-bin when accessing the URL http://localhost/toys-cgi on their web browsers.

---

■ **Note:** Be sure to disable SElinux when testing out the examples that follow. SELinux enforces rules that can restrict your web server tests with Apache.

---

## Creating Another Document and cgi-bin Directory

You can try out some of the directives just discussed by creating another document directory that has an equivalent cgi-bin directory. Take the following steps.

1. Create a directory called otakai inside /var/tmp by running

   `mkdir /var/tmp/otakai`

2. Make an html directory inside otakai by running

   `mkdir /var/tmp/otakai/html`

   This will hold our web pages.

3. Make a cgi-bin directory inside otakai by running

   `mkdir /var/tmp/otakai/cgi-bin`

   We will let this directory handle CGI scripts.

4. Open the httpd.conf file and add the following at the bottom:

   ```
   Alias /otakai "/var/tmp/otakai/html"

   <Directory /var/tmp/otakai/html>
           Options Indexes FollowSymLinks
           AllowOverride None
           Order allow,deny
           Allow from all
   </Directory>
   ```

   You added two directives, an Alias for the /var/tmp/otakai/html directory that is referenced by adding /otakai in the URL, and a Directory for additional access information for displaying web pages, in the /var/tmp/otakai/html directory. This will let users retrieve the sample web page, which shows a greeting that you will create later, at http://localhost/otakai.

5. You will now create a cgi-bin directory for your new document root. Add the following lines after the new entry you added in step 4.

   ```
   ScriptAlias /otakai-cgi-bin "/var/tmp/otakai/cgi-bin"
   ```

```
<Directory /var/tmp/otakai/cgi-bin>
        Options None
        AllowOverride None
        Order allow,deny
        Allow from all
</Directory>
```

Here you've added a ScriptAlias directive; this means that the server uses the /var/tmp/otakai-cgi-bin directory when a client requests a file from /otakai/cgi-bin in the URL. You also added a Directory directive to allow clients to use the contents of the new otakai/cgi-bin directory Save the file and restart the Apache server by issuing service httpd restart to enable your configuration changes.

6. Create a file called index.html in /var/tmp/otakai/html containing the code shown in Listing 13-1.

*Listing 13-1. A Basic Welcome Starting Page*

```
<html>
<body>
        Welcome to the Otakai community mirror site!
</body>
</html>
```

This code contains HTML tags that will display a welcome message when you visit the URL http://localhost/otakai. The DirectoryIndex directive will take action by appending the value it has to the URL. When you type the URL http://localhost/otakai on your web browser later, Apache will look for the DirectoryIndex directive and append the first value it finds there, if the directory has multiple values. The URL becomes http://localhost/otakai/index.html, and then Apache will try to find a match for the index.html file in the /var/tmp/otakai/html directory. In this example the index.html file in the /var/tmp/otakai/html directory exists, and that file is served on your web browser. If the file is not found, Apache will try the next value after the first.

7. Create a file called firstscript.cgi in /var/tmp/otakai/cgi-bin with the contents shown in Listing 13-2.

*Listing 13-2. A Test Perl-CGI Script*

```
#!/usr/bin/perl

print "Content-type: text/html\n\n";
print "<html>";
print "<body>";
print "Welcome to the CGI-BIN of Otakai community mirror site!";
print "</body>";
print "</html>";
```

The Perl source code contains header information to help Apache to interpret the script properly before sending it as a response to the client. After the script is interpreted, the expected HTML output will be rendered to the client's web browser. Save the file.

8. Change the permission of firstscript.cgi to make it executable. Run this command:

   chmod 755 /var/tmp/otakai/cgi-bin/firstscript.cgi

   to allow Apache to run it. If you do not, you will see a Premature end-of script header entry in the error_log.

9. Access your Otakai document directory by entering http://localhost/otakai in your web browser. It should look like Figure 13-3.

*Figure 13-3. The index.html file running for your local Otakai community web site*

10. Next, test the PERL-CGI script you made by accessing it using http://localhost/otakai-cgi-bin/firstscript.cgi in your web browser's address bar. The display should look like Figure 13-4.

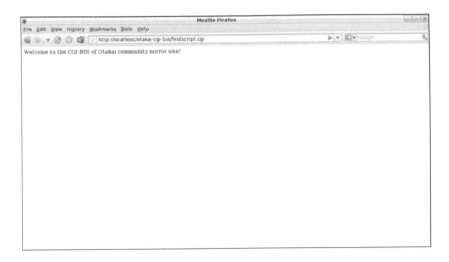

*Figure 13-4. The firstscript.cgi output from the Otakai CGI-BIN directory*

If you can see both screens, you have successfully created another document directory to hold your web site contents and CGI scripts.

# Virtual Hosts

Virtual hosts can let you serve more than one domain from the same Apache web server. This is a good approach compared to setting up different machines for additional web sites. You can see a depiction of virtual hosts in Apache in Figure 13-5.

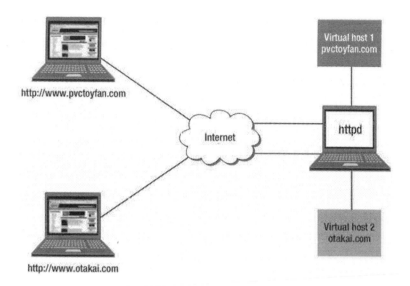

*Figure 13-5. Virtual hosts with Apache*

In this example, the Apache server is hosting two separate virtual hosts. The first virtual host is for the domain http://www.pvctoyfan.com, and the second is for http://www.otakai.com. When a client requests the content of http://www.pvctoyfan.com, Apache will serve the content from the first virtual host. The content of the second virtual host will be given if the client connects to the Apache server with the URL http://www.otakai.com.

## IP-Based and Name-Based Virtual Hosting

Virtual hosting can be either IP-based or name-based. IP-based virtual hosting requires that each virtual host have an IP address. You have to prepare the IP address for each domain because when requests arrive, the Apache server will look at the IP address to serve the correct web content. Name-based virtual hosting only needs the DNS server to be configured so that both hostnames point to the same IP address. Apache will be configured to differentiate hostnames to return web content.

Assume that the Apache web server is using virtual hosting to host two domains, pvctoyfan.com and otakai.com. When IP-based virtual hosting is used, both domains must have valid IP addresses assigned to them. For example, the www.pvctoyfan.com hostname has the IP address 202.124.120.1, and the www.otakai.com hostname has 202.124.120.2, and both domain name and IP addresses are configured in the web server as virtual hosts. If a client connects to 202.124.120.2 after a DNS lookup, the content for www.otakai.com will be returned. Similarly, the www.pvctoyfan.com content will be returned if the client goes for 202.124.120.1.

For name-based virtual hosting, the pvctoyfan.com and otakai.com domains need only a single IP address assigned for both web sites. The proper content will be served back to the client based on the domain name it requested. For example, suppose the web server has the IP address 202.124.120.1 and is configured to handle both www.pvctoyfan.com and www.otakai.com virtual hosts. If a client connects to the web server using the http://www.pvctoyfan.com domain name, the content for that domain that resides on the virtual host will be served. The same goes for http://www.otakai.com if the client requests it.

Name-based virtual hosting is easier to set up, but it is only effective on requests that use HTTP version 1.1 (HTTP/1.1). Only in HTTP/1.1 is the HTTP Host header available. For web browsers that still use HTTP/1.0, the name-based virtual server will not work properly because the HTTP request does not have the Host header. If you think there will be old web browsers connecting to your site, or if your clients will use SSL, it's better to use IP-based virtual hosting. SSL cannot be used in name-based virtual hosting because of an order conflict. For Apache to know the correct virtual host from the request, it will need to read the Host header of the HTTP request. It cannot do that unless the SSL connection is already established. The secure connection cannot be completed because the correct virtual host name cannot be determined by Apache due to the SSL's restriction. Otherwise, use name-based hosting.

To use virtual hosting in Apache, you will need the VirtualHost compound directive, discussed next.

## The VirtualHost Directive

Syntax:

```
<VirtualHost domain[:port]>
    directiveOption1 value1
    :
    directiveOptionN valueN
/VirtualHost>
```

The VirtualHost directive requires a domain name as its main argument. You can specify a port number if you need to have the virtual host serve content on a different port. Because it's a compound directive, you can put in additional directives that can change the way the virtual host behaves.

When the server receives a request for a document on a particular virtual host, it uses the configuration directives enclosed in the VirtualHost section. The domain part can be an actual domain name or an IP address. The port number is useful for setting up test instances of a web site even if you don't have control of the DNS or IP space.

You will configure two virtual hosts in your Apache server, one for www.pvctoyfan.com and one for www.otakai.com. The scheme we are going to use is name-based instead of IP-based.

## Configuring Name-Based Virtual Hosting

We will create a separate document root for the www.pvctoyfan.com domain. Note that both www.otakai.com and www.pvctoyfan.com are fictional domains and are for practice only!

1. Open the httpd.conf file and add the code shown in Listing 13-3 at the bottom.

*Listing 13-3. The Directory Directive for the www.pvctoyfan.com Domain*

```
<Directory /var/tmp/pvctoyfan/html>
        Options Indexes FollowSymLinks
        AllowOverride None
        Order allow,deny
        Allow from all
</Directory>
```

This will introduce the pvctoyfan.com document root directory for Apache. Save the file.

2. Create the directory in /var/tmp/pvctoyfan/html by issuing

   mkdir -p /var/tmp/pvctoyfan/html

   to store the web documents for the www.pvctoyfan.com domain later.

3. Open the httpd.conf file and uncomment the line

   NameVirtualHost *:80

   This will make the Apache accept requests for any IP address on port 80.

4. Add the VirtualHost directive shown in Listing 13-4 at the bottom for the www.pvctoyfan.com domain

   *Listing 13-4. The First VirtualHost Directive*

   ```
   <VirtualHost *:80>
       DocumentRoot /var/tmp/pvctoyfan/html
       ServerName www.pvctoyfan.com
   </VirtualHost>
   ```

   The first virtual host will also become the default. This means that if a domain points to the server (or an IP) that does not have a specific virtual host, the first host will be shown.

---

■ **Note:** Earlier, we said that certain directives can be contained in compound directives. VirtualHost is a good example because both the DocumentRoot and ServerName directives that are found Section 1 of the httpd.conf file are in this container. Also note that whatever the values of the DocumentRoot and ServerName in Section 1, they will not have any effect while inside a VirtualHost container. What is happening here is that the DocumentRoot and ServerName directives in the VirtualHost container are owned by that container only.

---

If you look at the example VirtualHost directive in the configuration file, you'll see other directives included such as the ServerAdmin. You can add these directives if you want but for now, our focus is to see how name-based virtual hosting works. The minimal configured directives will suffice.

5. Create the document root directory for www.otakai.com on /var/tmp/otakai/html by entering

   mkdir -p /var/tmp/otakai/html

   at the shell prompt.

6. Add the VirtualHost directive for the www.otakai.com domain, shown in Listing 13-5, at the bottom of the file.

*Listing 13-5. The Second VirtualHost Directive*

```
<VirtualHost *:80>
    DocumentRoot /var/tmp/otakai/html
    ServerName www.otakai.com
</VirtualHost>
```

After adding the entry, save the file and head back to the shell prompt.

7. Create a file called index.html within /var/tmp/pvctoyfan/html and give it the content shown in Listing 13-6.

*Listing 13-6. The Index Page for the www.pvctoyfan.com Domain*

```
<html>
<body>
        Welcome to the PVC Toy Fan site.
</body>
</html>
```

This will be the starting page for the www.pvctoyfan.com domain. Save the file.

8. Create a file called index.html in the /var/tmp/otakai/html directory and give it the code shown in Listing 13-7.

*Listing 13-7. The Index Page for the www.otakai.com Domain*

```
<html>
<body>
     Welcome to the Otakai community mirror site!
</body>
</html>
```

9. Open the /etc/hosts file using a text editor and look for the line

```
127.0.0.1                 localhost.localdomain localhost
```

Change it to

```
127.0.0.1                 localhost.localdomain localhost www.pvctoyfan.com
www.otakai.com
```

We are going to role-play the www.pvctoyfan.com and www.otakai.com domains as separate in our system. This is our only solution because we still do not have valid domain names for both. You can do better later after you learn DNS by adding records for both domains for a better feel of virtual hosting. Save the file.

10. Restart the Apache server by running service httpd restart.

11. Assuming you are running GNOME and Firefox on your CentOS server, type in
    http://www.pvctoyfan.com at the address bar. The resulting display should
    look like the one in Figure 13-6.

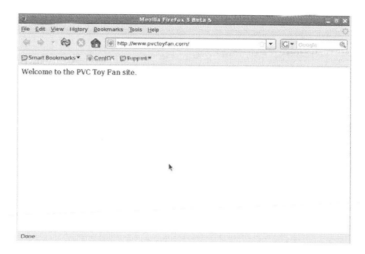

*Figure 13-6. The www.pvctoyfan.com virtual host accessed on Apache*

12. After verifying that www.pvctoyfan.com exists, enter http://www.otakai.com
    next, and the output should be similar to Figure 13-7.

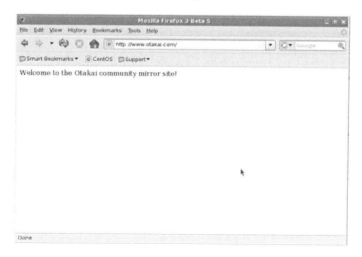

*Figure 13-7. Output from entering http://www.otakai.com*

When you see both domains, you have successfully used name-based virtual hosting with the Apache server.

You may want to see the internal details of how the result appeared as expected. Here is a step by step summary of what happens when a user wants to see the www.pvctoyfan.com site using our Apache server enabled for virtual hosting:

1.  Using an HTTP/1.1 browser, the site visitor sends a request for http://www.pvctoyfan.com to our Apache server.

2.  The Apache server accepts the request and tries to find the Host header. It does, and the header contains www.pvctoyfan.com.

3.  Our server then checks whether the NameVirtualHost directive is enabled. It is, and Apache starts to search for each VirtualHost container.

4.  It starts with the first VirtualHost container (the one that contains the ServerName directive ServerName www.pvctoyfan.com). It tries to match the hostname from the Host header to the ServerName directive, and it matches.

5.  After the match, the Apache server prepares the required response by using the contents of the chosen VirtualHost container, and it gives it back to the requesting client.

There are more virtual host setups available, and you can find them in the Apache documentation.

# Adding PHP to Apache

PHP is one of the most important open source scripting languages available. It can generate web pages similar to CGI and has extensive libraries and add-ons that can be used in creating applications. The latter attribute has made it popular with web developers. PHP has support for regular expressions that you can use to filter user input and can connect with major databases such as PostgreSQL and MySQL. With PHP integrated in Apache, web developers can create robust online applications that do things rather than just show things. This will also complete your Linux-Apache-Middleware-Programming setup (LAMP) for web development.

In this section, we will install PHP and enable it on our Apache server by loading it as a module.

1.  Install PHP with PostgreSQL and MySQL database support to the system with the following command:

    ```
    yum install php php-pgsql php-mysql
    ```

2.  Find the directive DirectoryIndex in the main section of the httpd.conf file and change it to

    ```
    DirectoryIndex index.html index.html.var index.php
    ```

    You've added index.php as a starter page, and that page will be used if it is on the web directory. Save the file and reload the server using service httpd restart.

3.  Create a test file called welcome.php inside the default document root directory of the www.pvctoyfan.com domain (/var/tmp/pvctoyfan/html) and give it the code shown in Listing 13-8.

*Listing 13-8. A Sample PHP Script*

```
<?php

        print "We are now PHP-enabled.";
?>
```

Save the file afterwards.

4.  Type `http://www.pvctoyfan.com/welcome.php` in the address bar and the result should appear as in Figure 13-8.

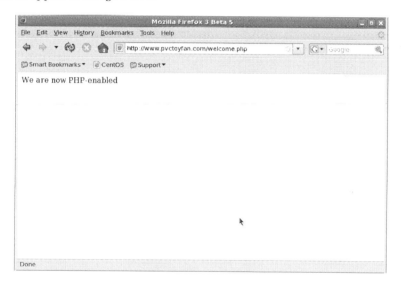

*Figure 13-8. Your first PHP script running on the www.pvctoyfan .com domain*

You can now start PHP scripts in your Apache web server. If you need database connectivity with PHP using PostgreSQL and MySQL, it is already included and all you need to do is to use the proper functions for each database. You can learn more about PHP and its database programming libraries at `http://www.php.net`.

# Secure Apache with SSL

In the chapter so far, all of our HTTP requests and responses have been sent in the clear. That approach is prone to cracker attacks such as sniffing, and transferring sensitive data can be hazardous. To complete this chapter you will apply what you have learned to create OpenSSL certificates here in Apache that will wrap your information through encryption.

## Securing with OpenSSL

Take the following steps to secure web traffic on your Apache server with OpenSSL:

1.  Install the SSL module for Apache by entering

    `yum install mod_ssl`

    This module will enable Apache to use SSL certificates for encryption.

2.  Create an RSA private key file called `private.key` with this command:

    `openssl genrsa -des3 -out private.key 2048`

    Provide a passphrase when you are prompted.

3.  Generate a sefl-signed certificate file called `certificate.pem` based on the `private.key` file just created, using

    `openssl req -new -x509 -key private.key -out certificate.pem -days 1095`

    Then answer the questions that follow to create the `certificate.pem` file.

4.  Copy the `private.key` file into the `/etc/pki/tls/private` directory:

    `cp private.key /etc/pki/tls/private`

5.  Copy the `certificate.pem` file into the `/etc/pki/tls/certs` directory:

    `cp certificate.pem /etc/pki/tls/certs`

---

▓ **Note:** We assume that both the `private.key` and `certificate.pem` files are in the current directory, which is `/root`.

---

6.  Open the Apache SSL configuration file `ssl.conf,` which is located in `/etc/httpd/conf.d,` and find this line:

    `#SSLCertificateFile /etc/pki/tls/certs/localhost.crt`

    Change it to

    `SSLCertificateFile /etc/pki/tls/certs/certificate.pem`

    Next, find the key file line

    `#SSLCertificateKeyFile /etc/pki/tls/private/localhost.key`

    and replace it with

    `SSLCertificateKeyFile /etc/pki/tls/private/private.key`

    Save the file and restart the Apache web server using `service httpd restart.` Before the Apache server can start, you will be asked for the passphrase you gave earlier for the private key you created.

7.  Enter https://localhost/otakai in the address bar of the browser. If it warns you of an exception, accept it for now to see if our secure site is working. The web page must have a small padlock in the lower-right corner of the browser window similar to Figure 13-9.

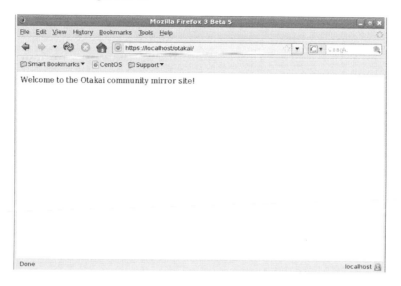

*Figure 13-9. The Apache server with https running*

If you can see the small padlock, your web browser is now talking in secure OpenSSL.

## Startup Without a Passphrase

If you want Apache not to ask you for a passphrase whenever it starts up with https, you need to remove the passphrase from the private key file it uses. If you did the previous steps, you now have the private.key and certificate.pem files in your root's home directory (/root). You will use the private.key file to create another private key file without any passphrase. To achieve that, take the following steps:

1.  Copy the private.key file into private.key-old by entering

    ```
    cp private.key private.key-old
    ```

2.  Create a new private.key file without the passphrase from the copy by decrypting it, entering

    ```
    openssl rsa -in private.key-old -out private.key
    ```

    After the command is run, and you have supplied the original passphrase when prompted, the new private.key file will have no passphrase on it.

3.  Copy the new private.key file into /etc/pki/tls/private this command:

    ```
    cp private.key /etc/pki/tls/private
    ```

311

4. Restart Apache by using `service httpd restart`. You will not be prompted for any passphrase.

---

■ **Caution:** Be sure to use certificates validated by a CA when you deploy your web site with OpenSSL. People will not take kindly to self-signed certificates even if the web site is legitimate.

---

## Summary

In this chapter you first learned about the role of web servers in the Internet, how they handle requests and responses using the HTTP protocol. One of the most widely used web servers, Apache, is provided with CentOS, and you also saw how to set up Apache in different configurations ranging from simple web pages to generating HTML pages on the fly using CGI and PHP. Securing web site traffic with OpenSSL is a must if the HTTP transactions will involve sensitive information. In the next chapter, you will learn about file sharing services that are available in CentOS to use in your network.

# CHAPTER 14

■■■

# File Sharing Services

In today's networked world, file sharing is an essential function needed by almost all computer users. Modern operating systems support different types of file sharing services such as anonymous FTP downloads, network printing, and remote directories. Since Linux was created with networking in mind from the beginning, we can seamlessly implement frequently used file sharing services when the need arises.

For this chapter, you are going to install three servers to allow your intended users to share resources: an FTP server to allow users to download and upload files to their computers, a Linux/Unix network using NFS to allow sharing large files, and finally, a Samba server that can allow our Linux computer to share files and printers with Windows computers.

## Very Secure FTP Daemon

The vsftpd (Very Secure FTP daemon) is an FTP server developed by Chris Evans. vsftpd was created with security from the start to prevent the common problems that affect most FTP servers, and it includes the restriction of privileges by letting the server run with a less-privileged user and the use of chroot(). Having chroot() limits directory visibility and thus lessens the chances of an attacker roaming the system if one does break in. When you need a stronger security mechanism with vsftpd, you can use OpenSSL to encrypt the file transfers.

As an FTP server, vsftpd supports both passive and active file transfers. It also listens on the default port 21, unless you change the port number on the configuration file.

You can install vsftpd in your CentOS system by typing the command yum install vsftpd in the shell as the root user. After the command completes, the tools and the configuration file for vsftpd will be available for your use.

## Configuring vsftpd

You can configure how vsftpd runs using its configuration files located on /etc/vsftpd. The /etc/vsftpd directory contains four files: userlist, and vsftpd_conf_migrate.sh. The last file is a shell script designed to migrate older vsftpd configuration files to be compatible with the newer version that you just installed.

### vsftpd.conf

The vsftpd.conf file is the main configuration file of vsftpd. It contains directives that control the execution of vsftpd. These directives are separated into lines and it follows the format `directive_name=value`

where `directive_name` is the directive you are going to use and `value` is the assigned value to be used on this directive. Here is an example directive on the default configuration file:

`anonymous_enable=YES`

The name of the directive is `anonymous_enable`; it allows anonymous users such as ftp and anonymous to use your FTP server and is enabled by the value of `YES`. Be careful when specifying directives, because vsftpd will complain if it finds spaces beside the assignment operator (=). Lines that start with a hash symbol (#) are generally referred to as "comments" and are ignored by vsftpd.

You can run vsftpd using the default configuration file and test out things on your network. It will use the default unprivileged user called `ftpsecure` and will run with `chroot()` to prevent attacks on your FTP server. You can change directives later that will match the requirements of your network using this file and running `service vsftpd restart` to make your changes effective. Other directives that you can use are found on the man pages of `vsftpd.conf`.

## ftpusers

The `ftpusers` text file can be used to restrict users who can use your FTP server. The file uses a simple syntax, which is separated line by line, where you specify the usernames of the users you do not want to be able to connect to your FTP server . Lines that start with the hash symbol are comments and are ignored by vsftpd when `ftpusers` is consulted for user access.

## user_list

The `user_list` file almost has the same function as the `ftpusers` file except that the way it restricts users can be changed. To do so, modify the `userlist_deny` directive of the main configuration file. If you set the `userlist_deny` directive to `YES`, the usernames contained in the `user_list` file will not be able to use the FTP server and will not be even be given a login prompt. If the said directive is set to `NO`, the users contained in this file will be able to log into the FTP server.

Like you can in the `ftpusers` file, you can add users by putting their usernames in separate lines. Lines that start with the hash (#) symbol are also treated as comments.

## Testing vsftpd

Now that you have been oriented about the vsftpd configuration files, you can test the server on your CentOS system. You have to start the server by using `service vsftpd start` on the shell prompt, and the vsftpd daemon will run on the background, waiting for FTP connections. You will create a user and use it to make a test connection on your FTP server.

1.  Create a user called pusa in your system to log into the FTP server. You need to do this because vsftpd will reject the root user instantly if you try logging in with it. Create the user pusa on the shell prompt as the root user by using the `useradd pusa` command. Give the new user a password by using the passwd command. Make sure to remove this user from your system after this chapter for safety.

2.  Change into the pusa user by running `su - pusa` and log into the FTP server by using `ftp localhost`. That will connect the pusa user into your locally running vsftpd server. You will be asked for the username and password you want to log into, and you can use the username and password of the pusa user.

After you log into your FTP server, you will be given the FTP prompt so you can download and upload files that the currently logged in user has access to. You can use the usual FTP commands, such as ls, get, put, mget, and mput. A sample FTP session using the pusa user on my system is shown in Figure 14-1.

```
530 Please login with USER and PASS.
KERBEROS_V4 rejected as an authentication type
Name (localhost:pusa): pusa
331 Please specify the password.
Password.
230 Login successful.
Remote system type is UNIX.
Using binary mode to transfer files.
ftp> ls
227 Entering Passive Mode (127,0,0,1,172,229)
150 Here comes the directory listing.
226 Directory send OK.
ftp> ls -la
227 Entering Passive Mode (127,0,0,1,129,253)
150 Here comes the directory listing.
drwx------   3 500     500        4096 May 26 04:16 .
drwxr-xr-x   3 0       0          4096 May 26 04:12 ..
-rw-------   1 500     500          19 May 26 04:16 .bash_history
-rw-r--r--   1 500     500          33 May 26 04:12 .bash_logout
-rw-r--r--   1 500     500         176 May 26 04:12 .bash_profile
-rw-r--r--   1 500     500         124 May 26 04:12 .bashrc
drwxr-xr-x   4 500     500        4096 May 26 04:12 .mozilla
226 Directory send OK.
ftp>
```

*Figure 14-1. Transferring files via vsftpd using the pusa user*

After you have finished practicing, you can quit the session by typing bye on the FTP prompt. You can also use a graphical FTP client to connect to your FTP server if you have one on your desktop.

■ **Note:** If you need to deploy your vsftpd server on your network immediately, I recommend uncommenting the line chroot_local_user=YES, or adding it if the line is not present on the configuration file, and running service vsftpd restart to apply the directive. This will turn on the chroot() function of vsftpd to increase security by forcing attackers that logs into the system to view only the current victim's home directory.

# NFS

The NFS protocol enables disk partitions residing on remote computers to be mounted as a local disk. With a mounted partition and the right permissions, you can create and delete files just like any other local directory. The backbone of NFS is RPC (Remote Procedure Call) that lets a host to call a procedure or subroutine that is owned by another computer on the network. With RPC, NFS servers and NFS clients send information to each other when file updates are made on the remote shared directory, so the NFS server and NFS clients know what files have been added, removed, or modified on an NFS connection.

There are some things to watch for when doing file sharing with NFS. As a user with the correct privileges, you have to make sure that whatever you do with a shared file on a shared NFS disk should not harm other users. You have to assume that what you use in the mounted remote disk is also accessible to other users. If you plan to remove or change a file, be sure to double-check if other users are also accessing the file.

Ultimately, though, any user is only allowed to do what the administrator has given permission to do.

---

■ **Note:** You can use NFS version 2, 3, or 4. These versions differ, for example, in the way they perform write operations on the shared remote files. You can read more about NFS on `http://nfs.sourceforge.net`. CentOS uses version 4 by default.

---

## Configuring NFS

NFS uses a configuration file called `exports` that is located on the `/etc` directory. With the `exports` file, you can specify what directories you want to share from this NFS server. The syntax on specifying a shared directory is

```
directory host(option1[, optionN])[ hostN(option1[, optionN])]
```

and contains the following elements:

`directory`: This is the directory to be shared. You can choose to share any directory you want. The chosen directory's subdirectories will also be shared once included in the configuration file.

`host`: These are the client computers that can use this shared directory. You can specify each computer's hostname provided you have a working DNS server. It is possible to use IP addresses of the computers directly if you prefer. Using IP addresses is recommended, because it will help you avoid failed NFS mounts when the DNS server goes down. Most people use either hostnames in the `/etc/hosts` directory or IP addresses for this reason.

`option1`: The options are the access restrictions you want for the shared directory to apply when being shared by users. You can place any number of restrictions as long as you separate them with commas. Some of the available access restrictions follow:

- `ro`: This will make the shared directory readable only and is the default access for shared directories. No changes can be made by the user once this is specified.
- `rw`: This will make the shared directory readable and writable. With this option, the user can make any changes to the directory.
- `no_root_squash`: The root user is automatically mapped to `nobody` unless this option is used. Because NFS trusts the remote computer, anyone who gains root access on a local computer would then have root access on the NFS server. Although you can use this option, do so sparingly.
- `no_subtree_check`: If only part of a partition is exported, a routine called subtree checking verifies that a file that is requested from the client is in the appropriate part of the partition. If the entire partition is exported, disabling this check will speed up transfers.
- `async`: This will make NFS answer requests immediately regardless of whether or not the data is safely stored on the disk.
- `sync`: This will make NFS reject requests until the data is actually written on the disk.

You can put any number of entries in the configuration file to represent the directories you want to share. In addition, you can also put any number of hosts that can access the shared directory separated with spaces per host.

The example entry in Listing 14-1 shares the /var/tmp directory with read and write access of this NFS server for the computer that has an IP address of 192.168.1.11.

*Listing 14-1. A Sample exports File Entry*

```
/var/tmp          192.168.1.11(rw)
```

When the computer that has that IP address mounts the /var/tmp directory of this NFS server, that user will be able to add and remove files on it. If you want to share a directory to more than one host, you can add them after the first host, separated with a space, for example:

```
/var/tmp          192.168.1.11(rw) 192.168.1.102(ro)
```

The previous line will share the /var/tmp directory to both hosts having the IP address of 192.168.1.11 and 192.168.1.102. The first host will have read and write access to the /var/tmp directory while the second host will only have read access.

Instead of listing each host on the line that needs to mount the same directory, you can also use wildcards instead of listing each IP address or hostname. You will use the asterisk character (*) in place for the substituted value, for example:

```
/var/tmp          192.168.1.*(rw)
```

This will allow any computer with the IP address starting with 192.168.1 to mount the /var/tmp directory on this NFS server. If you prefer the network notation, you can do that too like so:

```
/var/tmp          192.168.1.0/255.255.255.0(rw)
```

---

■ **Caution:** Be careful not to put spaces between the host and the option; that is, *do not* type /var/tmp 192.168.1.11 (rw). This will give everyone read and write access regardless of their hosts.

---

## Sharing a Directory Using NFS

Let's assume that there are two computers for our NFS setup. The first computer has the IP address of 192.168.1.11, and the second computer, 192.168.1.12. The first computer will be our NFS server, and you will edit the exports file on this server share the /var/tmp directory for the second computer. Later, you will use the second computer to mount the directory being shared by the first to share files.

1. Open the exports file in /etc, and add the lines shown in Listing 14-2 at the bottom of the file. This means that you want to share the /var/tmp directory of first computer to the second computer and allow read and write access to it. Save the file, and exit the text editor.

2. Next, copy a file for the second computer to use later when it mounts the shared directory you just added. The services file found in /etc is a good one, and you can put a copy on /var/tmp as follows using cp /etc/services /var/tmp. Then start the NFS server by issuing service nfs start. That will start the daemons that enable NFS to share files on NFS clients.

*Listing 14-2. Let the second computer have read and write access to this directory.*

```
/var/tmp        192.168.1.12(rw)
```

If your NFS server is running on a network with a firewall, it won't work because RPC does not use fixed ports when sending and receiving requests. Keep this in mind when you are experiencing problems in your NFS setup.

## Sharing Directories Using NFS Daemons

When you start your NFS server, five daemons activated:: rpc.nfsd, rpc.lockd, rpc.statd,rpc.mountd, and rpc.rquotad. You will see how these daemons play a role in sharing directories with NFS.

The rpc.nfsd daemon is the main server process for NFS, and it accepts RPC calls made by the NFS clients. These RPC calls hold the operations that are required to be done on a file, such as updating or deleting.

The rpc.statd daemon implements NSM (Network Status Monitor) RPC protocol. The rpc.statd daemon also provides information that helps the rpc.lockd daemon do file lock recovery procedures in case the NFS server goes down.

The rpc.lockd daemon provides locking services for NFS and will prevent users who are trying to change a file that is currently being used by another user. For example, if you are editing a document, only you will be able to make changes to it, and other users who want access will have to wait for you to finish. They can still read the document if they want to.

The rpc.mountd daemon handles the mount requests of the available shared directories by the NFS clients through the NFS mount protocol. If an NFS client wants to mount on a shared directory on the NFS server, rpc.mountd will check the contents of the configuration file if the NFS client can use the shared directory. When the NFS client is validated, the NFS server will provide the NFS client a handle that indicates that the share is acquired. The client will use this handle to mount the share. Users cannot mount available shared directories without this daemon running on the server.

Similar to regular filesystem quotas, rpc.rquotad provides quota support for remote filesystem shares. With rpc.rquotad, you can put a quota on a mounted NFS filesystem to provide limitations to file storage use in remote shares when required.

## Mounting a Shared Directory As the Client

Earlier, you added a directory that can be mounted by NFS clients to the exports file and started the NFS service to accept NFS requests. This time, you will see how an NFS client will mount the shared directory on the NFS server by using the second computer with the IP address of 192.168.1.12 on our example setup.

To mount an NFS shared directory, you will use the mount command, the same command used to mount partitions on your system. The difference in mounting a local partition and an NFS share lies in specifying the NFS server's hostname or IP address along with the server's shared directory. The syntax to mount NFS shares as a client follows:
mount server_name:shared_directory mount_point
where server_name is the hostname or IP address of the NFS server that has the remote shared directory you want to mount to. The shared_directory is the directory path of the NFS share that is being shared

by the NFS server, as specified on its exports file. The mount_point is the directory where you will attach or mount the remote NFS share into your system.

We will now mount the /var/tmp directory of the first computer on a directory called nfsshare on the second computer.

1. Create a directory called nfsshare on root's home directory on the second computer using mkdir /root/nfsshare. You will mount the remote directory of the first computer on this directory.

2. On the second computer, mount the /var/tmp directory of the first computer on /root/nfsshare as follows:

    mount 192.168.1.11:/var/tmp /root/nfsshare

That will mount the first computer's /var/tmp directory inside the /root/nfsshare directory in the second computer. After mounting the shared directory, you can use the mount command without any arguments to see the NFS share on the second computer listed along with your local mounted partitions. Here is the line that tells about the remote NFS share on the second computer:
192.168.1.11:/var/tmp on /root/nfsshare type nfs (rw,addr=192.168.1.11)

The mount command lists the remote share /var/tmp as coming from the first computer with the IP address of 192.168.1.11 and is of type nfs. The server allowed read and write access (rw) on this share.

Browsing the shared directory using ls -l on the second computer will show you the services file you copied earlier from the /etc directory of the first computer as shown on listing 14-3.

*Listing 14-3. The services File on the Mounted Remote Shared Directory*

```
[root@pusa ~]# mount 192.168.1.11:/var/tmp nfsshare/
[root@pusa ~]# ls -l /root/nfsshare/
total 360
-rw-r--r-- 1 root root 362031 Sep 15 16:37 services
[root@pusa ~]#
```

You can open it for reading, but when you try to make changes, you will be told that you do not have write access for this file. This happened because the services file on the first computer has only read permissions set for the group and others. Only the owner of the file, the root user of the first computer, can make changes to it. The permissions and ownership of the contents of the first computer's remote share applies to the NFS client. If the root user of the first computer changes the permissions to allow you to write to the file; that is the only time you can make changes to it.

## Unmounting a Shared Directory as the Client

To unmount a remote share, you can use the umount command, much like unmounting a local partition. For our mounted NFS share, that is on the second computer's /root/nfsshare directory, and you issue the following command on the shell:

umount /root/nfsshare

That will unmount the /var/tmp NFS share of the first computer from the second computer.

## Using exportfs

NFS has a tool called exportfs that you can use to maintain NFS shares on your NFS server. It can list the available NFS shares that NFS clients can mount to or even reload the exports file for the NFS server to know the changes of that file. If you want to list all of the available NFS shared directories or exported file systems, you can run exportfs without any arguments. With the first computer on our example, running exportfs itself will show this:

```
/var/tmp        192.168.1.12
```

That tells you about the /var/tmp directory can be mounted by the second computer with the IP address of 192.168.1.12. Assuming you added another directory to be shared on your NFS server, you can have NFS reread the exports file to update itself instead of restarting the nfs service by running

```
exportfs -r
```

The preceding command will let your NFS server mount new NFS clients that has been added on the exports file.

## Mounting Shared Directories at Boot Time

Earlier, you mounted remote shared directories from an NFS server using the mount command. You will have to do this every time you restart the second computer or any NFS client that you want to use for the NFS server. Fortunately, you can mount the shares automatically through the fstab file.

The fstab file is not only capable of maintaining local static filesystem information on your system but can also handle NFS shares that you want to be mounted at boot time. The syntax to add a remote NFS share to be mounted on boot time using fstab is

```
sourceHost:sharedDirectory     mountPoint    nfs     options        0 0
```

where the following information is needed:

- sourceHost: This is the NFS server that hosts the shared directory. You can specify either its host name or IP address.
- sharedDirectory: This is the shared directory that our NFS server hosts and the one we want to mount during boot time.
- mountPoint: This is the local directory that will contain the remote shared directory after a successful mount.
- options: These are the NFS directory options that we want to impose on our mounted directory. If several options are to be specified, they need to be separated by commas. Note that the permissions that the NFS server imposed on the remote share will always preside on the ones you give. For example, if the NFS server gave only ro for your computer and you specified rw in the fstab entry, the remote share will still be read-only, and you will not be able to make changes to it. The async, sync, hard, and soft options affect how the shared directory is used.

For the second computer to automatically mount the /var/tmp directory inside the /root/nfsshare directory at boot time, you add this line to the fstab file:

```
192.168.1.11:/var/tmp   /root/nfsshare nfs     rw,hard,intr    0 0
```

The preceding command will mount the /var/tmp directory of the NFS server with the IP address of 192.168.1.11 in the mount point directory located in /root/nfsshare. The type of filesystem for this entry is nfs, which tells the system to mount a remote NFS share. There are the options specified for this entry: rw, hard, and intr.

---

■ **Note:** The last two zeros in an `fstab` entry are placeholders for the use of the `dump` command and the `fsck` command respectively. The first placeholder is used by the `dump` command to know which filesystems are needed to be dumped or backed up. It has the value zero and it tells the `dump` command not to backup this filesystem. The second placeholder is used by the `fsck` command to know which filesystems require repairs. A value of zero indicates that this filesystem does not need to use fsck for repairs. Most of the time, these options are left as zeros when the entry is going to be used for NFS.

---

The rw option means that the files can be read and written, that is, modified. The hard option will make the NFS server wait indefinitely for connectivity to be restored. The soft option will timeout after a period of time. Using the hard option is the best choice to ensure data integrity, but if an NFS server goes down and it won't be coming back for a while, this option can cause problems.

With the hard option, the waiting process cannot be stopped, but if you add the intr option, it can be. This will give you control to stop the waiting NFS process by killing it if the NFS server crashed.

NFS can be a good way to share files with Unix and Unix-like operating systems, but you have to consider some of its disadvantages when deploying it in large, busy networks. It can become slow because of the number of RPC calls being made by both the NFS server and its connected NFS clients. You should also double-check the directory if it can be accessed and file permissions on your NFS shares, because those are some of the favorite entry points of attackers who want to enter your system using NFS.

Keep these issues in mind when you are planning to deploy or have deployed NFS in your network. Even with these disadvantages, NFS is still the standard way of sharing files in Unix, and most people still use it (though CIFS through Samba is really catching on).

# Setting Up a Samba Server

According to the Samba web site, "Samba is an open source/free software suite that provides seamless file and print services to Server Message Block/Common Internet File System SMB/CIFS clients." In other words, SAMBA allows Linux or Unix servers to work with windows clients. When you need to have a file and print server to share files and printers within a Windows network, a SAMBA-enabled Linux computer can actually provide the needs for those computers.

In addition, Samba can also join an existing Windows network by being a primary domain controller or a domain member. As a primary domain controller, Windows clients will be able to join the domain that the Samba server is running just like an actual Windows server. These clients will be able to use the shared resources such as directories, files, and printers that the Samba server offers after they have authenticated themselves. As a domain member, the Samba server can join an existing Windows network that is being hosted by a domain controller just like an actual Windows client. You can also make the Samba server a WINS (Windows Internet Name Service) server for your windows clients that uses NetBIOS names on the network.

For now, we are going to share and print files with Samba as a standalone server. As a standalone server, it will act on its own workgroup and it will not be affiliated with a domain. The good thing is what we will learn here can also be applied to more advanced server setups that you might want to use later such the domain controller you are going to setup on chapter 16.

## Installing Samba

Samba is not included in the default installation. You can install Samba by using the command yum install samba as the root user. This will install the required tools and configuration files needed to run Samba on your CentOS system.

## Configuring Samba

The configuration files of samba are stored in the /etc/samba directory. The files are smb.conf, lmhosts, and the smbusers.

The smb.conf file is the main configuration file of Samba. With this file, you can change the way the Samba server runs and add or remove shares. The lmhosts file can be used to resolve NetBIOS names to IP addresses and is similar to the hosts file in the /etc directory. The smbusers file contains Unix to SMB name mapping. Of the three files mentioned, the main configuration file will be of most use to us.

### lmhosts

The lmhosts file is Samba's NetBIOS host file. This file is similar to the hosts file found on the /etc directory except it maps the NetBIOS name to its IP address counterpart. Each line on the lmhosts file follows the syntax

```
ip_address      netbios_name
```

where ip_address is the IP address of the computer that will have the NetBIOS name given by the netbios_name. An example entry in this file follows

```
192.168.1.11    DIANA
```

The NetBIOS name DIANA will be used by your Samba server for the host with the IP address of 192.168.1.11. Lines that start with the hash symbol are ignored by Samba.

### smbusers

The smbusers file contains the mapping of Linux usernames to Samba usernames. Each entry is separated by a newline and takes the following syntax:

```
linux_username = samba_username1 [samba_username2 .. samba_usernameN]
```

where linux_username is a Linux user in your system and the samba_username is the Samba username this Linux user will be known as on the Samba server. You can put more than one Samba username on a Linux username if you want to refer a Linux user by those Samba usernames. You must separate the additional Samba usernames by a space. Here is an example entry:

```
root = administrator admin
```

The entry tells that the root user will be known as the administrator and the admin users on your Samba server. Lines that start with the hash symbol are treated as comments and are ignored by Samba.

## smb.conf

The smb.conf file contains sections that describe what you want the Samba server to do and the resources you want to share to your windows network. Each section can contain parameters that can be used to alter the section functions when Samba uses it. The section and parameters take on the following syntax:

```
[section_name]
parameter_name = value
        :
parameter_name = value
```

where section_name is the name of the section and must be enclosed in square brackets. The parameter_name is the name of the parameter to be used in this section, and value is the value that will be used for this parameter. There can be any number of parameters on a section, and each parameter must be separated into lines. Both section names and parameter names are case insensitive. Lines that start with the hash symbol (#) or a semicolon are comments and are ignored by Samba.

Here is an example section with a parameter:

```
[global]
workgroup = MYGROUP
```

The section name is [global], and the parameter workgroup is assigned the text value MYGROUP. Because this is a [global] section, the value you assign to the workgroup parameter will appear on the Windows client, and it will be used by the remaining related sections of the configuration file such as share definitions.

There are two kinds of definitions in the smb.conf file. The first is the global definition, and the second is the share definition. The global definition holds the [global] section that contains parameters that apply to the whole server. You can tell Samba to act as a primary domain controller, a domain member, or a stand-alone server. In addition to making the Samba server act as your chosen Windows server, you can specify what kind of password backend must be used for authenticating users and what printing system you want to use for Samba.

The share definition contains the resources that can be shared on your Windows network. The smb.conf file defines the [homes] section and [printers] section by default. The [homes] section lets users access their home directories in your Samba server. The [printers] section allows users to use the printer that can be accessed by Samba. You can create new sections to share other directories or printers in this definition.

In the remaining sections of this chapter, you will see how you can configure Samba to share directories and printers in your windows network.

# Configuring Stand-Alone Server Options

Here are some of the parameters of the [global] section that you might want to change when running a stand-alone server in addition to the workgroup parameter discussed in the previous section. There is no need to change any of these values at the moment, as the defaults are fine for practice use.

## server string

The server string parameter will hold the value that will be shown on the comment box in the print manager and the network neighborhood window. The default value is Samba Server Version %v, where %v contains the version of this running server. You can put any descriptive text here and even use the %h variable to show the hostname of the computer that the Samba server runs on.

## netbios name

The value of the netbios name parameter will be used by the Samba server when it joins into your Windows network. This will make it easier for your Windows clients to find your Samba server in their network neighborhood window. This is not set by default and instead defaults to the hostname of the computer.

## passdb backend

The passdb backend parameter will tell the Samba server what kind of backend or password storage mechanism to use when authenticating users. By default, it is assigned the tdbsam value that maps Windows users to Unix user accounts. You can change it to ldapsam if you want to use OpenLDAP for authentication. Integrating Samba and OpenLDAP will be explained further in Chapter 16.

## Adding a Samba User

Before you let your users access the shares you define in your Samba server, you will need to create Samba user accounts for them. Samba will use these accounts when authenticating your Windows users and giving them access to your shared files and printers.

To create a Samba user, you will first need to create a local system user in your CentOS system. This is required because Samba maps Windows users to Unix user accounts that will give them their proper directories while connected to it. Second, you will use the smbpasswd tool to give a password for that created Unix user account. The password you will give with this tool for this user will be the one your Windows users will use.

■ **Note:** Because of different methods of hashing, Samba has to have a separate password store to the main system. In other words, it is possible for the system password to be different from the Samba password. There are ways to get around this (such as using LDAP and centralized password changing scripts), but the initial difference might not be obvious.

3.  Create a local system account. We will use the sample username ging and create it using the useradd tool:

    useradd ging

4.  Use the smbpasswd tool to assign a Samba password for the user ging:

    smbpasswd -a ging

    The -a flag will tell smbpasswd to add the user ging and its associated password on the Samba server's password database. You will be asked to enter and verify a password, just like when using the passwd command.

Later, you will use the sample user ging to access its home directory on your Samba server while on a Windows computer.

## Testing the Samba Stand-Alone Server

You will need to have your Samba server and a Windows computer such as Windows XP running on your network to try this out. You will make your Windows computer join the MYGROUP workgroup that is being used by the workgroup parameter in the smb.conf file.

1.  Open the smb.conf file in /etc/samba and find the line

    ;           netbios name = MYSERVER

    And remove the semicolon in front of it. That will let your Windows client see your Samba server as MYSERVER in your network instead of localhost.localdomain. Save the file, and run service smb restart to put the changes into effect.

2.  On the Windows computer, click Start ➤ Control Panel, and select Performance and Maintenance.

3.  In the Pick a Task window, click "See basic information about your computer" to open the System Properties window.

4.  Click the Computer Name tab and the Change button next to the text "To rename this computer or join a domain, click Change."

5.  Make sure that the Workgroup option is selected on the "Member of" box, as shown in Figure 14-2. Type **MYGROUP** in the box, and click OK. Wait for a few seconds, and you will be told that your computer has joined the MYGROUP workgroup, your Samba server. Reboot your Windows computer to reflect the changes.

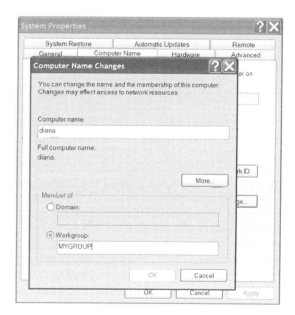

*Figure 14-2. Letting the Windows client join the MYGROUP workgroup*

6. Double-click the My Network Places icon on the desktop, and click the "View workgroup computers" on the left pane. You will find your Samba server, along with the description as specified on the server string parameter. Double-click that icon, and you will be prompted for a user to connect to your Samba server. Type **ging** as the username, and give the password you have assigned to that username. After you have logged in, you will see two icons: the ging user's folder and the Printers and Faxes folder, as shown in Figure 14-3. Those are the shared files that are usable by the Samba users as specified on the Share definition section of the smb.conf file.

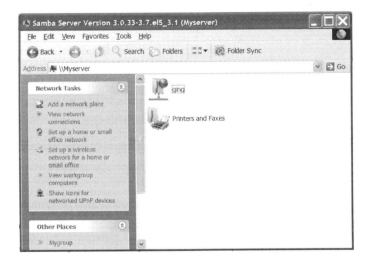

*Figure 14-3. The shared directory contents of the ging user on the Myserver workgroup*

You can now put files on your shared server using the logged account. You can do that by double-clicking the ging directory and copying some files on it.

## Adding Shares

Having the home directories and a printer would be fine for practice in a Samba server. But that will not be enough when you have deployed the server on your network, because certain requirements will make you organize the shared resources. For example, you might need to group files by department, or your users may want a central place to put public documents that can be retrieved by all, instead of having one user become the distributor. You can organize your shared files by adding shares, and you can control the access restrictions of the shares.

To create your own shared directory, create a section for it, and add the necessary parameters to tell Samba that this directory is a new share. The syntax for creating a share follows:

```
[share_name]
        comment = your_comment
        path = directory_path
        public = yes
```

```
writable = yes
printable = no
```

where [share_name] is the name of the share you want to create, comment is a short description about this share, and path is the absolute path of the directory that this share will use. The yes value of the public parameter tells Samba that this share is accessible by any user. The writable parameter will let users make changes on this directory if it has the yes value. Giving the printable a value of no will make Samba treat this share as a directory (if you make printable yes, Samba will view this as a printer instead).

You are going to create a share called [ourfirst] that uses the depot directory inside the /var/tmp directory. You are going to create that directory, add the required section on the smb.conf file, and see if there are any syntax errors. After the verification, you will restart the Samba server and try to access the new share.

1. Create a directory called depot inside the /var/tmp directory:

   mkdir /var/tmp/depot

2. Open the smb.conf file in /etc/samba, and add the content in Listing 14-4 at the bottom of the file. In Listing 14-4, you're defining a Windows shared directory by creating a section called [ourfirst]. Within the section, there are five parameters that affect how this shared directory works. The comment parameter gives some detail about the shared directory. The path parameter tells Samba to use the /var/tmp/depot directory for as the shared directory. The public parameter is set to yes to allow any user to access this shared directory. The writable parameter allows users to make changes on this directory and it set to yes. Because this is a shared directory, the printable parameter is set to no.

3. Test the configuration file to see if you have added the new share definition properly by issuing testparm on the shell. The testparm command will verify the contents of the smb.conf file for correctness. If you see any errors, open the smb.conf file again, and make the required changes. Otherwise, testparm will show you the shares that Samba will show to your Windows clients and the definitions afterward.

4. Restart the Samba server using service smb restart.

5. In the Network Places window, double-click the Myserver icon, and you will see that the ourfirst shared directory is now included on the available shares as shown in Figure 14-4.

*Listing 14-4. The New Directory's Share Definition*

```
;     Our first defined share
      [ourfirst]
                comment - My first shared directory
                path = /var/tmp/depot
                public = yes
                writable = yes
                printable = no
```

327

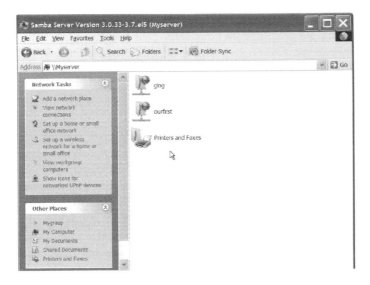

*Figure 14-4. The ourfirst shared directory is now included on the Myserver Samba server.*

As an experiment, open the ourfirst shared directory by double-clicking it, and try to create a new folder or text file inside it. You will be given the message "Access is denied" instead being able to create the folder or document. This happened because your Samba server still follows the Linux permissions rules. By default, your depot directory has only read and execute permissions for the group and others attributes. To allow full write privileges on this directory, change the permissions to allow write for both of those attributes by running chmod 777 /var/tmp/depot. After doing the permission change, you will now be able to create files and folders on that shared public directory.

## Sharing a Printer

There are many ways to set up a printer to be shared in Samba, and one of them is through CUPS (Common Unix Printing System), the default printing software for modern Linux/Unix distributions. While CUPS in itself is a big subject, you will only need to utilize the bare minimum of the system to make your Windows clients print to your Samba server's shared printer. You will make use of the raw form of print data and pass it directly to the printer. By passing the raw form, your Samba server does not perform any additional steps, such as applying the required font format and colors during the printing. The Samba server assumes that the Windows client has already prepared the document for printing, including the formatting, and will simply pass the document to the printer hardware.

You do not need to install Linux/Unix versions of the printer driver software on your Linux system, but the Windows clients do. They need the Windows printer driver software, because those computers will put the required instructions on the document for the printer hardware. In short, the Samba server acts as a middleman for the Windows clients and the printer hardware. Also, Linux drivers aren't necessary, because Windows has already done the work. Linux is just passing it to the printer for printing.

This setup has some minor problems though. One is the native Windows driver software itself: you should try to use a uniform version of the driver to avoid future incompatibilities with the printer hardware. Another is the additional administration overhead in setting up the Windows clients to do the filtering work prior to submitting it to our Samba server; we must make sure that those computers have the correct printer driver software installed on them. Last, both Samba and CUPS must be built so they can talk to each other. If you are using another distribution and your printer connections don't work out as expected, you can start your troubleshooting on the communication of Samba and CUPS. After solving those problems, Samba printing is a snap.

In our printer share example, these are the prerequisites:

- *Printer hardware* must be detected by the Linux system. Be sure to check your log files (through the use of the dmesg command or by checking /var/log/messages) after you connect the printer and turn it on to see if it got detected.
- *CUPS* must be installed in your system. Otherwise, use the yum install cups command to add it.

For our example, we are going to use my printer, the Canon iP1000. I just plugged in the printer, and it has been detected as a USB device. We will begin by configuring your computer using the CUPS web interface to prepare it for sharing.

## Preparing the Printer to Pass Print Data in Raw Form

We are going to change two files related to CUPS. Both files tell CUPS to allow raw print data to be used and passed to the printer.

1. Open the file called mime.convs located in /etc/cups using a text editor, and find the following line:

   ```
   #application/octet-stream          application/vnd.cups-raw          0          -
   ```

   Uncomment the line, and save the file.

2. Still in the /etc/cups directory, open the file mime.types, and find the following entry:

   ```
   application/octet-stream
   ```

   If you have that line on the file, you're done! Otherwise, add it at the end of the file and save.

3. Become root again, and restart CUPS using service cups restart to apply your changes

4. Open a web browser on the server, and point it to http://localhost:631 to display the CUPS web interface. This has to be done on the server itself, and the result is shown in Figure 14-5.

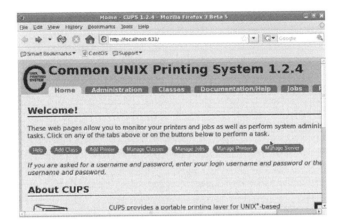

*Figure 14-5. The main screen of the CUPS printer server*

Depending on the type of printer you have, CUPS may or may not detect it. If it has been detected, you will be told to accept its best driver for.65 your printer by default, which is not what we want. Let's look at how you can change this behavior, in case you encounter this situation.

5. Click the Add Printer button, and give a name to your to-be-installed printer, as shown in Figure 14-6. I typed generic details for practice. You have to put in the actual parameters in the deployment.

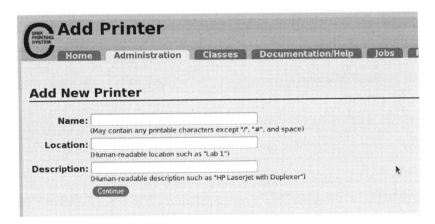

*Figure 14-6. The Add New Printer screen*

My generic sample printer information follows:

- *Name*: RawPrinter
- *Location*: Our Samba server
- *Description*: My installed USB printer

You need to specify the type of printer you have in the Device drop-down box. I chose Canon iP1000 (Canon iP1000 because CUPS detected my printer hardware and named it like that.). If you cannot find your model, and you know what type it is, you should still be able to select a printer. For example, if you have a USB printer, your selection may include entries such as USB #1. For more information on finding out on how to choose your printer type, visit the CUPS web site at http://www.cups.org. Click Continue after you've made your selection.

6. For Model/Driver for RawPrinter, let CUPS have its way for now by clicking Add Printer. You will see it has selected a driver that may not be suitable for your printer. This is shown in Figure 14-7. Next, we fix the newly added printer so it uses the raw driver instead of its chosen one for us.

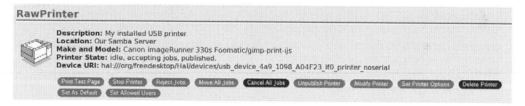

*Figure 14-7. Raw is not the Make and Model.*

7. Click the Manage Printers button from the Home tab, and you will see your newly added printer, RawPrinter. Click Modify Printer.

8. You don't need to change the information given earlier to describe your printer. You can click Continue here.

9. The same goes for the Device information, so click continue again.

10. For the Make/Manufacturer, you now have a wider selection instead of having a fixed set for each vendor. Select Raw here, and click Continue. This is shown in Figure 14-8.

### Make/Manufacturer for RawPrinter

Make:
- Pentax
- Postscript
- QMS
- Raven
- Raw
- Ricoh
- Samsung
- Savin
- Seiko
- Sharp

Continue

Or Provide a PPD File: [ ] Browse...

Modify Printer

*Figure 14-8. Setting the RawPrinter to be of Raw make*

11. For Model/Driver, choose the "Raw Queue (en)" option, and click the Modify Printer button to finalize the changes. You will see that the make is now changed to Local Raw Printer similar to Figure 14-9.

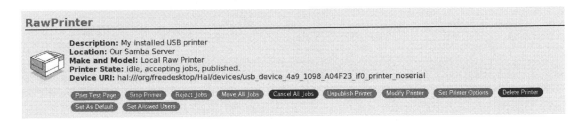

*Figure 14-9. The printer is now a Local Raw Printer.*

After setting up the printer, go back to your Samba server to configure printer sharing for Windows clients. If your printer is still not detected, you can find additional troubleshooting information in the CUPS web site.

## Configuring Samba to Share a Printer

Next, let's configure Samba to share a printer. To begin, open the smb.conf file located at /etc/samba with a text editor, and find the entries as shown on Listing 14-5 in the global definitions.

*Listing 14-5. The Options for Printing in the Global Definitions*

```
        load printers = yes
        cups options = raw
;       printcap name = /etc/printcap
        #obtain list of printers automatically on SystemV
;       printcap name = lpstat
;       printing = cups
```

If you have the entries in Listing 14-5, your Samba server is almost ready to accept printing requests from its Windows clients. The load printers parameter tells Samba to load the printers in the printcap file that was created when we were adding a printer using CUPS. That file is specified in the printcap name parameter, and it uses the file called printcap in the /etc directory. The cups options parameter lets you give options that can be used by your CUPS server when printing documents. It uses the raw value, because we do not want CUPS to do anything on the document that is about to be printed. The cups options parameter is only usable if you are going to use the CUPS server to print documents with Samba. You can do that by setting the printing parameter to cups to tell Samba to use the CUPS server for printing. Without these lines, the Samba server will not be able to share the available configured printers.

In addition, the [printers] section in Listing 14-6 will let the Windows computers see our printer, so they can send their print data to it.

*Listing 14-6. The [printers] Section of smb.conf*

```
[printers]
```

```
comment = All Printers
path = /var/spool/samba
browseable = no
guest ok = no
writable = no
printable = yes
```

The [printers] share lets Windows clients use the printers loaded earlier in the [global] section. In the share, the comment parameter gives some description about the shared printer on this server. The path parameter tells Samba what spool directory to use when printing documents. This serves as a temporary directory for Samba to sort out documents to be printed. Because this is a printer share, users must not be able to browse it, which is done by setting the browseable parameter into no. We do not want guest users or users that do not give a password to print on the server by setting guest ok to no. Users cannot write into the printer like a directory, so we set writable to no. The last line tells Samba that this share is a printer and users can print with it. Without these lines, the Samba server will not be able to share the its available configured printers.

You can close the file after checking if these entries are present.

## Installing the Samba Printer to the Windows Client

Follow the steps in this section for each Windows client you intend to allow printing to your Samba server. And as stated earlier, install the same Windows printer driver version on each Windows client to avoid incompatibility problems. Also, be sure to install the native Windows drivers of the printer hardware before installing the Samba printer.

1. Install the driver for your printer (Canon iP1000 for me). Usually, the printer driver setup prompts for the port of the printer and then for a test print. Play along by setting the printer port to LPT:1.

---

■ **Note** If you do not have the driver CD or installer package for your printer, you can search for it on the Internet. Take note of the model of the printer, and include that in your search for printer driver downloads.

---

2. Open the Network Neighborhood window, and double-click the Myserver workgroup we created earlier. If you cannot see the workgroup, you can manually type in \\myserver in the address bar of any Windows Explorer window to see the available shares you created.

3. The RawPrinter icon is now available for use. Double-click it, and Windows will ask if you want to install this printer. Click OK.

4. You will be told that the server does not have the proper driver installed. Click OK to allow installation of the actual driver for this printer, which we installed on our Windows client.

5. Select the vendor and make of your printer from the window, and you will be told that the printer has been successfully added to your computer.

6. With your Samba server ready and printer turned on, do a test print using the RawPrinter Samba shared printer. It works! And that concludes our shared printer setup with Samba as an anonymous server.

# Summary

In this chapter, you have seen how you can share resources in multiple ways for both Linux and Windows networks, as well as the ways that FTP, NFS, and Samba come into play. FTP can be a good solution if you only want to distribute files for everyone to download. NFS is best for Linux- or Unix-based file sharing in real time. Samba is the server for sharing files, and even printers, on a Windows network.

But your options do not stop here, because each server has many features and enhancements. For example, you could improve security of each server through pluggable authentication modules. Also, for Windows administrators who want to manage bigger Windows networks, the stand-alone server can be transformed into a full-pledged domain controller for the task. And Samba can fuse with OpenLDAP to create a lightweight directory mechanism for unified authentication when required.

In the next chapter, you will see how use mail servers to provide mail services to your networks and manage user mailboxes.

■■■

# CHAPTER 15

# Linux Mail Servers

If you need email service on your network, CentOS can provide it for you. With CentOS, you can install various mail servers that can send and retrieve email for your users.

In this chapter, we will create a small email system on which you can send and receive email. You will see the essential software for email, including MTAs (such as sendmail and Postfix) and IMAP or POP servers. After testing the email system, you will configure an email client to test whether the setup works as expected.

## Basic Email Concepts

Before you start installing email server software, you must know how email is sent and received in the network.

When you create and send email, you do the following:

1. Open an email client such as Evolution.

2. Type in a message.

3. Provide the recipient email address

4. Send the email.

Figure 15-1 illustrates this process.

*Figure 15-1. Sending an email*

In Figure 15-1, there are two components that are used when sending email: *the mail user agent* and the *mail transfer agent*. They interact whenever you send email to a recipient. The next sections explain the differences between these two components and the roles they play in email.

## The Mail User Agent

Mail User Agents (MUAs) let users manage email on their email accounts. The email account is usually assigned by an administrator within a company or is created personally on an email service provider. With MUAs, users can create, read, send, retrieve, and remove messages on their email accounts. MUAs send the user's email account information, such as username and password, when connecting to the email server for validation before being able to access their email.

MUAs are also known as email clients, and there are many to choose from when you manage email. For example, there is Mozilla Thunderbird and the integrated email software in the Mozilla Seamonkey. You can also use the Evolution email client included in the default desktop installation of CentOS, as you'll do in examples later in this chapter.

---

▓ **Note:** You can try Mozilla Thunderbird by visiting its web site at `http://www.mozilla. org`. If you also want to try the email client, Mozilla Seamonkey, you can visit its site at `http://www.seamonkey-project.org`.

---

After an email is created and then sent with the MUA, it will go to a mail transfer agent, which will handle the next steps.

## Mail Transfer Agent

Mail Transfer Agents (MTA) are the software responsible for delivering messages from one computer to another. This software makes sure that each email message is valid prior to sending by adding the proper headers so that it will be received properly by the target computer.

While the main job of an MTA is to send email, it also organizes messages through queuing. There will be times when email cannot be sent immediately for various reasons, such as high server load or too much network traffic. If this happens, email is queued until it can be sent.

An MTA can forward email to another MTA, a capability called *email relaying*. With this, you can assign an MTA within your private network and an MTA on your outside network. The computers on your network can send their emails on your internal MTA without worrying about outsiders snatching those off. The internal MTA can use email relaying to the outside MTA that will send the emails to the proper recipients. The outside MTA is hardened against attacks, and if an attacker manages to crack into it, he will have to find a way to enter your private network. This provides another layer of protection for your network setup because attackers must enter not only one but at least two MTAs to get into your network.

MTAs use the Simple Mail Transfer Protocol (SMTP) to send email prepared by the MUA. With SMTP, an MTA can send email to another MTA that understands the protocol. Because MTAs use SMTP, these mail servers wait for email to be sent on port 25.

There are many MTAs to choose from when you are going to deploy an email server in your network. You can choose from sendmail, Postfix, qmail, or exim, for example. Once you set up an MTA and the email accounts, your users will be able to send email to that server with their chosen email client.

## Mail Delivery Agent

Mail Delivery Agents (MDAs) handle the delivery of email to its intended recipients. They are usually implemented as separate software that is called by an MTA after it accepts email and is included on the same computer. When the MDA runs it sorts the email, for example by subject or sender. Some MDAs can also sort email into assigned individual user directories. Mail sent through an MDA will be ready for other mail servers such as POP3 or IMAP. Examples of MDAs include procmail for sendmail and maildrop for Postfix.

## POP3 and IMAP

After you create and send an email message, the user retrieves it using another set of software, the POP3 server and the IMAP server. Figure 15-2 illustrates their roles.

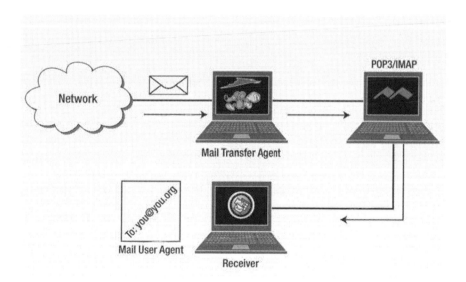

*Figure 15-2. Retrieving email from an MTA using POP3 or IMAP*

When a user retrieves an email message, the following steps happen:

1. The user connects to the assigned email server using his or her MUA.

2. After the email server authenticates the user, it retrieves the message from its hard drive.

3. The retrieved message is downloaded by the user's MUA and is now readable.

Going further, when an email message arrives at a target domain, that domain's MTA will receive it and save it on the computer's hard disk. To retrieve their email, users must connect to their assigned incoming email server, which can be either a Post Office Protocol version 3 (POP3) server or an Internet Message Access Protocol (IMAP) server. Both protocols allow the server to retrieve emails from the MTA's assigned directory for email storage that can be retrieved by the user's email client, but the way they retrieve email is different. They can be a lot more flexible than this although for a basic setup this is true.

The POP3 protocol was designed to allow users to retrieve email whenever they want on their email client. To get the latest email, they use their email client to connect to their assigned POP3 server, retrieve the email, and then disconnect. Once the new messages have been downloaded, users can read them offline at their leisure. By default, POP3 servers remove emails that have been retrieved by user, but this can be overridden if required. In summary, email is managed by the user's email client, locally.

There are some problems when you are going to use )POP3 for your emails. These include email maintenance, and speed. If you use multiple email clients to connect to a single POP3 server, your emails will end up on one of the email clients. For example, you have configured an email client at home and an email client at work. Using both email clients, some of your emails will be downloaded at home, while the others on your work email client. You have to make sure which email client to use when retrieving email from your POP3 to avoid missing out emails.

The IMAP protocol was designed to provide a better way for users to retrieve and manage email, and as an alternative to POP3. With IMAP, the user's messages reside on the server by default, and must be managed from there by email clients. Because messages are on the server, the user can access them anywhere using an IMAP-compatible email client. Any message that the user downloads, reads, and removes is saved on the server instead of the user's email client.

A user can also choose which messages to download on his or her email client using IMAP. This is possible because the email client downloads the message headers instead of the whole message. From these headers, the user can choose what email to read and, via the email client, instruct the IMAP server to send the data part of the message from that selected message header. Messages can still be downloaded to the user's email client as in POP3, but those serve only as copies. The original messages stay on the server unless the user removes those from the server. This solves the POP3 problems noted earlier and is why IMAP is often used on large networks.

If both POP3 and IMAP servers can download emails, which of those will you use? IMAP is generally prescribed unless there are specific reasons why POP3 would be better suited, such as for a work queue or if network connectivity is an issue.

# Sendmail

Sendmail is one of the oldest MTAs available and was written by Eric Allman. Sendmail is a derivative of his other work, delivermail, that was used in the Advanced Research Projects Agency Network (ARPANET), the precursor of the Internet. The delivermail program sends email using the Network Control Program (NCP) that provides network connectivity between hosts on the ARPANET. This program was also available on Berkeley Software Distribution (BSD) Unix during the ARPANET days.

When ARPANET began using TCP/IP, Eric used delivermail as reference and created sendmail to use the new protocol. With sendmail using TCP/IP, it can send email to a wider network and platform instead of being limited to the original Unix methods of sending email such as Unix to Unix Copy Program (UUCP) ) and FTP.

As an MTA, sendmail can send email using the SMTP protocol. It can send email that originates from an email client or another MTA. Sendmail can also relay email to another MTA if required.

Sendmail is installed in CentOS by default and is ready for use, but the additional configuration files to help you create the main configuration file need to be added to your system. You can do this by issuing yum install sendmail-cf in the terminal as root. After the installation completes, you will be able to configure sendmail easily, as you will see later.

# Sending Email with Sendmail

To send email with sendmail, use the `sendmail` command, which follows the syntax

```
sendmail target_emailaddress
```

where *target*_emailaddress is the email address of the recipient. This can be a complete email address that contains the receiver's domain name or just the username if the receiver is local to the computer. To practice sending email with the sendmail command, try sending an email to yourself, the root user.

1. Run the command

```
sendmail root
```

   That will make the cursor go down a line and wait for you to type in your message. Type something like **Test email** and press Enter.

2. Type a period to end the message and press Enter. That will make sendmail send your email to your target, yourself at the moment. Your terminal should look similar to the following:

```
[root@localhost #] sendmail root
Test email
.
[root@localhost #]
```

   If you get the prompt back, you're done.

# Checking Mail with the mail Command

After sending an email to yourself, you can check it by using an email client. You will use the `mail` command for now, a command-line email client that can let you manage email using the shell. To read the email you just sent, run the `mail` command on its own, like this:

```
mail
```

   In response, it will display the list of emails that you can view, as shown in Listing 15-1.

*Listing 15-1. The mail Command Interface with Your New Email*

```
[root@localhost ~]# sendmail root
Test email
.
[root@localhost ~]# mail
Mail version 8.1 6/6/93.  Type ? for help.
"/var/spool/mail/root": 1 message 1 new
>N  1 root@localhost.local  Tue Jun 30 06:43   14/608
&
```

   In Listing 15-1, the `mail` command points to your new email by using the >N symbol. Pressing Enter again will open the newest email in your account's mailbox. The sample email you created will show up, similar to Listing 15-2.

*Listing 15-2. The Contents of the New Email*

```
Message 1:
From root@localhost.localdomain  Tue Jun 30 06:43:28 2009
Date: Tue, 30 Jun 2009 06:43:25 +0800
From: root <root@localhost.localdomain>

Test email
```

Here you are currently viewing message 1 on your mailbox. This message has headers that tell you where it came from, what time it was received, and who sent it to you. The header part of the email is generated by the MTA to provide additional information to other MTAs that will receive your email.

After the header comes a blank line. This separates the header information from the body of the message.

The last part of the email is the message itself, 'Test email', that you wrote earlier.

If there are other unread messages left, you can view them also by pressing Enter and the mail command's interface will show you the next one. It will also tell you that there are no new messages to be read after you have browsed all new emails. If you want to reread an email, you can type its message number on the prompt followed by the Enter key and the mail command interface will show you the contents of that email.

You can exit the mail command's interface by typing **q** and pressing Enter.

Now that you have sent email to yourself and received it as root, it is time to learn how sendmail stores and organizes email messages, using the mbox mailbox format.

## THE MBOX FORMAT

The mbox format is widely used by MTAs, including sendmail, to store email. User emails to be sent and those to be received are placed into separate files for each user. With this format, emails are added or removed by an MTA on those individual files. While an MTA is making changes to an individual mbox file, that file is locked to avoid accidental modifications by other programs. After the changes have been made, the mbox file will be unlocked and ready for use by other programs.

To see how mbox files work, send yourself two new emails with different messages using the steps shown in the section "Sending Mail with Sendmail" earlier. The second should have the message "Second email" and the third should have the message "Third email." I will use those in the listings that follow.

After sending the two new emails, do not use the mail command to view them. Instead, use a text editor to open the text file that the sendmail command used for the recipient. Go to the /var/spool/mail directory and find the file called root in there. Open that file and the contents may look like this:

```
From root@localhost.localdomain  Tue Jun 30 07:33:41 2009

Return-Path: <root@localhost.localdomain>
```

```
Received: from localhost.localdomain (localhost.localdomain [127.0.0.1])
     by localhost.localdomain (8.13.8/8.13.8) with ESMTP id n5TNXfxD004935
     for <root@localhost.localdomain>; Tue, 30 Jun 2009 07:33:41 +0800
Received: (from root@localhost)
     by localhost.localdomain (8.13.8/8.13.8/Submit) id n5TNXcjA004934
     for root; Tue, 30 Jun 2009 07:33:38 +0800
Date: Tue, 30 Jun 2009 07:33:38 +0800
From: root <root@localhost.localdomain>
Message-Id: <200906292333.n5TNXcjA004934@localhost.localdomain>
```

**Second email**

```
From root@localhost.localdomain   Tue Jun 30 07:33:47 2009
Return-Path: <root@localhost.localdomain>
Received: from localhost.localdomain (localhost.localdomain [127.0.0.1])
     by localhost.localdomain (8.13.8/8.13.8) with ESMTP id n5TNXlQ6004939
     for <root@localhost.localdomain>; Tue, 30 Jun 2009 07:33:47 +0800
Received: (from root@localhost)
     by localhost.localdomain (8.13.8/8.13.8/Submit) id n5TNXiEU004938
     for root; Tue, 30 Jun 2009 07:33:44 +0800
Date: Tue, 30 Jun 2009 07:33:44 +0800
From: root <root@localhost.localdomain>
Message-Id: <200906292333.n5TNXiEU004938@localhost.localdomain>
```

**Third email**

The boldface lines are the messages for the second and third emails that you sent to yourself. Notice that the third email is appended at the end of the second email. This is how the mbox mailbox format stores an email that has been received by the MTA and is yet to be retrieved by an MUA. The mbox format is sendmail's mailbox format.

When an email client retrieves email, the messages retrieved from the user's mbox file are removed, returning space to the MTA for new email.

Once additional users send email using the sendmail command, you will see in this directory additional mbox files for each user. This is how sendmail organizes email using the mbox format.

You will see how to configure sendmail using its configuration files next.

# sendmail.mc

The sendmail.mc file is used to make the changes on sendmail's main configuration file called sendmail.cf. It is included in the installation of the sendmail-cf package and is inside the /etc/mail directory. The contents are less cryptic than in the main configuration file because it uses the syntax of GNU M4, the GNU implementation of the Unix macro processor. With M4 and the sendmail.mc file, you can create a new sendmail.cf file that you can manage more easily. Updating sendmail's main configuration file using this approach is recommended.

Listing 15-3 contains a section of the sendmail.mc file in M4 format.

*Listing 15-3. The sendmail.mc File with Some Definitions*

```
dnl # Uncomment and edit the following line if your outgoing mail needs to
dnl # be sent out through an external mail server:
dnl #
dnl define(`SMART_HOST', `smtp.your.provider')dnl
dnl #
define(`confDEF_USER_ID', ``8:12'')dnl
dnl define(`confAUTO_REBUILD')dnl
define(`confTO_CONNECT', `1m')dnl
define(`confTRY_NULL_MX_LIST', `True')dnl
define(`confDONT_PROBE_INTERFACES', `True')dnl
define(`PROCMAIL_MAILER_PATH', `/usr/bin/procmail')dnl
define(`ALIAS_FILE', `/etc/aliases')dnl
define(`STATUS_FILE', `/var/log/mail/statistics')dnl
```

Creating custom Unix macros with M4 is beyond the scope of this book. What we will focus on is the way to assign and change values of the available sendmail options that have been created for us within the sendmail.mc file.

The dnl keyword at the beginning of a line stands for "Delete new line." This macro instructs M4 not to add a blank line following the current line in the resulting file. The options available in the sendmail configuration file that will be generated by M4 are controlled using the define macro, which takes the following syntax:

```
define(`optionname', `optionvalue')
```

where *optionname* is the name of the option that you want to modify and *optionvalue* is the value that you want to assign to the option. For example, one define macro found in Listing 15-4 specifies the path of the procmail program that sendmail will use.

*Listing 15-4. The define macro for sendmail's MDA, procmail*

```
define('PROCMAIL_MAILER_PATH', '/usr/bin/procmail')dnl
```

In this define statement, the optionname is PROCMAIL_MAILER_PATH, and the optionvalue is /usr/bin/procmail. The define macro also calls the dnl macro to avoid adding a blank line following this line in the sendmail.cf that will be generated.

One thing you must not forget when specifying *optionnames* and *optionvalues* is the way to quote them. The opening quote must be the reverse apostrophe (`) and the closing quote is the apostrophe ('). If you do not enclose *optionnames* and *optionvalues* in this way, M4 will flag it as an error.

Some options in the sendmail.mc file do not use the define macro, because you set the value in the macro itself. One such option is the MASQUERADE_AS macro, which instructs sendmail to change the local hostnames of outgoing email to a different hostname. This macro is useful in domains that require local emails to be sent using the same domain name as the site's domain.

As an exercise, you will change two options in the sendmail.mc file. First, you'll make outgoing emails appear be coming from the pvctoyfan.com fictional domain, by changing the value of the macro MASQUERADE_AS. Second, you want sendmail to be able to listen to the network to accept email that must be sent by email clients. Assume that the hostname of the computer sendmail runs on has the domain pvctoyfan.com and its IP address is 192.168.1.11. Be sure to make a copy of the original sendmail.cf in case things go wrong. Here is what you are going to do.

1. Find the entry

   ```
   dnl MASQUERADE_AS(`mydomain.com')dnl
   ```

   and change it to

   ```
   MASQUERADE_AS(`pvctoyfan.com')dnl
   ```

   This will give all email coming from this computer the domain pvctoyfan.com.

2. Find the line

   ```
   DAEMON_OPTIONS(`port=smtp,Addr=127.0.0.1, Name=MTA')dnl
   ```

   and change it to

   ```
   DAEMON_OPTIONS(`port=smtp,Addr=0.0.0.0, Name=MTA')dnl
   ```

   This change instructs sendmail to listen for incoming email on all IP addresses including 192.168.1.11. If you don't do this, sendmail will only listen to the local loop IP address, 127.0.0.1, and your email clients on the network will not be able to send email to your server. Be sure to inform your users about the IP address you have used on this line, which will serve as the outgoing mail server for their email clients. You'll learn more about this later in the chapter, when you set up an email client to use your local mini-email system.

3. Run the command

   ```
   m4 /etc/mail/sendmail.mc > /etc/mail/sendmail.cf
   ```

   The m4 command accepts your modified sendmail.mc M4 file and generates the new configuration file sendmail.cf in machine language that sendmail understands, in the /etc/mail directory. Restart sendmail to make the changes active, by running service sendmail restart.

# sendmail.cf

The sendmail.cf file is the main configuration file of sendmail and resides in /etc/mail. This file contains options, rules, and rulesets that are used by sendmail during execution. Among the sendmail.cf options are the directory paths for the sendmail administrative configuration files and the type of MDA that sendmail will use during email delivery. The file also has rules and rulesets that are used by sendmail to process email information, such as rewriting destination email addresses from incoming messages. The contents of this file can be generated by using the sendmail.mc file and m4 discussed earlier. You can even opt to edit the contents of sendmail.cf to change the required options instead of using sendmail.mc if you really understand its syntax.

You can open the sendmail.cf file using a text editor but do not make any changes at the moment. Listing 15-5 shows sample contents of the file.

*Listing 15-5. A Section of the sendmail.cf File*

```
##################
#   local info   #
##################

# my LDAP cluster
# need to set this before any LDAP lookups are done (including classes)
#D{sendmailMTACluster}$m

Cwlocalhost
# file containing names of hosts for which we receive email
Fw/etc/mail/local-host-names

# my official domain name
# ... define this only if sendmail cannot automatically determine your domain
#Dj$w.Foo.COM
```

You can see that this sendmail.cf file follows some of the same syntax conventions as other administrative configuration files, such as comment lines starting with hash symbols and lines separated by newlines. But the way options are enumerated is different. For example, the line

```
#Dj$w.Foo.COM
```

specifies the domain name that sendmail will use if it cannot determine the domain name of the host computer. It uses the following syntax

```
optionvalue
```

where *option* is the name of the option that will be used and *value* is the value for this option. Note that the option in the example is specified as the capital Dj, the domain, and the value is $w.Foo.COM. If you know how to use regular expressions, the value of the Dj option uses one, the $w token to match words. In the example it is commented out.

From this sample content alone, you can start to see why configuring sendmail is challenging for most users. Some options look like this example, but others are defined differently, like the rulesets to rewrite email headers. Even experts occasionally get stumped when editing this file directly because most of its options use regular expressions that can match a value while sendmail is processing email. You can browse further in the file to see the rulesets if you want to test yourself.

■ **Note:** If you want to master configuring the `sendmail.cf` file by hand, you can start by reading *Pro Open Source Mail : Building an Enterprise Mail Solution*, by Curtis Smith (Apress, 2006). You can check the book at `http://www.apress.com`. Also be sure to practice a lot, and for safety, back up your original `sendmail.cf` file before you try changing it!

# The Sendmail Administrative Configuration Files

Sendmail is not limited to sending and receiving mails as originally designed. You can also change the way it behaves when certain domains or hosts are involved. You can allow some emails to pass or reject them if needed. In order to change the behavior of sendmail, you need to know what available configuration files it depends on. The sendmail administrative configuration files include `local-host-names`, `aliases`, `access`, `trusted-users`, `virtusertable`, and `mailertable`. They are located in /etc/mail.

## local-host-names

The `local-host-names` file contains all of the alternate names or aliases of the host computer where sendmail runs. If your computer has more than one name, enumerate them here. For example, if your computer's host name is example.com and it is also known as example.org and example.net, list those in the file in separate lines, as shown in Listing 15-6.

**Listing 15-6.** Sample Contents of the local-host-names File

```
example.com
example.org
example.net
```

Lines that start with a hash symbol (#) are treated as comments and are ignored by sendmail when the `local-host-names` file is read.

Whenever sendmail sees any of those host names, it will know that the email it is processing came from this host. If you leave the `local-host-names` file empty, sendmail will still be able to send email, but it will take a while because sendmail will try alternative ways to find who owns the hostname it encounters. You can treat `local-host-names` as sendmail's version of /etc/hosts in Linux.

## aliases

The `aliases` file is used by sendmail to translate a recipient to another. This is located inside the /etc directory. The format of an entry in the `aliases` file is like the following

```
original_recipient:    new_recipient
```

A snippet of the actual `aliases` file is shown in listing 15-7.

*Listing 15-7. Some Contents of the aliases File*

```
# Basic system aliases -- these MUST be present.
```

```
mailer-daemon:        postmaster
postmaster:           root

# General redirections for pseudo accounts.
bin:                  root
daemon:               root
adm:                  root
```

The aliases file must include the first two entries for sendmail to work properly. The mailer-daemon and postmaster are special aliases required by every MTA to accept system-related mail for the root user. We can see here that if you send a local email to the postmaster user, that email will be sent to the root user. Or if sendmail suddenly encounters a problem and needs to notify the administrator, it will send a copy of the error to the mailer-daemon user, which is also the postmaster and is translated to the root user.

The aliases file has an entry for the marc user on that file like this:

```
#root:                marc
```

You do not have to worry about it because that entry serves as an example only. It is also commented and you can remove it if you want to.

Here are some sample entries that can be added to the aliases file assuming the users redeye, ryan, and joel exist on your system:

```
ging:     redeye
bake:     redeye,ryan,joel
```

Whenever an email addressed to ging is accepted, sendmail forwards that mail to the redeye user. For the bake alias, the received email will be given to three users, redeye, ryan and joel. This forms a basic mailing list that can be implemented using aliases.

As usual, lines that start with # are comments and are ignored by both the sendmail and newaliases commands.

Whenever you add or change entries in the aliases file, you need to rebuild its corresponding database file, called aliases.db, which sendmail uses to process email aliases. If you do not, the new entries will not be seen by sendmail. This file is rebuilt every time you restart sendmail, but you can rebuild it manually by using the newaliases command without any arguments. If you manually ran newaliases, it will report that it has successfully recreated the file by stating the total number of aliases along with the new size of the file if there are no problems.

## access

The access file enables sendmail to filter out domains you specify as legitimate or not. With the access file, you can assign actions whenever a particular domain name satisfies your filtering. The format of a file entry is as follows:

```
target        action
```

where *target* is the domain, user, or network that we want to track down and *action* is the result we want to happen when a target satisfies our filtering. Listing 15-8 shows an example access file.

***Listing 15-8.*** *Filtering Out the Good Domains from the Bad*

```
ryan@example.com            OK
```

```
spamattacker.example.net    REJECT
192.168.1.10               RELAY
Connect:192.168.1          REJECT
```

This access file contains four lines that control how sendmail will handle email received from clients before sending it. The first line will allow emails from ryan@example.com to be sent, with the OK action. The second line will stop mail from the domain spamattacker.example.net from being sent, with the REJECT action. The third line will allow email from the computer with the IP address 192.168.1.10 to be sent using your mail server to its proper target host, with the RELAY action. The last line covers the rest of the 192.168.1 network and will reject emails from those computers, with the REJECT action. The Connect: keyword gives additional information about the source of the email. You can leave this out like in the third line and the action will still work.

There are other actions that can be used, and Table 15-1 lists the common ones.

*Table 15-1. Actions Available for the access File*

| Action | Result |
| --- | --- |
| OK | Accept local email. |
| REJECT | Reject the email and tell the sender that the sending failed. |
| RELAY | Accept the email and allow it to be relayed via SMTP. The mail server will act as a bridge to the sender's intended domain in case this server is not that domain. |
| DISCARD | Drop the email. |
| *NNN your_text* | *NNN* is one of the errors listed in RFC821, and *your_text* is your own custom message. |

Lines that start with # are treated as comments and are ignored by both sendmail and makemap.

Whenever you change the contents of the access file, you need to recreate those contents to be placed on its database file, called access.db so the situation here is similar to that for aliases. The access.db file is the one referenced by sendmail during the filtering process and it provides a way to update that database. This enables sendmail to provide fast filtering of your rules as you have enumerated them in the access file. You can update the contents of access.db along with the rest of the database files by restarting sendmail, or you can do it manually by using the makemap command. The makemap command creates a database map equivalent of a source file, which sendmail can use. The makemap command uses the following syntax:

```
makemap maptype resultfile < givenfile
```

where *maptype* is the type of map you want to use for the resulting database map *resultfile* based on the source file represented by *givenfile*. You can use the btree value to create B-tree-formatted maps or the hash value to create hash-formatted maps. We will use the hash value for the *maptype* to use hash tables on the resulting database file.

To update the access.db file based on the contents of the access file, enter the following at the terminal:

```
makemap hash /etc/mail/access.db < /etc/mail/access
```

Once the command runs, your access.db file is updated. You can also use the makemap command to manually update the database files of both virtusertable and mailertable, which will be discussed later in this chapter. Using the access file for security is a good measure, but it is inadequate for anything serious such as protecting a mailing list. You must not rely too much on this file for security.

## The trusted-users File

The trusted-users file lets you specify which users can use sendmail's –f flag, which lets users alter the email's original sender. In other words, it says which users are allowed to say where a message has come from. Most users, when they send a message, can only say that it came from them. Sendmail will silently throw away email from any user trying to use the –f flag who is not included in this file. This mechanism prevents unauthorized email forging for better security. This is a good security measure but again is inadequate for anything serious, such as protecting a mailing list.

For example, suppose you have assigned the users redeye and ryan the ability to make announcements on the example.com community mailing list any time you as the moderator are not available. In order for these users to generate mail coming from administrator@example.com, you need to add them to the trusted-users file; its contents would look like listing 15-9.

*Listing 15-9. Users Who Can Use the –f Switch Contained in the trusted-users File*

```
redeye
ryan
```

## The virtusertable File

The virtusertable file lets sendmail associate domains into new addresses. It is a bit like the aliases file but works for any domain. With virtusertable, sendmail can accept email sent to a specific user at a domain (or any user in that domain), and forward it to a local or remote user. The format of an entry in the virtusertable file is

```
givendomain     target
```

where *givendomain* is the domain you are expecting to receive from and *target* will be the user to receive the email when *givendomain* is matched. The *givendomain* can also be specified so that only a particular user at that domain should be accepted. The *target* can be a local user or a user from another domain. Listing 15-10 shows what this file might look like.

*Listing 15-10. A virtusertable File*

```
ryan@example.com               ryan
@otakai.ipbfree.example.org    mangaman@example.net
admin@tl29.example.org         jssicam@guru.example.net
```

In this virtusertable file, you can see how email is translated from its original recipient to the new one. The first line says that an email sent to ryan@example.com will be given to the local user ryan. In the second line, any email intended to the domain otakai.ipbree.example.org will be given to the user whose email address is mangaman@example.net. Finally, another specific user, admin@tl29.example.org, will be assigned to the user jssicam@guru.example.net. You can see a lot of room for flexible email translation using the virtusertable file, especially since the domains and users to be accepted need not be present to your email system. Of course, you can only control where things that come through this MTA go.

## mailertable

The `mailertable` file enables sendmail to accept email and have it sent to another MTA. It is mostly used when providing backup mail services. You can do the same thing with `virtusertable`, but that causes the destination to be rewritten— `mailertable` doesn't rewrite the destination; it simply forwards the mail.

An entry populating the `mailertable` file has the following syntax:

```
target_domain          new_mta_type:new_mta_host
```

where *target_domain* is the domain of the email to be accepted, *new_mta_type* the type of the new MTA, and *new_mta_host* is the hostname on which the MTA resides. You might mistakenly think that `virtusertable` duplicates `mailertable` because of the similarities in entries. The former is designed to accept email from domains and send them to their new recipient. The latter accepts emails and sends hands them over to another MTA to do the sending.

Another attribute that differentiates `mailertable` t from `virtusertable` is the way the type of MTA is specified for the new MTA to send the accepted email. In the `mailertable` syntax, *new_mta_type* can be `esmtp`, `smtp`, or `error`. Both `esmtp` and `smtp` values will forward the email to another source, such as another MTA assigned as a relay host. The `esmtp` value is used for MTAs that implements the Extended SMTP and is faster when sending email. Some of these MTAs include Postfix and qmail. The `smtp` value is used for MTAs that does not implement the Extended SMTP. You will usually use `esmtp` on your `mailertable` entries. The `error` value will send an error message back to the sender.

Listing 15-11 is an example `mailertable` file, and I'll briefly explain how it handles each type of MTA.

*Listing 15-11. Sample mailertable Contents*

```
tl28.example.com                      esmtp:tl29.example.org
nonexistent.example.net               error:This is not a valid domain.
```

The first entry assigns any email addressed to the tl28.example.com domain to the other MTA, called tl29.example.org. For SMTP-type lines, it really is to a hostname.

The second entry shows how emails with bad domain names can be handled using the error MTA. With the error MTA, an error message that you specify is returned to the sender.

If you want to forward email from subdomains to a domain, you can do that by prepending the *target_domain* part with a dot like this:

```
.tl28.example.com       esmtp:tl29.example.org
```

Emails coming from tl28.example.com subdomain will be forwarded to the tl29.example.org domain.

# Postfix

The Postfix mail server was created by Wietse Venema to be an alternative MTA to sendmail. As an MTA it can send and receive email, and it supports the mbox format used by sendmail. So if you migrate from sendmail to Postfix, you will have no problems using your existing mbox files.

Because Postfix was designed to be an alternative to sendmail, it includes compatibility features for the most-used programs in sendmail. For example, Postfix has a `sendmail` command that can be used like the original sendmail command. This will help existing sendmail users feel comfortable when using Postfix as their new MTA.

Beyond its support for sendmail, Postfix also has additional features that you can use. First is an alternative to mbox, the maildir mailbox format. This stores email messages in a set of directories instead of a single file and is explained later in the chapter. Second is the ability to use databases, such as Berkeley DB, LDAP, and PostgreSQL, for example. With the use of databases, you can have Postfix store and manage email in your chosen database in addition to mailboxes. There are other features you can use with Postfix, and you can learn more about them on the Postfix web site at http://www.postfix.org.

To begin using Postfix, you need to install and configure it on CentOS, starting in the next section.

## Installing Postfix

Postfix is not included in the default installation of CentOS. To install Postfix, run the command yum install postfix as the root user. This will install the required binaries and configuration files on your system.

If you have sendmail running, be sure to turn it off by executing service sendmail stop. This will free up port 25, the default port for sending mails by SMTP that is held by sendmail when it is running. After sendmail is out, you can start Postfix by issuing service postfix start in the terminal.

## Switching MTAs

You can choose which MTA to send emails if you have both sendmail and Postfix in your system using CentOS's system-switch-mail command and GNOME's Mail Transport Agent Switcher window. The former can be used on the terminal and the latter within your GNOME desktop. To install both tools, use yum install system-switch-mail system-switch-mail-gnome.

If you have GNOME installed, you can use the Mail Transport Agent Switcher by clicking the System menu then selecting Administration ➤ Mail Transport Agent Switcher. The Mail Transport Agent Switcher will appear as in Figure 15-3.

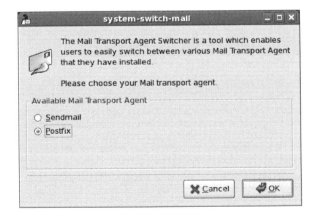

*Figure 15-3. The Mail Transport Agent Switcher window*

You can choose "Postfix" here and click Ok to use Postfix when sending emails in the next section. You can use this window again to use sendmail later if required.

## Sending Email with Postfix

You can use any mail client to send email with the Postfix MTA running on your system. As an example, follow the steps you learned in the section "Sending Email with sendmail" on the terminal, but this time send an email with the content `Postfix first email`. Then open the mbox file for root in the /var/spool/mail directory and see if the email with the Postfix message is there, as in Listing 15-12.

*Listing 15-12. The mbox File for root Changed by the Postfix MTA*

```
Third email

From root@localhost.localdomain  Fri Jul  3 13:31:19 2009
Return-Path: <root@localhost.localdomain>
X-Original-To: root@localhost.localdomain
Delivered-To: root@localhost.localdomain
Received: from localhost.localdomain (localhost [127.0.0.1])
    by localhost.localdomain (Postfix) with ESMTP id 24057705F9
    for <root@localhost.localdomain>; Fri,  3 Jul 2009 13:31:19 +0800 (PHT)
Received: (from root@localhost)
    by localhost.localdomain (8.13.8/8.13.8/Submit) id n635VEIx012603
    for root; Fri, 3 Jul 2009 13:31:14 +0800
Date: Fri, 3 Jul 2009 13:31:14 +0800
From: root <root@localhost.localdomain>
Message-Id: <200907030531.n635VEIx012603@localhost.localdomain>
To: undisclosed-recipients:;

Postfix first email
```

Our test worked because Postfix supports mbox as the default mailbox format. This will help you ease the transition from the sendmail MTA to Postfix.

You can use the `mail` command email client to see your email on its command line interface.

## The Postfix Main Configuration File

Postfix's main configuration file is called `main.cf` and is located in the /etc/postfix directory. The contents of the file are more reader-friendly than in sendmail's main configuration file, `sendmail.cf`. When you need to make modifications, you simply change the required lines and save the file. You can open the file now and browse through its contents.

The `main.cf` file follows syntax similar to that found in most Linux configuration files. Options that change the behavior of Postfix are called *parameters*. A parameter looks like this:

```
parameter_name = parameter_value
```

where *parameter_name* is the name of the parameter that you want to use and *parameter_value* is the value that you want to assign to your chosen parameter. Here is an example parameter in the `main.cf` file

```
#myhostname = host.domain.tld
```

Here, the parameter name is myhostname and the value assigned to it is host.domain.tld. Lines that start with # are comments and are ignored by Postfix. This line is currently commented and will not be used by Postfix.

The main.cf file lists a lot of parameters and there are others that you can use in addition to those. You can learn more about the other parameters by reading the man pages of the postconf command, Postfix's configuration utility.

Whenever you change something in the main.cf file, you must restart Postfix so it can update itself. In the following exercise you will make some changes to that file in order to have it ready to accept email for sending and make it use different method to store email.

We assume that the hostname for this mail server computer is called mail and is within the fictional pvctoyfan.com domain.

Open the main.cf file using a text editor.

1.   Find the lines

     ```
     #myhostname = host.domain.tld
     #mydomain = domain.ltd
     ```

     and change them to

     ```
     myhostname = mail.pvctoyfan.com
     mydomain = pvctoyfan.com
     ```

     The myhostname parameter will let Postfix know the name of the host it resides on. The mydomain parameter will inform Postfix the domain name it belongs to. Both parameters are used by other parameters within the configuration file.

2.   Uncomment the line

     ```
     myorigin = $mydomain
     ```

     to make Postfix append the domain name to locally sent mail. Notice that the myorigin parameter takes a parameter with a dollar sign instead an actual value. This is fine because Postfix understands that parameters prepended with a dollar symbol are variables and will take what is being held by them. Because mydomain has pvctoyfan.com as the value, myorigin becomes

     ```
     myorigin = pvctoyfan.com
     ```

     when Postfix interprets this line.

3.   Comment the line

     ```
     inet_interfaces = localhost
     ```

     and uncomment the line

     ```
     inet_interfaces = all
     ```

     to make Postfix accept and send email from all available network interfaces in the computer it resides on. If you do not uncomment this line, Postfix will only accept email from localhost, where it resides.

4. Find the line

   ```
   home_mailbox = Maildir/
   ```

   and uncomment it. This parameter instructs Postfix to use the maildir format instead of mbox to store email.

5. Save the file and restart the Postfix server by running `service postfix restart` as root. Send an email to yourself by following the steps in "Sending Email with sendmail" and put the message "The maildir format now" as the message body to root@localhost. You need to append the @localhost this time because Postfix's sendmail command will not be able to find the fictional pvctoyfan.com domain at the moment.

## MAILDIR

Maildir is another mailbox format that mail servers can use. It allows MTAs to store email messages into separate directories instead of a single file as in the mbox format. Each maildir directory contains three subdirectories to sort email depending on what the mail server should do with it. These directories include the new, the cur, and the tmp subdirectories. You can view a user's maildir directory by opening the Maildir contained in their home directory. For the root user, you can change into that directory by using the cd /root/Maildir command. From there you will see the three subdirectories.

The new subdirectory holds the new emails that have been received by the MTA for this user. Because you sent yourself an email, you received your own email, and Postfix placed it in the new subdirectory. If you browse the new directory now, you will see a file with a long name. That is your new email, and you can open it with a text editor to view its contents. A sample mail in the new directory looks like this:

```
Return-Path: <root@mail.pvctoyfan.com>

X-Original-To: root@mail.pvctoyfan.com

Delivered-To: root@mail.pvctoyfan.com

Received: from mail.pvctoyfan.com (localhost [127.0.0.1])

    by mail.pvctoyfan.com (Postfix) with ESMTP id 34F97705E1

    for <root@mail.pvctoyfan.com>; Sun,  5 Jul 2009 05:34:01 +0800 (PHT)

Received: (from root@localhost)

    by mail.pvctoyfan.com (8.13.8/8.13.8/Submit) id n64LXq6G004893

    for root; Sun, 5 Jul 2009 05:33:52 +0800

Date: Sun, 5 Jul 2009 05:33:52 +0800

From: root <root@mail.pvctoyfan.com>
```

```
Message-Id: <200907042133.n64LXq6G004893@mail.pvctoyfan.com>
To: undisclosed-recipients:;

This is the maildir format
```

How did it end up in the new directory? The steps are as follows. First, the MDA puts the email in the tmp directory and assigns it a unique name. Algorithms are applied in this step to make sure there will be no name conflicts between emails. Second, the renamed email is placed in the new directory. This will prevent maildir-enabled programs from reading incomplete email within the tmp directory because the content of the new directory is assumed to be copied completely. Last, when email is about to be retrieved the email in the new directory is placed in the cur directory by the user's MUA. The user's email content within his or her email client is then updated.

You have seen that delivered email goes through a set of directories in the maildir format. This prevents emails that are partially processed from being given back to the user and avoids file corruption that can occur if the mailbox is on a network drive such as NFS. The chance of an mbox file being corrupted is increased when placed on NFS, so it is not recommended. Even though mbox has some disadvantages compared to maildir, the former is faster than the latter for processing delivered mail. Appending a file at the end is faster than moving files from one directory to another.

The mailbox format to use really depends on your setup. If your mail server does not need network drives for storing email and you need speed, use mbox. Otherwise, use maildir and ignore the very small speed decrease in delivering email to your users.

## Postfix Administrative Configuration Files

Postfix has its own set of administrative configuration files that you can use to change the way it handles email. With these configuration files, you can restrict email, change its destination by setting an alias, or relay email to another MTA, much as you do in sendmail. These configuration files are located in the /etc/postfix directory.

Here is a quick look at each Postfix configuration file and how to use it.

### access

The access file lets Postfix filter email based on its domain. It functions in the same way as sendmail's access file; you specify given domains and select whether to accept (OK) or reject (REJECT) the email if it matches. Listing 15-13 shows some example entries for that file.

*Listing 15-13. A Sample access File for Postfix*

```
example.com          OK
192.168.1.10         OK
192.168.1            REJECT
```

Here, any email that originates from the example.com domain will be accepted and will be sent by Postfix. The same can be said for the host, which has the IP address of 192.168.1.10. For the rest of the computers in the 192.168.1 network, all of their emails will be rejected by Postfix.

There are other actions that you can use in Postfix's access file, and you can see them in the access file itself; it's located in the /etc/postfix directory.

After you make changes to this file, run the postmap command on it. The postmap command is Postfix's equivalent of sendmail's makemap command that creates the equivalent database file of a given source file. The syntax of the postmap command is

```
postmap targetfile
```

where *targetfile* is the source file that is needed to create the database file. The resulting database file will have the same name as the source file and have the .db extension by default. The database file will also be created on the same directory as the source file. Running postmap on Postfix's access file like this:

```
postmap /etc/postfix/access
```

will recreate the database file for access, the access.db file in the /etc/postfix directory. Like sendmail, Postfix will use this database file to match rules that you have encoded in the access file for speed. To use the access file in Postfix, you must include the line

```
smtpd_client_restrictions = check_client_access hash:/etc/postfix/access
```

in your main.cf file.

The smtpd_client_restrictions parameter lets Postfix restrict which clients can send messages to this server. The check_client_access will search for the given client information such as hostnames, IP addresses, or domains in the mapfile. Entries in the mapfile take the form *maptype:mapfile*, and for the access database file that uses hash tables, the value will be hash:/etc/postfix/access. If you add this entry to main.cf, you must restart Postfix to use this feature.

## aliases

Postfix uses the entries in the aliases file to translate one recipient to another. This is the same file that sendmail uses (/etc/aliases), and you follow the same rules in updating entries in this file that you would with sendmail. After making the required changes, you will need to run the newaliases command to recreate the database file that Postfix will use. You can also use Postfix's own version of sendmail's newaliases command, postalias, to recreate the database. If you use postalias, you need to specify the source alias file by running postalias /etc/aliases.

The aliases file in Postfix is enabled by default because of the lines

```
alias_maps = hash:/etc/aliases
alias_database = hash:/etc/aliases
```

Both the alias_maps and alias_database parameters take the aliases file in the /etc directory using the maptype:mapfile format, similar to the access file. The alias_maps parameter uses the aliases file, while the alias_database parameter uses the aliases.db database file.

## virtual

The virtual file allows Postfix to rewrite recipient addresses for all email destinations. It behaves the same way as virtusertable in sendmail and follows the same syntax. After making the additions to the virtual file, you must run postmap /etc/postfix/virtual to update the contents of its equivalent database file for faster lookups.

To use the virtual file in Postfix, you need to add the virtual_alias_maps parameter in your main.cf file like this:

```
virtual_alias_maps = hash:/etc/postfix/virtual
```

and restart Postfix.

## transport

The transport file enables Postfix to accept email and have it sent to another MTA or delivery agent. It is similar to sendmail's mailertable file, where you must specify the type of the new MTA that will process the email to be sent. The available types include local and smtp, for example.

After making changes to the transport file, you need to update its database version for faster lookup by running the postmap /etc/postfix/transport command.

To use the transport file in Postfix, you need to add the transport_maps parameter in your main.cf file like this

```
transport_maps = hash:/etc/postfix/transport
```

and restart Postfix.

## generic

If your mail server does not have a valid domain, your emails need additional address translation to make them valid on the Internet and to avoid bouncing. You can do this with the generic file, where you add entries to transform local email to a valid domain. The format of an entry is

```
local_email_account          valid_email_account
```

where local_email_account is the local computer account with an address like localhost that requires translation, and valid_email_account is a live email account that has a valid domain on the Internet. Usually you put the email account given to you by your ISP in place of the valid_email_account because you can be sure that it has a valid domain.

Here is an example entry assuming that my ISP, called validisp.net, gave me an email account called ryan@validisp.net. I can use that to transform mail from my local computer account to the domain of my valid ISP:

```
ryan@localhost.localdomain    ryan@validisp.net
@localhost.localdomain        ryan@validisp.net
```

On the first line, mail sent from my local account, ryan@localhost.localdomain, will have its address rewritten to the value on its right side, ryan@validisp.net, before being sent by Postfix. Because it is assumed that validisp.net is a valid domain, we are certain that my rewritten email will not be rejected by my target recipient.

The second line behaves like the first except that it will rewrite emails coming from the local computer, which has @localhost.localdomain as its domain name, instead of only from the local ryan user, to the ryan@validisp.net value. After you modify the file, you must run postmap /etc/postfix/generic to update its equivalent database file.

To use the generic file, you will need to add the smtp_generic_maps parameter in your main.cf file like this:

```
smtp_generic_maps = hash:/etc/postfix/generic
```

and restart Postfix.

## canonical

The canonical file works almost the same as the generic file but will translate received messages instead. This will rewrite messages that have may have invalid or incorrect domains or usernames to valid ones that are present on the server. The format of the canonical file is

```
sourceaddress          newaddress
```

where *sourceaddress* is the incoming email address and *newaddress* will be its translated address. For example, Ms. Ging's local email username ging.ging was changed recently to ging. Her colleagues will be certain to use her old local email username to send messages to her, which will result in bounced email. This can be solved by adding the following entry to the canonical file:

```
ging.ging              ging
```

When emails are received by Postfix for the ging.ging email address, it will be rewritten to ging. The new value will be used by the other database files such as aliases and will be given to the correct user. If you change entries on the canonical file, you will also have to update its database file by running postmap /etc/postfix/canonical. To use the canonical file in Postfix, you will need to add the canonical_maps parameter in your main.cf file, like this;

```
canonical_maps = hash:/etc/postfix/canonical
```

and restart Postfix.

## relocated

If you have users who have changed locations within the organization, such as to another building, relocated can help inform senders about it. An entry in the relocated file looks like this:

```
pattern        new_location
```

where *pattern* is usually the email address that the transferred person has and *new_location* is a helpful message that can inform the sender of the new whereabouts. The sender will be notified based on the value of *new_location* and the email will not be sent. Here are sample entries for the relocated file:

```
ging@example.com       Ms. Ging changed her address to ging@example.org
ging                   This address is not valid anymore
```

The first line will send the message "Ms. Ging changed her address to ging@example.org" back to the sender when the email address ging@example.com matches. The second line will match the local user email ging and send the message "This address is not valid anymore" back to the sender. In both entries, the original email will be bounced back to the sender.

You need to run postmap /etc/postfix/relocated to update its equivalent database file. To use relocated in Postfix, you need to use the relocated_maps parameter in your main.cf file like this:

relocated_maps = hash:/etc/postfix/relocated

and restart Postfix.

Now that you have seen the administrative configuration files, it's time to explore how Postfix can be modified through its main configuration file.

## Mail Servers and DNS

Earlier in this book, you learned how to set up different kinds of DNS servers. You also configured a domain for pvctoyfan.com by setting it as a master. This time, you will introduce your mail server into that domain by using a new record, called the *mail exchanger*. The mail exchanger resource record, or MX record, informs the sending MTA about the target domain's mail server. A sending MTA queries the domain for its mail server by the following process.

First, the sending MTA does a DNS query to the target domain about its MX record. If it finds one, the sending MTA will then initiate contact with the host specified by the domain's MX record and run SMTP. This way, sending MTAs will be guaranteed to talk to the domain's mail server with the MX record.

An MX record for named has the following syntax

MX     priority_number     mailserver_hostname

where MX is the mail exchanger keyword, which informs named that this resource record is for the mail server. The *priority_number* is a given number to specify the mail server's precedence when an MTA asks for the first mail server it talks to on this domain. Assuming you have configured two mail servers to run on your domain and have assigned 10 for the first's priority number and 20 for the second's priority number. If email is sent or received from your domain, your DNS will select the MX record with the higher priority number, and that is the first mail server. If you assigned both mail servers with the same priority number, your DNS server will use both mail servers. If both equal priority servers have been tried by the DNS and do not work, the next MX record with the lower priority will be used. This will be useful if you have many mail servers in your domain. The *mailserver_hostname* is the complete fully qualified domain name of the mail server for this domain. Make sure the host in the *mailserver_hostname* part has an address (A) record in the domain.

Listing 15-14 shows the modified contents of the db.pvctoyfan.com database file from Chapter 11 for the pvctoyfan.com domain with the MX record and the correct address record both included.

**Listing 15-14.** *The MX Record Added to the db.pvctoyfan.com Database File*

```
$TTL 1D
@               IN    SOA    ns.pvctoyfan.com. hostmaster.pvctoyfan.com. (
                             1         ; Serial
                             3H        ; Refresh
                             2H        ; Retry
                             1W        ; Expire
                             1D)       ; Minimum TTL
                      NS     ns.pvctoyfan.com.
                      MX     10   mail.pvctoyfan.com.

ftp                 A     192.168.1.7
www                 A     192.168.1.8
```

```
ns2          A    192.168.1.9
proxy        A    192.168.1.10
mail         A    192.168.1.11
```

In this example, the MX record was given a priority of 10, and the hostname of the mail server ends with a period. The priority number can be any value, and I used 10 for now. The period rule found in an NS resource record is still applicable to MX resource records to avoid the DNS server append the domain name at the end after the period.

Note that a new address record has been added for the mail host. This is a must in order for your DNS to resolve your mail server correctly when other computers query that host in addition to using the MX record.

When you make these changes on your DNS server, be sure to restart it so that they take effect, by entering service named restart.

# Dovecot

Dovecot is an IMAP and POP3 server for Linux/Unix systems. It was developed by Timo Sirainen, who designed it to be a secure and extensible server. For security, you can use software such as Secure Sockets Layer (SSL) or its own implementation of the Secure Authentication and Security Layer (SASL). Dovecot is also capable of handling mailboxes on NFS and clustered filesystems.

Because Dovecot is extensible, it supports plugins, or external libraries, to add features that are not activated or not readily available on it. Some of the plugins that you can use with Dovecot include acl for access control lists, quota for controlling mailbox space, and antispam to detect and stop spam mails. You can learn more about Dovecot by visiting its web site at http://www.dovecot.org.

In this section you will install and configure Dovecot in your system. You will learn the important configuration options used such as specifying what protocols Dovecot must provide when running. You will also send email with your current Postfix MTA and retrieve them with Dovecot using the Evolution email client included with CentOS.

## Installing Dovecot

Dovecot is not initially installed in a default CentOS setup. To add it, use the command yum install dovecot as root. That will place the required binaries and configuration files of Dovecot into your system.

## The dovecot.conf Configuration File

The main configuration file for Dovecot is called dovecot.conf and is located in the /etc directory. Lines that start with # are treated as comments and are ignored by Dovecot. Options are used to change the way Dovecot runs and follow the syntax

```
optionname = optionvalue
```

where *optionname* is the name of the option you want to use and *optionvalue* is the value you want to assign to that option. An example option that can enable or disable debugging information of Dovecot is

```
#mail_debug = no
```

If you put the value yes here, debug information will be shown. This is useful for developers who extend the Dovecot server. You will not have to use this feature, and it is commented out by default.

Some options that you can use in the main configuration file can be compound options. Compound options may contain attributes that are enclosed in curly braces that can change what the option can do.

An example of a compound option is protocol, which defines what must be done further to configure the specified protocol, such as IMAP or POP3. You can explore this option in the configuration file.

There are other options that you can use within the file, and you can learn more about them by reading the dovecot.conf file and consulting the Dovecot documentation site at http://wiki.dovecot.org.

## Configuration Options

Here are some configuration options that you might want to use in dovecot.conf when customizing Dovecot's behavior.

### protocols

**Syntax:** protocols *givenprotocol1* [*givenprotocol2*]

The protocols option lets you specify what protocols you want Dovecot to use when running. You can specify imap, imaps, pop3, pop3s, or none here. You can even put a combination of them here, depending on your setup. The default values are to listen for both types of IMAP and POP3 connections. If you put multiple values in the protocol option, you must separate them with a space, like this:

```
protocols imap imaps
```

To make Dovecot listen to IMAP requests on port 143, you can give the imap keyword here. If you need Dovecot to accept secure IMAP connections, you can use the imaps keyword to make it listen to port 993.

For POP3 connections on port 110, you can use the pop3 keyword here. If you want secure POP3 connections to be accepted by Dovecot, you can use the pop3s keyword to make it listen on port 995.

If you want Dovecot to be used for authentication with dovecot-auth, you must only use the none keyword here.

### ssl_cert_file

**Syntax:** ssl_cert_file = *givencertificatefile*

The ssl_cert_file option lets you specify the SSL or TLS certificate file that Dovecot will use to make secure connections when using both imaps and pop3s values for protocols. In the configuration file, this defaults to the generated self-signed certificate called dovecot.pem in the /etc/pki/dovecot/certs/ directory:

```
ssl_cert_file = /etc/pki/dovecot/certs/dovecot.pem
```

### ssl_key_file

**Syntax:** ssl_key_file = *givenkeyfile*

The ssl_key_file option lets you specify the SSL or TLS private key file used to create the certificate given on the ssl_cert_file option. This defaults to the generated key file called dovecot.pem in the /etc/pki/dovecot/private directory:

```
ssl_key_file = /etc/pki/dovecot/private/dovecot.pem
```

## ssl_key_password

**Syntax:** ssl_key_password = *givenpassword*

If you created a password-protected private key file, you will have to supply its password in ssl_key_password for Dovecot to use the private key when running. This defaults to a blank in the configuration file because the included generated private key does not require a password.

## mail_location

**Syntax:** mail_location = *mailboxtype:mailboxdirectory*

The mail_location option lets you specify the type of mailbox and its directory that Dovecot will use. The mailbox type can be mbox for mbox mailboxes, maildir for Maildir mailboxes, or Dovecot's own mailbox format, dbox. You can learn more about the dbox mailbox format at http://wiki.dovecot.org/MailboxFormat/dbox.

The mail_location option is set as blank and tells Dovecot to search for the mailboxes automatically. It will try to search for the Maildir, mail, or Mail directories inside each user's home directory, or the /var/mail directory. It is recommended to set the mailbox value in this option to inform Dovecot in case it fails to find the mailboxes uses autodetection.

To use the Maildir format, you will set the mail_location like this:

mail_location = maildir:~/Maildir

This means that the type of mailbox will be maildir and the directory Dovecot will use is the Maildir directory inside each user's home directory.

To use the mbox format, you will use the mbox keyword like this:

mail_location = mbox:~/mail:INBOX=/var/mail/%u

In this line, Dovecot will use the mail directory inside each user's home directory to store emails. The INBOX keyword makes Dovecot use the mbox file located in the /var/mail directory as the user's inbox. The %u is a variable in Dovecot that translates to the user's full username. For example, if %u is mintlentil, then the value of INBOX will be /var/mail/mintlentil when Dovecot uses it.

# Configuring Dovecot for Maildir

Because Postfix is running as your MTA, and you still have not downloaded your mail from its maildir mailbox, you will configure Dovecot to retrieve it.

1. Open the dovecot.conf inside the /etc directory using a text editor.

   Find the line

   #   mail_location = maildir:~/Maildir

   and uncomment it. The effect will be to make Dovecot retrieve emails on the user's maildir mailbox in their home directory.

2. Save the file and restart Dovecot by entering service dovecot restart as the root user.

# Configuring an Email Client to Send and Receive Email Using IMAP

We will now access mail through Dovecot using the Evolution email client. You will create a regular user called ipit for this exercise because the root user is not allowed by Dovecot to retrieve email by default. You will use the ipit user to send and retrieve sample messages using Postfix and Dovecot. Last, you will use the localhost when specifying both Postfix and Dovecot server names. This is because both servers are running locally and there is no need to send email away from your computer for practice.

1. Log in as the root user using the GNOME desktop and create the ipit user and give it a password using the User Manager by clicking System ➤ Administration ➤ Users and Groups. Make sure to remove this sample user after the exercise for security.

2. Start Evolution by clicking Applications ➤ Internet ➤ Email. We will assume that this is the first time you have run the email client. A welcome prompt will appear. Click Forward.

3. Do not click the Restore from Backup checkbox. Click Forward.

4. Type in some information. Enter ipit@localhost as the Email Address, as shown in Figure 15-4, and click Forward.

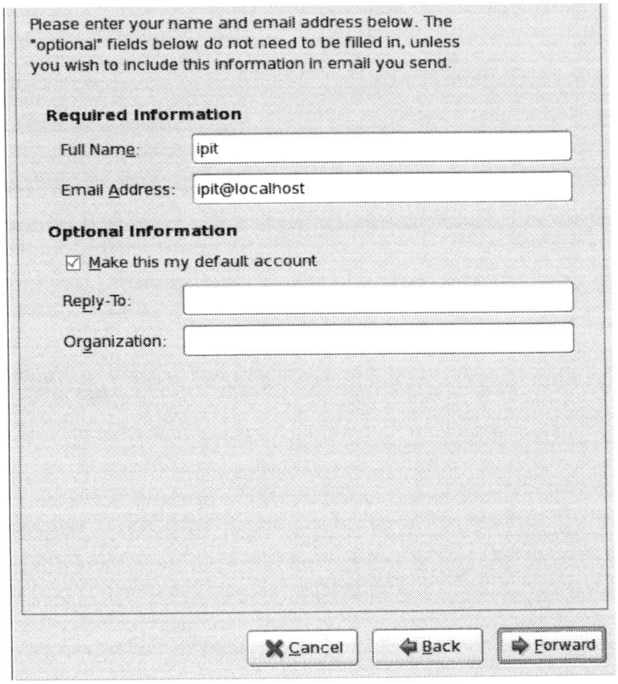

*Figure 15-4. Entering user details into the client*

5. In the Receiving Mail screen, select IMAP on the Server Type dropdown box.

6. In the Server text box, type in localhost as the mail server computer.

7. For security, select no encryption for now.

8. Leave the Authentication type as Password and You can compare your settings to Figure 15-5. When you are ready, click Forward.

*Figure 15-5. Configuring the IMAP server on your email client*

9. For the receiving options, accept the defaults and click Forward.

10. In the Sending Mail window, the server type must be SMTP; enter localhost as the server on the Server text box. Uncheck the Server Requires Authentication box for now. Both Postfix and Dovecot are running in this computer and your mail client will use them. Your screen should look like Figure 15-6.

*Figure 15-6. Configuring the SMTP on your email client*

11. Leave the rest of the settings at their defaults and click Forward.

12. Accept the default value in the Account Information window and click Forward.

13. Select the proper timezone for accurate email time stamps and click Forward.

14. Click Apply in the Done window.

15. You will be prompted for a password. Type in the password for ipit, and your mailbox should look like Figure 15-7.

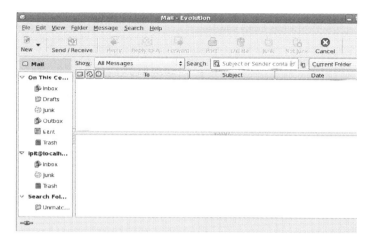

*Figure 15-7. **The message for ipit pulled from Dovecot IMAPReceiving Email with IMAP***

You will now test your email system by sending an email to yourself and retrieving it using IMAP.

16. Click on the ipit@localhost account on the left pane to highlight it, and then click the New button.

   Write a sample message to be sent to ipit@localhost. My message is shown in Figure 15-8.

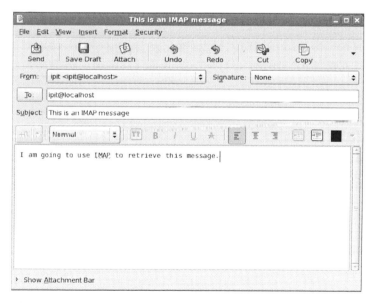

**Figure 15-8.** *Composing a message*

2.  Click the Receiving Email tab and select POP from the Server Type dropdown box. Your selection should look similar to Figure 15-12.

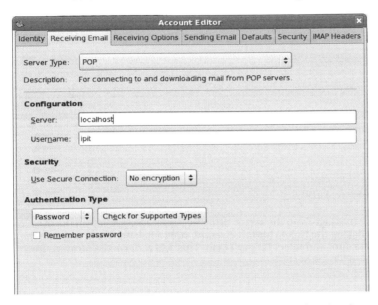

*Figure 15-12. Changing the Server Type to POP3 for email retrieval*

After selecting POP from the Server Type dropdown box, click OK. Click Close on the Evolution Preferences window. You will notice on the left pane that the ipit@localhost account is not visible anymore. What happened is that account is now the default POP3 account being used by Evolution.

3.  Compose a new message for the ipit@localhost email similar to what you did earlier by clicking New on the Evolution main window. My sample message is shown in Figure 15-13.

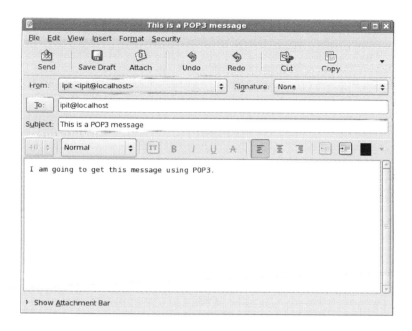

*Figure 15-13. The message to be retrieved using POP3*

4.  Click the Send button to send the message using POP3.

# Checking the POP3 Maildir contents

When you send the message, the MTA will save it in the new subdirectory of ipit's Maildir directory. The message will stay there until you download the message using the ipit@localhost account of Evolution. This is shown in Figure 15-14.

```
[root@localhost new]# pwd
/home/ipit/Maildir/new
[root@localhost new]# ls -l
total 4
-rw------- 1 ipit ipit 662 Oct  1 17:38 1254389934.Vfd00Ic10a4M764570.localhost.
localdomain
[root@localhost new]# tail 1254389934.Vfd00Ic10a4M764570.localhost.localdomain
To: ipit@localhost.pvctoyfan.com
Content-Type: text/plain
Date: Thu, 01 Oct 2009 17:38:54 +0800
Message-Id: <1254389934.5807.8.camel@localhost.localdomain>
Mime-Version: 1.0
X-Mailer: Evolution 2.12.3 (2.12.3-8.el5)
Content-Transfer-Encoding: 7bit

I am going to get this message using POP3.

[root@localhost new]# 
```

*Figure 15-14. The message inside the ipit's Maildir directory on the POP3 server*

If you click the Send/Receive button on Evolution, the message will be downloaded and erased from the server. The message download result is shown in Figure 15-15.

```
[root@localhost new]# pwd
/home/ipit/Maildir/new
[root@localhost new]# ls -l
total 0
[root@localhost new]#
```

*Figure 15-15. The message is removed from the server after the download.*

# Dovecot and OpenSSL

What you've done so far was not hard, right? Well it's time to crank up Dovecot by adding better security through OpenSSL. When you installed Dovecot, it automatically generated a self-signed certificate called dovecot.pem, which is located in the /etc/pki/dovecot/certs/ and /etc/pki/dovecot/private/ directories.

You can use self-signed certificates here for practice, but be sure to acquire a real Certificate Authority-validated one when sending your server into production. This way, users can verify your computer's security when accessing their email, and you can proudly tell them that you are serious about email security!

## Using Evolution with OpenSSL

Take the following steps to retrieve OpenSSL-secured email using the Evolution client:

1. Open Evolution if you have closed it and select Edit ➤ Preferences.

2. Select the ipit@localhost account and click Edit.

3. Click the Receiving Email tab and select TLS Encryption from the Use Secure Connection dropdown box. This is shown in Figure 15-16.

*Figure 15-16. Adding security when downloading messages using OpenSSL*

4.  Click OK after the selection.

5.  Click Close on the Evolution Preferences window. Create a sample message for
    ipit@localhost and send it. Retrieve it by clicking the Send/Receive button. You
    will be shown a confirmation screen similar to Figure 15-17.

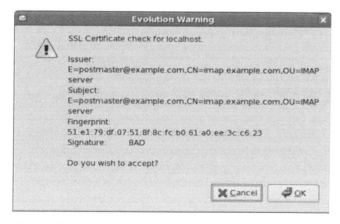

*Figure 15-17. Security confirmation screen when downloading messages*

This appeared because your Dovecot server is using the included self-signed certificate. It is fine to click OK here for now, but be alert if you see this message on another IMAP or POP3 server.

The same procedure applies if you want to test this using IMAP. By now you have downloaded your new email just like before. But the difference is that the mail is now very secure because the connection utilizes OpenSSL. Anyone who attempts a man-in-the-middle attack while you are retrieving your mail with OpenSSL will certainly be disappointed.

## Troubleshooting Tactics

Be sure to periodically check the contents of the mail server log file, called `maillog` and located in the `/var/log` directory, if things are working properly. If you experience problems, you can also consult the contents of the `message` log file in `/var/log` for added information.

# Summary

This chapter covered a lot of ground for Linux mail servers. You saw how email is handled in a full-fledged email server through the use of both sendmail and Postfix mail transfer agents. You also learned the different roles of mail transfer agents and IMAP and POP servers in an email deployment, and you learned a way to secure email access through OpenSSL.

In the next chapter, you will see how you can use directory services to provide uniform authentication on your network. This will help you administer user accounts, as you'll be able to maintain a computer to hold all user accounts instead of manually updating separate computers for each user.

■■■

# CHAPTER 16

# Directory Services

When you start your Linux administration duties, you will be given a handful of Linux servers to maintain. Let's suppose you are being given two or three servers at the beginning of your Linux career. That is manageable, and you'd only need to keep up with a few configuration files such as passwords and groups. In addition to those configuration files, you will also to keep track of which users are assigned to each server that will hold their individual data. Later, additional servers will be given to you as you gain experience with Linux administration. Most of the time, the new servers you will handle will contain a different set of system users. You will have to be twice as careful not to confuse which account belongs to what host and vice versa. As a result, the more Linux servers you are going to maintain, the more diverse and/or complex your administration of them will be.

## The Need for Unified Authentication

In this chapter's scenario, you have a computer laboratory containing three Linux computers for the students. Each computer contains programming tools for their studies. As an administrator, you have set each computer to include the required tools and user accounts. You and the faculty have also agreed that each student of each class will be assigned a user account (a *username*) and computer to log into for their laboratory session. For example, in the first computer laboratory Joel of class S11 will be assigned machine number 1 using user1. Eric of class S12 will be assigned to the same computer and have his data files kept under user2. The second laboratory will hold a different set of users for the other classes.

Computer laboratories are not often used for classes. If there aren't any, those rooms can also be used by students for research. Going back to our setup, suppose Joel wants to log into his computer to continue programming his assignment. When he gets into the computer lab, he cannot do his work because Eric logged into it first and is doing his research. Joel will have to wait for Eric to finish before he can continue.

The solution for this potential problem in your Linux administration job is to have a unified method of authentication. This means having a single account for you and your users to use for identification in your network. When you use a unified authentication mechanism, you are making the resources of your users available anywhere. They can log into any computer and have their work files available for them. In our example, Joel does not have to wait for Eric to finish, because all he has to do is to use another machine and log in with his user account. His personal files and configuration will be available to him as if he was using the same hardware Eric is currently using. With this solution, you also made the network transparent by letting your users log into the network using a single account. Figures 16-1 and 16-2 illustrate the difference between the two approaches.

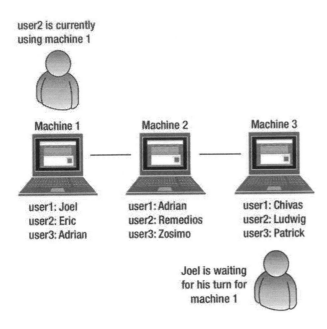

*Figure 16-1. Using an independent account per machine*

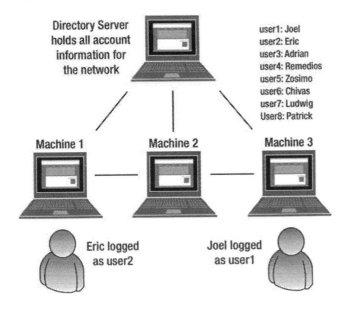

*Figure 16-2. Using a directory service*

In Figure 16-2, a directory server is used to store all account information in the network. This will be referenced by the laboratory computers when a user logs into a computer. With a directory server, both user1 and user2 can log into the network using their personal configuration.

There are two servers available for you in Linux if you want to have a unified authentication mechanism with directory services: NIS and OpenLDAP. In this chapter you will see how to use each directory service and how it can help in this chapter's scalable Linux network.

# Network Information System

The Network Information System (NIS) is a generic directory system for Unix systems. It was developed by Sun Microsystems to provide Unix systems a simple network lookup service that consists of a collection of databases and processes. In the past, when new computers were added to a network, system administrators needed to update certain network configurations for the existing computers. These include passwd, group, and hosts files for example.

With NIS, Unix machines can now determine which computer resides at a given location by using NIS as a directory. It can be compared to looking for information about someone using a telephone directory such as the yellow pages or white pages. Sun actually created NIS with this comparison in mind as the Unix version of the telephone directory.

---

■ **Note:** NIS was originally called the Sun Yellow Pages. The name had to be changed because "Yellow Pages" is a trademark of British Telecom, but the origin is reflected in utility names such as ypserv and ypbind.

---

To send and receive network information, NIS uses the RPC protocol similar to NFS. Remote procedures are generated by both the client and server to pass arguments and messages, this time for directory access.

If you need a directory service created for Unix and Linux machines, NIS can help you out in your network.

## Setting up NIS

The server component of NIS, ypserv, is not installed by default. Install it now by running yum install ypserv. That will put the binary in /usr/sbin and its configuration file in /etc.

## The NIS Server

The NIS server that holds the lookup databases and that the NIS clients talk to for information is ypserv. The databases ypserv uses to distribute network information to clients are stored in /var/yp. The contents of the /var/yp directory include a Makefile to generate the database and to update it later when network information needs to be changed.

NIS uses the concept of *domains* to determine the scope it can refer to in distributing host information. Domains also allow NIS clients to join the scope of the NIS server to receive host information. As long as both NIS server and NIS clients are within a domain, they can do directory lookups on the other computers in the domain.

To create a domain, you use the domainname command. It has the following syntax:
domainname newdomainname

where *newdomainname* is the name of the new domain you want to create in an NIS network. If you do not specify a new domain name for the domainname command, it will print out the NIS server's current domain.

---

▦ **Note:** The value that you assign for the domainname command is not persistent. If you reboot your system, the NIS domain name will revert to its default value, none. To make your setting persistent, be sure to add the domainname command to a startup script, such as the rc.local file. You can read more about the syntax of the rc.local file in Chapter 3. You can also add the entry NISDOMAIN=yourdomain where yourdomain is the name of your NIS domain in the network file in /etc/sysconfig.

---

You will now create your first NIS network. Name this domain toysdomain. It will have an NIS user named bakie that you will use to test for authentication within the domain. Finally, you will generate the database for your first domain by running the Makefile within /var/yp. These procedures will have our NIS server waiting for NIS clients for directory requests. We assign the NIS server the IP address 192.168.1.104 for this exercise. (If you are going to use that IP address, make sure it is available to avoid conflicts with other computers that might be using it.)

## Creating Your First Domain

Take the following steps to create your first domain:

1. Assign toysdomain as the name of the domain, using the domainname command:

   domainname toysdomain

   This will tell the Makefile found in the database directory which database it should create later.

2. Create a regular user account called bakie by running useradd bakie. Give it a password the same as its username for practice using the passwd command. (Don't worry if the passwd command complains about having a weak password, because this is only an example account. Just don't forget to remove the account after you've learned NIS, for safety.)

3. Start the NIS server by issuing service ypserv start. This will acknowledge the database that will be created by the Makefile in the next step.

4. Open the /var/yp directory and verify that the file called Makefile is there. If it is, run make to generate the database files for the domain. You will see something like Figure 16-3.

```
[root@localhost ~]# domainname toysdomain
[root@localhost ~]# service ypserv start
Starting YP server services:                    [  OK  ]
[root@localhost ~]# cd /var/yp/
[root@localhost yp]# make
gmake[1]: Entering directory '/var/yp/toysdomain'
Updating passwd.byname...
Updating passwd.byuid...
Updating group.byname...
Updating group.bygid...
Updating hosts.byname...
Updating hosts.byaddr...
Updating rpc.byname...
Updating rpc.bynumber...
Updating services.byname...
Updating services.byservicename...
Updating netid.byname...
Updating protocols.bynumber...
Updating protocols.byname...
Updating mail.aliases...
gmake[1]: Leaving directory '/var/yp/toysdomain'
[root@localhost yp]#
```

*Figure 16-3. The toysdomain database being created*

## ypserv.conf

The ypserv.conf file is the configuration file for ypserv and is located in the /etc directory. You can set options that can change the way ypserv runs or put access restrictions on hosts through the use of rules.

An option follows the syntax

optionname: optionvalue

where *optionname* is the name of the option you want to use for ypserv, and *optionvalue* is the value you want to assign for that option. For example, in the configuration file, ypserv will not use DNS lookups by default if the target host is not found on its own host list on the domain's database file. This behavior is controlled by the dns option, and the declaration looks like this:

dns: no

A rule uses the format

host_ip:target_domain:target_map:security_type

where *host_ip* is the IP address of the host that you want to apply this rule. This can be a single IP address such as 192.168.1.110, or multiple IPs, such as 192.168.1. for several computers. The *target_domain* is the name of the NIS domain for this rule. The *target_map* is the database map file whose usage you want to restrict to hosts. You can select a map file from the database directory of your created domain, such as /var/yp/toysdomain found in Figure 16-3. The *security_type* is the result of the rule if ypserv matches it. This can contain values of none, port, or deny. The none value will allow access if the rule is matched. The port value will allow access only if the originating port number is less than 1024. The deny value will deny access if the rule is matched. You can also use wildcards to match multiple values by using the asterisk (*) character in place of a rule's value. The following example rule

*:toysdomain:passwd.byname:port

states that any host that will access the passwd.byname database map of the toysdomain domain will be allowed only if the originating port is less than 1024. If no rule matches, ypserv will allow access to the target map the host wants to use .

Lines that start with the hash symbol (#) are comments and are ignored by ypserv (and other configuration tools covered in this chapter).

You can read more about the ypserv.conf file by consulting its man pages.

## The NIS Client

The tool a client uses to connect to an NIS server is called ypbind. When ypbind is started, it will search for NIS domains and talk to its ypserv process. Once it finds an NIS domain it can connect to, the ypbind process will try to bind itself to the domain. If it successfully binds or joins a domain, it can then access the host information held by the domain's NIS server.

This time, you will use the installed ypbind tool to bind yourself to the NIS domain created, toysdomain. You will use the IP address 192.168.1.100 for the NIS client.

---

■ **Caution:** If you are going to test the client set up on Fedora 9 or 10, be sure to turn off the NetworkManager service (http://www.mailinglistarchive.com/fedora-list@ redhat.com/msg157217.html). This can be done by going to the System menu and choosing Preferences ➤ System Services. As shown in Figure 16-4, find the NetworkManager service entry. Disable it and then stop it. NetworkManager might have some conflicts with NIS, so it is best to implement this workaround for the moment.

---

*Figure 16-4. Turning off the NetworkManager service on Fedora*

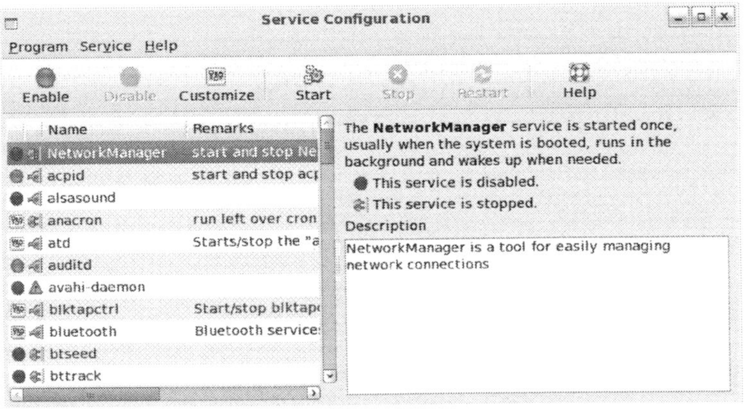

## Binding to an NIS Domain

Take the following steps to bind an NIS client to an NIS server:

1. Set the client's NIS domain name to your NIS server's domain, toysdomain. You will use the domainname command on the client, like this:

   domainname toysdomain

2. Run the ypbind tool to bind to your assigned domainname:

   service ypbind start

3. That's it!

If the way to bind an NIS client to a NIS server looks easy, it is. Just make sure that your machines can see each other on the network by configuring them properly, with an IP address and a valid hostname.

## yp.conf

The ypbind command also has a configuration file that you can use to change how it runs when connecting to an NIS server. Called yp.conf, it is located inside the /etc directory. For example, to set the NIS domain as toysdomain and the NIS server's hostname as toysdomainserver, you can use the domain option, like this:

domain toysdomain server toysdomainserver

You can find other options for yp.conf by consulting its man pages.

## nsswitch.conf

The nsswitch.conf file in /etc is the configuration file for system databases and name service switches that is used by services to look up information. ypbind uses the file to determine where to start finding the information requested by the client such as system users and passwords. If you open and look into the file, as shown in Listing 16-1, you will see the sequence in which the system searches the required information.

*Listing 16-1. The Search Order for passwords, shadow, and group*

```
passwd:     files
shadow:     files
group:        files
```

The listing shows that when a request for an entry in the passwd file is made, the search starts and ends on the system's password file, /etc/passwd. For example, if our client needs the account information for the user bakie, who is not on that computer, it will search locally in the /etc/passwd file. Because the bakie user is not included on the system, the search will fail and report a logon error. The same treatment is given by the rest of the configuration files, the shadow and the group files. Right now our goal is to make a transparent network and even if the user bakie is not present on the client computer, we want the system to search also for the account information on the NIS domain it joined. If the user bakie is on the NIS domain, the NIS client will request additional information on the user from the domain.

To implement this approach, add the keyword nis to each entry as shown in Listing 16-2.

*Listing 16-2. The Search Now Includes NIS*

```
passwd:     files nis
shadow:     files nis
group:         files nis
```

Because we know that the bakie user is on the NIS domain, you will have a successful logon, as you will see later.

## Testing the Setup

Let us see if your NIS client can talk to your NIS server on the toysdomain NIS domain. On the NIS client, run the command ypcat passwd. You'll see the display shown in Figure 16-5.

```
[root@localhost ~]# ypcat passwd
pusa:$1$7e7Z7jpP$Mzbd1XflqvMRY3GSPO6pO0:500:500::/home/pusa:/bin/bash
ging:$1$fpXVLaIL$zs.TtEPxAmI51PEbRr4jP0:501:501::/home/ging:/bin/bash
ipit:$1$lJVc35KO$K7XzRZcH/Hqwg6Gbj9Z0S1:503:503::/home/ipit:/bin/bash
bakie:$1$IYmMg3MI$4yTlWXVcju46Chtna89h6.:1025:1025::/home/bakie:/bin/bash
bake:$1$lXGbOfDT$QoLh/8ZwW6Z87zIjDLhV6.:502:502::/home/bake:/bin/bash
[root@localhost ~]# █
```

*Figure 16-5. Running ypcat on the NIS client*

What happened here is that the NIS client showed us a part of the network information that is being distributed by the toysdomain NIS server. You can also run the same command on the NIS server, but be sure that ypbind is running as well. It will display the same output as the NIS client.

The NIS client was able to communicate with the NIS server because it has made a successful bind with ypbind. In Figure 16-6 you can see the files created by ypbind after it has connected to the NIS server in /var/yp on the NIS client.

```
[root@localhost binding]# pwd
/var/yp/binding
[root@localhost binding]# ls -l
total 8
-rw-r--r-- 1 root root 14 Jul 14 07:39 toysdomain.1
-rw-r--r-- 1 root root 14 Jul 14 07:39 toysdomain.2
[root@localhost binding]# █
```

*Figure 16-6. The files created by ypbind on the NIS domain, toysdomain*

---

■ **Note:** ypcat is part of the NIS utilities you can use on your NIS domain. You'll learn more about it later in the chapter.

---

Before we go explore the NIS utilities, you need to understand how NIS manages information on its databases for distribution. This is through the use of maps.

## Maps

Maps in NIS are the set of files that contain information about an NIS domain. These files hold information about passwords, groups, networks, hosts, protocols, services, aliases and ethers for Ethernet addresses. These map files are contained in a directory named after the NIS domain in the NIS database directory. In our current setup, the NIS server's database directory has a subdirectory called toysdomain that holds the map files for the toysdomain NIS domain. If you look at the contents of the /var/yp/toysdomain directory, you will see a set of files similar to Figure 16-7.

```
[root@localhost toysdomain]# cd /var/yp/toysdomain
[root@localhost toysdomain]# ls -l
total 2180
-rw------- 1 root root   12477 Jul 14 02:44 group.bygid
-rw------- 1 root root   12483 Jul 14 02:44 group.byname
-rw------- 1 root root   12622 Jul 14 02:44 hosts.byaddr
-rw------- 1 root root   12818 Jul 14 02:44 hosts.byname
-rw------- 1 root root   13191 Jul 14 02:44 mail.aliases
-rw------- 1 root root   13607 Jul 14 02:44 netid.byname
-rw------- 1 root root   12777 Jul 14 02:44 passwd.byname
-rw------- 1 root root   12771 Jul 14 02:44 passwd.byuid
-rw------- 1 root root   29211 Jul 14 02:44 protocols.byname
-rw------- 1 root root   14573 Jul 14 02:44 protocols.bynumber
-rw------- 1 root root   16384 Jul 14 02:44 rpc.byname
-rw------- 1 root root   14236 Jul 14 02:44 rpc.bynumber
-rw------- 1 root root  766110 Jul 14 02:44 services.byname
-rw------- 1 root root 1470490 Jul 14 02:44 services.byservicename
[root@localhost toysdomain]# 
```

*Figure 16-7 The map files for the toysdomain NIS domain*

If you try to open a file using a text editor, you will only see unreadable information. The file's contents are encoded in this way because it is in dbm format (see note), which allows NIS to perform fast lookups to give information to NIS clients. It uses a key-value pair for its contents. These files were generated by using the Makefile found in /var/yp.

---

■ **Note:** You can find out more about Berkeley DB at http://www.oracle.com/technology/products/berkeley-db/index.html

---

Notice that most of the map files have two versions, such as passwd.byname and passwd.byuid. When an NIS server performs a search on an NIS domain, it will determine how it can most efficiently find the information on its databases. If the NIS client tries to look for an account using usernames, the NIS server will first look in the passwd.byname file. There is no need for you to concern yourself with these database files, because they are used only by the ypserv process. The files you can modify in order to update the associated database files are contained in the nicknames file within the /var/yp directory of the NIS server, shown in Figure 16-8.

```
passwd          passwd.byname
group           group.byname
networks        networks.byaddr
hosts           hosts.byname
protocols       protocols.bynumber
services        services.byname
aliases         mail.aliases
ethers          ethers.byname
```

***Figure 16-8.*** *Contents of the nicknames file*

The contents of the nicknames file tell you which files you can modify to update the NIS server database. For example, the passwd entry of the nicknames is associated with the system /etc/passwd file; the group with /etc/group, and the hosts with /etc/hosts.

Assuming that you need to change the password for our user bakie, you will run the passwd command as root. Next, you will need to update the NIS server databases to reflect the change by running make on the /var/yp directory. After you run the make command, the database files associated with the passwd nickname will be updated as well. That way, the new password can be used by your NIS clients.

Bottom line: You will need to run make on the /var/yp directory on the NIS master every time you make changes to the files represented in the nicknames file.

With the concept of maps out of the way, it's time to see the utilities you can use for our NIS setup.

## NIS Utilities

Here are useful some tools you can use to find out more about NIS in a network, such as which domain it currently runs on and specific values in the domain's map files.

### ypwhich

The ypwhich command will return the name of the NIS server of an NIS domain. If you run it without any arguments, it will show the NIS client's NIS server for the domain it is currently affiliated with. Here is the syntax for the ypwhich command:

```
ypwhich given_options
```

where *given_options* are the options you want to supply on ypwhich. For example, to see the translation of the maps table, you can run ypwhich -x.

Running ypwhich in either NIS master or NIS client will return the IP address of the NIS server of the toysdomain. In our example, it will return 192.168.1.104. It will return the NIS master's hostname if it has an entry on your DNS.

If there are other NIS domains in your network, you can use the –d flag to find the master of that domain. For example, if there is an NIS domain called toystatues in your network, running ypwhich –d toystatues will return its NIS server name.

## ypcat

The ypcat command will print the values of all keys from the NIS database. Here is its format:

```
ypcat given_options given_mapname
```

where *given_options* are the options you want to use with ypcat and *given_mapname* may be a map name or a map nickname. Earlier, you ran the command ypcat passwd,where the map is the nickname of the actual map file, passwd.byname, which showed you all the keys in the passwd map. You can use ypcat to display the values of the other database maps as needed.

## ypmatch

The ypmatch command can be used to search for a certain map value using its key. The syntax of the ypmatch command is

```
ypmatch key mapname
```

where key is the selected key in the chosen map table given by *mapname* for the value to be searched.
To further illustrate the key-value pair, take a look at this sample entry of the passwd map file

**bakie**:$1$VeB.1qOW$DN.fnliYrV7vTrOhpC3v..:503:503::/home/bakie:/bin/bash

The underlined part is a key, while everything that follows is the value of the key. The ypmatch command will show whatever value a key holds in your search. As an exercise, assume you want to find the value of the key bakie in the group map. To do that, you enter this:

```
ypmatch bakie group
```

The ypmatch command will return the value contained in the bakie key of the group map if one exists. In our setup, it should return this:

```
bakie:!:503:
```

## yppasswd

The yppasswd command lets you change the NIS password of the target user. This will change both the system user's password and the one contained in the NIS database map, passwd. Here is the syntax for the yppasswd command:

```
yppasswd target_user
```

where *target_user* is the user, within this NIS domain, whose password to change.
When you run this command, you do not have to manually update the map file as discussed earlier, because yppasswd will do it for you. Before you run this command, make sure you run its RPC server process with the same name to accept NIS password changes. To do so, enter service yppasswdd start.

# NIS with NFS

A very good use for NIS is to pair it with NFS. By having an NFS server sharing remote directories and NIS to provide uniform authentication and network information, we can have a very transparent Linux network. We will combine the two servers in this exercise, so it is best that you read about NFS on Chapter 14 before diving in here.

In this exercise, we will let our NIS server on toysdomain run an NFS server and have it share the /home directory. The client will mount the remote /home directory and let it bind to the server. Note that our client initially does not have the bakie user. After this exercise, you will see that even if the user is virtually nonexistent to the NIS client, it will appear to be there because of the bakie user's mounted home directory (/home/bakie) and having a single authentication with NIS.

We will continue with our fictional network setup where the IP address of the NIS and NFS server is 192.168.1.104 and the NIS client, 192.168.1.100.

## Using NIS with NFS

Take the following steps to run an NFS server on your NIS server:

1. Start the NIS server, ypserv on the server machine. Be sure that the NIS domain toysdomain has been set by using the domainname command explained earlier.

2. Open the exports file located in /etc and add the following entry:

   ```
   /home    192.168.1.100(rw)
   ```

   This will cause the /home directory of the NIS server to be shared by NFS. Save the file and run the NFS server by entering service nfs start.

3. Create a blank file called nisblankie in the home directory of bakie by entering

   ```
   touch /home/bakie/nisblankie
   ```

   You will use this file to verify our setup later on the client.

4. In the NIS client, unmount the /home directory by running umount /home. You will mount the remote shared /home directory of the NFS server by using mount 192.168.1.104:/home /home. Be sure to double-check the operation by running the mount command without any argument on the client to confirm that the remote shared directory has successfully mounted on the client machine.

5. Run the NIS client on the client machine by issuing service ypbind start. As in step 1, make sure that the NIS domain name toysdomain has been registered through the domainname command.

6. Log into the toysdomain NIS domain on the client by doing an su - bakie. Supply the password (if you're not logged as root initially) and see the contents of the directory, shown in Figure 16-9. If your display is the same as the figure, you have successfully created an NIS and NFS combination.

```
[root@localhost ~]# domainname
toysdomain
[root@localhost ~]# su - bakie
[bakie@localhost ~]$ ls -l
total 0
-rw-rw-r-- 1 bakie bakie 0 Jul 14  2009 nisblankie
[bakie@localhost ~]$
```

*Figure 16-9. The home directory of bakie on a transparent network*

If your display is the same as the figure, you have successfully created an NIS and NFS combination.

With NIS, you now have the capability to create a transparent network by having a central authentication system to be referenced by Linux and Unix systems. The second directory service software, OpenLDAP, can further help us in making our network more diverse by authenticating computers using other operating systems.

# OpenLDAP

NIS can be a good solution for central authentication if your machines are all Linux or Unix. Other operating systems and server software that need directory services cannot use it, however. This opened up opportunities for making other directory access software; one of the first of these is the Directory Access Protocol (DAP).

DAP was developed during the late 1980s to access the X.500 directory service, which was intended for client systems. It lets clients use Bind, Read, List, Search, Compare, Modify, Add, Delete and ModifyRDN operations on the directory it holds. It also uses the Open Systems Interconnection (OSI) protocol as its basis for networking. DAP's usage did not become widespread because not many machines used the OSI protocol at the time'.

DAP was also considered a "heavyweight" as it needed to contain a lot of programming code for some clients. That led to the development of another directory service implementation, whose objective was to be more accessible and easier to maintain and also to use TCP/IP as its underlying networking layer. The new implementation, created by Tim Howes, Steve Kille and Wengyik Yeong in the 1990s, is named the Lightweight Directory Access Protocol (LDAP). It can also use the X.500 protocol and make updates to the directory when needed. Thanks its flexibility, additional features have been integrated, such as security mechanisms with Transport Layer Security (TLS).

As LDAP became popular, the open source community created its version of the protocol, called OpenLDAP. It was originally created by Kurt Zeilenga, who used the LDAP reference implementation for the project. This eventually led to the creation of an OpenLDAP community, and additional maintainers joined the project. Howard Chu and Pierangelo Masarati joined Kurt Zeilanga's project and the three became the core maintainers of the community, which they named the OpenLDAP project. More contributors and maintainers joined the community because OpenLDAP is more extensible and is targeted to more platforms.

In the remainder of this chapter, you will see how we can install OpenLDAP on our system, and use its directory services capabilities to make our first set of test records.

## Setting up OpenLDAP

There are two packages that need to be installed to have OpenLDAP on our system. The first package contains the server binaries and configuration files. The second contains the tools required by clients to connect to the server. To install both packages, type in the following command

```
yum install openldap-servers openldap-clients
```

## slapd

The slapd command is used to run the slapd process, the standalone LDAP daemon. This is the server component of OpenLDAP. The server will accept all LDAP connections and requests on its default port, 389. When run on its own, it can accept arguments that can affect its behavior such as listening to certain types of IP addresses. slapd also has its set of configuration files, ldap.conf, which is located in /etc, and slapd.conf, in /etc/openldap.

The slapd command can also be configured to have its data replicated on another OpenLDAP server for greater availability. This can be done through the use of slurp, the standalone LDAP update replication daemon. You can learn more about LDAP replication at http://www.openldap.org/doc/admin24/ replication.html.

## ldap.conf

The ldap.conf configuration file is used to set system-wide defaults to be applied when running LDAP clients. It also holds the configuration for LDAP's name service switch library and its PAM (Pluggable Authentication Modules) module, which will be discussed in the following pages. This file is located in the /etc directory.

When you open the file, you will see a lot of entries, and most of them are prepended with hash symbols. Those lines are comments, used for notes and information about the options. These are ignored when slapd runs; it executes the lines that are not commented.

Configuration options used to change system defaults follow the format

```
option_name option_value
```

where *option_name* is the name of the option you want to use and *option_value* is the value to be assigned to it. For example, assume that the LDAP server runs on the local machine and you want your LDAP clients to connect to that server. You will use the host command like this:

```
host 127.0.0.1
```

If you want to enable other features of slapd, such as adding PAM and SSL for additional security, you can do so with the ldap.conf file. Be sure to restart the server so that any changes you make in the file will be in effect when it is run.

## slapd.conf

The slapd.conf file contains the configuration for the slapd daemon. Lines commented out with # are treated the same way as in ldap.conf. Blank lines are also ignored and are used to make the file more readable. The slapd.conf file is used not only by the slapd process, it is also used by other OpenLDAP utilities as well; slapadd and slapcat for example.

The configuration file is divided into two parts, the global definitions and the database definitions. If you browse the configuration file, you will see the format illustrated in Listing 16-3.

*Listing 16-3. The Structure of the slapd.conf File*

```
# comment - these options apply to every database
```

```
<global configuration options>

# first database definition & configuration options

database <backend 1 type>

<configuration options specific to backend 1>

# subsequent database definitions & configuration options
:

# Nth database definition & configuration options

database <backend Nth type>

<configuration options specific to backend Nth>
```

The following sections discuss the role of each section in running slapd.

## Global Definitions

The global definitions contain directives for additional reference files, modules to be loaded, libraries for encrypting connections and access definitions for security. The directives declared here will be followed by the directives used by the database definitions section, such as using TLS (if it's enabled) when providing data to the requesting LDAP client.

## Database Definitions

The database definitions have directives that tell the OpenLDAP tools where data can be placed, the type of storage, and the data directory in which to store the created databases. You will use the slapd.conf file to create our databases for our directories. Before you start using the first database, you need to understand the concepts of modules and the schema.

# Modules

OpenLDAP allows you to use additional features through the use of *modules*. A module is a set of extra code that can be loaded into the slapd process. There are two types of module directives that you use in the slapd.conf file: the modulepath directive and the moduleload directive.

The modulepath directive lets you specify the directory or directories where the modules reside. The directive uses the following syntax:

```
modulepath target
```

where *target* can be a directory where the modules are located. To put multiple directories in *target*, separate each directory with a colon (:). Here is an example modulepath line that tells slapd the modules are found in both /usr/lib/openldap and /usr/lib64/openldap directories:

```
modulepath      /usr/lib/openldap:/usr/lib64/openldap
```

The `moduleload` directive lets you specify the module files to use with OpenLDAP. The module files contain the extra code that can add features and change the way `slapd` runs. Those modules must be accessible in the directories declared in the `modulepath` directives.

The `moduleload` directive uses the following syntax

```
moduleload target_module
```

where `target_module` is the name of the module you want to load. Here is an example `moduleload` line that loads the SQL *backend*—the routines that can let OpenLDAP use SQL:

```
moduleload back_sql.la
```

The entries are commented out at the moment and the default backend library that OpenLDAP will use is the bdb format. You can change these later when you want a more advanced backend library to be used on your databases.

## Schemas

Creating a directory for your OpenLDAP server is like making an object out of some set of attributes. For example, take a look at the shirt you are wearing. What is its size? Its brand? Its color? Its material?

Let's say the size of your shirt is XL, the brand is Crispa, the color is white, and its material is cotton. If we are to create a structure for our object, it would look something like Figure 16-10.

| object type | clothing |
|---|---|
| type of clothing | shirt |
| size | xl |
| color | white |
| material | cotton |
| name | Crispax |

*Figure 16-10. The structure of our shirt object*

The way we created the structure to store shirt information is not much different from making LDAP directory structures. LDAP directories use predefined attributes through schemas.

---

■ **Note:** Making LDAP directory structures is similar to making RDBMS tables, discussed in Chapter 12. The difference is that the attributes are already predefined.

---

LDAP schemas contain attributes that can be used to define the structure of a directory. These attributes are categorized into object classes. You can think of object classes as being the "supertype" of attributes. For example, the attribute for the owner of a hardware device is owner, and for some of the usage instruction is in description, which belongs to the object class device. Figure 16-11 shows the device object class and its attributes

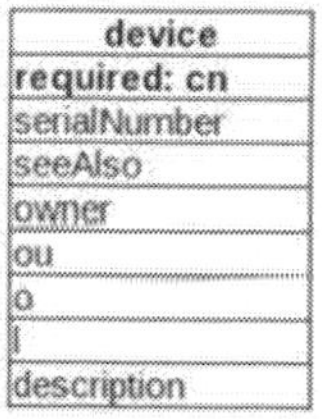

| device |
|---|
| required: cn |
| serialNumber |
| seeAlso |
| owner |
| ou |
| o |
| l |
| description |

*Figure 16-11. LDAP schemas for the top and person object classes*

Some object classes require you to use certain attributes before you can use them to create structures and entries for your database. Those attributes are marked with the MUST keyword within their object class definition. In Figure 16-11, if you are going to use the device object class, and you must use the cn (common name) attribute. Otherwise, your LDAP server will complain and will not continue with your database operation.

If you are going to create the structures for the clothing example in Figure 16-10, you might use the groupOfNames, the organization, and the device object classes. For the groupOfNames object class, you would use the member attribute for the type of clothing and cn attribute for the size. For the organization object class, you would use the searchGuide attribute to store the color of the shirt. For the device class, you would use the description attribute for storing material and owner attribute for the clothing name. There is an attribute that must be used even if you don't need it in this example, and that is the o (organizationName) attribute of the organization object class. You need to do this because using the organizationName attribute has a MUST keyword in the definition of the organization object class in the core.schema file. This is how you create your own structures by selecting the object classes and using their attributes.

The object classes in the schema files are also categorized according to the way they hold data. The categories are the abstract, the structural, and the auxiliary.

Abstract object classes serve as template classes to create object classes. The top object class is an abstract object class and all structural object classes inherit attributes from this class. Not all auxiliary object classes derive from the top object class.

Structural object classes have attributes that you can use to define the structure of your database. You can use the attributes of structural object classes to create entries that can be used in your directory's database. The person object class is an example of this kind.

Auxiliary object classes have attributes that can complement the structures being created for additional detail only. If you need to maintain optional secure certificate information in your database, you can use the certificationAuthority auxiliary object class.

---

▓ **Note:** The rest of the object classes and attributes used in Figure 16-11 can be found in the file called

/etc/openldap/schema/core.schema.

---

Where can you retrieve the available object classes and attributes when you are going to create the directories? You load them using the include directive, and the commonly used schemas are loaded by default with the lines shown in Listing 16-4.

*Listing 16-4. The Commonly Used Schemas of OpenLDAP Loaded for Our Use*

```
include          /etc/openldap/schema/core.schema
include          /etc/openldap/schema/cosine.schema
include          /etc/openldap/schema/inetorgperson.schema
include          /etc/openldap/schema/nis.schema
```

To find out more about the available attributes and their object classes, you can view them in /etc/openldap.

# Your First Database

The slapd.conf file included during the installation is configured with a practice database. Find the section shown in Listing 16-5.

*Listing 16-5. A Database Entry*

```
####################################################↵
################
# ldbm and/or bdb database definitions
#############################################   ↵
#####################

database      bdb
suffix         "dc=my-domain,dc=com"
rootdn         "cn=Manager,dc=my-domain,dc=com"
```

The database, suffix and rootdn directives are used by OpenLDAP to create a database on the server. With these three directives, you can create additional databases, depending on the requirements of your organization.

The database directive is used to announce the start of a database definition that slapd will use. It takes the type of backend as the argument that will be used for this database. Backends are the storage formats that can be used by slapd to store database data. Some backend types include bdb, hdb, and sql. The bdb type will use the Berkeley Database for this database. The hdb type will use the hierarchical database, a modified version bdb that lets slapd do subtree renaming within the database. The sql type will let slapd send LDAP information as a subtree to an RDBMS. You can learn about other backend types you can use with the database directive by viewing the slapd.conf man pages or by visiting http://www.openldap.org/doc/admin24/backends.html.

The suffix directive is used to specify distinguished names (DNs) of queries that will be passed to the backend of this database. You can view this as the name of the database, and the proper way to name it is using LDAP attributes of the object classes in the schema files.

From the value of suffix above, you can see that the way we name our databases is similar to domain names. This is to ensure that the databases are unique every time, just like domain names. This naming scheme also makes it easier to associate the directory contents based on the domain it represents.

In our first database, the name is derived from my-domain.com and contains two components, my-domain and com. We used two instances of the domainComponent attribute (dc) to assign the values for the two parts. Note also that it uses the equals (=) operator to assign the values. This naming scheme is also how DNs are created.

The rootdn directive is used to tell OpenLDAP the distinguished name that is not affected by the access command or limitations for this database. This line identifies the superuser for this database, who is known as the *directory manager*. Just like the superuser accounts in Relational Database

Management Systems such as PostgreSQL, the DN you will use here can do anything on this database. Similar to suffix, the rootdn directive uses three attributes: twp dc attributes and one cn attribute. The cn attribute holds the username of the superuser of this database. That superuser is under the domain my-domain.com and is specified using the 2 dc attributes, one for my-domain and one for com.

Because OpenLDAP requires security to protect its databases, you can provide a password for the directory manager by entering a value for the rootpw directive. The configuration file already has this entry, but it is commented out. Find the line

```
# rootpw          secret
```

and remove the # and the space after the hash symbol to use the "secret" as the password for the directory manager of this database. If you do not remove the space after the hash symbol, OpenLDAP will not be able to recognize the rootpw directive properly..

The database files will be stored physically using the value specified in the directory directive. The files are used by OpenLDAP to reference the my-domain.com database encoded using the selected backend, bdb. Because we are going to use bdb, be sure to copy the file called DB_CONFIG.example into the database directory as DB_CONFIG:

```
cp /etc/openldap/DB_CONFIG.example /var/lib/ldap/DB_CONFIG
```

This file contains the constants required by the bdb or hdb backend to use for fast lookup on the databases. Without the file, OpenLDAP will complain, displaying the message

```
bdb_db_open: Warning - No DB_CONFIG file found in directory /var/lib/ldap:
```

and you will not be able to perform LDAP data operations successfully.

■ **Note:** OpenLDAP has support for SASL and TLS for stronger security. You can enable them by using the TLSCACertificateFile directive for example when you are going to use the server in a production environment.

## Using the my-domain.com database

The next thing to do to our database is to populate it with records. Before you actually do that, we will create a fictional IT organization called "My Domain organization." It consists of two groups: the programmers and the testers. You will record each user's name, serial number, and group to make things simple. Figure 16-12 shows the organizational table structure for our database.

| serialNumber | 1 | 2 | 3 |
|---|---|---|---|
| sn | Baclit | Sicam | Pohlmann |
| cn | Ryan | Jaime | Frank |
| member | Chief Programmer | Programmer | Tester |

*Figure 16-12. Organizational table structure for the my-domain.com database*

To create groups for our organization, you will create subtrees under the base DN. Subtrees can help you organize information into groups. They can be thought of as OpenLDAP's equivalent of the table in an RDBMS. The subtree will be added after the database's base DN, which will be discussed next.

---

■ **Note:** Although you can create databases without using subtrees in OpenLDAP, doing so will mean that additional filtering will be required in your searches to find specific records. You always need to filter starting from the base DN. For example, if you remove both the `programmers` and the `testers` subtrees in Figure 16-12, all data will be placed in the `my-domain.com` node. If you need to find a specific tester named `testmaster`, you will have to search all the data within the `my-domain.com` node just to find that person. With subtrees, you can immediately start refining your search by selecting the potential group in which you believe your target record resides. Going back to Figure 16-12, assuming that `testmaster` is within the subtree `testers`, you can start your search on that subtree, instead of hacking your way from the top, the `my-domain.com` node.

---

The next thing to do is to learn the proper format to encode the information using attributes that can be understood by OpenLDAP.

## LDIF Format

The LDAP Data Interchange Format (LDIF) is the format the LDAP protocol requires for storing data on its database. It was designed by Tim Howkes, Mark Smith, and Gordon Good at the University of Michigan during the 1990s. The format was extended and became a standard known as RFC 2849 (http://tools.ietf.org/html/rfc2849).

The format's syntax is almost the same as with most Linux configuration files, where the lines are separated by blank lines and comments prepended with #. But in this case the entry to be saved in the database must be followed by a colon (:) and then its associated value.

Listing 16-6 shows the LDIF entry for the first record.

*Listing 16-6. The Base DN*

```
dn: dc=my-domain,dc=com
objectclass: top
objectclass: dcObject
objectclass: organization
description: My domain database
dc: my-domain
o: My Domain organization
```

Why did we create this entry instead of the first one shown in Figure 16-11? This is called the Base Distinguished Name record and must always be the first record in every database you create. The Base DN will use it as a reference in every operation, such as searches. This will be our first record for the my-domain.com database and you should save it in a file called first.ldif.

Let us take a closer look at the contents of the first.ldif file. Listing 16-7 shows a more section-oriented version of the contents.

*Listing 16-7. The Base DN Contents Segregated*

```
dn: dc=my-domain,dc=com

objectclass: top
objectclass: dcObject
objectclass: organization

description: My domain database
dc: my-domain
o: My Domain organization
```

As stated earlier, each entry has two parts, the left side and the right side, separated with a colon. The left side contains the variable, which can be an attribute or an object class. For the first section, which consists of the first line, the variable side contains the dn attribute.

The right side holds the value assigned to the attribute defined on the left side. As you can see in the first line, contents of the value side can also be attributes with values of their own, like dc. Or the value side can contain only one value, as illustrated in the objectclass attributes. Some single-valued attributes can contain spaces, such as the description attribute. To learn more about which attributes can accept which values, refer to the supplied schema files.

In every LDIF file you are going to create, you must specify a dn entry to help OpenLDAP identify individual records. For the next records you create, you will see how to distinguish them further from the Base DN and from one another.

The second section is the object class section. Here you put the object classes that are required by the attributes you will use. For example, the dc attribute depends on the dcObject object class.

The third section is the attributes assignment section. This is where we assign values to our selected attributes based on the loaded object classes. For example, we put the value *"My Domain Organization"* for the o attribute within the organization class.

## Starting OpenLDAP

Before you add the contents of the first.ldif file, you need to start the OpenLDAP server to accept LDAP requests. Enter the command service ldap start to run it.

## Adding Entries with ldapadd

The ldapadd command lets us insert entries to the database. It accepts input that is in LDIF format. The syntax for ldapadd is

```
ldapadd -x -D "target_DN" -W -f target_file
```

The –x flag tells ldapadd to use simple authentication instead of the SASL library. It will use the value found in the rootpw directive of the target database. The –D flag assigns the target database using its distinguished name, specified by *target_DN* (shorthand for target Distinguished Name), to add the contents. The –W flag will let ldapadd ask for the value of the directory manager's password interactively in the shell. The –f flag lets you specify the LDIF file, given by *target_file*, that contains the new entry to be added to the database. To add the contents of the first.ldif file, we use

```
ldapadd -x -D "cn=Manager,dc=my-domain,dc=com" -W -f first.ldif
```

> ■ **Note:** We assume that the LDIF files are contained in the root's home directory (/root). Be sure to change to the root's home directory before running any of the LDAP tools starting with ldapadd.

Here, the –D flag states that the contents of the file pointed to by the –f flag must be stored in the my-domain.com database.

> ■ **Note:** If you look closely at the value of the –D flag, cn=Manager is included as the name of the database. You need to specify the name of the directory manager of the target database every time you use the LDAP tools. As said earlier, the directory manager has the capability to change things inside the database it is assigned to, and adding records is one of those changes.

After you run the command, ldapadd will display

```
adding new entry "dc=my-domain,dc=com"
```

if everything goes well.

The next thing to do is to create the subtree for our fictional IT organization. Create another file called second.ldif and give it the contents shown in Listing 16-8.

*Listing 16-8. Subtrees for the my-domain.com Database*

```
dn: ou=Programmer,dc=my-domain,dc=com
ou: Programmer
objectClass: organizationalUnit

dn: ou=Tester,dc=my-domain,dc=com
ou: Tester
objectClass: organizationalUnit
```

The entries are similar to the contents of first.ldif but there are slight differences. First, a new object class is introduced, the organizationalUnit. This is one of the object classes that can be used to group data in your databases. There are others, such as groupOfNames and groupOfUniqueNames, but for this example, organizationalUnit will suffice. If you need additional information to describe the groups in your organization, explore the other object classes mentioned.

Second, the dn attribute uses the ou attribute of the organizationalUnit object class to help distinguish it from other related records. With the ou in the dn, OpenLDAP can tell groups apart from each other.

Third, the dn and dc attributes are used without specifying their object classes, the top and dcObject. These two object classes are implicitly included in every LDIF entry that you make to be used on OpenLDAP. There is no harm done if you do not put them in the new records.

Add the contents of the second.ldif file into the my-domain.com database by entering

```
ldapadd -x -D "cn=Manager,dc=my-domain,dc=com" -W -f second.ldif
```

The last step is to put actual data as records in the database. Create another file called third.ldif and add the contents shown in Listing 16-9.

*Listing 16-9. Data to Be Added*

```
dn: uid=ryan,ou=Programmer,dc=my-domain,dc=com
uid: ryan
cn: Ryan Baclit
ou: Programmer
givenName: Ryan Baclit
sn: Baclit
objectClass: organizationalPerson
objectClass: inetOrgPerson

dn: uid=chivas,ou=Programmer,dc=my-domain,dc=com
uid: chivas
cn: Chivas Sicam
givenName: Chivas Sicam
ou: Programmer
sn: Sicam
objectClass: organizationalPerson
objectClass: inetOrgPerson

dn: uid=frank,ou=Tester,dc=my-domain,dc=com
uid: frank
cn: Frank Pohlmann
ou: Tester
givenName: Frank Pohlmann
sn: Pohlmann
objectClass: organizationalPerson
objectClass: inetOrgPerson

dn: uid=lisa,ou=Tester,dc=my-domain,dc=com
uid: lisa
ou: Tester
cn: Lisa Hayase
givenName: Lisa Hayase
sn: Hayase
objectClass: organizationalPerson
objectClass: inetOrgPerson
```

Your third LDIF file contained four records that are to be added to the my-domain.com database. Here is a record:

```
dn: uid=lisa,ou=Tester,dc=my-domain,dc=com
uid: lisa
ou: Tester
cn: Lisa Hayase
givenName: Lisa Hayase
sn: Hayase
objectClass: organizationalPerson
objectClass: inetOrgPerson
```

You might be wondering why there is a need to use the uid attribute coming from the inetOrgPerson object class. And why is the organizationalPerson object class used to provide the ou attribute instead of the usual organizationalUnit object class?

In our example, we used the uid attribute of the inetOrgPerson object class instead of the cn. The uid attribute is usually used to hold unique values similar to usernames in Linux. In our example, the cn attribute contains the real name and may contain nonunique values. The sn attribute is used to store the surnames while givenName is used to store the full name for additional information for this example.

We chose organizationalPerson as the object class to represent the ou attribute because of the type of information in the record being added to the database. Earlier, you created the Programmer and Tester groups and you used organizationalUnit because it is well suited for the task. This time, you are not making a unit, but an actual representation of the person within the group you created earlier. In the code snippet above, Lisa belongs to the Tester group, as defined in her dn (uid=lisa, ou=Tester, dc=my-domain, dc=com).

Add the entries now, using

```
ldapadd -x -D "cn=Manager,dc=my-domain,dc=com" -W -f third.ldif
```

You will learn how to retrieve the records next.

## Searching Entries with ldapsearch

The ldapsearch tool allows you to search for records contained in the OpenLDAP databases. You can also filter the results made by ldapsearch for more accuracy. It uses the following syntax:

```
ldapsearch -x -D "target_DN" -W -b "starting_point" "(filter)"
```

where *target_DN* is the database we want to search records using the distinguished name. The –b flag accepts the starting point of the search. If it is left blank, OpenLDAP will start its search from the distinguished base DN from the top down to the last record. The "(*filter*)" argument will narrow down the search based on the pattern you provide. The pattern must use an attribute and it can also accept wildcard characters. Similar to ldapadd, the –W flag will make ldapsearch ask for the value of the directory manager's password interactively in the shell before making the search.

As an example, to search for the records that are affiliated with the Programmer organizational unit (ou), you use the following

```
ldapsearch -x -D "cn=Manager,dc=my-domain,dc=com" -W -b "ou=Programmer,dc=my-domain,dc=com"
```

The –D flag tell OpenLDAP to use the my-domain.com database with the directory manager to do the search. The –b flag will make the search start from the records within the my-domain.com database containing the Programmer value on ou attributes. The output will show three records and a result such as this:

```
# search result
search: 2
result: 0 Success

# numResponses: 4
# numEntries: 3
```

The search will also include the name of the group, ou=Programmer, in the result.

This example uses filters to search for a tester with the givenName value starting with Lisa:

```
ldapsearch -x -D "cn=Manager,dc=my-domain,dc=com" -W -b "ou=Tester,dc=my-domain,dc=com"
"(givenName=Lisa*)"
```

The new entry in the command is the filter part, (givenName=Lisa*), which tells OpenLDAP to narrow down the records that have been searched to retrieve only the ones starting with Lisa. It will show one record, and the result similar to this:

```
# search result
search: 2
result: 0 Success

# numResponses: 2
# numEntries: 1
```

## Changing Entries with ldapmodify

You can change the values of the attributes, add and delete attributes by using the ldapmodify command, which uses the following syntax:

```
ldapmodify -x -D "target_DN" -W -f target_file
```

The –x flag tells ldapmodify to use simple authentication instead of the SASL library. It will use the value found in the rootpw directive of the target database. The –D flag assigns the target database using its distinguished name given by target_DN to add the contents. The –W flag will let ldapmodify ask for the value of the directory manager's password interactively in the shell. The –f flag lets you specify the LDIF file.

Notice that this syntax is almost the same as for the ldapadd command, because ldapmodify is also the ldapadd command. The ldapadd command actually stands for the command ldapmodify –a. The only difference between the two commands aside from the name and flag it uses is the ability to use the changetype attribute in the LDIF entry.

The changetype attribute must use the value modify to signal OpenLDAP that a change to an entry will be made. The change will have to be specified using the format

```
dn: target_DN
changetype: modify
operation_attribute: target_attribute
target_attribute: target_attribute_value
```

The **dn** must point to the record that needs to be changed, as given by *target_DN*. The **operation_attribute** is the required modify attribute to be used, and its value can be add, replace, or delete. Using add will add an attribute, replace will replace the current value of the attribute, and delete will remove the attribute along with its value. The **target_attribute** is the actual attribute of the record, and *target_attribute_value* is the value that we will change.

Create a file called fourth.ldif with the content shown in Listing 16-10.

*Listing 16-10. Changing the Two Tester Records*

```
dn: uid=frank,ou=Tester,dc=my-domain,dc=com
changetype: modify
add: description
description: Expert Senior Software Tester

dn: uid=lisa,ou=Tester,dc=my-domain,dc=com
changetype: modify
replace: givenName
givenName: Misa Hayase
```

In the first Tester entry, Frank's record is given a new attribute, description, which is assigned the value Expert Senior Software Tester. The last two lines tell OpenLDAP what attribute to add and what value to put into the new attribute for the target record.

For the second Tester entry, the givenName attribute of Lisa's record will be changed into Misa Hayase from Lisa Hayase. This time, no attribute has been added for this tester.

To make the modifications, run the following command

```
ldapmodify -x -D "cn=Manager,dc=my-domain,dc=com" -W -f fourth.ldif
```

You will see the following if there are no problems

```
modifying entry "uid=frank,ou=Tester,dc=my-domain,dc=com"
modifying entry "uid=lisa,ou=Tester,dc=my-domain,dc=com"
```

Now try performing a search for the new attribute you added for the Tester Frank. Enter the following:

```
ldapsearch -x -W -D "cn=Manager,dc=my-domain,dc=com" -b "ou=Tester,dc=my-domain,↵
dc=com" "(description=*Senior*)"
```

This tells OpenLDAP to find and display all Testers who have the word Senior in the description attribute, and Frank's record will appear. If we try to look for Misa's record using her given name as before

```
ldapsearch -x -W -D "cn=Manager,dc=my-domain,dc=com" -b "ou=Tester,dc=my-domain,↵
dc=com" "(givenName=Lisa*)"
```

No record will show up, because her givenName attribute now contains Misa Hayase.

## Removing Entries Using ldapdelete

OpenLDAP can also remove unwanted entries from a database, using the ldapdelete command. It has the following syntax:

```
ldapdelete -x -D "target_DN" -W "target_entry"
```

The *target_DN* is the distinguished name of the database and directory manager to use. The *target_entry* is the record to remove. It must be the full distinguished name of the record.

In our scenario, suppose that Frank becomes the Project lead and must be removed from the my-domain.com database. To remove his record, use the following command:

```
ldapdelete -x -D "cn=Manager,dc=my-domain,dc=com" -W "uid=frank,ou=Tester,↵
dc=my-domain,dc=com"
```

## Creating a Backup

To make a backup of your database, you can use the slapcat command. This database-to-LDIF converter utility can convert your bdb or hdb database into the more human-readable LDIF format we learned in this chapter. The syntax for slapcat is

```
slapcat -b "target_DB" -l "target_backup_file"
```

The -b flag accepts the value of *target_DB*, which is the suffix value of the target database you want to back up. The -l flag will identify the file where slapcat should it put the converted database after the backup. That file will be created if it does not exist yet. You must keep this file because it will contain the backup of the database.

To make a backup of the my-domain.com database, we issue the following
```
slapcat -b "dc=my-domain,dc=com" -l my-domain.ldif
```
You can restore the backup using slapadd, another tool to add entries to the OpenLDAP databases.

---

▓ **Note:** slapcat is among the OpenLDAP utilities that can be used even if the server is not running. The same is true of slapadd and slapauth for example. By contrast, the ldapadd, ldapmodify, and ldapdelete commands need the server running before they can be used. But why two sets of utilities for a single operation? The slapcat and slapadd commands are more suited for offline administration of the OpenLDAP server. They are recommended when you are trying to restore a backup that contains a large number of entries. The ldapadd and ldapdelete commands are better suited if a server that can accept requests is running. Avoid using both the slap and ldap commands at the same time, because that can lead to inconsistent data searches.

---

## OpenLDAP and Samba

Now that you have learned the basics of OpenLDAP, it is time to put it to practical use. You will combine OpenLDAP with Samba to create a setup similar to the earlier NIS/NFS combination. The Samba server for this section will be a domain controller that will provide shares and can accept Windows clients for its domain. The OpenLDAP server will be referenced by the Samba server for account information such as file shares and printers for the connected Windows client. We are not going to cover additional Windows client setup such as roaming profiles or saving current user desktop data changes.

Unlike the NIS/NFS combination, setting up OpenLDAP with Samba will require additional tools to help us make the configuration files and starting domain accounts. The following sections discuss each of these tools as you use it during the setup process.

# Installing Perl Modules

Some Perl modules will have to be added into your system before you can use the other tools to make your OpenLDAP and Samba setup. They are `Crypt::SmbHash`, `Digest::SHA1`, `Net::LDAP`, and `Unicode::MapUTF8`.

---

■ **Note:** You can learn more about the Perl programming language by visiting their web site at `http://www.perl.org` and its library at `http://www.cpan.org`. You can also use *Beginning Perl* by James Lee (Apress, 2004).

---

The `Crypt::SmbHash` module is the pure Perl implementation of Lanman and Windows NT 4-style passwords. It's used to make password entries in `smbpasswd` format for Samba users. The `Digest::SHA1` module contains interface codes to enable Perl to use the SHA1 encryption algorithm. The `Net::LDAP` module contains programming code that can let Perl programs connect to an LDAP server. The `Unicode::MapUTF8` module enables Perl to convert characters to and from Unicode or UTF8.

You will now install each of these modules in your system in preparation for the OpenLDAP and Samba tools later.

1. Install the GNU Compiler tools, which contain the gcc compiler, by entering `yum install gcc`. This is needed because some of the Perl modules may require compilation before they can be installed into your system. It will also prevent `/usr/bin/make -- NOT OK` messages during installation.

2. You will use Perl's CPAN shell, which can let you query, download, and install Perl modules found on the CPAN (Comprehensive Perl Archive Network) sites. Start the shell by entering

   `perl -MCPAN -e shell`

3. The first time you run this command, you will be asked to manually configure the network settings for the CPAN package sources similar to Figure 16-13.

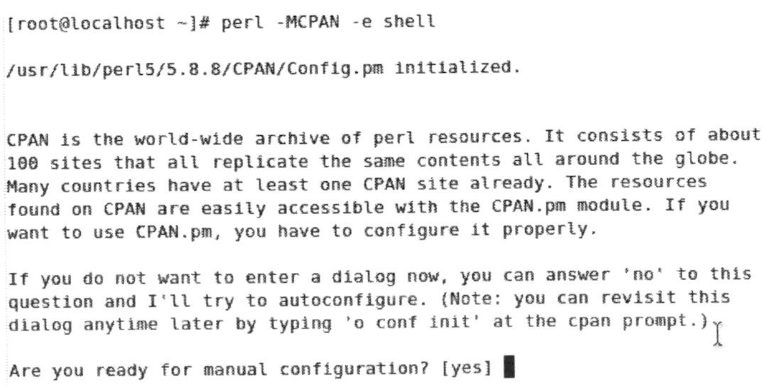

```
[root@localhost ~]# perl -MCPAN -e shell

/usr/lib/perl5/5.8.8/CPAN/Config.pm initialized.


CPAN is the world-wide archive of perl resources. It consists of about
100 sites that all replicate the same contents all around the globe.
Many countries have at least one CPAN site already. The resources
found on CPAN are easily accessible with the CPAN.pm module. If you
want to use CPAN.pm, you have to configure it properly.

If you do not want to enter a dialog now, you can answer 'no' to this
question and I'll try to autoconfigure. (Note: you can revisit this
dialog anytime later by typing 'o conf init' at the cpan prompt.)

Are you ready for manual configuration? [yes] █
```

*Figure 16-13. The network configuration prompt of the CPAN shell*

Type **no** here to make it autodetect your network settings. You will then be given the CPAN shell prompt on your terminal; it looks like this:

```
cpan>
```

---

▒ **Note:** Be sure that you are connected to the Internet before starting the CPAN shell. The CPAN shell will need to update itself by querying CPAN sites when run for the first time and while downloading the Perl modules. Also, if you need to reconfigure your CPAN shell network settings, you can run the command `o conf init` while on it.

---

4. Install each required module using the CPAN shell prompt with the `install` command:

```
install module_name
```

where `module_name` is the name of the Perl module that you want to install in your system. For example, to install the `Crypt::SmbHash` module, you will use

```
install Crypt::SmbHash
```

at the CPAN prompt. You will see a lot of output, including the current progress of the module's download and compilation if necessary.
There will be times where CPAN will ask you for additional information during installation, such as when you are running tests or installing additional modules. A sample question is shown in Figure 16-14.

```
CPAN.pm: Going to build G/GB/GBARR/perl-ldap-0.39.tar.gz

*** Module::AutoInstall version 1.03
*** Checking for Perl dependencies...
[Core Features]
- Convert::ASN1     ...loaded. (0.20 >= 0.07)
[SASL authentication]
- Authen::SASL      ...missing. (would need 2.00)
==> Auto-install the 1 optional module(s) from CPAN? [n] █
```

***Figure 16-14.** An additional module to be installed in your system*

It is safe to accept the defaults and press Enter each time you are asked. After the installation completes, you will be given back your CPAN prompt. Use the `install` command again for the `Digest::SHA1`, `Net::LDAP`, and `Unicode::MapUTF8` modules.

5. After you are done with the installations, you can exit the CPAN shell by typing **quit** at the prompt.

# nss_ldap

The nss_ldap package contains code that allows clients to use an LDAP server as the source of hosts and groups information. It also contains the pam_ldap library, which allows LDAP to interface with Linux-PAM (Pluggable Authentication Modules for Linux) for changing passwords. This library will be installed inside the /lib/security directory. You can learn more about nss_ldap at http://www.padl.com/OSS/nss_ldap.html.

1. Install the package by entering

    ```
    yum install nss_ldap.
    ```

2. Open the system-auth PAM file in the /etc/pam.d directory using a text editor and add the text bolded in Listing 16-11.

    *Listing 16-11. Changes for the system-auth PAM File*

    ```
    #%PAM-1.0
    # This file is auto-generated.
    # User changes will be destroyed the next time authconfig is run.
    auth        required      pam_env.so
    auth        sufficient    pam_unix.so nullok try_first_pass
    auth        sufficient    pam_ldap.so use_first_pass
    auth        requisite     pam_succeed_if.so uid >= 500 quiet
    auth        required      pam_deny.so

    account     required      pam_unix.so
    account     sufficient    pam_succeed_if.so uid < 500 quiet
    account     sufficient    pam_ldap.so
    account     required      pam_permit.so

    password    requisite     pam_cracklib.so try_first_pass retry=3
    password    sufficient    pam_unix.so md5 shadow nullok try_first_pass use_authtok
    password    sufficient    pam_ldap.so use_authtok
    password    required      pam_deny.so

    session     optional      pam_keyinit.so revoke
    session     required      pam_limits.so
    session     [success=1 default=ignore] pam_succeed_if.so service in crond quiet
    use_uid
    session     required      pam_unix.so
    ```

    In the file, a new rule was added for each of the auth, the account, and the passwordmanagement groups to make use of the pam_ldap.so module. Each of these rules is given a sufficient control flag, making LDAP another secondary source of authentication for the system on each management group.

    Adding the pam_ldap.so module on these management groups makes it possible for other PAM-enabled Linux software to authenticate with an LDAP server. Save the file afterwards.

3. Open the samba PAM file in the /etc/pam.d directory and add the lines bolded in Listing 16-12.

*Listing 16-12. New Entries for the samba PAM File*

```
#%PAM-1.0
auth            required        pam_nologin.so
auth            include         system-auth
auth            sufficient      pam_ldap.so

account         include         system-auth
account         sufficient      pam_ldap.so




session         include         system-auth
password        include         system-auth
password        sufficient      pam_ldap.so
```

Additional rules for the auth, the account, and the password management tasks were also added to use the pam_ldap.so module. This will allow Samba to use an LDAP server to access account information for its domain, such as users, for example. This is possible because the Samba server that was installed in your system includes PAM support and is capable of using other PAM services if needed. Save the file after you have added the new lines.

---

▓ **Note:** You can learn more about PAM concepts in Chapter 8.

---

## The nss_ldap Configuration File

The configuration file for nss_ldap is called ldap.conf and is stored in the /etc directory. It contains options that can change how nss_ldap behaves when a program tries to access an LDAP server it is configured with.

An option in the ldap.conf file takes the format

```
option_name option_value
```

where *option_name* is the name of the option that you want to use and *option_value* is the value that you want to use with the chosen option. Lines that start with # are comments, and nss_ldap ignores them.

You will make changes to this file in order for nss_ldap to interface with your OpenLDAP server later by specifying its distinguished names and binding passwords for example.

1.  Open that file in the /etc directory and find this line:

    ```
    base dc=example,dc=com
    ```

    Replace it with the new distinguished name, like this:

    ```
    base dc=dctoys,dc=com
    ```

2.  This new base value will be used as the default distinguished name in searches.
    Next, find the line

```
#binddn cn=manager,dc=example,dc=com
```

and change it to

```
binddn cn=Manager,dc=dctoys,dc=com
```

3.  The binddn option takes a value using the distinguished name in LDAP format. That value will be used in LDAP operations if the user is not root. Next, find the line

```
#rootbinddn cn=manager,dc=example,dc=com
```

and change it to

```
rootbinddn cn=Manager,dc=dctoys,dc=com
```

4.  This is similar to the binddn option, but the rootbinddn option will be used only when root is doing the LDAP operations. Last, find the line

```
#bindpw secret
```

and uncomment it. The value you give on the bindpw option will be used as the password when regular users are going to connect to OpenLDAP. Save the file after you make the changes.

## ldap.secret

In the nss_ldap configuration file, you gave a value for the bindpw that will be used by non-root users when connecting to OpenLDAP. You can also give the root user a binding password, but it must be placed in a text file called ldap.secret in the /etc directory. This is needed because the nss_ldap configuration file content can be accessed by anybody on the network.

You will now make this file and configure it.

1.  Using a text editor, create a file called ldap.secret containing the word

```
secret
```

This value is the same as the bindpw option you gave in the slapd configuration file slapd.conf.

2.  Save the file and enter the command chmod 600 /etc/ldap.secret to change the permissions so that it is readable only by the root user.

## nsswitch.conf

You will make changes to the nsswitch.conf file so that the name server switch (NSS) recognizes your OpenLDAP server as another reference for users and groups. You can do this by adding the ldap keyword to the required lines.

1.  Open the nsswitch.conf file in /etc and find the lines

```
passwd: files nis
shadow: files nis
group:  files nis
```

Change them to

```
passwd: files nis ldap
shadow: files nis ldap
group:   files nis ldap
```

2.  Save the file after you make the changes.

# OpenLDAP

With PAM and NSS configured to connect to an LDAP server, you will prepare OpenLDAP next to have it accept Samba users on a new LDAP database.

1.  Make sure that Samba is in your system, or install it by running yum install samba.

2.  Copy the Samba OpenLDAP schema file, named samba.schema, from /usr/share/doc/samba-3.0.33/LDAP into the OpenLDAP schema directory in /etc/openldap/schema. To do that, use the following command

    cp /usr/share/doc/samba-3.0.33/LDAP/samba.schema /etc/openldap/schema/samba.schema

3.  Open the slapd.conf file in /etc/openldap and find the lines

    ```
    include          /etc/openldap/schema/core.schema
    include          /etc/openldap/schema/cosine.schema
    include          /etc/openldap/schema/inetorgperson.schema
    include          /etc/openldap/schema/nis.schema
    ```

    Add the Samba OpenLDAP schema file using the include directive:

    ```
    include          /etc/openldap/schema/core.schema
    include          /etc/openldap/schema/cosine.schema
    include          /etc/openldap/schema/inetorgperson.schema
    include          /etc/openldap/schema/nis.schema
    include          /etc/openldap/schema/samba.schema
    ```

    This will allow your OpenLDAP server to create LDAP databases that can be used with Samba.

4.  You are going to create a new LDAP database by using another distinguished name in place of my-domain.com. You are now going to use dctoys.com for "domain controller for toys.com"). Find the lines

    ```
    suffix          "dc=my-domain,dc=com"
    rootdn          "cn=Manager,dc=my-domain,dc=com"
    ```

    and change them to

    ```
    suffix          "dc=dctoys,dc=com"
    rootdn          "cn=Manager,dc=dctoys,dc=com"
    ```

    Save the file after you make the changes.

# OpenLDAP Client Configuration File

OpenLDAP has a configuration file it can use when running LDAP clients. This file is also called ldap.conf and is located in the /etc/openldap directory. With this file, you can specify the default values of certain options when LDAP clients connect to the OpenLDAP server. Do not confuse this file with the configuration file for nss_ldap, which has the same name.

You can use options to tell the clients which host the LDAP server resides on and the distinguished name it uses. This file follows the syntax of nss_ldap's configuration file in specifying options and comments. You will now add lines that OpenLDAP will use when LDAP clients connect to it.

1.  Open the file ldap.conf in the /etc/openldap directory and add the following lines:

```
HOST 127.0.0.1
BASE dc=dctoys, dc=com
```

The first line uses the HOST option to tell LDAP clients what hostname or IP address the LDAP server is using. You can specify more than one hostname here but for this example, your current machine will suffice. The BASE option identifies the default distinguished name the OpenLDAP server will use in LDAP operations. The value must follow the LDAP format.

2.  After adding the lines at the bottom of the file, save it. Then start the OpenLDAP server by using the service ldap start command.

## Samba

You will now configure the Samba server to interface with your prepared OpenLDAP server. After configuring Samba, you will create the required user and machine accounts with the OpenLDAP and Samba tools.

1.  Open the main configuration file, smb.conf file, located in the /etc/samba directory, and find the lines

```
workgroup = MYGROUP
server string = Samba Server Version %v

;     netbios name = MYSERVER
```

Change them to

```
workgroup = DCTOYS
server string = Samba Server Version %v

netbios name = PDC-DCTOYS
```

These lines introduce the Samba server to your network with the DCTOYS domain controller and identify it as PDC-DCTOYS to netbios.

2.  Find the lines

```
security = user
passdb backend = tdbsam
```

under the Standalone Server Options and comment them out. You will not configure your Samba server as a standalone server.

3.  Find the following lines under the Domain Controller Options:

```
;     security = user
;     passdb backend = tdbsam
```

```
;     domain master = yes
;     domain logons = yes
```

and change them to

```
  security = user
  passdb backend = ldapsam:ldap://127.0.0.1
```

```
domain master = yes
domain logons = yes
```

By removing the semicolons, you are making this Samba server act as a domain controller. It can now accept Windows client logons for this domain. The passdb backend directive is changed to use the ldapsam backend to tell Samba that it will refer to an LDAP server for user passwords. Following the ldapsam backend is the location of the LDAP server this Samba server is going to use. You can see that the LDAP URL ldap://127.0.0.1 is pointing to the same machine, the localhost. You can change this line later if you need to separate the OpenLDAP server from the Samba server.

4. After the domain logons = yes line, add the following

```
ldap admin dn = cn=Manager,dc=dctoys,dc=com
ldap suffix = dc=dctoys,dc=com
ldap group suffix = ou=Groups
ldap user suffix = ou=Users
ldap machine suffix = ou=Computers
ldap password sync = yes
```

```
add machine script = /usr/sbin/smbldap-useradd -w "%u"
```

The ldap admin dn option tells Samba what distinguished name to use when connecting to an LDAP server for user account information. The value to be assigned here must be a qualified distinguished name in LDAP format.

The ldap suffix option contains the value that will be used for all LDAP suffixes for the sambaDomain object in the LDAP database. In addition, the value you provide here will be appended to the other related options, such as the ldap group suffix, for example, when Samba is going to access a user's group information.

The values for the ldap group suffix, the ldap user suffix, and the ldap machine suffix will tell Samba where to put the group, the user, and the machine information in the LDAP database. The value of the ldap suffix option will be appended to these values when Samba is about to send information to the LDAP server. This will help the LDAP server know where to put the information in its database. For example, if user information is to be added, the value of the both ldap user suffix and ldap suffix will be used by Samba to create the distinguished name ou=Users,dc=dctoys,dc=com. That distinguished name will be sent along with the information that will be added to the LDAP server.

The ldap password sync option will let Samba update user passwords using the LDAP server. The LDAP server will store the updates on the userPassword object of the database.

The add machine script line will specify what external program or script Samba will use when adding machines into its domain. The value here uses a script called smb-ldapuseradd, which is used to add user accounts to both Samba and OpenLDAP.

If you notice, the LDAP options you have added in the smb.conf file use certain database objects to store user, group and machine information the LDAP database. But we have not changed an entry in the database on the slapd.conf file to make those objects. Not to worry because the database objects will be created using the Smbldap-tools, discussed next.

5. After you have added the entries, save the file and run testparm to see if you need to make corrections. The testparm command will tell you if you have misconfigured anything in the smb.conf file.

# Smbldap-tools

Smbldap-tools is a set of Perl scripts created to help administrators manage Samba user and group accounts stored in an LDAP directory. These tools allow administrators to create users and assign passwords to them, for example. They also include scripts that will help administrators create the required LDAP database for OpenLDAP and Samba to use. Other scripts can be used to create configuration files that its tools will use such as smbldap-useradd. You can learn more about smbldap-tools by visiting its website at http://www.gna.org.

Earlier, you installed certain Perl packages into your system using the CPAN shell. Those Perl packages are required by smbldap-tools to run properly. Without those libraries in your system, smbldap-tools will not be able to connect to your OpenLDAP server when your Samba server is going to retrieve account information during authentication.

## smbldap.conf

The smbldap.conf file is the main configuration file of the smbldap-tools package. It is placed inside the /etc/smbldap-tools directory. This file is used to specify options that will be used by its tools when interfacing Samba with OpenLDAP. You can specify the master and slave LDAP servers that the smbldap-tools scripts will use here.

To specify options in the file, follow the format

```
option_name="option_value"
```

where *option_name* is the name of the option you want to use and *option_value* is the value that you want to assign for this option. The value for *option_value* must be enclosed in double quotes. An example option line that assigns the LDAP suffix using the suffix option is

```
suffix="dc=dctoys,dc=com"
```

Lines beginning with # are comments and are ignored by the smbldap-tools scripts.

## smbldap_bind.conf

The smbldap_bind.conf file contains options that specify credential information that the smbldap-tools will use when connecting to the assigned LDAP servers. This file is also located in the /etc/smbldap-tools directory. It holds the distinguished names and binding passwords for both master and slave

LDAP servers. The distinguished name for the master LDAP server information is given using the masterDN option and the binding password as masterPw. For the slave LDAP server, enter slaveDN and slavePw for its distinguished name and binding password respectively.

The syntax for this file is identical to the smbldap.conf syntax.

## Installing and Configuring smbldap-tools

You will now install smbldap-tools into your system to complete your setup.

1. Download the smbldap-tools-0.9.5-1.noarch.rpm RPM package from http://download.gna.org/smbldap-tools/packages/smbldap-tools-0.9.5-1.noarch.rpm and save it in root's home directory. Change to that directory and install the package by entering

   rpm -Uvh --nodeps smbldap tools-0.9.5-1.noarch.rpm

   The --nodeps option will force the smbldap-tools package to be installed to avoid the warning messages that the prerequisite Perl modules are not present. Also, you did not use RPM packages to install the required Perl modules and they are not listed in the RPM database of your system.

2. Start the Samba server by entering service smb start. The running Samba server is needed later by smbldap-tools when creating its updated configuration files.

3. Run the smbldap-tools configuration file script, named configure.pl and located in /usr/share/doc/smbldap-tools-0.9.5, by using the command

   /usr/share/doc/smbldap-tools-0.9.5/configure.pl

   The configure.pl file is a Perl script included to help you create both smbldap.conf and smbldap_bind.conf files interactively. Once the script starts, it will access the Samba server to get information such as what LDAP server will be used and the domain's SID (security descriptor), and it will prompt you for some information. You can answer the questions by giving the default answer enclosed in the square brackets. Press Enter to all questions except

   . ldap master bind password [] >

   and

   . ldap slave bind password [] >

   You need to give the root binding passwords you specified on the ldap.secret file in the /etc directory (which is secret for now) for these two questions. It is safe to use the same password for both questions because you are running a single OpenLDAP server.

4. The final prompt is

   unix password encryption: encryption used for unix passwords
   unix password encryption (CRYPT, MD5, SMD5, SSHA, SHA) [SSHA] >

   You will need to use MD5 in place of the default answer. The MD5 algorithm is used for your system's shadow file in the /etc directory.

When the script finishes, the updated smbldap.conf and smbldap_bind.conf files will be in the /etc/smbldap-tools directory. The old configuration files will be renamed smbldap.conf.old and smbldap-tools.old for your reference.

5. Add the starting entries for your OpenLDAP server so that it can handle domain logon requests by the Samba server. You can do that by running the smbldap-populate command. A sample output is shown in Figure 16-15.

```
[root@ging smbldap-tools]# smbldap-populate
Populating LDAP directory for domain DCTOYS {S-1-5-21-1519240468-4156490655-4011
731066}
(using builtin directory structure)

adding new entry: dc=dctoys,dc=com
adding new entry: ou=Users,dc=dctoys,dc=com
adding new entry: ou=Groups,dc=dctoys,dc=com
adding new entry: ou=Computers,dc=dctoys,dc=com
adding new entry: ou=Idmap,dc=dctoys,dc=com
adding new entry: uid=root,ou=Users,dc=dctoys,dc=com
adding new entry: uid=nobody,ou=Users,dc=dctoys,dc=com
adding new entry: cn=Domain Admins,ou=Groups,dc=dctoys,dc=com
adding new entry: cn=Domain Users,ou=Groups,dc=dctoys,dc=com
adding new entry: cn=Domain Guests,ou=Groups,dc=dctoys,dc=com
adding new entry: cn=Domain Computers,ou=Groups,dc=dctoys,dc=com
adding new entry: cn=Administrators,ou=Groups,dc=dctoys,dc=com
adding new entry: cn=Account Operators,ou=Groups,dc=dctoys,dc=com
adding new entry: cn=Print Operators,ou=Groups,dc=dctoys,dc=com
adding new entry: cn=Backup Operators,ou=Groups,dc=dctoys,dc=com
adding new entry: cn=Replicators,ou=Groups,dc=dctoys,dc=com
adding new entry: sambaDomainName=DCTOYS,dc=dctoys,dc=com

Please provide a password for the domain root:
Changing UNIX and samba passwords for root
New password:
```

*Figure 16-15. Output from the smbldap-populate command*

After you run the smbldap-populate command, your LDAP server will now have its database configured to accept account information that your Samba server will send and retrieve. These include subtrees for users, groups, computers, and domain users that are required for a Samba domain.

6. Run the command smbpasswd -w secret. The secret keyword is the binding password you provided earlier, in the ldap.conf file in the /etc directory. This value will be saved in the file called secrets.tdb inside the /etc/samba directory. The -w flag of the smbpasswd will use the password you gave to the LDAP server when it accesses the ldap admin dn for authentication. It should show a line like this after a successful run:

```
Setting stored password for "cn=Manager,dc=dctoys,dc=com" in secrets.tdb
```

7. Create a user called toyuser1 for this domain by using the smbldap-tools script called smbldap-useradd. This command has the following syntax:

```
smb-useradd given_options new_username
```

where *given_options* are the options that you want to pass to smb-useradd and *new_username* is the username of the new user. To create the toyuser1 for your setup, use the command

```
smbldap-useradd -m -a toyuser1
```

The –m flag tells smbldap-useradd to create a home directory for this user to store his files. The –a flag will create both Samba and Linux accounts for this user.

8. Change toyuser1's password by entering smbldap-passwd toyuser1. When prompted for a password, enter it as toyuser1 also for now. This acts the same as the passwd command of Linux but is targeted to change both Samba and OpenLDAP user passwords.

## Joining the DCTOYS Domain Controller

The last thing to do is to use a Windows computer to join your DCTOYS domain controller setup. We are going to use Windows XP for this section.

1. As the administrator user, click Start ➤ Control Panel ➤ Performance and Maintenance ➤ System. This will open the System Properties window.

2. Click the Computer Name tab and click the Change button. Click the Domain radio button under the Member Of section of the Computer Name Changes window and type **DCTOYS** as shown in Figure 16-16.

*Figure 16-16. Joining the DCTOYS domain using the Computer Name Changes window*

3. Then click OK.

4. The Computer Name Changes window will now ask for a user name and password to be used to join this domain. Use **root** as the user name and **secret** as the password. You will be joined to the DCTOYS domain and will need to reboot afterward. Only the root user has the administrator privileges to allow machines to join your domain controller. You can add users with that privilege but it is beyond the scope of this book.

5. Log into the DCTOYS domain as shown in Figure 16-17 using the toyuser1 network user.

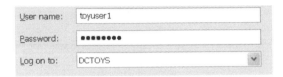

*Figure 16-17. The DCTOYS domain is now a choice in the Log On To dropdown box.*

If you logged into the domain successfully, you will be greeted by two User Environment warnings. These warnings tell you only that Windows cannot find the copy of your roaming profile in the domain controller or the local profile to be used on your current session of the desktop. Click OK to both windows to close them. After those two windows, you will see the of toyuser1's desktop.

## Testing the Samba and OpenLDAP Setup

As a final test, click Start ➤ My Computer and find the network drive icon. It should look like the one in Figure 16-18.

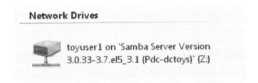

*Figure 16-18. The network drive for toyuser1 as drive Z*

1. Double-click on that icon to open its folder window.

2. Right-click in that folder window and select New ➤ Text Document. Name that document from_win_client.txt.

3. Go back to the DCTOYS domain controller machine and as root, type the command ls -l /home/toyuser1. You will see the empty text document you have created from the Windows machine while logged as the toyuser1 network user as shown in Figure 16-19.

```
[root@localhost toyuser1]# pwd
/home/toyuser1
[root@localhost toyuser1]# ls -l
total 0
-rwxr--r-- 1 toyuser1 Domain Users 0 Jul 20 12:24 from_win_client.txt
[root@localhost toyuser1]#
```

*Figure 16-19. The from_win_client.txt text document that the toyuser1 network user created*

If you see the file, you did it!

## Troubleshooting Tactics

If your setup does not work, you can do some fixes on it. Here are the common pitfalls in implementing this server combination and their solutions.

### Pitfall #1: Cannot log into the domain controller

First, check your machines to see if the network is set up properly. Can they see each other using the ping command? Second, a reboot may be needed for each virtual machine if you are doing this setup on a virtualized environment. It is a good idea to restart the sample Windows machine as well, and then try joining again.

### Pitfall #2: Cannot start the Samba server properly because only the nmbd process is running

With this problem, it is most likely that you have misconfigured or corrupted your LDAP database along the way. The Samba server is trying its best to connect to the LDAP server but cannot, because of a problem with the current database. All you have to do is to redo the setup from scratch using a new database named with a different distinguished name. For example, suppose you tried step 2 of the "Installing and Configuring smbldap-tools" procedure a few times and the Samba server still won't run with OpenLDAP using the distinguished name dc=dctoys,dc=com. Just rename the database to something else such as dc=dctoys1,dc=com, for example, and things will be fine.

If you still cannot fix the problem, it is recommended that you browse the log files of Samba in the /var/log/samba directory and the general log file, messages, in the /var/log directory. From there, you can check the Samba, OpenLDAP, and SmbLdap-tools web sites to see if the problems you are experiencing have been solved by other users.

# Summary

You have learned the importance of having a centralized authentication server for both Linux/Unix networks and hybrid services networks. NIS can be used if the network is a Linux network only. For other services that need directory services such as Samba, OpenLDAP can be used to provide a single authentication reference.

In the next chapter, you will learn how to change the Linux kernel to match your operating system needs. You will modify the existing kernel, use modules, and even make a new one fresh from the Internet.

# CHAPTER 17

■■■

# The Linux Kernel

The kernel is the core of an operating system. It is responsible for allocating and managing system resources for both hardware and software. Much as the human brain controls the muscular system, the kernel issues commands to the rest of the operating system that enable it to function properly. Instead of managing muscles and cells, though, the kernel communicates with the hardware by keeping tabs on device drivers, which interface with the hardware. The kernel also allocates computer resources to the user software.

In this chapter, you will learn about the origins of the Linux kernel and the types of kernels you can build. You will also learn how to use kernel modules that can let us add and remove features to a Linux system. Finally, you will see how to rebuild a new kernel that can be used for deployment.

## History of the Linux Kernel

The development of the Linux kernel was initiated by Linus Torvalds, a graduate student at the University of Helsinki in Finland, in 1991. It started out as a hobby, because he wanted an operating system similar to Minix, a Unix-like system. Later, he decided to make his software not just as capable as Minix, but better.

He released the source code to the Minix community (comp.os.minix) after reaching version 0.02 using the GNU Public License (http://www.linux.org/info/gnu.html). Because the source code is freely available, the community began to add features and code to the kernel source. That lead various organizations, both user-based and commercial, to lend support to further its advancement.

You can easily grab yourself a copy of the Linux kernel sources at its web site at http://www.kernel.org.

## Types of Linux Kernels

The kernel is actually a small binary file, which resides in the /boot directory. You can have more than one kernel in the /boot directory and choose which to implement based on the way each one uses libraries and handles processes. The two types of kernels used in Linux are the modular kernel (shown in Figure 17-1) and the monolithic kernel (Figure 17-2).

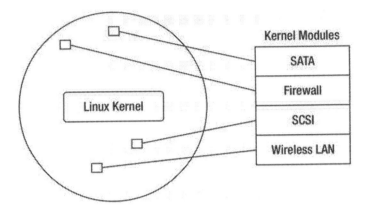

Figure 17-1. *The modular kernel in memory*

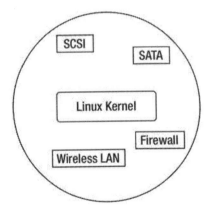

Figure 17-2. *The monolithic kernel*

*Modular* kernels, also known as *microkernels*, use software libraries called *modules*, which can be loaded and unloaded during runtime. These libraries reside in a designated directory that can be referenced by the kernel when it is needed. Because modular kernels use modules, the kernel binary file is smaller than with the other type. In addition, the kernel is easier for beginners to build and maintain.

*Monolithic* kernels do not use modules. They are carefully built and when run, can actually perform faster than their modular counterpart. The reason for their speed is that they omit a step that is essential for modular kernels—loading and unloading modules. Monolithic kernels can also load modules if needed, but they do not have to, because only the required libraries are combined into them.

When is one type of kernel better than the other? It really depends on the purpose of the Linux machine you are going to build. If you require graphics, multimedia, and office software, you should use the modular kernel. This will allow the kernel to use required libraries that cannot fit into memory all at the same time. If your Linux machine focuses on a core service, such as providing name services only, it is better to use a monolithic kernel.

For now, we will explore the modular kernel, the default kernel type for Linux systems that beginning administrators can immediately use after a fresh installation.

# Kernel Modules

Most of the Linux systems you are going to install are using the modular kernel. This is true even for CentOS. To verify that you are using modules, take a peek at the /lib/modules directory. You will see a directory called 2.6.18-92.el5, the same name as the loaded Linux kernel on your machine. This directory holds all of the additional libraries that the Linux kernel can use, and some of those were already loaded on your machine during boot.

Another way you can see modules in memory is to use the shell command lsmod, (shorthand for "list modules"), which will display all of the loaded modules in your system. The command does not take any arguments, and you can try it now; you'll see a display like that shown in Figure 17-3.

```
[root@localhost ~]# lsmod
Module                   Size  Used by
autofs4                 24517  2
hidp                    23105  2
rfcomm                  42457  0
l2cap                   29505  10 hidp,rfcomm
bluetooth               53797  5 hidp,rfcomm,l2cap
sunrpc                 144893  1
ipv6                   258273  16
xfrm_nalgo              13765  1 ipv6
crypto_api              11969  1 xfrm_nalgo
dm_mirror               29253  0
dm_multipath            22089  0
dm_mod                  61661  2 dm_mirror,dm_multipath
video                   21193  0
sbs                     18533  0
backlight               10049  1 video
i2c_ec                   9025  1 sbs
button                  10705  0
battery                 13637  0
asus_acpi               19289  0
```

*Figure 17-3. Modules loaded on the running system*

The output of the lsmod command is divided into three columns: Module, Size and Used By. The Module column shows the name of the module that is loaded, the Size column shows its size in bytes, and the Used By column shows which other modules use this module and how many such modules there are. If the kernel itself is using a module directly, the module will not be included in the output.

Take a look at the Bluetooth module. It is being used by five modules, some of which are the hidp, the rfcomm, and the l2cap modules.

When will you use the list generated by the lsmod command? You will use it when you are about to recompile the kernel, because you will need to know what modules the new kernel needs to have loaded. You will see later some ways to filter the modules to make your system run using the newly built kernel.

# Loading Kernel Modules

Linux lets you load kernel modules if you know which ones you need to load. There are three ways to load a module in a running Linux system, and each is discussed in the following sections.

## insmod

The insmod command lets you load a Linux module in the running kernel. Its syntax is

```
insmod filename
```

where *filename* is the module's filename. Modules that are loaded into memory come from their physical file, located in the /lib/modules directory of the running kernel. These files always end in with the .ko extension. For example, the ide-cd module is loaded from the file called ide-cd.ko, which is located in the /lib/modules/2.6.18-92.el5/kernel/drivers/ide directory.

Assuming you have not loaded the ide-cd module into memory, you can use the insmod command to load it, by issuing

```
insmod /lib/modules/2.6.18-92.el5/kernel/drivers/ide/ide-cd.ko
```

This will add the ide-cd module into the list of modules that can be generated by the lsmod command. When loading modules using insmod, you must include the path of the module file if it is not within the current directory.

If you try to use insmod on a module that depends on other modules before it can be loaded, you will be told to load the other modules first. That is probably OK if the number of modules you want to load is few, but it can be bothersome if the list goes greater than five, for example. The next command will do all the dependency loading for you in situations like that.

## modprobe

The modprobe command can automatically load the dependent modules for a module you want to load. It will look for the module and its dependent modules in the current running Linux kernel modules directory. The syntax of the modprobe command is

```
modprobe options modulename
```

where *modulename* is the name of the module you want to load. Note that modprobe does not require you to specify the filename of the module, unlike the insmod command. You can add options to the modprobe command, such as the −v flag, which shows messages while the command is running. If you want to load the ide-cd module using modprobe, you enter the following:

```
modprobe ide-cd
```

# modprobe.conf

The `modprobe.conf` file is the configuration file for the `modprobe` command and is located in the `/etc` directory. With the `modprobe.conf` file, you can add options to the modules you want to load and even provide aliases to the modules to be loaded for easier access. Each line of the file uses a command for a module you want to load, whether it is giving the module aliases or adding options when it is loaded. Lines that start with the hash symbol (#) are treated as comments and are ignored by `modprobe`.

In addition to the `modprobe.conf` file, the `modprobe` command also reads the files in the `/etc/modprobe.d` directory when it loads modules. The files in that directory each have the same name as the corresponding module. They contain `modprobe` commands that are to be run when that module is being loaded or unloaded. For example, the `floppy-pnp` file on my setup contains specific `modprobe` commands that are to be executed when the `floppy-pnp` module is loaded or unloaded by `modprobe`. The files in the `/etc/modprobe.d` directory follow the same syntax as the `modprobe.conf` file.

Some common `modprobe` commands that can be used in both `modprobe.conf` and the files in the `/etc/modprobe.d` directory are `alias`, `options`, `insert`, `remove`, and `include`.

The `alias` command lets you give another name for a module to be loaded. You can use this command to simplify loading a module that has a long name by creating a more manageable name for it. The `alias` command uses the syntax

```
alias new_name target_module
```

where *new_name* is the new name you want to assign to the module to be loaded, which is identified by *target_module*. Here is an example `alias` command:

```
alias snd-card-0 snd-hda-intel
```

When `modprobe` reads this entry in `modprobe.conf`, the `snd-hda-intel` module will be known as `snd-card-0` after it is loaded.

The `options` command allows you to give arguments to a module when it is loaded. You can use this command to customize the module that you will use on your system. It follows the syntax

```
options target_module new_arguments
```

where *target_module* is the name of the module that you want to give arguments specified by *new_arguments*. The *target_module* can also be an alias. You can provide more than one argument in *new_arguments* by separating them with spaces. Here is an example `options` command:

```
options snd-card-0 model=hp-dv4 enable=1
```

The `snd-card-0` module will use the values that both the `model` and the `enable` arguments contain when it is loaded by `modprobe`.

The `install` command will let `modprobe` run your own set of commands that you assign on a target module instead of loading it. You can use any shell command for the target module. The format for the `install` command is

```
install module_name your_commands
```

where *module_name* is the name of the module on which to run the set of shell commands in *your_commands* when loading the module. Here is an example `install` command that displays two messages. First you'll see

```
IDE-CD module being loaded
```

before loading the module and

```
IDE-CD module loaded
```

after loading the ide-cd module. The ide-cd module is going to be loaded using the `insmod` command. Here's the complete command:

```
install ide-cd echo "IDE-CD module being loaded" ; ↵
insmod /lib/modules/2.6.18-92.el5/kernel/drivers/ide/ide-cd.ko ; echo "IDE-CD module loaded"
```

There are three custom shell commands being used when loading the ide-cd module, and they are separated by semicolons. If you know shell programming, you can add more commands just as in any shell script. The two messages will appear if the command `modprobe ide-cd` is used.

The `install` command can be useful if you have a newer module for a hardware driver that you want to load in place of the one included in the kernel. It's also useful when you are testing a module to verify that it is actually loaded by modprobe.

The `remove` command is similar to the `install` command, but the custom commands are executed first in place of the removal of the target module using the -r flag of modprobe. The `remove` command uses the following syntax:

```
remove module_name your_commands
```

where *module_name* is the name of the module on which to run the set of shell commands in *your_commands* when unloading the module. Altering the earlier custom `install` command for ide-cd to display messages when unloading it results in this command:

```
remove ide-cd echo "IDE-CD module being unloaded" ; rmmod ide-cd ; ↵
echo "IDE-CD module unloaded"
```

If you want to add module files or configuration files other than those in /etc/modprobe.d, use the `include` command, which has the syntax

```
include target
```

where *target* can be a directory or a file that modprobe can use. Assuming you have created a custom modprobe configuration file called pentablet.testload to load a new pen tablet driver you just compiled, you will use this command:

```
include /root/pentablet.testload
```

If the files you have included have a similar alias in the modprobe.conf file, the former will use the value of the latter. For example, pentablet.testload has the content

```
alias snd-card-0 snd-hda-woofer
```

That value will be used in place of the one in the modprobe.conf file:
```
alias snd-card-0 snd-hda-intel
```

Listing 17-1 shows an example of modprobe.conf content.

*Listing 17-1. Sample modprobe.conf Content*

```
alias eth1 tulip
alias snd-card-0 snd-via82xx
options snd-card-0 index=0
options snd-via82xx index=0
```

In the example code, we can see that the contents use two alias commands and two options commands. The first alias command binds the tulip module to the name eth1. Whenever the Linux kernel uses the eth1 name, it will reference the module associated with it. The kernel will do the same for the second alias command, for the snd-via82xx module being bound to the snd-card-0 alias. For the options command, we can see that it has assigned the argument index=0, tosnd-card-0, the alias for the snd-via82xx module after it is loaded. The same argument will be given to the actual snd-via82xx module in case the Linux kernel accesses it directly.

You can learn more about the modprobe.conf configuration file by consulting its man pages.

# Unloading Kernel Modules

Linux allows you to unload kernel modules when they are not needed anymore. There are several ways to unload modules, as you'll see in the following command explanations.

## rmmod

rmmod lets you remove modules from a running Linux kernel. Unlike insmod, it only requires you to specify the module's name when removing it. The syntax for rmmod is

```
rmmod modulename
```

For example, to remove the ide-cd module in memory, you will use

```
rmmod ide-cd
```

This will unload the ide-cd module, assuming that it is not being used by other modules. If there are modules that depend on ide-cd, you will have to unload those prior to this module.

## modprobe

Unloading dependent modules on the target module you want to unload can be a pain, but modprobe can take care of that for you. You need to specify the -r flag for the module you want to unload, which instructs modprobe to look also for modules that depend on the target module you want to remove from memory. For example, to remove the ide-cd module along with the modules depending on it, you will use

```
modprobe -r ide-cd
```

The command will fail if you try to remove a module that depends on other modules that are still being used in the kernel. A good exercise is to unload the bluetooth module using the modprobe -r command.

## blacklist

If you do not want to load certain modules, you can use the blacklist file to instruct the Linux kernel not to load them. The Linux kernel will refer to the blacklist file during boot time, and any module you add into the file will not be loaded. The blacklist file is located in /etc/modprobe.d, and the syntax to flag modules not to be loaded is

```
blacklist modulename
```

where modulename is the name of the module you want to prevent from loading. For example, if you do not want to load the ide-cd module when the system runs, because you know that your system does not have any IDE CD-ROM drives, you will add the following entry to the blacklist file:

```
blacklist ide-cd
```

You can mark off additional modules by adding them to the file. If you think your system is functioning improperly because of a module you did not load, you can temporarily load it on the next reboot by putting a hash symbol in front of the module in the blacklist file. This will comment out the instruction, and the Linux kernel will ignore it, thus loading the module as if it were not blacklisted at all.

Now that you have learned how to load and unload modules, it is time to find out when a kernel needs to be rebuilt.

# When to Recompile the Kernel

Rebuilding the Linux kernel seems a mystic art for many new Linux administrators. This may be because the kernel sources are readily available, and there are many possible ways of using the kernel. You can build a new kernel, keep the old one handy, or stay with the old kernel. Or you can use the newly installed kernel on your system as the replacement for the stock kernel provided during the installation.

If the kernel you are currently using contains all the functions needed for the service you are going to provide, stay with it. The same applies if you are beginning to learn Linux. The stock kernel is capable in production environments, as long as all the hardware you need can be used by it.

Once you gain more Linux administration experience, if you want to see how far your Linux system can go given the current hardware, or if some hardware required is not supported in your current stock kernel installation, it is best to rebuild a new one.

To dispel the mystique of kernel recompilation, you will build a new one, starting in the next section.

# Getting a New Linux Kernel

You can download the latest kernel source code at `http://www.kernel.org`. The kernel we are going to use is the newer of the 2.6 series, version 2.6.28.7, at the time of this writing. Download the file called `linux-2.6.28.7.tar.bz2` at

```
http://www.kernel.org/pub/linux/kernel/v2.6/linux-2.6.28.7.tar.bz2
```

and save it into your home directory (/root). You will prepare the kernel sources in the following section.

---

■ **Note:** The kernel archive web site also offers the patch edition of the latest kernel, called `patch-2.6.28.7.tar.bz2`. You can use these patches as long as you have an earlier kernel source available in your system. For example, if you have the sources for 2.6.28.6, and you don't want to download a bigger complete 2.6.28.7 kernel source, you can use `patch-2.6.28.7.tar.bz2` to update your available kernel sources. But which is better, patching kernels or getting the complete sources? It really depends on your preference, and I prefer the bigger ones because I have the bandwidth to get them.

---

## Preparing to Configure the New Linux Kernel

Take the following steps to prepare for configuring the new Linux kernel:

1. Make sure that you have the compiler tools installed in your system such as gcc, make, and ld. These tools are not included in the default install, and if you need to add them, use the command

```
yum install gcc
```

2. Copy the downloaded Linux kernel to /usr/src. You will put the kernel sources and the future versions here to tidy things up:

```
cp /root/linux-2.6.28.7.tar.bz2 /usr/src
```

3. Change to that directory by using cd /usr/src.

4. Extract the kernel sources using the tar command

```
tar xvfj linux-2.6.28.7.tar.bz2
```

That will create a directory called linux-2.6.28.7 in the /usr/src directory.

---

■ **Note:** Do not panic if you see a lot of output in your screen while the extraction is taking place. The kernel is a very big archive and it contains a ton of source code that has been contributed by the community. Just wait until the shell prompt returns.

---

5. Create a symbolic link for the extracted kernel. Your future applications will reference the new kernel using the symbolic link when you need to compile them yourself.

```
ln -s linux-2.6.28.7 linux
```

6. Change to the /usr/src/linux directory:

```
cd /usr/src/linux
```

You are now ready to configure the new kernel to be built.

# Ways to Configure the Kernel Sources

The configuration file for your kernel is called .config and is normally found in /usr/src/linux. There are three ways to create it. The first is using the command line for configuration, where you specify the kernel parameters on each prompt, the second is by configuring the kernel graphically, and third is by using the text user interface. Each of these configuration methods will be discussed in turn.

---

■ **Note:** A default configuration file is included in the archive. This configuration file contains generic options that are selected to build a kernel that can run on most systems. Those options may be sufficient if you are practicing kernel compilation, but it is recommended that you create your own for a system to be deployed.

---

## Configuring the Kernel with the Command Line

You can configure the kernel with the command line by using the command make config to display the dialog shown in Figure 17-4.

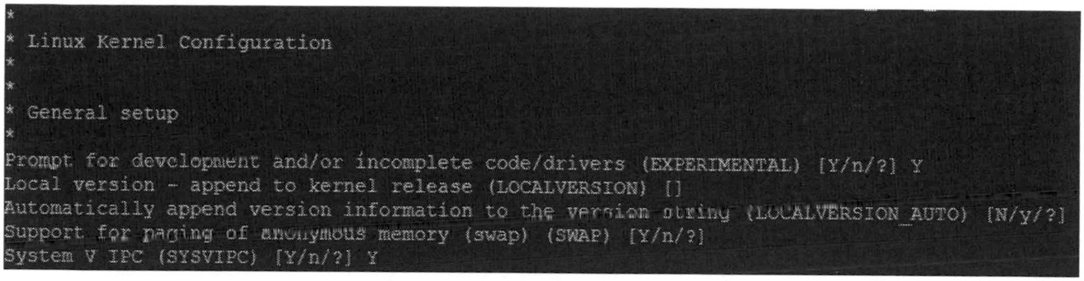

```
*
* Linux Kernel Configuration
*
*
* General setup
*
Prompt for development and/or incomplete code/drivers (EXPERIMENTAL) [Y/n/?] Y
Local version - append to kernel release (LOCALVERSION) []
Automatically append version information to the version string (LOCALVERSION_AUTO) [N/y/?]
Support for paging of anonymous memory (swap) (SWAP) [Y/n/?]
System V IPC (SYSVIPC) [Y/n/?] Y
```

*Figure 17-4. Configuring the kernel using the command line*

The format of each entry is as follows:

```
Main Section
[Subsection]
Feature_1 query_1
Feature_2 query_2
        :
Feature_N query_N
```

Referring to Figure 17-4, the main section you are currently in is the General Setup section, with descriptions of its features. Some sections can contain subsections; for example, Processor Types and Features contains a Device Drivers subsection.

In the figure, one selected feature is `Prompt for development and/or incomplete code/drivers?`, which will inform you if any driver is still in an experimental stage. Next to it is the Query section, which includes the options you can type in as the answer for that kernel feature. The options include `y`, if you want the module to be included in the kernel itself, `n`, if you do not want the feature to be included, `m`, if you want the feature to be compiled as a module that you can load and unload, and `?`, if you need more information about the current feature being asked. For example, if want to know more about the `Kernel .config support (IKCONFIG)` feature, you can type `?` and press Enter. The display shown in Figure 17-5 will appear.

```
0) [N/y/?]
Support for paging of anonymous memory (swap) (SWAP) [Y/n/?]
System V IPC (SYSVIPC) [Y/n/?]
POSIX Message Queues (POSIX_MQUEUE) [Y/n/?]
BSD Process Accounting (BSD_PROCESS_ACCT) [Y/n/?]
  BSD Process Accounting version 3 file format (BSD_PROCESS_ACCT_V3) [N/y/?]
Export task/process statistics through netlink (EXPERIMENTAL) (TASKSTATS) [Y/n/?
]
  Enable per-task delay accounting (EXPERIMENTAL) (TASK_DELAY_ACCT) [Y/n/?]
  Enable extended accounting over taskstats (EXPERIMENTAL) (TASK_XACCT) [N/y/?]
(NEW)
Auditing support (AUDIT) [Y/n/?]
  Enable system-call auditing support (AUDITSYSCALL) [Y/n/?]
Kernel .config support (IKCONFIG) [N/m/y/?] ?

This option enables the complete Linux kernel ".config" file
contents to be saved in the kernel. It provides documentation
of which kernel options are used in a running kernel or in an
on-disk kernel.  This information can be extracted from the kernel
image file with the script scripts/extract-ikconfig and used as
input to rebuild the current kernel or to build another kernel.
It can also be extracted from a running kernel by reading
/proc/config.gz if enabled (below).

Kernel .config support (IKCONFIG) [N/m/y/?]
```

*Figure 17-5. Additional information requested by giving the question mark (?) as an answer*

Then you can provide the required answer for the feature after learning more about it. For options that are capitalized, such as N in Figure 17-5, simply pressing Enter will use N as the default answer to the feature. In effect, you are telling the configuration not to include the kernel feature as default. That goes the same for other options that are capitalized.

The good thing about configuring the kernel this way is its accessibility. You do not have to install any special libraries to configure the kernel, just the compiler tools. The bad thing is that you need to complete the configuration up to the end to save it. If you quit halfway, all of your previous configured features will be lost.

This approach is best used if you have only the shell prompt on your system to build a kernel. You can stop configuring the kernel now by using Ctrl+C to get back to the prompt.

## Configuring the Kernel Graphically

If you installed the GNOME Desktop in your CentOS system, you can configure the kernel graphically. This tool allows you to select kernel parameter options by clicking and searching, which is easier because you can navigate through all the options. And you can save the configuration anytime you want.

Configuring the kernel graphically requires g++, the C++ compiler tool chain based on the GNU Compiler Tools (gcc). This will let the gcc compiler generate C++ code with the QT development libraries. To install both, use the command

```
yum install gcc-c++ qt-devel
```

After the installation, type the following in the kernel directory (/usr/src/linux):

```
make xconfig
```

You will see the graphical interface to help you configure the kernel, similar to Figure 17-6.

---

■ **Note:** To learn more about making graphical Linux applications using the QT library, read *Foundations of QT Development* by Johan Thelin, (Apress, 2007).

---

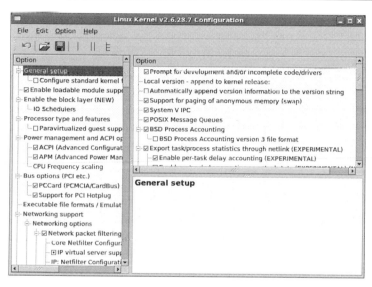

*Figure 17-6. The graphical interface for kernel configuration*

The left panel contains the main configuration sections and their subsections. Selecting an item from the left pane will either open a subsection or display the available features you can select, in the right pane. The lower right pane contains the description of the currently selected item, which is highlighted.

Selected kernel features can take on three forms, as shown in Figure 17-7. A blank checkbox means that the kernel feature is not to be included in any way during the kernel compilation. A checked box will include the kernel feature within the kernel, and not as a loadable module. A circle in a box will compile the kernel feature as a loadable module that you can load and unload. You can cycle through these selections by clicking the checkbox.

☐ Feature not selected

⦿ Feature will be a module

☑ Feature will be compiled-in

*Figure 17-7. The button states when selecting kernel features*

After selecting the features you need, you can save your configuration by clicking the Save button on the main toolbar.

You can quit the graphical configuration by selecting Quit on the main menu.

## Configuring the Kernel with menuconfig

The last way to configure a kernel is a hybrid of the two previous methods. Using the ncurses library enables a simple text interface to be used in the shell, much like the early DOS applications. With this method, you do not need a full-blown graphical interface installed in your Linux system to have a flexible way of configuring a kernel.

You need to add the ncurses library headers on your system by using the command

```
yum install ncurses-devel
```

After the installation completes, run the make command for menuconfig inside the kernel source directory:

```
make menuconfig
```

The menuconfig interface will look like Figure 17-8.

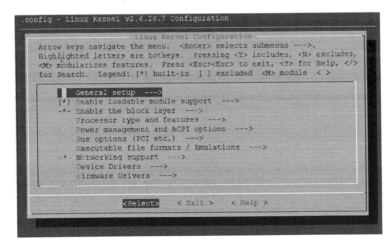

*Figure 17-8. The ncurses interface for menuconfig*

Pressing Enter on a main section will open a subsection or display the set of features it contains. Pressing the left or right arrow keys will navigate through the bottom options, enabling you to Select a kernel parameter, Exit the configuration, or get Help on the selected kernel parameter. If you exit the configuration, you will be prompted whether to save the changes you made.

In Figure 17-9, the Processor Type and Features section has been selected and its features are displayed.

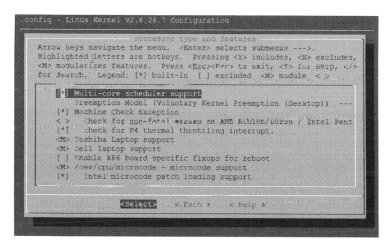

*Figure 17-9. The kernel parameters of the Processor Type and Features section*

As in the main configuration window, you can use the Select option at the bottom to explore a kernel parameter further. Choosing Exit will return you to the previous window.

Selecting a kernel parameter works in almost the same way as on the command line, but it's more visual and user-friendly. Pressing **y** on a kernel parameter compiles it in the kernel. This appears as an asterisk on the selection. Pressing **n** instructs the compiler not to build the kernel parameter and leaves the selection beside it blank. Pressing **m** builds it as a module and appears as a capital *M* on the selection.

You can search for a kernel parameter or description by pressing the slash (/) key to display the Search Configuration Parameter window, which lets you specify a text to be searched. In Figure 17-10, I am searching for the Tulip network card driver.

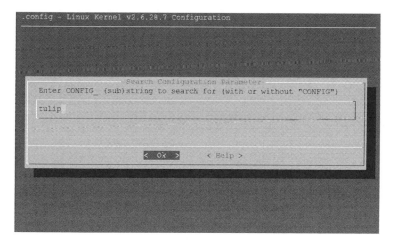

*Figure 17-10. Searching for the Tulip network card driver*

After selecting OK, I see the information shown in Figure 17-11, which tells me the kernel sources have my driver.

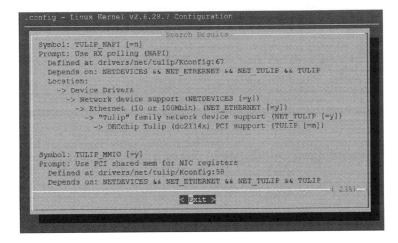

*Figure 17-11. Additional information found for the tulip network card driver*

You can navigate within the window by pressing the up- and down-arrow keys. After reading the text it offers on the result, you can go back to the main configuration window by selecting **Exit.**

In the next section we will build a new kernel for practice, using some practical rules that can be applied to production systems as you gain more experience. Because a kernel is necessarily machine-specific, I'll describe the steps I took, and you're encouraged to follow along on a lab machine using my settings.

# Preparing for Kernel Compilation

Once you learn how to configure the kernel, the next thing to do is to list all of the available hardware you have on your machine. These can include hard disks and external CD-ROM drives. Ideally, you still have the manuals for your computer hardware. Otherwise, you will have to resort to finding out the hardware you have installed on your machine manually.

Fortunately, there are utilities available in Linux to help you find out more about your hardware. One is the Hardware Lister tool (lshw), which can generate a nice list of hardware on your machine. It will detect each device based on its attributes, and can be enough for you to single out the hardware. You can learn more about it at http://ezix.org/project/wiki/HardwareLiSter.

For this exercise, you should use my hardware as a reference. My hardware specifications include an Athlon XP processor, 1GB RAM, 40 GB hard drive (IDE), a Davicom Network card and an internal combo DVD Writer optical drive. Checking the output of lsmod shows me a lot of modules, but I only need to know if there are any modules for my network card, because most of the time, the network card is the sensitive hardware. Based on my research, it uses the tulip or dmfe modules, and the output of lsmod confirms that it does:

```
tulip                50657  0
dmfe                 22757  0
```

It is time to select a method of configuring the kernel, and I choose the menuconfig version. Knowing that my processor is an Athlon XP, I select the Athlon/Duron/K7 kernel parameter, found in the Processor Family subsection of the Processor Type and Features.

Next is my network card. I went to the Device Drivers from the main section, and then to Network Device Support ➤ Ethernet (10 or 100Mbit) ➤ "Tulip" Family Network Device Support, and finally checking to see whether Davicom DM910x/DM980x Support is selected with an asterisk or compiled as a module with an M. The latter is already selected, and there is nothing left to be done on the network card.

Browsing the other kernel parameters can be daunting at first, but once you get the hang of it, you will instantly see what to change. For this exercise, what we've done is enough because the Linux developers made sure that the most-used kernel features are already selected, if not to be compiled in, then as a module. It is now safe to exit the configuration and save it.

## Building the Kernel

With the configuration over, I now issue the command make bzImage in the /usr/src/linux directory. This will start compiling the new kernel based on the configuration selections made earlier. The build will take some time, and it will display many messages, as illustrated in Figure 17-12. I will need to wait for the build to finish before going to the next step.

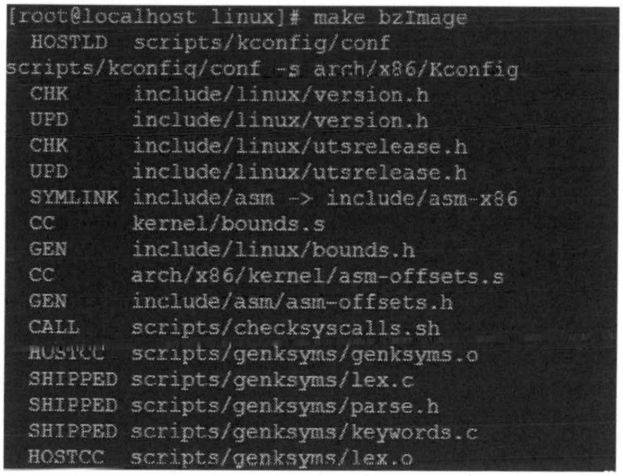

*Figure 17-12. The compilation of the kernel begins.*

After the build finishes, the compiler will show that the kernel has been built, and it will be named bzImage. The build process will display more information about the kernel, such as the size and its location:

```
Root device is (3, 2)
Setup is 12312 bytes (padded to 12800 bytes).
```

```
System is 1822 kB
CRC 6a9913df
Kernel: arch/x86/boot/bzImage is ready  (#1)
```

In my machine, the kernel resides on the arch/x86/boot directory within /usr/src/linux. The next thing to do is to copy and rename the bzImage file into the /boot directory as newkernel by using

```
cp /usr/src/linux/arch/x86/bzImage /boot/newkernel
```

## Building the Kernel Modules

The kernel modules are essential for my kernel because it is modular. To build the modules, run the make modules command. That will start building all the kernel modules, starting from the processor up to the cryptographic extensions configuration. This compilation takes much longer than that of the kernel, and again, you have to wait until it finishes.

After the modules have been compiled, and you have the prompt back, type make modules_install to copy the compiled modules into their final destination, in the /lib/modules directory. Specifically, the kernel modules for the kernel you just compiled will now be in /lib/modules/2.6.28.7, the current version of the kernel.

## Making the Boot Loader Initialized RAM Disk

All modular kernels need a special file for the boot loader that contains references to the modules under the /lib/modules directory. Without this file, the boot loader will not be able to load the Linux system properly, because it doesn't know what instructions to use for your hardware.

To make a boot loader initialized RAM disk for the new kernel, I use the mkinitrd command. The mkinitrd command uses the following syntax:

```
mkinitrd new_boot_image kernel_version
```

Because I named the new kernel as newkernel, name the image file as newkernel.img for easier reference. Use the following command:

```
mkinitrd /boot/newkernel.img 2.6.28.7
```

## Adding the New Kernel into the GRUB Boot Loader

The new kernel is almost ready. An entry for it is needed in the GRUB configuration file, grub.conf, in the /etc directory.

Before opening the file for changes, I need to know which partitions hold my root (/)and /boot partitions. The mount command shows that my root partition is on /dev/hda2 and my /boot partition is on /dev/hda1.

The grub.conf file is opened and I find the entry

```
title CentOS (2.6.18-92.el5)
```

```
root (hd0,0)
kernel /vmlinuz-2.6.18-92.el5 ro root=LABEL=/1 rhgb quiet
initrd /initrd-2.6.18-92.el5.img
```

This entry is the default kernel for my CentOS installation. I need to make a new entry for my new kernel, and I follow the syntax

```
title kernel_name
    root (hard_disk_number,partition_number)
    kernel (hard_disk_number,partition_number)/kernel_name root=which_device
    initrd (hard_disk_number,partition_number)/kernel_image_name.img
```

The title command takes a descriptive text to describe the new kernel. The root command tells the GRUB boot loader where to find the root partition of the system. The kernel command takes two main parameters; the first is the location of the new kernel, and the second is the device name of the kernel's location, as specified by the subcommand root. The initrd command takes the location of the kernel RAM disk file's location.

For my new kernel, enter the following:

```
title My New Kernel
    root (hd0,1)
    kernel (hd0,0)/newkernel root=/dev/hda1
    initrd (hd0,0)/newkernel.img
```

Notice that the notation for specifying the partition location for root, kernel, and initrd is somewhat unusual compared to the root subcommand. This is GRUB's way of identifying what partition is assigned per hard disk. Let's take (hd0,1) as an example. The first part, hd0, tells GRUB that it is the first hard disk. If the given value is hd1, it is the second hard disk, and so on. Indices start with 0 and increase from there.

The second number specifies the partition to use on the given hard disk. For (hd0,1), I require GRUB to use the second partition of the first hard disk. As with the index of the hard disk drive, the indices for partitions also start with 0.

The line initrd (hd0,0)/newkernel.img tells GRUB to use the newkernel.img file located in the first hard disk's first partition. I noted earlier that the /boot partition resides in /dev/hda1, and this is the direct translation of that partition as an argument for the initrd command. The same concept is applied in the kernel command.

There are other ways to specify hard drive and partitions in GRUB; to learn more about them, refer to its man pages.

The contents of the grub.conf file must look like the following (for my machine):

```
title CentOS (2.6.18-92.el5)
        root (hd0,0)
        kernel /vmlinuz-2.6.18-92.el5 ro root=LABEL=/1 rhgb quiet
        initrd /initrd-2.6.18-92.el5.img

title My New Kernel
    root (hd0,1)
    kernel (hd0,0)/newkernel root=/dev/hda1
```

```
initrd (hd0,0)/newkernel.img
```

The new kernel is added at the bottom of the default installed kernel. I did not delete the default kernel, because my new kernel may not run as expected. The next thing to do is to reboot the system and select the My New Kernel option on the GRUB prompt. If the boot continues and I gain a prompt, I'm fine. Running the command uname -r to report the version of the running kernel will reveal it is using 2.6.28.7. The new kernel indeed!

---

■ **Tip:** If your kernel looks good during boot-up but then hangs somewhere in the middle, that can be fixed. You can find a troubleshooting tactic specifically for that scenario in Chapter 19 in the "My new kernel is stuck!" section.

---

## Your Turn

To fully appreciate the kernel compilation process, try to follow the steps I just described on your own system. First, get as much of the information about your hardware as you can. You can use tools such as lspci and lshw for example. Second, configure the kernel according to your system. Third, build the kernel using the make commands discussed. Finally, test the new kernel on your system.

## Summary

Many new administrators do not want to compile a new kernel because of the thought of getting their hardware damaged by it in any way. This is not true at all, and the worst damage a new misconfigured kernel can do is to report that it cannot continue to load further. You must reboot the system and use the old kernel and see what kernel parameter should be removed, recompile it and put the new recompiled kernel into action.

Once you get the hang of compiling kernels, you can create more specialized kernels suited to your organization's requirements. All you need is patience and practice, and the kernels you will make will serve you well to the end.

■ ■ ■

# CHAPTER 18

# Linux Virtualization

In this chapter, you will learn the basics of what virtualization is and how to decide if it's right for you. After that, we'll look at some of the virtualization technologies that are available at present for your use. You will also learn how to use Xen in CentOS to create a separate operating system instance and run it within your Linux desktop.

## Understanding Virtualization

When an organization requires a certain computer setup, hardware and software need to be purchased to assemble it. As an example, suppose management asks the IT department to build an extension LAN (Local Area Network) to provide file and print sharing and FTP server and Web access for a new floor of the company's building. Given the requirements, the IT people will request separate hardware and operating systems for each type of service. After the IT components have been received, the team will assemble the extension LAN and get it running as expected.

Fast-forward a few months. The IT people saw that the extension LAN requires two additional computers to accommodate the data traffic of that new floor. The IT team must now go back to management, request new hardware and software, and build the required servers. And the cycle goes on.

Expansion and rebuilding cycle is beginning to disappear: new hardware with more instructions and computing power is being manufactured, and software that takes advantage of those kinds of hardware is being developed. Now, you can implement the requirements of a given computer setup with a single machine with specialized software designed to run multiple operating systems for each service. This concept of abstracting hardware, or configuring hardware to allow multiple separate operating system instances to run simultaneously on a single machine, is *platform virtualization*. The computer that has the virtualization software is often called the *virtualization host* or the *main host*. The operating system instances running inside the main host are called *guests* or *virtual machines*.

The basic virtualization configuration is illustrated in Figure 18-1.

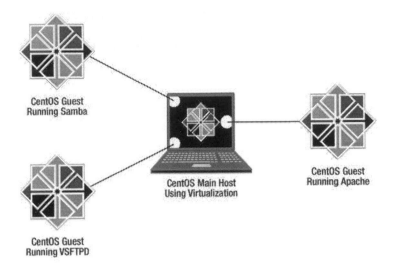

*Figure 18-1. The main host and guest operating systems running in a virtualized environment*

## Deciding to Use Virtualization

The extension LAN example in the previous section is not the only time to use virtualization. Some other uses include systems development, clustering, and security by isolation.

If you develop systems and you use application libraries that can tap the low-level instructions of your computer, you could freeze your system and lose your current data, which will cost you time and possibly require you to reinstall your system to continue your work. With virtualization, you can copy your development system and paste backup copy if your current copy goes down.

Then too, when you are administering a high-availability server cluster, such as a web server cluster, you will have to set up two or three computers to provide redundancy for that service. Those computers can be combined into a single computer with virtualization. Those separate computers for the web server cluster will become separate instances inside the single computer. Backing up and restoring a computer on a cluster will only require creating an instance.

If you are developing software that must be portable across different platforms, you can use virtualization to test the software. You can create instances of Linux or Windows operating systems and run your software in them. Or if you are going to deploy server software, such as a new version of Samba, you can just install it on an instance of CentOS Linux and let your instance of Windows XP connect to it. If everything is fine, you can deploy the new Samba installation on your network.

Also, virtualization provides some security. In the event of a network break-in, an attacker will most likely enter a guest in your virtualization setup. Damages will be done to the guest until the attacker leaves. After studying the attack, all you need to do is to get a clean backup of the guest, remove the damaged one, and configure and run the new copy. With this scheme, the attack was isolated on a guest. You must do everything you can to secure the main host in order not to compromise your virtualization setup by applying what you have learned in Chapters 8 through 10.

# Xen

The Xen project was initially developed at the University of Cambridge and was led by Ian Pratt. He also founded XenSource, a company to provide commercial support for Xen. His company was later acquired by Citrix (http://www.citrix.com), who provides commercial support for Xen and commercial Xen editions, such as XenServer Enterprise Edition. The Xen project's web site is now located at http://www.xen.org.

Xen uses paravirtualization for the x86 architecture. Its hypervisor can run multiple guests and those can almost match its native installed speed. Because of paravirtualization, your intended guests must have Xen support to run on your Xen system.

# Exploring Virtualization Technologies

It is important to know that Xen's virtualization technology is not the only kind of out there. There are other types of virtualization, and each has its own attributes with advantages and disadvantages. The virtualization technologies include full virtualization, hardware-assisted virtualization, operating system virtualization, and paravirtualization. Knowing these will help you decide on what kind of virtualization technology you are going to apply if you have the proper resources.

## Full Virtualization

Full virtualization lets a guest run unmodified on the main host. If you are going to run Windows XP, for example, you do not have to make modifications prior to installing it to your virtualization setup. After the installation, start the guest with your virtualization software, and it will run as expected. Full virtualization is possible, because the virtualization software safely translates instructions from the hardware back to the guest. By safely sending the instructions back to the guest, the modified instructions can be used by the guest as if they came from the actual hardware. In addition, those instructions cannot be used by a guest to change instructions being used by other guests, if there are any. The process of allowing the virtualization software to make these instruction changes is called *binary translation* and is an important attribute for full virtualization.

Examples of virtualization software that use full virtualization include VirtualBox (http://www.virtualbox.org) and VMWare Server (http://www.vmware.com).

## Hardware-Assisted Virtualization

Hardware-assisted virtualization enables virtualization software to use extra instructions available from the hardware to run guests. The extra hardware instructions eliminate the need for the virtualization software translate the instructions being used by the guest going to and back from the hardware. Eliminating the translation will result in better performance in your virtualization setup.

To use hardware-assisted virtualization, you must have hardware that supports virtualization like the AMD Athlon 64 x2 and Intel's Core 2 Duo processors. Your virtualization software must be able to use the additional instructions provided by these processors, such as the Linux KVM (kernel-based virtual machine) (http://www.linux-kvm.org), and Xen-HVM (Xen's Hardware Virtual Machine).

## Operating System Virtualization

In operating system virtualization, each guest has its own filesystem to store its tools, like shell commands and data, but each uses the kernel of the main host. Each guest that boots appears to running its own kernel when sending instructions to the hardware. When a guest sends its instructions, the main host's kernel is actually the one sending those instructions to the hardware. The hardware uses the instructions and provides the required output back to the main host's kernel. The main host's kernel sends those instructions to the originating guest. You can view this approach as an inverted tree, where the root is the kernel that is being shared, and the guests are the branches as shown in Figure 18-2.

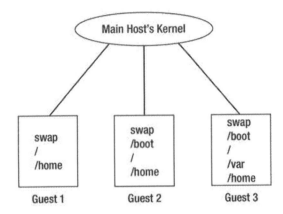

*Figure 18-2. The kernel being shared by the guests*

---

▓ **Note:** See Chapter 17 to review kernel concepts.

---

When you use this virtualization type, you have to make sure that the kernel can be shared by the guests. For example, if guests are created for the x86 architecture, the main host's kernel must be of the same architecture. Some examples of this type include OpenVZ (http://wiki.openvz.org) and Linux-VServer (http://www.linux-vserver.org).

## Paravirtualization

Paravirtualization uses a hypervisor or a virtual machine monitor to run guests. It uses two kinds of kernels, one that is built to be the hypervisor and the other for the guests to run. The hypervisor will be loaded on the main host and can be used to start guests. The guests will run their own kernels and boot as normal within the main host when started.

When instructions need to be sent to hardware, guests send those to the hypervisor. The hypervisor will take care of the instructions and send them to the hardware. The instructions that the guests send to the hypervisor are called *hypercalls*. Hypercalls can be made only by guest kernels designed to interface with a hypervisor. Some examples that use this approach are Xen (http://www.xen.org) and Wind River (http://www.windriver.com).

Paravirtualization makes use of its main host's available protection domains or protection rings when doing virtualization. Protection domains are an abstract concept used by operating systems to restrict processes to run according to their intended functions and use computer resources like memory and disk drives being accessed by those processes. Sometimes protection domains are implemented by the hardware itself such as the x86 architecture. This is also used to protect the main host from possible attacks by malware or wild processes that can crash the system.

There are multiple protection domains on a system starting with 0 as the highest domain. Figure 18-3 shows the protection domains available on the x86 architecture.

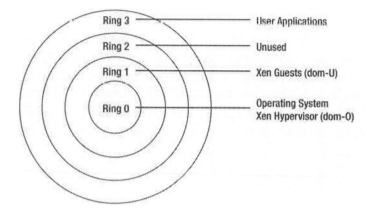

*Figure 18-3. The protection domains of an x86 architecture*

The processes that run on ring 0 can use the hardware directly. This is where the operating system and hypervisors are used because they need to access the hardware. The Xen hypervisor needs to run on level 0 to use hardware that is requested by guests. The guests are run on ring 1, because they must not access hardware. Only by making hypercalls to the Xen hypervisor on ring 0 can the guests use hardware. User applications are run on ring 3, because they do not need to use hardware. Ring 2 is unused at present.

■ **Note:** For Xen, the hypervisor is called dom-0, short for *domain 0*. The kernel the guest uses is called dom-U, for *domain unprivileged*, and is given for the guest kernels, which are on the lower rings.

## Hardware Requirements

To run Xen on your Linux machine, you need to make sure you have the proper CPU and enough memory. You should be one of the recent Pentium-class CPUs, such as Pentium Pro, Celeron, AMD Athlon, and AMD Duron. These CPUs have the x86 architecture instructions that Xen can use to provide virtualization. If you have the 64-bit equivalents to these, your Xen setup will perform even better.

Having lots of memory on your hardware is beneficial to your Xen setup. The more memory you have, the more virtual machines you can run. For example, in a machine that has 1 GB RAM, up to three virtual machines with 256 MB RAM can be run with decent speed and performance. You can start with 1 GB of RAM for your practice on Xen.

After you have the double-checked that your system meets these requirements, it's time to install Xen.

# Installing Xen

It is a good idea to disable SELinux before you begin the Xen installation. If SELinux is active, you might encounter permission problems when running guests and administering Xen. To turn it off, open the configuration file called config inside the /etc/selinux directory, and find the following line:

```
SELINUX=enforcing
```

Change it to this:

```
SELINUX=disabled
```

Then save the file.

Xen is not included in the default CentOS installation. To install the Linux kernel modified to run Xen and its tools, use the following command:

```
yum install xen
```

After the installation completes, your system will also update the contents of the GRUB configuration file and place the modified Linux kernel or the Xen kernel on top of the selection. You can open the GRUB configuration file (grub.conf) inside the /etc directory and see if the top entry has a title similar to this:

```
title CentOS (2.6.18-128.2.1.el5xen)
```

If you have this, you can boot the Xen kernel. Reboot the system, and choose the first entry in the GRUB menu (or the entry with the word xen on it) to load the Xen's hypervisor. If you do not see the line that contains the word xen, your Xen setup may have not completed successfully. Try to run the yum install xen command again and see if it gets installed properly.

---

▓ **Note:** GRUB is covered in Chapter 3.

---

After installing and rebooting the system into the Xen kernel, you should notice that the boot log contains a lot of Xen-oriented messages running through the screen. Those messages are informing you that the Xen kernel is being loaded. When you log into the system, you are now using the Xen kernel and are ready to create virtual machines for guest operating systems.

If you're not sure whether the kernel you are using is the Xen kernel, you can issue the command uname, which tells you what kernel version you have loaded. If the value uname shows contain the xen word, you are running the Xen kernel.

DyK3vVM2N/-1 of 1-/second/7613747 1SP

## cember 26, 2012 (Order ID 108-1319370-9732219)

|  | Item Price | Total |
| --- | --- | --- |
| of CentOS Linux: Enterprise Linux On the Cheap | $25.93 | $25.93 |
| --- Paperback |  |  |
| *) 1430219645 |  |  |

| | |
| --- | --- |
| Subtotal | $25.93 |
| Tax Collected | $2.24 |
| Order Total | $28.17 |
| Paid via credit/debit | $28.17 |
| Balance due | $0.00 |

ent completes your order.

back on how we packaged your order? Tell us at www.amazon.com/packaging.

amazon.com

**Your order**

Qty. Item

1

The installation of Xen package included libvirt, a set of utilities that can help you manage virtualization technologies available under Linux, including QEMU and OpenVZ as well as Xen. With libvirt, you can create guest images to install and administer guest operating systems. To learn about the many things you can do with libvirt, visit the web site at http://www.libvirt.org.

# The xend Daemon

After you have booted your hypervisor kernel, a daemon called xend is also started. The xend daemon included with Xen provides consoles to allow administrators to manage guests. With xend, the guests can be started and rebooted using Xen command line tools such as xm. You can start the xend daemon manually by using service xend start.

## The xend Configuration Files

The xend daemon stores its configuration files inside the /etc/xen directory along with the guest configuration files. The configuration files it uses are xend-config.sxp, xend-pci-permissive.sxp, and xend-pci-quirks.sxp. The last file called qemu-ifup is a shell script that lets Xen use QEMU for using networking on guests.

### xend-config.sxp

The xend-config.sxp file is the main configuration file of the xend daemon process. This file contains directives that can alter the xend daemon's behavior such as allowing Xen command-line tools like xm to connect to guests. Another is to change the location of files being used by xend like the directory to store log files.

The directives in the xend-config.sxp configuration file use the following syntax:

```
(directive_name argument)
```

where directive_name is the name of the directive that you want to change, and *argument* is the new value to be assigned for that directive. The main configuration file is long and Listing 18-1 shows part of its contents.

*Listing 18-1. Some Contents of the xend-config.sxp File*

```
#(logfile /var/log/xen/xend.log)
#(loglevel DEBUG)

#(xend-http-server no)
(xend-unix-server yes)

(xend-unix-path /var/lib/xend/xend-socket)
```

In Listing 18-1, the logfile directive tells xend to place log information into the xend.log file located inside the /var/log/xen directory. The loglevel directive takes the DEBUG argument that tells xend to record debug information in addition to other log entries. The xend-http-server directive tells whether xend should start the HTTP server that can accept commands from clients using HTTP: the no argument indicates that the server will not be started. The xend-unix-server directive controls the xend Unix server. With it, command line tools such as xm will be allowed to issue commands to xend to control guests. The xend-unix-path argument will let xend tell command line tools such as xm the Unix socket file to use when sending commands the Xen Unix server.

---

■ **Note:** Always enclose in parenthesis the directives you specify on the Xen configuration files for the xend daemon process to understand them.

---

Last, the lines that are preceded by a hash symbol are treated as comments and are ignored by the xend daemon. Values assigned to commented directives will be used by xend for those directives as default values. For example, the following line

```
#(logfile /var/log/xen/xend.log)
```

tells xend to use the xend.log file in the /var/log/xen directory to store log information by default if you have not uncommented the line and changed its value.

If you require additional information about the directives, you can consult the man pages of the xend-config.sxp file and the xend daemon itself.

## xend-pci-permissive.sxp and xend-pci-quirks.sxp

The xend-pci-permissive.sxp file is used to permit queries by PCI devices while the xend-pci-quirks.sxp file is used to control certain PCI devices under Xen. These files also follow the syntax of the main configuration file in specifying directives and comments. However, you do not need to worry about these files, because they are used to manipulate low-level hardware. If you know about the internals of the x86 architecture and require some feature to be added on a PCI device, you can ask for assistance from the Xen developers. You can start by joining the Xen Developers Mailing List at http://lists.xcnsource.com/mailman/listinfo/xen-devel.

## qemu-ifup

The qemu-ifup script file is used by xend to start the Universal TUN/TAP virtual network kernel drivers using QEMU. The TUN part of the driver is the virtual point-to-point network device that lets the kernel do low-level IP tunneling. The TUN driver creates the /dev/tunX character device and the tunX virtual point-to-point interface. Applications can write network packets from the /dev/tunX character device and receive network packets on the tunX interface. The TAP part of the driver is the virtual Ethernet network device that provides low-level support for Ethernet tunneling to the kernel. The TAP driver creates the /dev/tapX character device and tapX virtual Ethernet device. Applications can send Ethernet frames to the /dev/tapX character device and receive Ethernet frames on tapX device. The variable X here holds integer values that starts with 0 and helps in giving unique names for the devices. For example, the first TUN character device will be /dev/tun0 and the second will be /dev/tun1. You can learn more about TUN/TAP on http://vtun.sourceforge.net.

▨ **Note:** You can learn more about the QEMU open source processor emulator by visiting its web site at http://www.qemu.org. The site also contains tutorials on how to make QEMU image files and use the emulator to install your operating system on it with the QEMU emulator.

With TUN/TAP, guests can have their own network devices to use to connect to networks. The xend daemon will be able to assign network information, such as IP addresses, to each of the guest's network devices. There is no need to modify this file, because xend will use the qemu-ifup script when assigning network information to the started guests.

# The xend Network Configuration Scripts Directory

The /etc/xen/scripts directory contains the required network configuration scripts for xend when starting virtual machines. These scripts are used to provide NAT (network address translation), virtual interfaces, and network bridging for virtual machines to connect to the network. One of these network scripts, network-bridge, is used by the xend daemon process in its main configuration file. Do not change any of these files unless you really know shell script programming and are sure that you can achieve the desired result.

# Checking Dom-0

Before you can create and use guests on your Xen system, you need to know if dom-0 is running. You can do this by using the Xen Management User Interface that is run using the xm command. The xm command is the tool to manage the domains in Xen setup. It uses the syntax

```
xm command targetdomain options
```

where command is the command you want to apply to a guest or domain given by targetdomain. The targetdomain can be domain's name or numeric ID. The options value represents additional arguments that can included if the specific command requires them

To find out if dom-0 and any dom-U domains are running, run the command xm list on your terminal, and xm will show you all the domains running on your system. An example output for the xm list command is shown in Figure 18-4.

```
[root@aso ~]# xm list
Name                                      ID Mem(MiB) VCPUs State    Time(s)
Domain-0                                   0     942     1 r-----      38.8
```

*Figure 18-4. The xm list command shows dom-0 running.*

In Figure 18-4, only the hypervisor, or Domain-0, is running. If your dom-0 is not on the list, you will not be able to run guests. If you cannot see this table, you need to start the xend daemon by using `service xend start`. Figure 18-4 shows five columns that describe the information of the currently running domains:

Name: This column shows the name of the domain name. In Figure 18-3, only Domain-0 is shown. Domain-0 is always present on the hypervisor and is always displayed as the first domain.

ID: The ID column is the numeric equivalent of the domain name. You can use this or the domain name as the argument for the Xen commands that require you to specify a domain.

Mem(MiB): This column displays the amount of memory given to the virtual machine.

VCPUs: This column shows how many virtual CPUs have been given for this domain.

State: This column shows the virtual machine's current state. The state column is divided into six positions, and each position represents a state a domain can have. The positions starting from the left are running, blocked, paused, shutdown, crashed, and dying. For example, if a domain is currently paused, a letter p will appear on the paused position. A blank state is shown as a hypen (-).

- *Running (r)*: The domain is currently running on a CPU. If you have a single CPU computer, this will be left blank for all domains except Domain-0.
- *Blocked (b)*: The domain is blocked and not running or runnable. This state can be caused because the domain is waiting for some input or output such as coming from a network connection. It is also possible that the domain has gone to sleep because it has nothing else to do.
- *Paused (p)*: The domain has been paused, usually because the administrator runs xm pause. A paused domain will still use allocated resources such as memory and CPU, and it cannot be scheduled to run by the hypervisor.
- *Shutdown (s)*: The domain is being shut down, rebooted, or suspended. A shutdown state is also shown when the domain is in the process of being destroyed.
- *Crashed (c)*: The domain has crashed. Usually, this state can occur only if the domain has been configured not to restart on crash.
- *Dying (d)*: The domain is in process of dying but has not completely shut down or crashed.

Time(s): This column tells how long the domain has been running as calculated by Xen in seconds.

The list command of xm is one of the many commands that you can use to manage your Xen domains. You will learn additional xm commands later after you install your first guest.

## Making a Guest with virt-install

There are various ways to create a virtual machine to be used for your Xen setup. One is to clone the filesystem of the host system to a directory or an image file. Another is to use a remote repository to start an installation to create the virtual machine. The repository can come in the form of a YUM repository or something similar. Another alternative is to use the QEMU processor emulator to create image files to install the operating system of your choice and have it loaded by Xen. These steps are advanced, and if you want to know the other approaches in making virtual machines for Xen, you can find those on http://www.xen.org.

If these choices seem intimidating, you can use the virt-install a tool to ease the process. The virt-install script designed to create virtual machines from operating systems that come with Xen support and is great for administrators who are new to Xen. The script is part of the libvirt package that you installed along with the xen package earlier. Most recent Linux distributions, including CentOS, have a Xen kernel included that can be used to create a virtual machine in the unprivileged domain. You will use you CentOS installation CDs or DVD to create an instance of the Xen kernel in your system.

■ **Note:** You cannot use Fedora Core 9 or 10 as a guest operating system in your Xen setup. Neither of these distributions Xen kernels in the installation media, and you have to create the images yourself if you want either of them as a guest. Fedora 8 has Xen support in its installation media, and you can use it in place of CentOS in the examples that follow.

You can install a paravirtualized guest with `virt-install` using NFS, HTTP, and FTP. Unfortunately, you cannot use the local CD or DVD drive directly as an installation source because `virt-install` assumes that the installation files are distributed using the given protocols. That is what we are going to do to install a paravirtualized guest—using one of the protocols to "distribute" the local CD or DVD drive for `virt-install` to see the installation files. Also, the only time you can use the CD or DVD drive directly is when you are going to add an unmodified guest using the hardware-assisted virtualization method.

In the example in this section, you will create a virtual machine that contains another instance of CentOS using NFS with your installation DVD as a source.

■ **Note:** If you have several CDs, it is recommended to copy all of the CDs' contents into a single directory and export it using NFS. This will provide a smooth installation when creating virtual machines. Be sure to have enough hard drive space before copying! See Chapter 14 if you need a review of NFS.

When you run `virt-install`, you will be asked by a series of questions for the new guest to be created:

- What is the name of your virtual machine?: You have to give a unique name to help Xen identify guests from one another. Use it to start this guest.
- How much RAM should be allocated (in megabytes)?: Specify the amount of memory this guest will use when running.
- What would you like to use as the disk (file path)?: Specify the guest's image file, which holds the guest's kernel, filesystem, and system tools. You need to give the full path here to let `virt-install` know where to place it. You can name the image file using the name of the guest and append the `.img` extension, the shorthand for image.
- How large would you like the disk (...) to be (in gigabytes)?: In this question, the name of the image file you gave previously will replace the ellipses. Specify the size of the image file to be created for this guest in gigabytes. The file must be big enough to hold all of the operating system files your guest has. If you do not include a desktop environment during the install, you can allot 2 GB. Otherwise, allow 4 GB.
- Would you like to enable graphics support? (yes or no): If your guest can support graphical installation, say yes here. For CentOS as a guest, saying yes will start the graphical version of the Anaconda installer.

- `What is the install location?`: Specify the location of the guest source installation files that `virt-install` will use to install on your guest's image file. The guest installation files can come from an NFS server, an HTTP server, or an FTP server. For an NFS server, use the format `nfs://hostname/directorypath`. For an HTTP server, use `http://hostname/directorypath`. For an FTP server, use `ftp://hostname/directorypath`. The `hostname` is the host name or IP address of the machine of the source server, and `directorypath` is the location of the installation files being hosted by that server. For example, if the NFS server that has the IP address of 192.168.1.102 and shares the directory `/media/CentOS_5.2_Final` that contains the installation source files required to make a CentOS guest, you will use `nfs://192.168.1.102:/media/CentOS_5.2_Final`.

After you answer these questions, `virt-install` will create the required image file, perform the installation using the installation source, and reboot the guest in your system.

The remaining examples in this chapter assume that the hardware is Xen-capable and that the computer has 1 GB of available RAM, enough disk space to store the virtual machines. This machine will have the IP address of 192.168.1.102, which will be used instead of 127.0.0.1 to help the CentOS installation find your local NFS server.

## Preparing the Installation Media

We will prepare the CentOS installation DVD for use with `virt-install` later.

1. Put the CentOS 5.2 DVD on your drive. Wait for it to mount on your desktop.

2. Open the exports file in `/etc`, and add the following line:

   ```
   /media/CentOS_5.2_Final        *(ro,sync)
   ```

   This line allows any host to mount the remote shared directory of this NFS server, which permits the new instance of the CentOS installation to mount on the NFS server. Adding this line also avoids having to guess what IP address the installation process will get, since you're specifying it on the exports file.

3. Start the NFS server if it is not yet running by using `service nfs start`. If you have it running, you can use `exportfs -r` to reload the contents of the exports file so the new shared directories can be seen by NFS clients.

These steps will have the installation DVD visible later when using the `virt-install` script in making your first virtual machine.

## Using the virt-install Command

With the CentOS DVD accessible through your local NFS server, we will start installing your first guest OS using `virt-install` command.

Run the `virt-install` command without any arguments. That will start the series of questions discussed earlier that you need to answer to make the virtual machines. For this example, you can use the following responses:

- *What is the name of your virtual machine?*: MyCentOS
- *How much RAM should be allocated (in megabytes)?*: 256
- *What would you like to use as the disk (file path)?*: /var/lib/xen/images/MyCentOS.img
- *How large would you like the disk (/var/lib/xen/images/MyCentOS.img) to be (in gigabytes)?*: 4
- *Would you like to enable graphics support? (yes or no)*: yes
- *What is the install location?*: nfs://192.168.1.102:/media/CentOS_5.2_Final

The installation process will start. The installation will look like on the one shown Figure 18-5, which you should recall from when you first installed CentOS in your system. The graphical version of the Anaconda installer is used because you said yes on the "Would you like to enable graphics support?" question.

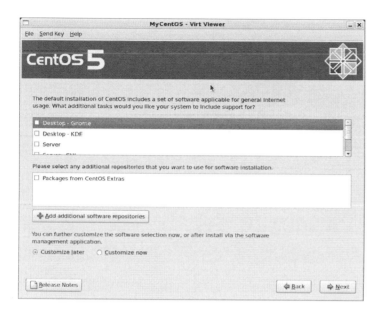

*Figure 18-5. Installing CentOS under Xen*

■ **Note:** It is better not to include a desktop environment in your virtual machines if you are just starting out with Xen. The memory that Xen requires may become inadequate and the virtual machines may slow down significantly. You can do this by unchecking "Desktop – GNOME" and "Desktop – KDE" when you see the screen shown in Figure 18-5 during the installation of your CentOS guest. This is what I did when I installed the CentOS guest for this chapter.

After the installation process completes, the installer will reboot, and Xen will handle the booting of the CentOS guest. A running session of your new virtual machine is shown in Figure 18-6.

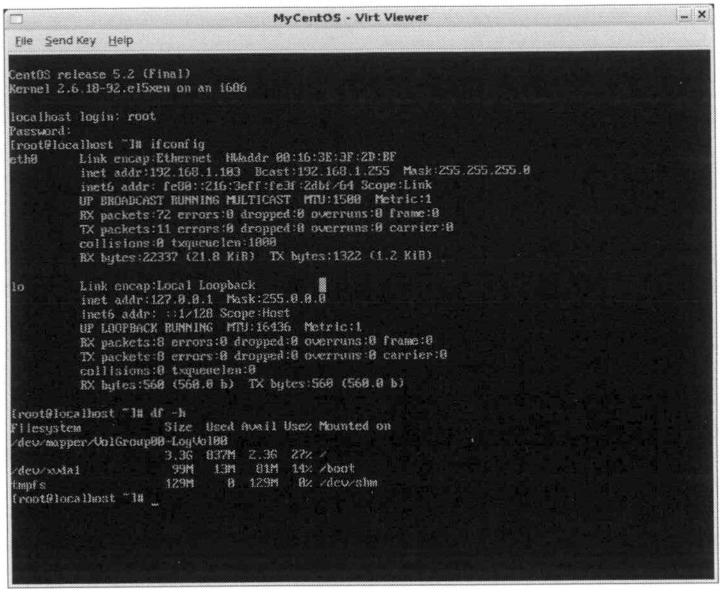

*Figure 18-6. Your new virtual machine!*

With your first CentOS guest running on your Xen hypervisor, you can log into it, run shell scripts, package installation, and set up servers—just like another system.

Let's look at the current domains running on your Xen setup using the xm list command. The output should be similar to Figure 18-7.

```
[root@localhost ~]# xm list
Name                                     ID Mem(MiB) VCPUs State    Time(s)
Domain-0                                  0     747    1 r-----      764.9
MyCentOS                                  4     255    1 -b----       22.7
```

*Figure 18-7. There are now two domains in your paravirtualized system.*

## Understanding the Guest Configuration File

When you create virtual machines using virt-install, a guest configuration file is created for each of them using the name of the domain. These configuration files are stored in /etc/xen. The guest configuration file uses directives to alter the behavior of the domain when run. Each directive uses the following form:

```
directivename = givenvalue
```

where directivename is the name of the directive that you want to use, and givenvalue is the value that you want to assign to that directive. Some values need to be enclosed in quotation marks, while others do not. Be sure to consult the man pages for xmdomain.cfg to find out about the options and their value formats. Lines that start with a hash symbol are comments and are ignored by the Xen tools.

If you browse the /etc/xen directory, you will find the configuration file for the first domain you have created called MyCentOS. The virt-install command named this file the same as its domain's name. This file will be used to start the MyCentOS domain and to change its directives to affect its performance. You can open the file using a text editor.

Listing 18-2 shows contents of the MyCentOS configuration file made by virt-install.

*Listing 18-2. The Contents of the MyCentOS Guest Configuration File*

```
name = "MyCentOS"
uuid = "2e76d0e9-bf47-016d-09b0-5d9ce1a62e8f"
maxmem = 256
memory = 256
vcpus = 1
bootloader = "/usr/bin/pygrub"
on_poweroff = "destroy"
on_reboot = "restart"
on_crash = "restart"
vfb = [ "type=vnc,vncunused=1" ]
disk = [ "tap:aio:/var/lib/xen/images/MyCentOS.img,xvda,w" ]
vif = [ "mac=00:16:3e:3f:2d:bf,bridge=xenbr0" ]
```

These are the directives need to start the MyCentOS domain:

- name: This directive identifies the domain's name, which must be unique to avoid conflicts with other domains.
- uuid: This directive will hold the 128-bit UUID (universally unique identifier) for the domain, which is used by Xen to identify domains using UUID. The default behavior is to create a UUID on each call to xm create if you do not give a value here.
- maxmem: This specifies the maximum amount of additional memory that this virtual machine can use when its initial allocated memory is used up. Using maxmem is possible with the xend daemon because of its balloon capability that can increase memory on running guests.
- memory: This directive is the amount of memory to be given by xend to this virtual machine.
- vcpus: This directive specifies the number of virtual CPUs that this domain can use.
- bootloader: This directive specifies the bootloader that must be used to start this domain. The pygrub script is used by default, but if you need to use another, you can specify it here.
- on_poweroff: This specified what will be done when the guest makes a proper shutdown or when xm shutdown is called. In this example, the guest will be cleaned up because of the destroy value.
- on_reboot: This directive specifies what will be done when the guest makes a proper restart or when xm reboot is called. In this case, the guest will be restarted because of the restart value.
- on_crash: Here, you specify what will be done when the guest crashes for any reason. In the example, the guest will be restarted because of the restart value.
- vfb: This directive specifies the type of virtual frame buffer to be used when connecting to this virtual machine using virt-viewer or a similar tool. This line can use either VNC or SDL. The default is VNC.

- disk: The disk directive specifies what device this virtual machine uses when it is run. The device can be a physical hard drive or an image file. In this entry, when the MyCentOS guest runs, it will use the MyCentOS.img image file, which contains its own guest kernel and filesystem located in the /var/lib/xen/images directory. That file will be known as the xvda device, and the guest will have write access on it.
- vif: The last directive is used to create the virtual interface to be used by the guest. Creating this interface is analogous to putting a network card on the virtual machine's hardware. The MAC (Media Access Control) address can be assigned and so acts as its bridge identifier.

The values given here are specifically assigned for the MyCentOS domain. After you have created the clone later called MyCentOS-1, its configuration file remains the same except for some adjustments to differentiate it from the original. Some of the adjustments are the MAC address value inside the vif directive and the value of the uuid directive. You can change the directives by hand, but that does increase the chances of your clone not working as expected.

There are other directives that you can add to customize your virtual machine, and those can be found in the xm and xmdomain.cfg man pages.

## Xen Guest Example Configuration Files

Xen has sample configuration files for each type of guest you can create using the xm command in the /etc/xen directory. These are the xmexample1, xmexample2, xmexample.vti, and xmexample.hvm. You can browse their contents and use them as templates in manually creating virtual machines.

## Connecting to a Guest

You can connect to a running guest in multiple ways, and we will cover the mostly used methods: using the xm command, the virt-viewer command, and the vncviewer.

### Using xm

You can use the console argument of the xm command to connect to your target guest. You will have to specify either the name or numeric ID of the guest, which you can get by running xm list.

After you have connected to a guest, you will be given a console that you can use to log into that guest. Assuming your MyCentOS guest is still running, open a new terminal, and use the command xm console MyCentOS. You will be given a terminal screen to connect to it similar to Figure 18-8.

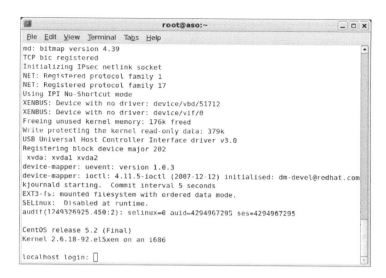

**Figure 18-8.** *A MyCentOS console given to you after using the xm console command*

When you are finished with the console, you can just close the terminal window. You can use the xm console command to reconnect to that guest or connect to another one when needed.

## Using virt-viewer

The virt-viewer command will display a graphical console on a running virtual machine. This is used by virt-install after rebooting to your new installed guest as shown in Figure 18-6. The virt-viewer command uses the following syntax:

```
virt-viewer target_domain
```

where target_domain can be the guest's name or numeric ID, which, again, you can discover in the output of the xm list command. As an exercise, close the virt-viewer window of the MyCentOS guest by clicking its close button in the upper right-hand corner. Open a new terminal, and use the command virt-viewer MyCentOS & to open a new virt-viewer window for the MyCentOS guest and allow you to run commands on the same terminal afterward.

---

**Note:** Using virt-viewer on a guest that has a running virt-viewer window on it will block the new one. You need to close the old virt-viewer window to see the new virt-viewer window for the same guest.

---

# Using vncviewer

When you start a guest, Xen also starts a virtual network computing (VNC) server for it. With VNC, you can connect to that guest and have a graphical console similar when using virt-viewer. You must have vncviewer on your system before you can use vnc to connect to your guest. To install it, you use the command yum install vnc.

Before you can connect to a guest, you must know two things about it: the host that the guest is running on and the port number that the guest's VNC server is listening to. To find out the port number of the guest's vnc server, you can use this command:

ps ax | grep **target_domain**

where target_domain is the domain name of the guest. If you like to know the VNC port number of the MyCentOS guest, you will use ps ax | grep MyCentOS, and it will show an output like this:

```
7249     ?    Sl     0:37 /usr/lib/xen/bin/qemu-dm -M xenpv -d 2 ↵
-domain-name MyCentOS -vnc 127.0.0.1:0 -vncunused
```

The bold part is the important entry here. You will use that bold argument for the vncviewer command, like this:

vncviewer 127.0.0.1:0

After running the command, your screen will look similar to the one shown in Figure 18-9.

*Figure 18-9. **Connecting to the MyCentOS guest with vncviewer***

You can log into your MyCentOS guest as the root user and browse your system. You can close the window after you explore the system.

# Shutting Down a Guest

You can shut down a running guest in two ways. The first is to enter the guest operating system and using its native shutdown command (shutdown -h now). The second is to use the shutdown command of xm. You use xm to gracefully shut down of a virtual machine as follows:

```
xm shutdown target
```

where target is either the name or ID number of the target domain. Use the following command now to properly shut down the MyCentOS domain:

```
xm shutdown MyCentOS
```

You can monitor the domain if it is already shutting down by using the xm list command.

# Starting a Guest

To start a guest that is not running, you can use the xm create command. The xm create command uses the following syntax:

```
xm create target
```

where target is the name of the guest as stated on the name option of its configuration file. To start the MyCentOS domain, you will use xm create MyCentOS. You can use xm list afterward to monitor its loading on your hypervisor.

If you want to start a guest automatically when the main host boots, you can do that by copying the configuration file of the guest inside the /etc/xen/auto directory. For example, you want to run the MyCentOS guest automatically when your Xen system boots. All you need to do is to copy the MyCentOS configuration file in /etc/xen into the /etc/xen/auto directory by using cp /etc/xen/MyCentOS /etc/xen/auto. The next time your Xen system reboots, you can expect that the MyCentOS guest will be booted as well.

# Cloning a Guest

If you need to make a copy of an existing guest and do not want to repeat the virt-install command, you can do that with virt-clone. The virt-clone command will clone a guest by copying the guest's image file created by virt-install and create a new configuration file with the same hardware configurations for it. The command will also take care of putting new values on certain options of the clone's configuration file such as the name option, and the uuid option to avoid conflicts when run together with the original. The syntax for virt-clone is the following:

```
virt-clone --original source_domain --name new_domain --file target
```

where --original flag must point to the source domain that you want to duplicate. The --name flag will take the new name of the new copy. The --file flag will indicate the name and destination of the virtual machine image file for the new domain. Be sure that the original domain is not running before using virt-clone; if it is, xend will not let you make the copy. This limitation preserves the contents of the original and makes the copy as close the original as possible.

As an example, you will clone the MyCentOS domain into MyCentOS-1. The virtual machine file will be named MyCentOS-1.img and is to be placed in /var/lib/xen/images. Run the following command:

```
virt-clone --original MyCentOS --name MyCentOS-1 ↵
--file /var/lib/xen/images/MyCentOS-1.img
```

The amount of time required to clone a virtual machine depends on the size of its virtual machine file or image file—the bigger the file, the slower the cloning. Like when you used virt-install, the name of the clone's configuration file will be the same as its domain name, MyCentOS-1.

After the cloning finishes, you can start the cloned guest using xm create MyCentOS-1 and view it with virt-viewer MyCentOS-1. In Figure 18-10, both the MyCentOS and MyCentOS-1 guests running and they have different IP addresses: MyCentOS has 192.168.1.103, while MyCentOS-1 has 192.168.1.104.

*Figure 18-10. The MyCentOS and MyCentOS-1 guests running*

# Cleaning Up

After experimenting with Xen, you should shut down NFS and then remove your CentOS installation DVD from the drive (you don't have to do so if you copied the contents on your hard drive):

1. Stop the NFS server using service nfs stop.

2. Open the exports file in /etc and comment or remove the entry

   /media/CentOS_5.2_Final          *(ro,sync)

   And save it.

3. Eject the DVD from the drive.

# Summary

In this chapter, we have covered several types of virtualization technologies, but we covered paravirtualization in more depth because of Xen. You have learned the roles of the Xen hypervisor and guests in running virtualization in CentOS. You also saw how to manage paravirtualized Xen guests, including starting a guest, stopping a guest, and cloning a guest. And last, we also covered how to connect to a running guest using multiple methods to administer them.

In the next chapter, you will learn the techniques to use when things go wrong on your Linux system.

■■■

# CHAPTER 19

# Linux Troubleshooting

In previous chapters, you learned how to install and configure CentOS. You also learned how to use the shell prompt to issue commands and change server-configuration files present on the system. At this point, you have a good starting point in your Linux administration career with CentOS.

The last lesson that you must learn is how to handle basic troubleshooting of your Linux system. Linux and its installed software are stable, but you will face times when you might have changed a file or two that makes your system unable to boot as expected. Or, some hard drive partition failure occurred that you want to take a closer look at, which is impossible for a non-bootable Linux system. You will need to use CentOS's rescue mode to rip open your non-booting system and investigate the cause of the problem.

## The CentOS Rescue Environment

Redhat-based systems such as CentOS and Fedora contain a rescue environment that you find in any of several locations: on the first installation CD or the DVD installer; on a USB flash drive containing the correct installer; or on the RHEL CD. The rescue environment includes a special kernel designed to run on minimal available memory. The environment also includes tools such as text editors and some shell utilities that can help you fix problems on your system. To run in the rescue environment, you must set your motherboard's BIOS media boot sequence to launch your booting sequence from an optical drive of your choice or from a USB port. You need to consult your motherboard's documentation for information on how to enter the BIOS and change attributes.

After you change the boot sequence of your BIOS so it launches the rescue environment, insert the first CD or the DVD of CentOS into the optical drive. Let the hardware boot; once the optical drive detects the inserted CentOS installation disc, you will see a start up screen similar to the one in Figure 19-1.

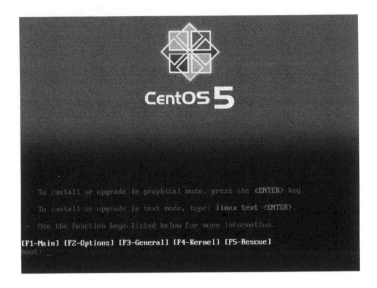

*Figure 19-1. The install start up screen of CentOS*

This is the same screen that you saw when you began to install CentOS in Chapter 1. Instead of pressing "enter" to start installing a new system, type this line at the boot: prompt to launch the rescue environment: linux rescue.

Pressing "enter" now instructs the CentOS installer to boot the rescue environment. You will be presented with a series of questions that cover how you want the rescue environment to behave, such as what language to choose, what keyboard type to use, whether to enable networking, and whether to attempt to mount the partitions. The controls are similar to text-based user interfaces in Linux: the "tab" key switches sections, the arrow keys let you navigate on the section's widgets, and the "spacebar" key lets you do something on the selected widget, such as push a button.

You can answer the questions based on your system when it comes to what language to use and the type of keyboard you have. The defaults are fine for those. You are learning the CentOS Linux rescue environment for now, so just say no to networking. This option is useful at a later stage, such as when you need the network, and you have an available backup Linux computer to transfer files to your problem machine using a network service such as FTP or SSH.

The rescue environment's final question informs you that it will try to find the available Linux partitions on the Linux installation and mount them. You have three options available: Continue, Read-Only, and Skip (see Figure 19-2).

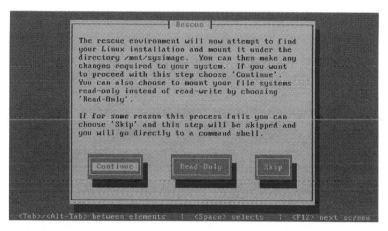

*Figure 19-2. The rescue environment mount partitions screen*

Both Continue and Read-Only locate the installed Linux system's partitions and mount these on the /mnt/sysimage directory. You can switch to that directory later and perform the required fixes, such as restoring configuration files or getting rid of the problem kernel. The Continue option lets you make changes to your Linux filesystem after mounting it. The Read-Only option lets you browse only the contents of the mounted partitions for observation. This is good for investigating why the system suddenly stopped booting normally.

Skip doesn't mount your Linux filesystem. This is useful if the rescue environment fails to locate the partitions, or you want to mount the partitions manually. The Skip option is best suited for experienced Linux administrators who can handle other Linux flavors. While this option is aimed at experienced Linux administrators, you will learn some of the things you can accomplish with it later in this chapter.

For now, select Continue and press the spacebar to make the rescue environment find your Linux system partitions and mount them on the /mnt/sysimage directory (see Figure 19-3).

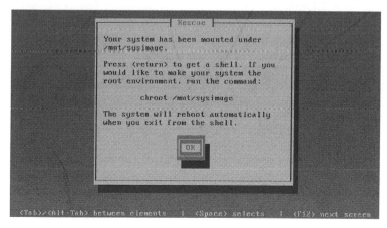

*Figure 19-3. The rescue environment found the partitions and mounted them on /mnt/sysimage*

459

If everything goes well, the rescue environment's shell prompt appears (see Figure 19-4). If you don't see the shell prompt, you must mount your Linux system's partition manually. Reboot your system using the rescue environment and choose the Skip option. Then follow the instructions on finding and mounting your Linux file system later in this chapter.

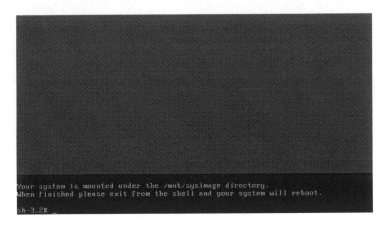

*Figure 19-4. The rescue environment shell prompt*

After you mount your Linux system's partitions, you must remember that the root (/) partition you're in is only the temporary root partition of the rescue environment. This isn't the same as the root partition during normal mode.

The rescue environment contains two virtual consoles. The first console appears one after the environment loads. You can start using this console to run shell commands to troubleshoot your system. If you need to do something else like examine a configuration file while a command is running on the first console, you can use the second console to view it. You can access the second virtual console by pressing Ctrl+Alt+F2 and it gives you a prompt to run commands. To go back to the first virtual console, use Ctrl+Alt+F1.

# Exploring the Rescue Environment

The rescue environment is a complete but compact Linux system that runs in memory. You can use most of the repair common tools for Linux administration from the rescue environment. For example, you can use ls, cd, more, and less. When editing configuration text files, you can use vi, pico, and ed.

Before diving more deeply into how to use the rescue environment, you need to understand how it differs from the affected Linux system you're troubleshooting. You can run ls -l now and see the contents of the rescue environment's root filesystem, then run ls mnt/sysimage to view the mounted partitions of the affected Linux system (see Figure 19-5).

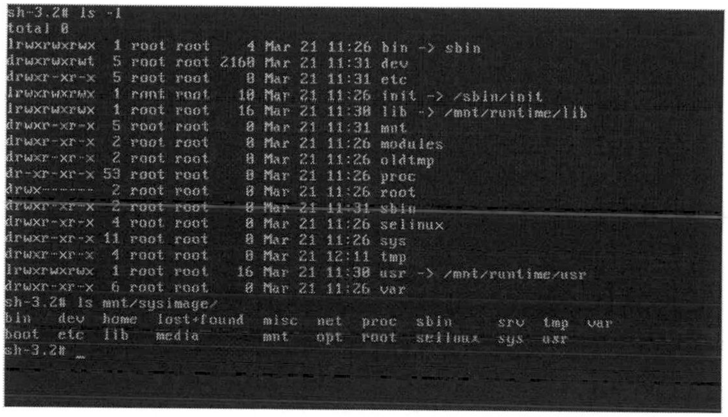

*Figure 19-5. The rescue environment and the affected Linux filesystem*

If you look closely at Figure 19-5, you can see that there are minor differences between the rescue environment directories and the Linux system mounted on /mnt/sysimage. For example, the media and opt directories aren't present on the root filesystem of the rescue environment. Both directories reside inside /mnt/sysimage, your Linux system's root filesystem. In case you get lost in a directory and cannot tell whether you're in the rescue environment or the Linux system you're troubleshooting, you can always use pwd to determine where you're working.

You're now ready to learn how to solve common problems on a non-booting Linux system using the rescue environment.

# Troubleshooting Checklist

Common causes for some of the problems you encounter in a production Linux system include:

- The root password changed.
- The Bootloader was overwritten.
- You're experimenting with the files in /etc.

You will learn how to recover from each of these problems using the CentOS rescue environment. Before continuing with the exercises, I recommend you run a chroot to your Linux system partition: chroot /mnt/sysimage.

This command puts you inside the /mnt/sysimage directory and makes it the current root partition of the rescue environment. Doing this makes it easier to run commands and access personal data as if you were logged into your system. For example, you need to run ls /mnt/sysimage/home if you didn't use the chroot command to check the contents of your own system's home directory. If you did use the chroot command, you can use ls /home instead.

## Changed the Root Password

A changed root password—whether the change was implemented manually or through automation—can sometimes confuse the Linux administrator.

This can lead to using the wrong password on the wrong system. Alternatively, it can lead to forgetting the password after the change. Being locked out of your own Linux system can be frustrating, but you can use the rescue environment to change the root password, and then use your new password to get back into the system.

To change the root password of the affected system, open the shadow file contained in the /etc directory using vi or pico, then find root's entry. For example, the root's shadow file entry looks like this:

```
rroot:$1$Ptp2PgoF$NWZNuTH18YY8lI4GWlGLP.:14310:0:99999:7:::
```

According to the format of the passwd and shadow files, the second column contains the user's password. You want to be able to log into the affected system as root without any password, and then change it later for safety reasons. The root's shadow file entry should look like this when you remove the characters of the second column:

```
root::14310:0:99999:7:::
```

Save the file and exit your text editor. Next, type reboot; this logs you out of the rescue environment automatically and begins to load the affected Linux system. Be sure to remove the rescue CD or DVD from the drive to avoid having to reload the rescue environment. After you boot into the affected system, log in as root, which won't prompt you for a password. Be sure to change the root user's password immediately and write it down, so you won't be locked out again.

---

■ **Warning:** Sometimes administrators forget to change the blank password of root after doing this fix. Doing this leaves your system wide open, not only to outside attackers, but to anyone who tries to log in as root. All anyone would have to do is to use the root username and hit the "enter" key for the password. Watch out!

---

## Bootloader Was Overwritten

Linux bootloaders such as GRUB are used to start a Linux system. This bootloader usually resides on the master boot record of the hard disk. Sometimes the bootloader gets overwritten by another OS's bootloader, disabling your Linux system. If this happens, you need to restore the bootloader and add an entry to the newly installed OS that makes both OSes available for selection during start-up. Before you can do that, you need to restore the bootloader using the rescue environment.

For the purposes of this example, let's assume you want to restore GRUB for CentOS as your bootloader.

Begin the process of restoring the bootloader by booting up the rescue environment as instructed, and then use the chroot command against /mnt/sysimage. Next, you need to determine how the hard disk is represented as a block device. It can be hda for the first IDE hard disk or sda for the first SCSI or SATA hard disk. You can use the mount command to give you a clue on how it is represented. Assuming your hard disk is represented as hda inside /dev, you issue the following command to restore GRUB back on the master boot record:

```
/sbin/grub-install /dev/hda
```

Review your system's `grub.conf` file for corrections, if there are any. Next, you can test for the presence of the bootloader by rebooting your affected system.

---

■ **Note:** This is a good time to double-check the contents of GRUB's configuration file, `grub.conf`, inside `/etc`. You're checking to see whether there the file contains any incorrect entries. You can also add the entry of the OS that overwrote your bootloader before rebooting.

---

## You're Experimenting with the Files in /etc

During your Linux administration duties, you will need to perform certain configuration file changes on the system for a variety of reasons. For example, you will need to allow a new kernel to see the filesystem during its boot cycle. Assume you have backed up the configuration files contained in `/etc` and changed the contents of `fstab` so the new kernel can see the hard disk. Some kernels see SATA hard drives as hda, while others see them as `sda`. Now consider the case where your current CentOS system represents the SATA hard drive it resides on as hda and the new kernel needs to see it as `sda`. You make the required changes and reboot the system using the new kernel, but then the new kernel stops working because a missing module is missing. Rebooting back to the old kernel is a problem because it knows that the SATA hard drive is represented as hda inside the `fstab` file. This situation can spell a lockout.

To fix this problem, reboot the rescue environment and revert the entries of the affected Linux system's `fstab` file to their original condition. If that isn't possible, restore the `fstab` file from a backup. After you reboot, you'll be back on track.

## Skipping /mnt/sysimage

You will find yourself in situations where you need to troubleshoot non-CentOS systems, such as Ubuntu or Slackware distributions. The mounting of the actual system might not perform as expected, so you will need to mount the partitions yourself. To accomplish this, you need to know the available partitions of the affected Linux system. You can use the `fdisk -l` command to list your available partitions on your affected system's hard disk (see Figure 19-6).

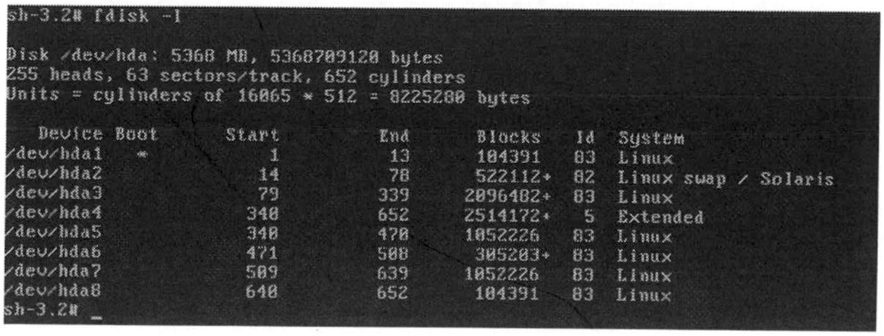
```
sh-3.2# fdisk -l

Disk /dev/hda: 5368 MB, 5368709120 bytes
255 heads, 63 sectors/track, 652 cylinders
Units = cylinders of 16065 * 512 = 8225280 bytes

   Device Boot      Start         End      Blocks   Id  System
/dev/hda1   *           1          13      104391   83  Linux
/dev/hda2              14          78      522112+  82  Linux swap / Solaris
/dev/hda3              79         339     2096482+  83  Linux
/dev/hda4             340         652     2514172+   5  Extended
/dev/hda5             340         470     1052226   83  Linux
/dev/hda6             471         508      305203+  83  Linux
/dev/hda7             509         639     1052226   83  Linux
/dev/hda8             640         652      104391   83  Linux
sh-3.2# _
```

***Figure 19-6.** A sample output of the `fdisk -l` command*

## Finding the Affected System's Root (/) Directory

It's important that you find the root (/) directory if you're troubleshooting a Linux system and you skip the option of making the rescue environment mount the partitions on /mnt/sysimage. Linux distributions place important configuration files and block devices in /etc and /dev respectively. Sometimes, the problems originate from a configuration file, as in the fstab example already discussed. In other unusual cases, the distribution might have a buggy udev setup.

To find the root directory successfully, you need to see if the /etc and /dev directories exist on the mounted partition. You will learn how to do that in this simple exercise:

1.  Create a directory called temp inside the /mnt directory. This directory serves as your mount point for the affected system's root directory.

2.  Use the output given in the fdisk -l to start mounting each partition. For example, you could use this command to try to mount /dev/hda1 in /mnt/temp:

        mount /dev/hda1 /mnt/temp

3.  Check the contents of the partition. If the mounted partition doesn't contain the /etc and /dev directories, you need to unmount the partition to let other partitions use the mount point. You can unmount the mounted partition using the umount command. For example, you can use this command to unmount the partition contained in /mnt/temp:

        umount /mnt/temp

You need to continue Steps 2 and 3 until you find the /etc and /dev directories. You have found the affected Linux system's root partition once you see those two directories. All that remains is to perform the required fixes to recover from the problem.

After you fix the system, you need to unmount the mounted partition before you reboot you perform this step to ensure that your updates to the files saved successfully.

# Mounting Logical Volumes

If your fdisk -l output shows that a Linux LVM or logical volume System entry exists in your system, then you must take extra steps to mount it in your system (see Figure 19-7).

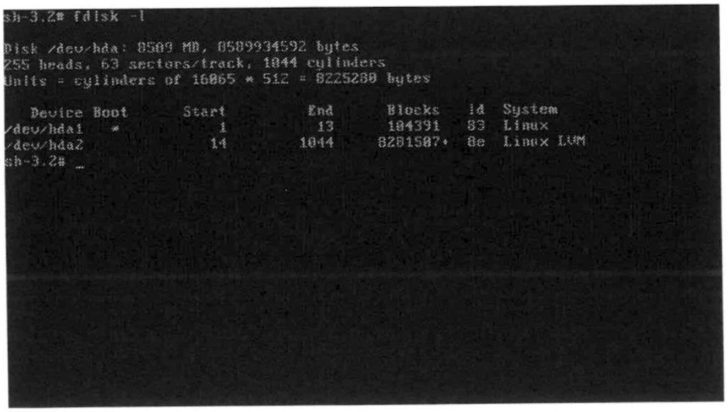

*Figure 19-7. A logical volume that might contain the root partition of your system*

This procedure replaces Step 2 in the preceding exercise if you're searching for your system's root (/) filesystem. You can use the logical volume management, or the lvm command, to search for and activate logical volumes in your system. Using givencommand with the lvm command takes this syntax:

```
lvm givencommand moreoptions
```

moreoptions can be additional values required by the command you use with lvm.

## Mounting Logical Volumes

Mounting logical volumes requires that you walk through a handful of steps:

1. Run the lvm vgscan command to search for all available volume groups in your system. For example, running this command with the filesystem example in Figure 19-7 produces this output:

```
Found volume group "VolGroup00" using metadata type lvm2
```

This message indicates that lvm vgscan found the VolGroup00 volume group, which is of type lvm2. This means you have a device that you can use to start searching for your system's root directory.

2. Activate all of the logical volumes of the volume groups in your system using the lvm vgchange -ay command. Note that the vgchange command of lvm can change the attributes of logical volumes. It accepts the -ay option, which changes the availability of the logical volumes in the volume groups to yes (y). By default, this command affects all volume groups. The output should look like this:

```
2 logical volume(s) in volume group "VolGroup00" now active
```

3. When you see this line, you can mount the logical volumes, just as you would any other storage device (such as hda1).

4. Mount a volume from a selected volume group. In the example system, you start off with the logical volumes found in VolGroup00 inside /dev/VolGroup00. There are two logical volumes, LogVol00 and LogVol01. Begin by mounting LogVol00 inside the /mnt/temp directory created earlier:

```
mount /dev/VolGroup00/LogVol00 /mnt/temp
```

5. Finally, check whether that is the root directory of your Linux system. If not, try mounting the next logical volume (LogVol01), such as in the first part of this step.

# Single-User Mode

It's possible to troubleshoot CentOS without using the rescue environment by booting into single-user mode. In single-user mode, the system boots on runlevel 1 and tries to mount the partitions. After the partitions are mounted, you can do the troubleshooting as if you were in the rescue environment. For example, assume your GNOME desktop won't start because your new video card driver for Xorg isn't compatible with it. All you need to do is boot into single-user mode, undo the edits to the required configuration file, and start your desktop.

You can use single-user mode to fix your system as long as you can still boot it up and log into it. Otherwise, you should use the rescue environment.

---

▓ **Note:** The network isn't started automatically in single-user mode. For example, you must configure the network interfaces manually to connect to the network using ifconfig.

---

## Booting into Single-User Mode

Booting into single-user mode can spare you from having to boot up the rescue environment. Follow these steps to boot into single-user mode:

1.  When GRUB runs and you see its splash screen, press a key. This puts you in GRUB's interactive menu.

2.  Press the "a" key so GRUB will let you add parameters on the kernel you're about to use—the default kernel, in this example.

3.  Type single after adding a space on the last parameter, then press the "enter" key.

In Figure 19-8, the grub prompt lists the ro and root=LABEL=/ parameters for the kernel. The ro parameter tells GRUB to make the root filesystem specified by the root parameter read-only. This helps you avoid accidental changes to your system's root filesystem when you boot your system. The root=LABEL=/ assignment tells GRUB that the kernel must use the device being represented by the LABEL=/. You can learn more about labels by reading the man pages of e2label, which you can use to change the label of an ext2 or an ext3 filesystem.

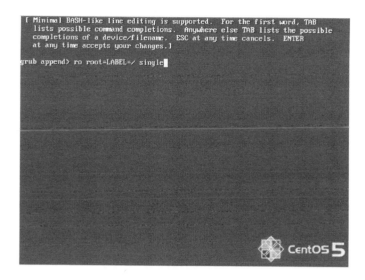

**Figure 19-8.** *The parameter you add to enter single-user mode*

At this point, the system assigns you the single-user mode shell on `runlevel 1`.

# My New Kernel Is Stuck!

In chapter 17, you learned how to download and compile a new Linux kernel from
http://www.linux.org. Assuming you tried to do this, you might have experienced the situation where
your new kernel didn't continue to load after the initial boot. Specifically, you might have seen an error
message complaining about a missing device, such as a `console`. Or your boot sequence might have
hung in a manner similar to what you see in Figure 19-9.

```
insmod used greatest stack depth: 2960 bytes left
Loading ata_piix.ko module.
Waiting for driver initialization.
Scanning and configuring dmraid supported devices
Creating root device.
Mounting root filesystem.
kjournald starting.  Commit interval 5 seconds
EXT3-fs: mounted filesystem with ordered data mode.
Setting up other filesystems.
Setting up new root fs
setuproot: moving /dev failed: No such file or directory
no fstab.sys, mounting internal defaults
setuproot: error mounting /proc: No such file or directory
setuproot: error mounting /sys: No such file or directory
Switching to new root and running init.
unmounting old /dev
unmounting old /proc
unmounting old /sys
ERROR opening /dev/console: No such file or directory
Trying to use fd 0 instead.
WARNING: can't access (null)
exec of init ((null)) failed!!!: Bad address
init used greatest stack depth: 2432 bytes left
Kernel panic - not syncing: Attempted to kill init!
```

• *Figure 19-9. **Your new kernel got stuck in the middle of a system boot***

If this happened to you, your system might be using an old version of udev. For example, this can happen if you have an older version of CentOS or Fedora. Linux uses the udev command to manage devices that your system uses, such as hard disks and/or optical drives. udev is responsible for creating special files—such as hda—to represent the first IDE hard disk inside the /dev directory of your system. The problem lies in the fact that udev can't create the required device entries because it might be an old version that contains problems.

Fixing this doesn't require that you re-create each device that the udev command must make during boot up. You need to create only three types inside the /dev directory of your system: the console, the null, and the tty devices. Linux uses the console device to leverage devices assigned as consoles. With console devices, you can enter commands to use your system. Linux uses the null device as a general garbage bin for useless data or unneeded output. The tty devices lets Linux create terminals for you to log into the system.

## Creating the Required Device Files

Begin by booting into the rescue environment and choosing Skip when prompted to mount your Linux system. This prevents the rescue environment from creating temporary special files in your system's /dev directory. Next, implement the commands shown in Listing 19-1.

```
ls -l /dev/console
ls -l /dev/null
ls -l /dev/ttyS0
ls -l /dev/ttyS1
ls -l /dev/ttyS2
ls -l /dev/ttyS3
```

*Listing 19-1. Getting the Details of the Rescue Environment's Special Files*

The list you create by running the code in Listing 19-1 probably looks similar to the list shown in Figure 19-10, but this could look different in future releases of CentOS.

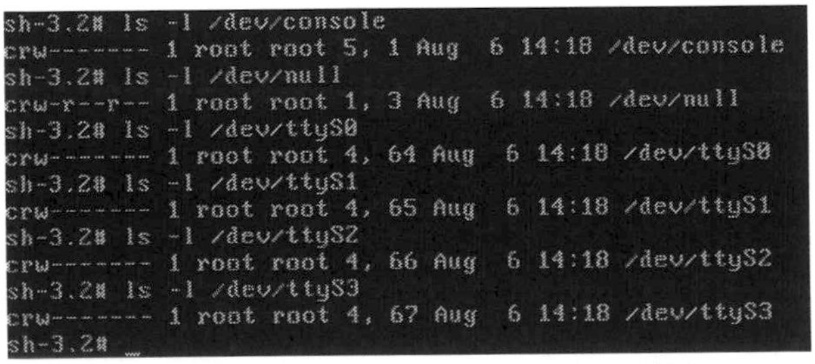

*Figure 19-10. The devices of the rescue environment*

So far you've listed the rescue environment's device files for console, null, and some tty devices. Next, you need to copy the major and minor numbers of each device onto a piece of paper. For example, the /dev/console special file of the rescue environment has the major number of five and minor number of one. Linux uses these numbers to identify individual devices. Next, you need to use these numbers to create the devices on your Linux system.

Make the required special files in the /dev directory of your Linux system using mknod command. This command was built for that purpose, and it uses this syntax, where specialfilename is the name of the special file you want to create:

```
mknod specialfilename specialfiletype givenmajornumber givenminornumber
```

Your file will be given the type of specialfiletype. The givenmajornumber and givenminornumber are the major number and minor number you need to assign to the special file once you create it.

Assuming that you mounted your Linux system's root directory in /mnt/temp, you can use the list in Figure 19-9 to run the commands listed in Listing 19-2 in succession.

```
mknod /mnt/temp/dev/console c 5 1
mknod /mnt/temp/dev/null c 1 3
mknod /mnt/temp/dev/ttyS0 c 4 64
mknod /mnt/temp/dev/ttyS1 c 4 65
mknod /mnt/temp/dev/ttyS2 c 4 66
mknod /mnt/temp/dev/ttyS3 c 4 67
```

*Listing 19-2. Making the Special Files on Your Linux System's Dev Directory*

Each command in Listing 19-2 creates the required special file inside the /dev directory of your system. For example, the first mknod command creates the console special file in the /dev directory of your system as a character device specified by the "c" character. You copy the major and minor numbers used here from the rescue environment's console special file shown in figure 19-9. If you make a mistake on any of the commands making the special files, such as mixing up the major and minor numbers, you can remove that file with the rm command and re-create it with the mknod command.

At this point, you should be able to reboot your system using the new kernel—which should load.

If you reboot to your new kernel, and it still won't continue to load, you will need to investigate the issue further. For example, you might have selected the kernel to use a Pentium CPU, but your machine is an Athlon CPU. Or you might have forgotten to select the filesystem your Linux system is using, such as xfs. Review your kernel configuration because the problem starts there most of the time.

# Summary

In this chapter, you learned how to use the rescue environment provided by the CentOS and Fedora CDs, and a DVD installer. You also learned some basic troubleshooting techniques, including how to reinstall the GRUB bootloader in case it gets overwritten and how to change the root password to avoid a lockout. You also learned how to use the single-user mode in Linux to troubleshoot the system in case the rescue environment is unavailable. Together, these techniques give you a fighting chance to troubleshoot your Linux system successfully. Later, as you gain more experience, your troubleshooting tactics will improve, and you'll become an expert Linux user with CentOS.

Good luck!

# Index

groupadd -g 1000 students command, 96
groupdel command, 96
groupmod <options> <groupname>
        command, 96
groupmod command, 96
groups
    adding, 91, 96
    changing properties of, 92, 96
    deleting, 93, 96–98
    managing quotas for, 101
<grp.> option, 94–95
<grpn> option, 94, 95
grpquota keyword, 99
GRUB (GRand Unified Boot) loader, 55
GRUB command, 56
grub.conf files, 59, 432–433, 463
grub-md5-crypt command, 59
guests, 435
gui section, 124

# H

h command, 43
-h option, 137–138
h323 protocol, 219
hard drive, provisioning, 71–77
hard link, 38
hard option, 321
Hardware Lister tool, 430
hardware-assisted virtualization, 437
--hash flag, 137
hash symbol (#), 32, 170, 345–347, 352, 359
hd prefix, 72
head command, 44
headers, sendmail, 340
hello.sh file, 52
--help parameter, 50
hints file, 246–247
history command, 52
/home directory, 34, 36, 89, 384
/home file, 82
host column, 279
host configuration. *See also* client/host
        configuration
host element, 316
Host header, 304

HostKey key, 230
hostmaster.pvctoyfan.com domain, 253
Hostname property, 2, 3
.htaccess files, 297
html directory, 292, 299
HTTP (Hypertext Transfer Protocol), 289
http_access ACL-operator, 258
http_access deny all directive, 259
http_port directive, 259
httpd_sys_content_t context, 199
httpd.conf directory, 291
httpd.conf file, 293–297
    commonly used directives, 294–297
        global environment section, 294–295
        main server configuration, 295–297
    configuration file sections, 293–294
hypercalls, 438
Hypertext Transfer Protocol (HTTP), 289

# I

I <days> option, 95
-i (info) command, 141
-i (install) option, 135, 137–138, 140
I command, 43
-I rule number, 213
i386 RPM architecture, 134
i8042.noloop parameter, 58
IANA (Internet Assigned Numbers
        Authority), 242
icons directory, 292
icp_port directive, 259
ID column, 444
ide=nodma parameter, 58
ide-cd module, 418, 420, 422
Identifier attribute, 108–110
IKCONFIG (Kernel .config support) feature,
        425
IMAP (Internet Message Access Protocol).
        *See also* Dovecot
    checking maildir contents, 366–367
    overview, 337–338
    sending and receiving mail using, 362–
        366
--import command, 136
importing keys, RPM, 136–137

of users, changing
with command line, 94–95
with graphical interface, 89–91
protocol compund option, Dovecot, 360
protocols option, Dovecot, 360
--provides keyword, 141
proxy server, 71
proxy.apress.com domain, 257
proxy.pvctoyfan.com domain, 257
proxy.pvctoyfanparent.com directive, 260
proxy.pvctoyfansibling1.com directive, 260
proxy.pvctoyfansibling2.com directive, 260
psql command, 278
public keys, 136–137
public parameter, 327
public_key_file file, 230
pvcreate command, 84
pvctoyfan.com document root directory,
304
pvctoyfan.com domain, 252–254, 303
PVs (physical volumes), 83–84
pwd utility, 35

## ▓Q

:q command, 43
:q! command, 43
-q option, 141–142
qemu-ifup file, 442–443
query argument, 126, 129
--query keyword, 141
querying packages, RPM, 141
queuing email messages, 336
quiet option, 57
quota <user> command, 101
quota command, 100
quota -g <group> command, 101
quota -g command, 101
quotacheck -cugv /home command, 99
quotacheck utility, 99
quotaoff <filesystem> command, 101
quotas. See disk quotas

## ▓R

r code, 183

-R rule number, 213
RAID (Redundant Array of
Independent/Inexpensive Disks), 9,
71
checking on, 81
partitioning using, 77–81
types and levels, 78–81
rc.local file, 376
rcp tool, 227
RDBMs (Relational Database Management
Systems), 261
read command, 51
Read-Only option, 459
receiving email
with POP3, 367–369
using IMAP, 362–366
Recent Documents submenu, 117
Redhat Package Manager. See RPM
redirection, 47
Redundant Array of
Independent/Inexpensive Disks.
See RAID
refresh attribute, 254
REJECT action, sendmail, 347
REJECT target, 212
reject-with command, 190
relabeling, 193
Relational Database Management Systems
(RDBMs), 261
relative paths, 39–40
RELAY action, sendmail, 347
reloading options, with gdmflexiserver, 125
relocated file, Postfix, 357–358
relocated_maps parameter, Postfix, 358
Remote Procedure Call (RPC), 315
remote_machine command, 228
remotemachine command, 229
remove command, 420
remove option, 146
removing
MySQL database, 267
packages, 140, 146–147
privileges, 269
renaming files, 40–41
--replacefiles option, 138

491

## ▓U

19583297R00281

Made in the USA
Lexington, KY
26 December 2012